Creating Components

Object Oriented, Concurrent, and Distributed Computing in Java

OTHER AUERBACH PUBLICATIONS

The ABCs of IP Addressing
Gilbert Held
ISBN: 0-8493-1144-6

The ABCs of LDAP
Reinhard Voglmaier
ISBN: 0-8493-1346-5

The ABCs of TCP/IP
Gilbert Held
ISBN: 0-8493-1463-1

Building an Information Security Awareness Program
Mark B. Desman
ISBN: 0-8493-0116-5

Building a Wireless Office
Gilbert Held
ISBN: 0-8493-1271-X

The Complete Book of Middleware
Judith Myerson
ISBN: 0-8493-1272-8

Computer Telephony Integration, 2nd Edition
William A. Yarberry, Jr.
ISBN: 0-8493-1438-0

Electronic Bill Presentment and Payment
Kornel Terplan
ISBN: 0-8493-1452-6

Information Security Architecture
Jan Killmeyer Tudor
ISBN: 0-8493-9988-2

Information Security Management Handbook, 4th Edition, Volume 1
Harold F. Tipton and Micki Krause, Editors
ISBN: 0-8493-9829-0

Information Security Management Handbook, 4th Edition, Volume 2
Harold F. Tipton and Micki Krause, Editors
ISBN: 0-8493-0800-3

Information Security Management Handbook, 4th Edition, Volume 3
Harold F. Tipton and Micki Krause, Editors
ISBN: 0-8493-1127-6

Information Security Management Handbook, 4th Edition, Volume 4
Harold F. Tipton and Micki Krause, Editors
ISBN: 0-8493-1518-2

Information Security Policies, Procedures, and Standards: Guidelines for Effective Information Security Management
Thomas R. Peltier
ISBN: 0-8493-1137-3

Information Security Risk Analysis
Thomas R. Peltier
ISBN: 0-8493-0880-1

Interpreting the CMMI: A Process Improvement Approach
Margaret Kulpa and Kurt Johnson
ISBN: 0-8493-1654-5

IS Management Handbook, 8th Edition
Carol V. Brown and Heikki Topi
ISBN: 0-8493-1595-6

Managing a Network Vulnerability Assessment
Thomas R. Peltier and Justin Peltier
ISBN: 0-8493-1270-1

A Practical Guide to Security Engineering and Information Assurance
Debra Herrmann
ISBN: 0-8493-1163-2

The Privacy Papers: Managing Technology and Consumers, Employee, and Legislative Action
Rebecca Herold
ISBN: 0-8493-1248-5

Securing and Controlling Cisco Routers
Peter T. Davis
ISBN: 0-8493-1290-6

Six Sigma Software Development
Christine B. Tayntor
ISBN: 0-8493-1193-4

Software Engineering Measurement
John Munson
ISBN: 0-8493-1502-6

A Technical Guide to IPSec Virtual Private Networks
James S. Tiller
ISBN: 0-8493-0876-3

Telecommunications Cost Management
Brian DiMarsico, Thomas Phelps IV, and William A. Yarberry, Jr.
ISBN: 0-8493-1101-2

Creating Components

Object Oriented, Concurrent, and Distributed Computing in Java

CHARLES W. KANN

CRC Press is an imprint of the
Taylor & Francis Group, an **informa** business
AN AUERBACH BOOK

CRC Press
Taylor & Francis Group
6000 Broken Sound Parkway NW, Suite 300
Boca Raton, FL 33487-2742

First issued in hardback 2017

ISBN-13: 978-0-8493-1499-5 (pbk)
ISBN-13: 978-1-1384-6854-2 (hbk)

Visit the Taylor & Francis Web site at
http://www.taylorandfrancis.com

and the CRC Press Web site at
http://www.crcpress.com

Library of Congress Cataloging-in-Publication Data

Kann, Charles W.
Creating components : object oriented, concurrent, and distributed computing in Java/
Charles W. Kann.
p. cm.
Includes bibliographical references and index.
ISBN 0-8493-1499-2 (alk. paper)
1. Parallel programming (Computer science) 2. Object-oriented programming (Computer science) 3. Java (Computer program language) I. Title.

QA76.642.K36 2003
005.13'3—dc21

2003048033

Contents

Preface

Purpose and Goals

The purpose of this book is to introduce concurrent programming using objects (which we refer to as *component programming*) to students who are familiar with procedural and GUI programming. The material in this book is largely tied to concepts used in the Java programming language and the supporting APIs and Java-based tools. Some of the ideas presented can be translated successfully to other languages or APIs; however, the intent of this book is to present the material primarily in a Java framework.

The types of programs that can be produced using the idea of component programming are growing in number and importance. As the use of Internet-based services grows, the need for programs that manage requests from many sources also grows. The tools required to handle these types of requests, such as RMI, CORBA, or J2EE, are all amenable to design and implementation using component techniques. This book covers those techniques and will help students to better understand how the concurrency in these systems affects the programs they implement.

This book is intended for courses in concurrent and object-oriented programming in Java taught at the junior/senior undergraduate level or first-year graduate level. It can also be used as an adjunct to several other courses, such as:

- *Concurrent programming or operating systems*, for which the first three chapters would serve to help students understand and implement concurrent programs in Java. Also, Chapter 13 could be used as part of a module on distributed computing.
- *Distributed programming*, for which the concepts from Chapters 3 and 7 could be used as templates for many distributed program implementations, and Chapter 13 could be used to cover aspects of Java RMI.

- *Object-oriented programming*, for which the discussion in Chapter 5 regarding the use of interfaces in Java and in Chapters 10 to 12 could be used to cover aspects of system design and management.
- *Advanced programming in Java*, for which the discussion in Chapter 2 could be used to cover threads in Java and in Chapters 4 to 6 to cover topics such as objects, interfaces, and exceptions.

Intended Audience

The material in this book assumes some familiarity with the Java programming language and the use of the Java API, such as would be gained in two semesters of Java or a course on Java as a second language for programmers fluent in another language. This book is not intended to be a text for an introductory course on Java and is not appropriate for students trying to learn Java for the first time, even if they are fluent in another programming language, such as C++. Minimally, students using this book should have a fairly good grasp of the Java programming language, including topics such as how to write a GUI program, how to design classes and instantiate objects, and the mechanisms used to invoke methods and pass parameters. Any additional background that the student has (such as an understanding of the processes from a course on operating systems, or memory usage such as would be covered in a course on programming languages) will help the student better understand the principles put forth in this text but are not necessary to understanding the material in the text.

Resources Needed

This text assumes that the reader has access to the *Java Standard Edition* (J2SE), which is sometimes called the *Java Developer's Toolkit* (JDK). The book uses features of JDK 1.4, so version 1.4 or higher of the toolkit is needed to run the programs in the text. This text assumes that the reader is familiar with the JDK and the commands for compiling and running Java programs. It also assumes that the reader has some familiarity with the standard Java APIs and can use these APIs for simple programs.

Approach

This book can be divided roughly into five main sections.

- Chapters 1 to 3 cover the basics of concurrent programming. Topics include a definition of concurrent programming, the types of concurrent programming and why multiple types of concurrent programming exist, how concurrency is implemented and supported in Java, and some basic techniques for implementing a concurrent program.

- Chapters 4 to 6 cover basic Java topics, such as what an object is, how objects impact the implementation details of a program, what an interface is, how to use interfaces to program, and some basic exception-handling techniques in Java.
- Chapters 7 to 9 cover some more advanced topics for implementing concurrent programming in Java, such as the Java Event Model and notification objects. Examples are given of how these techniques can be combined to produce powerful solutions to problems.
- Chapters 10 to 12 cover program design and management. OOP techniques such as composition and classification are covered, with an emphasis on how their use impacts components. Implementation decisions made specifically in the Java programming language that support program management are also discussed.
- Chapter 13 applies the material from the rest of the book to distributed programming using RMI.

Overview

Chapter 1 contains the background material for the rest of the book. Definitions of concurrent programming and components are given. This chapter points out that the intuitive definition of concurrency (i.e., multiple activities occurring at the same time) is not useful in understanding the problems in concurrent programming and the mechanisms required to solve those problems. A better definition is provided using activities that can interleave execution order, and the mechanisms to control that interleaving are discussed. The chapter also considers the different reasons for using concurrent programming and how they impact the type of solution generated.

Chapter 2 covers the basics of concurrency in computer programs. How concurrency is implemented is discussed to explain the behavior of the programs — for example, why stack-based local variables are safe in a concurrent program but instance variables are not. Chapter 2 also covers the mechanisms for synchronization in Java, how they are implemented, and why the decisions were made to implement them in these manners. It is important that students understand the reasoning behind the implementation details because often students try to memorize the effects of using synchronization constructs in programs. This normally leads to not understanding how to use the construct, invalid programs, and frustration with the language in general. All of these problems can be avoided simply by understanding why synchronization is implemented as it is.

Chapter 3 provides a simple method for designing concurrent programs around passive and active objects. The active objects are simple procedural entities, and the passive objects are designed using state diagrams that are translated using simple rules into Java classes. While this technique is not sufficiently powerful to implement all programs, the concepts are simple to understand and provide a good mechanism for evaluating many components.

Chapter 4 deals with the concept of an object in Java. Objects in Java differ from some languages, such as C++, and these differences are substantial enough that they affect the way a program is developed. The advantages of this model are discussed in detail.

Chapter 5 is an overview of programming with interfaces. While the Java programming language does not have parameterized data types (generics or templates), it is possible to work around this lack by using interfaces. This chapter explains what an interface is and how it can be used to implement classes that will work with generic objects.

Chapter 6 covers exceptions. Exceptions are covered in nearly every introductory text for Java. But the point of view of these texts is normally how to use exceptions in Java; however, an exception handling strategy is an important part of any design for a program. This chapter explains how exceptions can be used to effectively handle problems that occur at runtime.

Chapter 7 covers the Java Event Model using an animator program. This animator is a component that allows any object that is drawable to register with it and then allows the object to be animated. The animator is implemented using the Java Event Model and is built in stages by solving problems until the form of the Java Event Model has been completed.

Chapter 8 introduces examples of cooperative synchronization using the animator and several threads that suspend while they are moving in an animation. In this way, the effects of trying several different synchronization schemes is shown graphically so the race, deadlock, and starvation situations are obvious.

Chapter 9 combines techniques from Chapters 3, 7, and 8 and introduces some others such as confinement to show more robust solutions to concurrent problems.

Chapter 10 introduces object design in terms of reuse and specifically deals with how to do reuse with objects that are essentially utility objects or objects that are not part of the problem design but provide a service to one or more applications. Procedural as well as object-oriented reuse is covered, with object reuse being demonstrated using both composition and classification. The final result is to argue that composition should always be used for reuse of what essentially is a utility class.

Chapter 11 looks at the more traditional topics in OOP of composition vs. classification in regard to designing objects to solve a problem, which involves the simple "is" and "has" rules, as well as the concepts of aggregation and association of objects in composition design. This chapter covers these concepts in terms of the choices that need to be considered when designing a program and why some designs result in more robust systems than other designs. Also covered is the impact of concurrency on the different designs.

Chapter 12 looks at the topic of program management, or the issues involved in actually implementing a program after it has been designed. This chapter includes a number of Java-specific items that make enforcing good program management easier.

Chapter 13 applies the principles covered in the first 12 chapters to several distributed computing problems using RMI. This chapter shows how some distributed computing programs are just types of component programs.

Keywords

Many terms used in this book have specific meanings that either differ from the common usage of those terms or are not in the common vernacular. These terms have been italicized in text and are defined in the Keyword section at the end of the book (Appendix A).

Problems

At the end of each chapter are problems designed to reinforce the material covered in the chapter. Some of these problems are designed to be answered with paper and pencil to allow students to reason about how and why things are implemented as they are in Java. Some are extensions to programs implemented in the chapter to reinforce the concepts shown in those programs. Finally, some problems are programs to be implemented using the principles presented in the chapter.

References

Additional reading material is cited at the end of each chapter for readers interested in more in-depth analysis of the issues covered in each chapter. A reference list is provided at the end of the book.

Code Availability

The source code for this book is available from www.Auerbach-publications.com.

Chapter 1

Introduction to Concurrent Programming and Components

1.1 Introduction

This chapter introduces the topics of the book, particularly *concurrency* and *components*. Because the concept of concurrency, particularly as it applies to programming, is so poorly understood by novice programmers, this chapter begins by giving a working definition of concurrent programming. This definition abandons the largely useless definition of concurrency as two programs running at the same time, replacing it with a definition that deals with how concurrency affects the implementation of a solution to the problem.

Once the definition of concurrent programming has been given, special purpose objects called *concurrent components* are introduced. These objects are the most interesting objects in concurrent programming because they are the ones that coordinate the activities in a concurrent program. Without concurrent components a concurrent program is simply a set of unrelated activities. It is the components that allow these activities to work together to solve a problem. Components are also the most difficult objects to write. This is because the activities (or active objects) correspond closely to normal procedural programs, but components require a change in the way that most programmers think about programs. It is also in components that the problems specific to concurrent programming, such as race conditions and deadlock, are found and dealt with. The rest of the book is about how to implement concurrent programs using these concurrent components.

Finally, this chapter explains the different types of concurrent programs and how these programs result in various types of programs. Part of understanding concurrent programming is realizing that there is more than one reason to do concurrent programming. An important aspect of any program is that it should solve a problem. Concurrency improves the solution to many different types of problems. Each of these problem types looks at the problem to be solved in a slightly different manner and thus requires the programmer to approach the problem in a slightly different way.

1.2 Chapter Goals

After completing this chapter, you should be able to:

- Understand why concurrent programming is important.
- Give a working definition of a concurrent program.
- Understand the two types of synchronization and give examples of each.
- Give a definition of the term *component* and know what special problems can be encountered when using components.
- Describe several different reasons for doing concurrent programming and how each of these reasons leads to different design decisions and different program implementation.

1.3 What Is Concurrent Programming?

The purpose of this book is to help programmers understand how to create concurrent programs. Specifically, it is intended to help programmers understand and program special concurrent objects, called *concurrent components*.* Because these components are used only in concurrent programs, a good definition of a concurrent program is needed before components can be defined and methods given for their implementation. This section provides a good working definition of a concurrent program after first explaining why concurrent programming is an important concept for a programmer to know. The working definition of a concurrent program provided here will serve

* The term *component* is poorly defined and is used in object-oriented programming. Because some readers might use the term in non-concurrent contexts, the concept is introduced as *concurrent components* here; however, all components in this book are concurrent components, so the *concurrent* part of the term will be dropped, and the term *component* will represent a concurrent component.

as a basis for understanding concurrent programming throughout the rest of the book.

1.3.1 Why Do Concurrent Programming?

The first issue in understanding concurrent programming is to provide a justification for studying concurrent programming. Most students and, indeed, many professional programmers have never written a program that explicitly creates Java threads, and it is possible to have a career in programming without ever creating a thread. Therefore, many programmers believe that concurrency in programming is not used in most real systems, and so it is a sidebar that can be safely ignored. However, that the use of concurrent programming is hidden from programmers is itself a problem, as the effects of a concurrent program can seldom be safely ignored.

When asked in class, most students would say they that have never implemented a concurrent program, but then they can be shown Exhibit 1 (Program1.1). This program puts a button in a JFrame and then calculates Fibonacci numbers in a loop. The fact that there is no way to set the value of stopProgram to false within the loop implies that the loop is infinite, and so it can never stop; however, when the button is pressed the loop eventually stops. When confronted with this behavior, most students correctly point out that when the Stop Calculation button is pressed the value of stopProgram is set to true and the loop can exit; however, at no place in the loop is the button checked to see if it has been pressed. So, some mechanism must be present that is external to the loop that allows the value of stopProgram to be changed. The mechanism that allows this value to be changed is concurrency.

What is happening in Exhibit 1 (Program1.1) is that, behind the scenes and hidden from the programmer, a separate thread, the Graphical User Interface (GUI) thread, was started. This thread is a thread started by Java that is running all the time, waiting for the Stop Calculation button to be pressed. When this button is pressed, the GUI thread runs for a short period of time concurrently with the main thread (the thread doing the calculation of Fibonacci numbers) and sets the value of stopProgram to true. Thus, Exhibit 1 (Program1.1) is a very simple example of a concurrent program. Because nearly every Java programmer at some point has written a program that uses buttons or other Abstract Window Tool Kit (AWT) or Swing components, nearly every Java programmer has written a concurrent program.

This brings up the first reason to study concurrent programming. Regardless of what a programmer might think, concurrent programming is ubiquitous; it is everywhere. Programmers using visual components in nearly any language are probably using some form of concurrency to implement those components. Programmers programming distributed

Exhibit 1. Program1.1: A Program To Calculate Fibonacci Numbers

```
import java.awt.*;
import java.awt.event.*;

/**
 * Purpose: This program illustrates the presence of threads in
 *          a Java program that uses a GUI. A button is created
 *          that simply toggles the variable "stopProgram" to
 *          false, which should stop the program. Once the
 *          button is created, the main method enters an
 *          infinite loop. Because the loop does not explicitly
 *          call the button, there appears to be no way for the
 *          program to exit. However, when the button is pushed,
 *          the program sets the stopProgram to false, and
 *          the program exits, illustrating that the button is
 *          running in a different thread from the main method.
 */

public class Fibonacci
{
  private static boolean stopProgram = false;
  public static void main(String argv[]) {
    Frame myFrame = new Frame("Calculate Fibonacci Numbers");
    List myList = new List(4);
    myFrame.add(myList, BorderLayout.CENTER);
    Button b1 = new Button("Stop Calculation");
    b1.addActionListener(new ActionListener() {
      public void actionPerformed(ActionEvent e) {
        stopProgram = true;
      }
    });

    Button b2 = new Button("Exit");
    b2.addActionListener(new ActionListener() {
      public void actionPerformed(ActionEvent e) {
        System.exit(0);
      }
    });

    Panel p1 = new Panel();
    p1.add(b1);
    p1.add(b2);
```

(continued)

Exhibit 1. Program1.1 (Continued)

```
    myFrame.add(p1, BorderLayout.SOUTH);
    myFrame.setSize(200, 300);
    myFrame.show();

    int counter = 2;
    while(true) {
      if (stopProgram)
        break;
      counter + = 1;
      myList.add("Num = " + counter + "Fib = " +
      fibonacci(counter));
      myFrame.show();
    }

    //Note: stopProgram cannot change value to true in the above
    //loop. How does the program get to this point?
    myList.add("Program Done");
  }

  public static int fibonacci(int NI) {
    if (NI < = 1) return 1;
    return fibonacci(NI - 1) + fibonacci(NI - 2);
  }
}
```

systems, such as programs that run on Web servers that produce Web pages, are doing concurrent programming. Programmers who write UNIX ".so" (shared object) files or Windows ".com" or ".ddl" files are writing concurrent programs. Concurrency in programs is present, if hidden, in nearly every major software project, and it is unlikcly that a programmer with more than a few years left in a career could get by without encountering it at some point. And, as will be seen in the rest of the book, while the fact that a program is concurrent can be hidden, the effects of failing to account for concurrency can result in catastrophic consequences.

The second reason to study concurrent programming is that breaking programs into parts using concurrency can significantly reduce the complexity of a program. For example, there was a time when implementing buttons, as in Exhibit 1 (Program1.1), involved requiring the loop to check whether or not a button had been pressed. This meant that a programmer had to consistently put code throughout a program to make sure that events were properly handled. Using threads has allowed this checking to be handled in a separate thread, thus relieving the program of the responsibility. The use of such threads allows programmers to write code to solve their problem, not to perform maintenance checks for other objects.

The third reason to study concurrent programming is that its use is growing rapidly, particularly in the area of distributed systems. Every system that runs part of the program on separate computers is by nearly every definition (including the one used in this book) concurrent. This means every browser access to a Web site involves some level of concurrency. This chain of concurrency does not stop at the Web server but normally extends to the resources that the Web server program uses. How to properly implement these resources requires the programmer to at least understand the problems involved in concurrent access or the program will have problems, such as occasionally giving the wrong answer or running very slowly.

The rest of this text is devoted to illustrating how to properly implement and control concurrency in a program and how to use concurrency with objects in order to simplify and organize a program. However, before the use of concurrency can be described, a working definition of concurrency, particularly in relationship to objects, must be given. Developing that working definition is the purpose of the rest of this chapter.

1.3.2 A Definition of Concurrent Programming

Properly defining a concurrent program is not an easy task. For example, the simplest definition would be when two or more programs are running at the same time, but this definition is far from satisfactory. For example, consider Exhibit 1 (Program1.1). This program has been described as concurrent, in that the GUI thread is running separately from the main thread and can thus set the value of the stopProgram variable outside of the calculation loop in the main thread. However, if this program is run on a computer with one Central Processing Unit (CPU), as most Windows computers are, it is impossible for more than one instruction to be run at a time; thus, by the simple definition given above, this program is not concurrent.

Another program with this simple definition can be illustrated by the example of two computers, one running a word processor in San Francisco and another running a spreadsheet in Washington, D.C. By the definition of a concurrent program above, these are concurrent. However, because the two programs are in no way related, the fact that they are concurrent is really meaningless.

It seems obvious that a good definition of concurrent programming would define the first example as concurrent and the second as not concurrent; therefore, something is fundamentally wrong with this simple definition of concurrent programming. In fact, the simple-minded notion of concurrency involving two activities occurring at the same time is a poor foundation on which to attempt to build a better definition of the term *concurrency*. To create a definition of concurrency that can be used to describe concurrent programming, a completely new foundation needs to be built. A better, workable definition is supplied in the rest of Section 1.3.2.

1.3.2.1 Asynchronous Activities

Defining a concurrent program begins by defining the basic building block of a program which will be called an *activity*. An activity could be formally defined as anything that could be done by an abstract Turing machine or as an algorithm. However, what is of interest here is a working definition, and it is sufficient to define an activity as simply a series of steps implemented to perform a task. Examples of an activity would be baking a pie or calculating a Fibonacci number on a computer. The steps required to perform a task will be called an *ordering*.

Activities can be broken down into subactivities, each an activity itself. For example, baking a pie could consist of making the crust, making the filling, filling the crust with the filling, and baking the pie. For example, Exhibit 2 shows the steps in baking a pie, where the crust must first be made, then the filling made, the filling added to the crust, and the pie baked. If the order of these activities is completely fixed, then the ordering is called a *total ordering*, as all steps in all activities are ordered. In the case of a total orderings of events, the next step to be taken can always be determined within a single activity. An activity for which the order of the steps is determined by the activity is called a *synchronous activity*. Note that partial orderings are also controlled by synchronous activities; these are implemented by the programming equivalent of "if" and "while" statements.

In the case of making a pie it is not necessary to first make the crust and then make the filling. The filling could be made the night before, and the crust could then be made in the morning before combining the two to make a pie. If the order in which the crust and the filling are made can be changed, then the ordering is called a *partial ordering* (the order of steps to make the crust and the order of steps to make the filling remain fixed, but either can be done first).

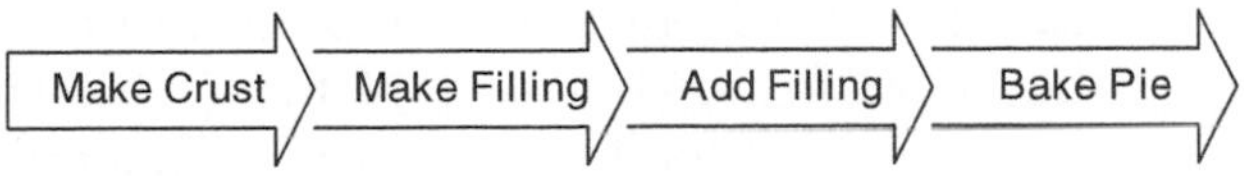

Make Crust → Make Filling → Add Filling → Bake Pie

Exhibit 2. Synchronous Activity to Make a Pie

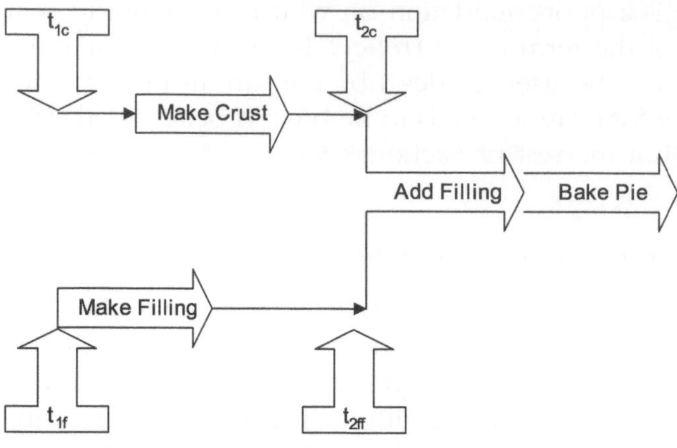

Exhibit 3. One Possible Example of Asynchronous Activities in Making a Pie

However, if one activity must always finish before the other begins, it is possible to implement this behavior with a synchronous activity.

A special case occurs when, for a partial ordering, the next step is not determined by a single activity. To show this, several values of time must be defined. The time after which preparing the crust can be started is t_{1c}, and the time that it must be completed is t_{2c}. The time after which preparing the filling can be started is t_{1f}, and the time that it must be completed is t_{2f}. Now, if $[(t_{1c} <= t_{1f} < t_{2c}) \| (t_{1f} <= t_{1c} < t_{2f})]$, then the activities of making the crust and the filling can (but do not necessarily have to) overlap. If the steps overlap, then the overall ordering of the steps cannot be determined within any one task or, thus, any one activity. One example of this situation for baking a pie is illustrated in the Gant chart in Exhibit 3. Note that many other timelines are possible, as the crust does not have to start at t_{1c}, nor does it have to end at t_{1f}; it simply has to occur between those two times. The same is true of making the filling. The two activities might not actually overlap; it is sufficient that they *can* overlap.

The only way that these two activities can overlap in this manner is if the lists of steps for the activities are being executed independently. For example, it is possible that two bakers are responsible for the pie, one making the filling and the other making the crust. It is also possible that one baker is responsible for both the crust and filling, but they are switching back and forth from doing steps from one part of the recipe (making the crust) to another part of the recipe (making the filling). However they are accomplished, by the definition given here the steps involved in the two subtasks are being executed independently, or asynchronously, of each other. This type of activity is called an *asynchronous activity*.

The definition of an asynchronous activity leads to a very simple definition of concurrency: *Concurrency is defined as the presence of two or more asynchronous activities.*

When asynchronous activities are present in a program, it is possible (but not necessary) for the steps for the two activities to interleave. As we will see in Chapter 2, the number of different ways they can interleave can be quite large, and the results can be quite unexpected. However, note that from the definition of asynchronous activities the two activities do not have to run at the same time; they simply have to be *able* to run at the same time. This is a useful distinction, because the problems that will be encountered in concurrency occur not because the activities execute at the same time but because they can interleave their executions. It is also useful because if a program allows activities to interleave, it must protect against the ill effects of that interleaving whether it occurs or not. As will be seen, this means that methods that might be used concurrently must be synchronized even if the vast majority of the time the use of the synchronized statement provides no benefit.

The importance of the improvement of this definition of concurrency over the definition of concurrency as multiple activities happening at the same time cannot be overemphasized. This definition implies the types of problems that can occur and the way to solve those problems. If a concurrent program does not actually run two activities at the same time, but it can do so, then action must be taken to make sure problems do not occur. Any argument as to whether these two activities are actually running at the same time, or if they generally run one after the other, is a moot point. Arguments about how the activities are actually implemented (for example, are priorities present in the system?) and how the implementation might affect the interactions (does the higher priority process always have to run first?) also do not matter. If the asynchronous activities are present, then the program must account for this behavior.

It should be noted that the definition of asynchronous activities solves the first problem with the definition of concurrency. The two threads running in Exhibit 1 (Program1.1) are asynchronous activities, thus they are concurrent. However, the two computers running in different cities are also asynchronous activities, so the definition of concurrent programming must be further tightened.

1.3.2.2 Synchronization of Asynchronous Activities

That two or more asynchronous activities are concurrent is a good definition of concurrency, but it is not a useful definition. As was mentioned before, two asynchronous activities that are unrelated are concurrent, but that does not mean that any particular action must be

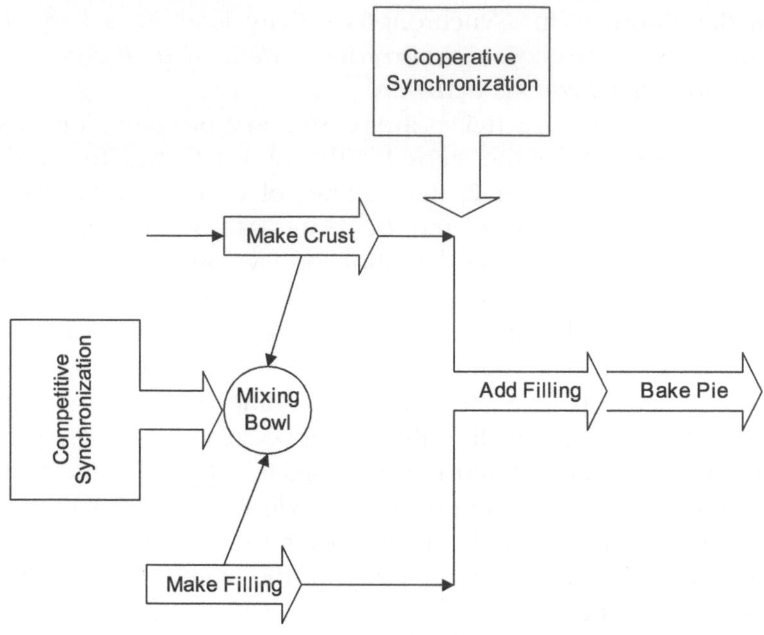

Exhibit 4. Competitive and Cooperative Synchronization

considered when reasoning about them. A useful definition requires that some interaction between the activities is needed. This interaction between activities requires that the activities must coordinate (or synchronize), so this section will define how synchronization affects the activities.

Sebesta [SEB99] says that, "Synchronization is a mechanism that controls the order in which tasks execute." In terms of activities, this definition suggests that, while the asynchronous activities represent separate control over the execution of steps in the activity, at times the asynchronous activities agree to come together and cooperate in order to create valid partial orderings within the activities. Sebesta defines two types of synchronization, *competitive synchronization* and *cooperative synchronization*. To see how synchronization affects the partial orderings within an asynchronous activity, examples of these two types of synchronization are given.

Exhibit 4 gives examples of both types of synchronization. The figure illustrates two asynchronous activities: making a pie crust and making a filling. These two activities will synchronize, first showing synchronization of a shared resource for competitive synchronization and, second, showing synchronization around an event for cooperative synchronization. To understand competitive synchronization, consider what would happen if both recipes called for mixing the ingredients in a large bowl but only one large bowl is available so both activities must use the same bowl. If both activities used the bowl without considering the actions of the other activity it would be possible to mix the filling and the crust at the same time, which would result in an incorrect solution to the problem of making the pie. Therefore, the two activities must compete for the use of the resource and synchronize on it with the rule that when one activity is using it the other cannot continue until the resource becomes free. In this example, the bowl is a shared resource that the two activities must synchronize on in order to correctly solve this problem, in this case referred to as *competitive synchronization*.

The second type of synchronization occurs when asynchronous activities must wait on an event to occur before continuing. In Exhibit 4, this occurs when the making of the pie crust and the filling must both be completed before the filling can be added to the crust and the pie baked. Because the two activities must cooperate in waiting for this event, this type of synchronization is called *cooperative synchronization*. Note that, while the synchronization does impose a partial ordering on the asynchronous activities, it does not make them synchronous. Except for when the activities must synchronize for some reason, they are still asynchronous.

1.3.2.3 Concurrent Programming

With the introduction of asynchronous activities and synchronization, the background is now in place to define concurrency. *Concurrency* is the presence of asynchronous activities that interact and thus must at some point in their execution implement either competitive or cooperative synchronization. This is a workable definition of concurrency as it requires activities that do not actually run at the same time but which behave as if they do. It also requires that they must synchronize to be considered concurrent.

Now that a workable definition of concurrency has been built, it is relatively easy to build a definition of a concurrent program:

> ***Concurrent Program:*** *A program that contains asynchronous activities which synchronize at one or more points or on one or more resources during execution.*

By design, this definition does not specify how asynchronous activities are implemented in the program. These activities might be Ada tasks, UNIX processes, Pthreads, or Java threads. It also does not say how the synchronization is achieved, which once again could be through Ada select statements, UNIX operating system calls, or use of a Java synchronized statement. Further, it does not say how the activities communicate, whether by method calls in a single process, interprocess communications such as UNIX pipes, or Remote Method Invocation (RMI), to processes on completely different computers. These are all just details of individual concurrent programs, but the basic principals of concurrency will always be the same.

1.4 Components

An interesting way to look at a concurrent program is to think of it as containing two types of units, activities that act on other entities or entities that control the interactions of these activities. If these units are objects, then in a concurrent program all objects in that program can be made to be either active (asynchronous activities such as threads) or passive (such as a shared resource or an event that is used for synchronization). Other types of simple, non-concurrent objects are used by active and passive objects, such as vectors or StringTokenizers, but these are not involved in the concurrency in the program.

Most programmers do not have problems understanding active objects, as they are simply instructions that are written and executed in a procedural order that, in principle, can be represented by a flow chart, nor do they have problems understanding non-concurrent objects. This is probably because the behavior of the object can normally be understood in the context of the activity within which it is being run, much like a procedural program. This is how students have been taught to program since their first introductory class.

However, passive objects, which from now on will be called *concurrent components* or simply *components*, are much more difficult for most programmers. This is likely because they provide the infrastructure for the asynchronous activities that executed in a concurrent program. This is a somewhat foreign concept to many programmers.

Components in the example of making a pie are the shared mixing bowl and the event that signifies that preparation of the crust and filling is completed. They control the behavior of the asynchronous activities so that they coordinate and produce a correct result. They also sit between asynchronous activities and are shared and used by multiple asynchronous activities.

Note that not all objects that are non-active are components. For example, a vector is safe to use in a multi-threaded program, but it is not a component because even if it is used by a number of threads it is not normally used to coordinate between those threads. Objects are added or removed from the vector, but the vector is used just to store data elements, not to coordinate the asynchronous activities. A special type of vector called a *bounded buffer* (presented in Chapter 3) is actually used to coordinate between asynchronous activities.

Because components provide an infrastructure for asynchronous activities and coordinate between these activities, they have a number of characteristics that must be considered that do not exist when implementing normal objects. Some of these characteristics are enumerated here:

- Because components coordinate between several threads, they cannot be created or owned by a single thread; therefore, some mechanism must be used to allow these objects to be registered, or to register themselves, with other objects representing the asynchronous activities. Many mechanisms are available to do this, ranging from using a simple parameter in a constructor to special purpose methods in GUI components to entire protocols such as Light-Weight Directory Access Protocol (LDAP) for remote objects.
- Because components are used in separate asynchronous activities and, in the extreme case of distributed computing, on physically different computers, some mechanism must be implemented to allow the components to communicate with the asynchronous activities. Once again, these mechanisms range from simple method invocation in the case of threads to entire protocols when distributed objects are used.
- Unlike objects for asynchronous activities, which can be designed using procedural flow, the logic in a component is generally organized around the state of the component when it is executed. Some mechanism needs to be designed to effectively implement the components to allow them to provide this coordination (see Chapter 3).
- Some harmful interactions, called *race conditions*, can occur if the objects are not properly designed. One way to avoid race conditions is to make all the methods in the object synchronized and not allow an object to give up the object's lock while it is executing. This is called *complete synchronization* and is sufficient for non-component objects such as a string or a vector; however, components must coordinate between several objects, and complete synchronization is too restrictive to effectively implement this coordination. Much of the rest of the book is concerned with how to safely relax the synchronized conditions.
- A second type of harmful interaction, called a *deadlock*, can result if the component is not properly designed. Deadlock can occur in any concurrent program when objects are improperly handled; however, the possibility of deadlock can actually be built into components that are not designed properly, even if the component is used correctly. Several examples of deadlock are provided in the text, particularly in Chapter 7 on Java events.

Two examples are given here to show how these conditions affect a component. The first example of a component is a button object. A button provides a service to the GUI thread by relaying the occurrence of an event (the button has been pressed) to any other objects that are interested in this event (the Listeners). In Exhibit 1 (Program1.1), the button is created in the main thread and then passed to the GUI thread by adding it to the Frame object. It is then used by other threads that are interested in knowing when the button is pressed through the addActionListener methods in the button. Thus, the button is independent of the threads that use it (the GUI thread or any threads associated with the ActionListeners). So, the button is an independent object that provides a coordination service between multiple other threads as well as the service of informing other asynchronous activities (in this case, threads) that the button was pressed. A special mechanism, called an *event*, is used to allow the button to communicate with the threads with which it is interfacing. For this simple program, it is not necessary to worry about the state of the button or race or deadlock conditions, but the reasons why these could affect even a simple button are covered in detail in subsequent chapters.

Another example of components is most distributed services that use distributed objects such as RMI, Common Object Request Broker (CORBA), or Enterprise Java Beans (EJB). When using distributed objects, the components exist on centrally located servers and provide services to remote clients, such as a Web browser on a PC, which are processes or programs running on other computers and can access the components through a network. In the case of distributed programs, all five of the problems that can occur in components (listed above) are of vital importance, as will be seen in Chapter 13.

1.5 Types of Concurrent Programming

Before continuing to describe component programming, it is necessary to clear up some misconceptions about concurrent programming. Programmers often believe that concurrent programming is something that involves just one type of problem. For example, some programmers believe that all concurrent processing involves speeding up very large simulations, such as simulations of weather or of seismic activity in the Earth's crust. Other programmers believe that concurrent programming addresses only problems that occur when an operating system is run on a computer. Still others believe that concurrent programming is required only in distributed systems. Because these programmers approach the problems of concurrency with preconceived biases as to the type of problem they want to solve, they do not understand the methodologies for concurrency that address problems other than the ones in which they are interested.

There is a very wide variety of reasons to use concurrency, and each of these reasons to implement concurrency in a program results in programs that are structured differently. There is really no one "best" way to implement concurrency and synchronization, as it really depends on the type of problem being solved. Below is a list of some of the reasons why concurrent programming might be used. Each type of concurrent program is accompanied by a description of how the type of problem to be solved affects the type of solution that is developed. This text is largely interested in using concurrent programming for soft real time, distributed, and modeling purposes. While the techniques used do apply to other systems, more appropriate solutions usually apply to those problems. Also, note that a program is seldom any one type of concurrent program; often it will exhibit characteristics of many of the program types:

- *Incidental concurrency.* Incidental concurrency occurs when concurrency exists but the asynchronous activities do not interact with each other. An extreme example would be a stand-alone computer in Washington running Word and a stand-alone computer in San Francisco running Excel. Incidental concurrency also occurs on operating systems such as UNIX, where multiple users are using a single computer but each user's program does not interact with any other program. So, while concurrency exists and must be taken into account in the operating system, from the point of view of the user's program no concurrent behavior must be considered. Incidental concurrency is really not very interesting and is not considered further in this book.
- *Resource utilization.* Resource utilization, which is often associated with operating systems, occurs when a program is built around shared resources. For example, concurrency was implemented in the first operating systems to keep the expensive CPU occupied doing useful work on one program while another performed Input/Output (IO). This same principal occurs in a PC where some parts of a program can be designed around special-purpose hardware, such as a graphics or IO processor, which is really a separate CPU and thus running asynchronously to the main processor. This type of concurrency is often handled by the compiler or the operating system and is normally transparent to the programmer. When doing this type of concurrent programming, the programmer writes the program around the special resources that are present and shared. This type of concurrent programming is normally covered in books on operating systems and are not considered further in this book.
- *Distributed programming.* In a distributed program, not all of the resources required by a program exist on a single computer but instead reside somewhere on a network of computers. To take advantage of these distributed resources, programs are designed around locating and accessing the resources. This can involve special methods and protocols to find the resources, such as with RMI using rmiregistry, and even writing entire protocols, as with socket-level protocols.

- *Parallel computing.* Parallel computing is used when a program requires a large amount of real (clock) time, such as weather prediction models. These models can be calculated more rapidly by using a number of processors to work simultaneously on the problem. Parallel programs are designed around finding sections of the program that could be efficiently calculated in parallel. This is often accomplished by using special compilers that can take language structures such as loops and organize them so that they can be run on separate processors in parallel. Some systems add extensions to languages to help the compiler make these decisions.
- *Reactive programming.* Reactive programs are programs for which some part of the program reacts to an external stimulus generated in another program or process. The two types of reactive programs are hard real time and soft real time.
  - *Hard real time.* Hard real time programs are programs that must meet a specific timing requirement. For example, the computer on a rocket must be able to guarantee that course adjustments are made every 1/1000th of a second; otherwise, the rocket will veer off course. Hard real time programs are designed around meeting these timing constraints and are often designed using timing diagrams to ensure that events are processed in the allotted time. The programs are then implemented in low-level languages, such as Assembly or C, which allow for control every clock cycle used by the computer.
  - *Soft real time.* Soft real time programs process the information in real time, as opposed to a batch mode, where the information is updated once or twice a day. These programs use current data but do not meet hard deadlines. One example is a Web-based ordering system that always has the most recent data but could take several seconds to provide it to the client. These systems are often designed around the services they provide, where the services are sometimes implemented as transactions. Objects that are components often process these transactions.
- *Availability.* For some programs such as E-commerce Web sites it is important that they are accessible 24 hours a day, 7 days a week. Concurrency can be used to replicate the critical parts of the program and run them on multiple independent computers. This guarantees that the program will continue to be available even if one of the processors fails. These programs are designed so that critical pieces can be replicated and distributed to multiple processors. These systems are often soft real time programs with special capabilities to ensure their availability; thus, they use components in their design.
- *Ease of implementation.* Using concurrent programming can make it easier to implement a program. This is true of most GUI programs, where concurrency with components makes it easier to implement buttons, TextFields, etc. Many of the objects used in these systems are designed as components.

- *System modeling.* Sometimes concurrent programming is used because it better supports the abstract model of the system. These programs are often simulation programs modeled using objects, where some of the objects are active and some are passive. These programs are designed around making the abstract program model as close to the real-world problem as possible. Many of the objects that are modeled in these systems are components.

1.6 Conclusion

The purpose of this book is to help programmers, particularly students, understand how to apply components in programs and the special issues that are involved in writing programs for concurrent environments. To accomplish this, this chapter has provided a definition of a concurrent program that will be used as a basis for the rest of the book. It has also given a basic definition of a component that will be expanded in the rest of the book. It is hoped that this book will help the reader understand how to apply components to problems where they are needed, thus adding another tool to their toolbox of ways to solve problems.

1.7 Further Reading

Among the many different ways to regard concurrent programs, the idea that an object-oriented concurrent program can be viewed as consisting of active and passive objects is only one. For example, ADA used the idea of a rendezvous to coordinate between tasks (see the *Ada 95 Reference Manual* [ADA95] and Barnes [BAR96]) and added the concept of protected types ([ADA95]), which is much closer to the concept of active and passive objects and is very similar to some of the methods used in this book, particularly in Chapter 3. Many other suggestions have been made regarding how to handle concurrent programming. A good text that covers many of the historical aspects of concurrent programming is Gehani and McGettrick [GEH88]. Concurrent programming is still a very active area of research. Two texts that give a very good overview of the issues involved are Bacon [BAC98] and Ben-Ari [BEN90]. Some good texts on concurrent programming specifically in Java are Hartley [HAR98] and Lea [LEA00]. Finally, concurrent programming has traditionally been taught as part of a course in operating systems. This is because problems associated with concurrent programming were first encountered and solved in designing and implementing operating systems, and it is still the responsibility of the operating system to provide a virtual concurrent environment to programs running under them. A number of good books on operating systems address the issues of concurrent programming; see, for example, Stallings [STA01].

That a program can be written completely using only active and passive objects was proposed in a doctoral thesis by Hathorn [HAT88] and forms the basis of what has been called a *coordination language* (see Gelernter and Carriero [GEL92]). Active and passive objects have also been present in a number of design methodologies (specifically, see Booch [BOO91] and Meyer [MEY88]) and eventually were included in UML (see Booch [BOO99]); however, none of these approaches treats passive objects exactly the same or exactly as they are presented here.

1.8 Problems

1. Consider two programs running on the same computer, but running in totally separate processes. To the programmers implementing them, are these programs concurrent?
2. Consider the same two programs as in Problem 1 but this time consider them from the point of view of the programmer implementing the operating system. Are these two programs now concurrent or not? Is your answer the same as before? Why or why not?
3. Two programs are being run on two separate computers, but both access the same database on a common server. Consider the programs from the point of view of the programmers writing the programs that access the servers. Are these two programs concurrent? What about from the point of view of the programmer implementing the server?
4. If the activities of making the crust and the filling for a pie can occur in either order, but one must be started and completed before the other can begin, are the two activities concurrent? What questions could you ask that might affect your answer?
5. The java.util.vector class is described in the Java API as being "synchronized." According to the definition of a component given in this chapter, is a vector then a component?
6. If something is *thread safe* it means that a call to a method on that object can be run safely in a program with many threads. Is a thread-safe object a component?
7. Describe some of the mechanisms of operating systems for implementing asynchronous activities in a computer program. Does the mechanism used for implementing these activities affect the definition of an asynchronous activity? Do the same for languages other than Java that support asynchronous activities (Ada, Modula2, OCCAM, Concurrent C, Co-Pascal, etc.).
8. Describe some mechanisms used in other languages or operating systems for implementing synchronization. Does the mechanism used for implementing synchronization affect the definition of an asynchronous activity?

9. Describe several problems where concurrency could be used effectively. What type(s) of concurrency would you use to implement such a program? How would that affect the design of the program?
10. Consider the following types of objects. Are any components? Why or why not?
    - Integer
    - Vector
    - Socket
    - Array of primitives
    - Array of objects
    - TextField
    - Button
    - Servlet
    - Enterprise Java Bean
11. Show that a JButton can indeed be linked to many objects by having the button notify multiple objects when it is pressed. Show that the button is independent of the GUI thread by adding and removing it from more than one frame.
12. What happens if the same ActionListener object is added to a JButton twice? Does this seem to be reasonable behavior?
13. In a single-tasking operating system, such as DOS, buttons were often displayed on the terminal and the program would then simply poll (busy wait) until something happened on the screen. Because this represents a type of GUI, are these buttons components? Why or why not?
14. Can a component contain a thread? Explain.

Chapter 2

Threads and Program Contexts

2.1 Introduction

Concurrent programs have some very different properties from the more common *procedural* programs with which traditional programmers are familiar. For example, if a procedural program is run repeatedly with the same input, one rightly expects the same result each time, which is nice because a program can be shown to be correct for at least the limited number of cases tested. It also means that any bugs will be reproducible and will occur each time the program is run. The same is not true of concurrent programs, where a program that is run repeatedly can legitimately produce a different answer each time.

This chapter explains what is happening while a program, either procedural or concurrent, is executing. Once the mystery of how a program works is revealed, the reasons why things happen the way they do should be much clearer. This understanding will be used to show how such mechanisms as *synchronized blocks* and *wait* and *notify* methods can be used to control concurrency in a program.

This chapter also introduces the mechanism in Java for creating an asynchronous activity, the *thread*, and describes how a thread differs from a *process*. This difference will be used to provide an overview of how the current generation of *Web servers* is implemented. Some problems unique to concurrent programming are then identified and solved. These problems involve *safety* (if it finishes, does it get the correct answer?) and *liveness* (does the program finish?) and are affected by the presence or absence of *race conditions* and *deadlock*.

2.2 Chapter Goals

After completing this chapter, you should be able to:

- Program simple Java programs that contain threads.
- Explain a simple memory management and execution model, similar to the one used in the *Java virtual machine* (JVM).
- Understand how programs use contexts to control multiple threads.
- Understand what *nondeterminism* is and why it occurs in concurrent programs.
- Identify race conditions in programs and be able to eliminate them.
- Understand how the synchronized statement and the wait and notify method calls work in Java, and know some of the rules for their use.
- Understand what *deadlock* is, how it can occur, and how to prevent it.

2.3 Writing Threads in Java

This section demonstrates how to write threads in Java and how the execution of threads differs from the traditional procedural programs with which most programmers are familiar. First, examples of simple procedural and concurrent programs illustrate how they differ in structure. Additional procedural and concurrent programs are then contrasted to show how a concurrent program can produce different, and nondeterministic, results.

2.3.1 Simple Procedural and Concurrent Programs

To demonstrate how to structure a program that uses threads, this section contrasts a simple procedural program with a single method call with a similar concurrent program that starts one thread. The program in Exhibit 1 (Program2.1) is a simple Java procedural program that starts executing in main. This program creates an object of type ProceduralExample and then calls the run method in that object. The main method then suspends executing, and the program continues executing in the run method. When the run method completes, the program returns to the main method, finishes executing in the main method, and then exits the program.

A similar program using threads is provided in Exhibit 2 (Program2.2). This program also starts in main and creates an instance of the RunnableExample object. The program does not then call the run method in the RunnableExample object, but instead creates a Thread object that is passed to the RunnableExample object as a parameter to its constructor. This "registers" the RunnableExample object with the thread.

Exhibit 1. Program2.1: Procedural Program

```
public class ProceduralExample {

  public void run() {
    System.out.println("In Run");
  }

  public static void main(String args[]) {
    ProceduralExample pe = new ProceduralExample();
    pe.run();
  }
}
```

Exhibit 2. Program2.2: Concurrent Program Created Using the Runnable Interface

```
public class RunnableExample implements Runnable {
  public void run() {
    System.out.println("In Run");
  }

  public static void main(String args[]) {
    RunnableExample re = new RunnableExample();
    Thread t1 = new Thread(re);
    t1.start();
  }
}
```

The start method is now called on the Thread object, and the thread begins executing. The main is now free to continue executing (as will be seen in Section 2.3.3), but so is the new thread object. When the start method of the Thread object is called, it starts by calling the run method in the object that was registered with its constructor (in this case, the RunnableExample object). The run method of this object prints out the message and ends. It does not return to the main; instead, because both the main and the created thread have completed executing, the program exits.

Note that the RunnableExample object needed to be declared as "implementing Runnable." This is because the Thread object is expecting to be able to call the run method on this object when its start method is called. Because the Thread object does not know about this RunnableExample object, the only way it can guarantee that the run method will be available is to require that any object that is to be passed to its constructor must implement Runnable, which in turn ensures that it will have a run method to call. This was not necessary in the ProceduralExample program because the definition of the actual object to be called (the ProceduralExample class) was available when the call to the run method was made. Interfaces are covered in greater detail in Chapter 5; for now, simply realize that when thread objects

Exhibit 3. Program2.3: Concurrent Program Created by Extending the Thread Class

```
public class ThreadExample extends Thread {
  public void run() {
    System.out.println("In Run");
  }

  public static void main(String args[]) {
    ThreadExample t1 = new ThreadExample();
    t1.start();
  }
}
```

are created they must be given an object that implements Runnable in their definition.

2.3.2 *Extending Class Thread*

Another way to create a thread does not involve passing an object that implements Runnable to the thread. This can be done by having the class extend the Thread class, as in Program2.3 (Exhibit 3). Because Thread already implements Runnable, the object that extends the Thread class automatically implements the Runnable object. The constructor now does not have an object passed to it because it is itself the Runnable object. The thread can determine if an object was passed to the constructor or not. If one was, it will call the run method on the passed object; otherwise, it will call the run method on the "this," or current, object.

These two mechanisms are very similar and can almost be used interchangeably; however, Java supports only a single inheritance model, used by the mechanism to create a thread that extends class Thread. Therefore, classes that extend Thread cannot be used in other inheritance hierarchies, which is a drawback. Because no corresponding negative behavior in regard to using objects that implement Runnable exists, this method is always applicable and preferred. This book always implement threads using the Runnable interface method.

2.3.3 *Programs with Multiple Threads*

Section 2.3.1 used various mechanisms to describe how the procedural and concurrent programs run; however, because they produced the same results, this is likely to be seen as a distinction without a difference. This section shows how different mechanisms can actually produce very different results.

Program2.4 (Exhibit 4) is a simple procedural program that creates two objects, giving them different numbers so that the outputs from

Exhibit 4. Program2.4: Procedural Program with Two Method Calls

```
public class Procedural {
  private int myNum;
  public Procedural(int myNum) {
    this.myNum = myNum;
  }

  public static void main(String argv[]) {
    Procedural a = new Procedural(1);
    Procedural b = new Procedural(2);
    a.run();
    b.run();
    try {
      Thread.sleep((int)(Math.random() * 100));
      System.out.println("in main");
      Thread.sleep((int)(Math.random() * 100));
      System.out.println("in main");
    } catch(InterruptedException e) {
    }
  }

  public void run() {
    try {
      Thread.sleep((int)(Math.random() * 100));
      System.out.println("in run, myNum = " + myNum);
      Thread.sleep((int)(Math.random() * 100));
      System.out.println("in run, myNum = " + myNum);
    } catch(InterruptedException e) {
    }
  }
}
```

Exhibit 5. Output from Exhibit 4 (Program2.4)

```
in run, myNum = 1
in run, myNum = 1
in run, myNum = 2
in run, myNum = 2
in main
in main
```

the objects can be distinguished. The run method of the first object is called, producing two lines of output. The program then returns to main, and the run method of the second object is called, again producing two lines of output. This second method completes, and control is returned to main where two more lines are printed out. This output, shown in Exhibit 5, will be the same no matter how many times this program is run. The order of execution is always the same, so we call this execution *totally ordered*.

Program2.5 (Exhibit 6) is similar to Program2.4 (Exhibit 4) except that now the calls to the methods have been replaced with threads. While Program2.5 looks similar to Program2.4, it behaves in a very different way. In Program2.5, the main creates two objects and uses

Exhibit 6. Program2.5: Concurrent Program with Two Threads and a Main Thread

```
  public Concurrent(int myNum) {
    this.myNum = myNum;
  }

  public static void main(String argv[]) {
    Concurrent a = new Concurrent(1);
    Concurrent b = new Concurrent(2);

    Thread t1 = new Thread(a);
    Thread t2 = new Thread(b);

    t1.start();
    t2.start();

    try {
      Thread.sleep((int)(Math.random() * 100));
      System.out.println("in main");
      Thread.sleep((int)(Math.random() * 100));
      System.out.println("in main");
    } catch(InterruptedException e) {
    }
  }

  public void run() {
    try {
      Thread.sleep((int)(Math.random() * 100));
      System.out.println("in run, myNum = " + myNum);
      Thread.sleep((int)(Math.random() * 100));
      System.out.println("in run, myNum = " + myNum);
    } catch(InterruptedException e) {
    }
  }
}
```

Exhibit 7. Two Possible Outputs from Exhibit 6 (Program2.5)

```
One Possible Output
    in main
    in run, myNum = 2
    in run, myNum = 2
    in main
    in run, myNum = 1
    in run, myNum = 1

Another Possible Output
    in run, myNum = 2
    in main
    in run, myNum = 1
    in run, myNum = 2
    in main
    in run, myNum = 1
```

these objects to create two threads, t1 and t2. The start method for thread t1 is called, and now both the main and thread t1 are free to execute. If the main executes first, it starts t2 and all three threads are free to run. Each thread now has an equal chance of running. Thus, the main could run first, followed by t2 twice, then main, and then t1 twice, as in the first example of output from this program provided in Exhibit 7. It is equally likely that t2 will run, followed by main, then t1, t2, main, and t1, as in the second example output shown in Exhibit 7. In fact, it is not very difficult to show that this simple program has 24 combinations of possible outputs.

Earlier, a procedural program was said to have a total ordering; that is, it had only one correct ordering of statements in the program. A concurrent program is a *partial ordering*. By this we mean that even though the threads themselves are ordered and the statements in each thread are actually procedural, the order in which the JVM chooses a thread for execution of its next instruction is not ordered. This allows the statements in the threads to be interleaved, as shown in Exhibit 7. From this example, it is not difficult to see that the number of correct total orderings consistent with the partial orderings imposed by the threads can be very large even for simple concurrent programs. For this program, the number of possible orderings of the output is actually $(n + 2)!$, where n is the number of threads we start. This large number of correct total orderings makes reasoning about concurrent programs quite complex, much more difficult than for procedural programs. Much of the rest of the text is dedicated to techniques for managing this complexity. How the JVM actually is able to produce this large number of partial orderings is the subject of the Section 2.4, which explains how the JVM builds a process and a thread and how it then uses the information to execute a program.

2.4 A Simple Execution Model

How a program is actually instantiated and executed on a computer is a complex subject often requiring several semesters' study of operating systems, programming languages, and compiler theory to sort out all the details. The JVM is no exception. Like most computer architectures, it is elegant and complex. Fortunately, for the purposes of this text, the basic behavior of concurrent programs can be explained without the complexity of creating a working computer architecture. This chapter develops such a model that is used to explain the behavior of programs in this and later chapters. At the end of this section, this simple model is used to explain the basic behavior of current-generation Web servers.

While the model developed in this chapter is true to the spirit of the JVM and explains all the behavior necessary to talk about the threads in this chapter, it does not claim to be *completely* true to the

JVM. In some cases, it alters details when those details add unneeded complexity, and large sections of the JVM are not discussed at all. In order to make it clear that the model used is not the JVM and does not implement the actual JVM memory model, the virtual machine described here is called a *simple virtual machine* (SVM) and implements a *simple memory model* (SMM). Readers interested in more in-depth treatment of the JVM or computer architectures in general should refer to the Further Reading section at the end of this chapter.

2.4.1 A Simple Memory Model (SMM)

Like most architectures, the SVM uses several different types of memory when running a program. The purpose of each part of this memory, as well as the ability of parts of a program to access it, is to logically partition memory to allow the program to execute correctly. The SMM used by the SVM will use four different types of memory:

1. A *program counter* (pc) register keeps track of the current instructions being executed; this would be an address in the JVM, but in this chapter it is a line of program code.
2. A *heap* is used to store all objects and object data; this area is shared by all the SVM threads.
3. A *method area* contains class definitions and compile program instructions for running the programs; this area is also shared by all SVM threads.
4. A *program context* contains information unique to each thread, such as the SVM *stack*. It can also contain other information, such as the PC associated with this thread. The SVM stack contains information such as the variables local to this method and the return address for the calling method.

Each separate SVM program (called a *process*) contains one PC, heap, method area, and one or more thread contexts, one for each thread. Exhibit 8 shows graphically how this would look on a computer running two SVM processes, the first with threads main and t1 and the second with threads main, t1, and t2.

One analogy that may help you to understand this concept of a process is to imagine a single builder who is working on several houses. He can only work on one task at a time. Assume that the builder is building a row of townhouses, using the same plans for each, and that he has a single set of tools for working on the houses; therefore, the builder can share the plans and tools. Because not all material to build the houses is available all the time, the builder moves between the houses, working first on one and then another as material for a specific task for a particular house becomes available.

By our analogy, the builder is the CPU, which can be working on one task at a time. The tools are the objects (heap), and the plans are

Process 1

pc = 12
Heap Method Area
Object_1 method_1()
Object_2 method_2()

Thread Contexts
main t1
pc = 7 pc = 12
Stack Stack

Process 2

pc = 24
Heap Method Area
Object_1 method_1()
Object_2 method_2()

Thread Contexts
main t1 t2
pc = 19 pc = 3 pc = 24
Stack Stack Stack

Exhibit 8. Graphic Representation of Two Processes in the SVM

the instructions we are using (the method area). Each townhouse (a thread) has its own status (PC), and the PC used by the builder (CPU) is the one for the townhouse on which he is currently working. The overall construction site is the process, with shared plans and tools but separate townhouses (threads). When the builder moves from working on one townhouse to working on another, this shift is called a *context switch*, as the context (townhouse) that is being worked on has changed.

This analogy can be extended to a process. If the builder is working on two different sets of townhouses at different locations, each construction site becomes a process. Each of these sites will have its own plans (method area) and tools (heap), so the plans and tools are not shared between the sites but are shared within the sites. Each site also has a set of townhouses to be constructed (threads). When the builder switches from working on one townhouse to another, either at the current site or at the other site, this change is still referred to as a context switch.

As with any analogy, this one between building townhouses and processes and threads can be carried only so far. At some point, the actual workings of the real system must be understood because extending the analogy without understanding the underlying system is likely to result in an invalid understanding of the how the real system works. So, the analogy should never be extended without an understanding of how the real system works.

2.4.2 Threads, Processes, and Web Servers

The SMM is a very simple model of memory with too many details left out to be of much use in actually implementing a real computer architecture. However, as will be shown in Section 2.4.3, it provides sufficient detail to explain the behavior of a concurrent program. This section uses it to explain how Web servers work and why mechanisms such as *servlets* are replacing older technologies such as the *common gateway interface* (CGI).

Operating systems were first written so that multiple programs could be run at the same time on a single computer. There was no thought given to the possibility that a single program could use more than a single thread or require more than one context. Each program was considered to be a single, complete entity that did not need to communicate with any other programs while running. Therefore, these operating systems combined the context into the process, and a process had a single heap, method area, and only one thread (or context). If a separate thread was needed, a new process was started. It was much later that programmers began to realize that they could effectively use more than a single thread in a program. A thread is much more effective than a process for handling multiple contexts for two reasons:

- Every process has its own heap and method area and therefore has much more baggage (or weight) than a thread. To create a thread, only a new context is created which shares the heap and method area with the context that created it; hence, a thread is more "lightweight" than a process. Threads are often referred to as *lightweight processes* and processes as *heavyweight processes.* Because a thread has much less overhead, it is less expensive to create a thread and to switch between two threads in the same process. In particular, creation of a thread can require several orders of magnitude fewer resources to create than a process.
- Because threads share a heap, they can communicate using the variables in the heap. This makes communication between threads easier than between processes, because processes do not share any runtime memory. To share data between processes, external data stores, such as files, must be used. These can be computationally expensive options for sharing data.

When Web servers were first introduced, they were used with programs such as Perl or C/C++ to process data from Web pages. These early programs were implemented as processes using the CGI mechanism. CGI always created a process to run the program, much as early operating systems did, which resulted in two major drawbacks to implementing Web servers as processes:

- Each time a new request came from a Web page, a new process had to be created to handle it. Because every Web page would produce a request, this required that a process be started for every Web page requested from the server. When the Web was new, the number of requests was small, and this was not a problem;

however, as use of the Web grew, some Web servers began to receive a million or more requests an hour. The overhead in creating a process became very large and threatened to swamp even very fast servers.

- Because all data associated with a request was contained in a process, when the process exited the data was no longer available on the server; however, persistent data between Web pages was necessary for tracking the current status of the user to know what actions to take when a request was processed. Several solutions to this problem were attempted by programmers. The data could be written to a file and retrieved with each request, but access to a disk is slow and bogged down the system. The data needed was sometimes put in hidden fields on the HTML page sent to the client computer, but this data was easily hacked and changed and was simply not secure. Other mechanisms to handle the need for persistent data were tried, but all had significant problems.

The problems of large overhead in starting a process and the inability to share data effectively have been solved by applying technologies that use threads, such as servlets.* The big difference between CGI and servlets is that, while CGI uses a separate process for each request, a servlet processes each request as a thread inside of a process, which solves the two problems encountered with CGI. Because threads require much fewer resources for creation and somewhat fewer resources for context switches, servlets and other technologies that use threads require much fewer resources than process-based technologies such as CGI.

Because many threads can share the heap, each request can create a thread and *cache* information in the heap. When the next request comes from the user, this cached information can be retrieved and the new thread created to process this request. This allows for the use of a simple mechanism for maintaining a persistent store on the server.

Using threads has solved a number of problems encountered when implementing programs to run on Web servers, but it has created many others. Because the requests running on the Web servers are now sharing data inside of a process, all the problems that occur with communicating asynchronous activities are present and need to be accounted for. The last two sections of this chapter outline these problems, and the rest of this textbook is concerned with how to handle such problems.

---

* Servlets are not the only technology that uses threads in a server. Languages such as Perl that originally were run only as processes can now be run as threads.

Exhibit 9. Procedural Program for Exhibit 10

```
1  public class PExec {
2    public void run() {
3      int counter = 0;
4      System.out.println("In run, counter = " + counter);
5      counter++;
6      System.out.println("In run, counter = " + counter);
7      return;
8    }
9    public static void main(String args[]) {
10     PExec pe = new PExec();
11     pe.run();
12     return;
13   }
14}
```

2.4.3 Program Execution for a Procedural Program

This section explains how asynchronous activities, such as threads and processes, can interleave execution. It begins by explaining how a simple procedural program executes and then uses the same model to show how the SVM can use thread contexts in the execution of a concurrent program. The model of execution is expanded in subsequent sections to explain concepts such as process states, the Java *synchronized* modifier, and *wait*, *notify*, and *notifyAll* methods.

This discussion begins by considering the procedural program in Exhibit 9. In this figure, the lines in the program have been numbered to show the statement in the program that is being executed in the PC. In a real program, the PC would be set to the address of an instruction in the method area.

The following details how the execution of the program would proceed. Each step corresponds to a frame in Exhibit 10, which shows the SMM state of the process after that step has been executed. This can lead to some confusion, as the PC always points to the next line to be executed, not the line that was just executed.

1. The program begins execution. The SVM creates the heap and thread context for main, initializing them to null. It also creates the method area and loads the methods for the PExec class into the method area. Finally, it creates a PC. Because the program is still starting up, the PC exists and might even be used, but its value for now is undefined.
2. The SVM pushes an *activation record* for the main method on the stack. As part of this activation record, a reference to the PExec object is created; however, the object itself is not yet created, so the reference is null. We will represent this reference using a convention similar to that in C: *pe. The SVM at this point also

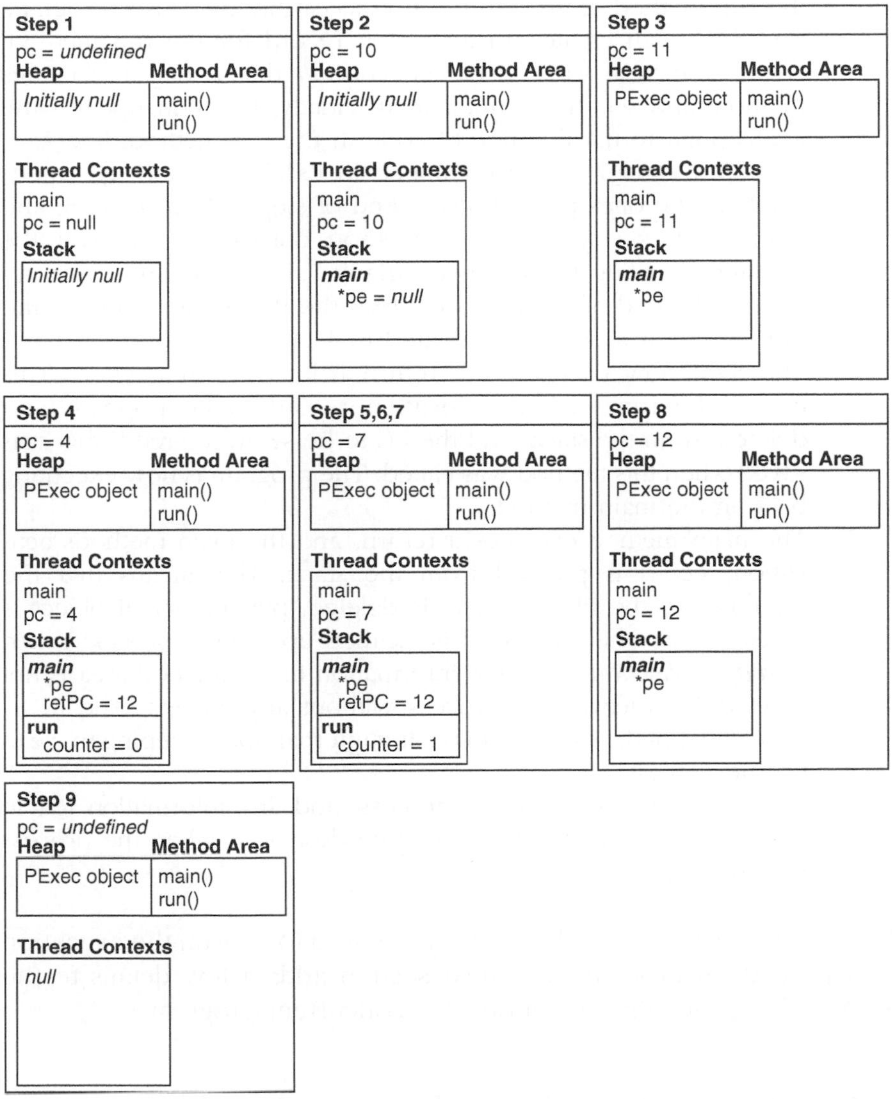

Step 1
pc = *undefined*

Heap	Method Area
Initially null	main() run()

Thread Contexts

main
pc = null
Stack
Initially null

Step 2
pc = 10

Heap	Method Area
Initially null	main() run()

Thread Contexts

main
pc = 10
Stack
main
*pe = *null*

Step 3
pc = 11

Heap	Method Area
PExec object	main() run()

Thread Contexts

main
pc = 11
Stack
main
*pe

Step 4
pc = 4

Heap	Method Area
PExec object	main() run()

Thread Contexts

main
pc = 4
Stack
main
*pe
retPC = 12
run
counter = 0

Step 5,6,7
pc = 7

Heap	Method Area
PExec object	main() run()

Thread Contexts

main
pc = 7
Stack
main
*pe
retPC = 12
run
counter = 1

Step 8
pc = 12

Heap	Method Area
PExec object	main() run()

Thread Contexts

main
pc = 12
Stack
main
*pe

Step 9
pc = *undefined*

Heap	Method Area
PExec object	main() run()

Thread Contexts

null

Exhibit 10. Steps in Executing a Procedural Program

assigns the process PC and the thread PC to the first executable line in the main method, line 10.

3. The SVM now executes the code at line 10, which creates an instance of the PExec class in the heap. The *pe reference points to this object in the heap (note that it is no longer null), and the SVM updates the PC in this context and the process PC to point to the next executable line in the program, line 11.
4. The SVM prepares to call the run method. First, the PC of the next line to be executed in the main, line 12, is stored in a special variable in the activation record of the main method that we will call the retPC. This is the line where execution will continue when

the run method returns and is not accessible by a user program. The SVM then creates an activation record for the run method, creates the local variable named *counter* that is declared in this method, and sets the counter to 0. Finally, the SVM updates the PC to point to the first line of code in the run method, line 4.

5. Steps 5, 6, and 7 are all combined in Exhibit 10, and the values used are the ones present at the end of step 7. In steps 4, 5, and 6, the SVM executes in the run method, outputting a line with the counter, updating the counter variable, and outputting a second line. At the end of this series of steps the PC points to line 7, and the counter has been incremented to 1 on the stack.
6. The SVM now executes the return from the run method. This causes the run methods activation record to be popped (and deleted) from the stack, and the PC to be set to the retPC that was saved when this method was called. The program is now executing back in the main method.
7. The main method executes a return, and the main methods activation record is popped from the stack. This means that the reference to the PExec object is deleted, but the actual object is deleted later when the stack is cleaned up using a process called *garbage collection*. Also, the information in the method area is not deleted. This leaves the process without any context. The PC is now undefined, as the SVM is doing internal housekeeping to clean up the process.
8. The SVM now destroys this process, and any information left in the heap or the method area will be destroyed when the process is destroyed.

This example shows how the SVM can be used to explain the execution of a procedural program. The next section adds a few details to the SVM and explains the execution of a concurrent program.

2.4.4 Program Execution and Context Switching with Threads

The execution of a concurrent process in the SVM is the same as for a procedural program with one major difference. Because a concurrent program has multiple threads, multiple contexts will exist in a concurrent process, and, because each context has its own PC, the SVM must choose which thread context to run at each execution cycle and hence which context's PC to use. Many factors can go into this decision, some of which can only be decided at run-time. For example, if a context has had several statements run without interruption, the SVM may decide to allow another context to run on the next cycle. Because it is impossible for the programmer to know all the factors that will go into deciding what thread context will be selected next, the rule

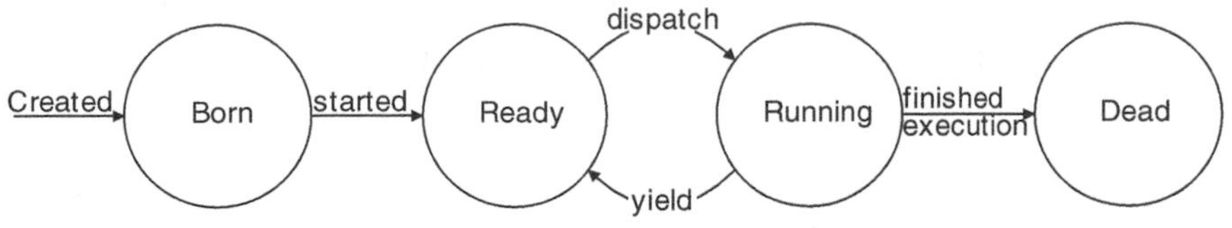

Exhibit 11. SVM Thread States

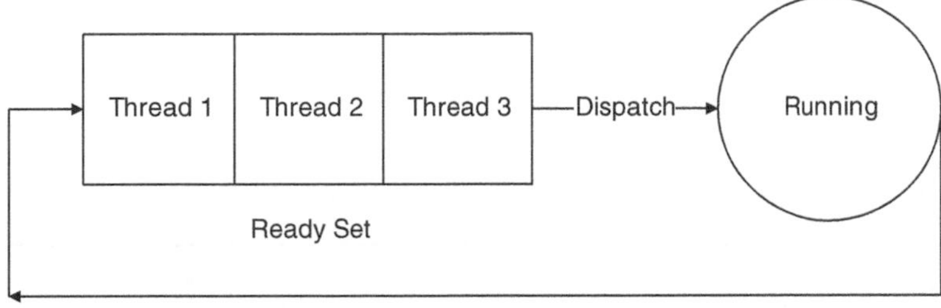

Exhibit 12. Relationship between Ready and Running States in SVM

for the SVM will be that at any time any valid and ready thread context can be selected. The programmer should never make any assumptions about what context, and hence what PC, will be selected.

This discussion of threads begins by answering the question of how a new thread context gets created and the thread started. When a thread is created, it is initially in a *born* state (see Exhibit 11). The start method is then called on the thread, and the thread is moved to the *ready* state, a state from which it can be run. Often, many threads are ready to run and must be managed by the SVM. This is done by placing these threads in a *ready set,** as shown in Exhibit 12. The thread that is currently executing using the CPU is in the *running* state. For a computer with a single CPU, only one thread can be in the running state at any time.

When the SVM chooses the next thread to execute, it can choose the thread that is currently in the running state or any thread that is in the ready set; the programmer cannot influence this decision,** and any one of these threads is equally likely to be chosen. If the SVM chooses the thread already running, it simply executes the instruction in the process PC. If it chooses a thread from the ready set, the process

* Note that the term *set* is intentionally used here to show that the threads are not ordered. This is consistent with the terminology used in [LIN99]. The more commonly used term in texts on operating systems is a *ready list,* but this implies an ordering that is not necessarily present.

** In the JVM, the programmer can influence this decision by the use of thread priorities; however, it is incorrect to use priorities to control the interactions between them. Priorities serve no useful purpose in this discussion and so are dropped from the SVM.

Exhibit 13. Concurrent Program for Exhibit 14

```
public class CExec implements Runnable{
  public void run() {
    int counter = 0;
    System.out.println("In run, counter = " + counter);
    counter++;
    System.out.println("In run, counter = " + counter);
    return;
  }
  public static void main(String args[]) {
    CExec ce = new CExec();
    Thread t1 = new Thread(ce);
    t1.start();
    System.out.println("in main");
    return;
  }
}
```

PC is written to the context for the currently running thread, its state is changed to ready, the PC of the new thread is loaded into the process PC, and the state of the newly executing thread is changed to running. Because the context (PC and stack that are used) has been changed when this occurs, the process of suspending one thread and starting another is referred to as a *context switch*. When a thread completes running, it is moved to the *dead* state. In the dead state, a thread still exists but it cannot be executed. The dead state is necessary to allow the SVM to maintain the context of the thread until it is safe to get rid of the thread.

Using these relationships, the execution of a concurrent program is explained in a manner similar to that used in Exhibit 10. A few things are added to the SMM to be able to support the addition of concurrency. First, the thread context must have a state variable added so that the state of the context can be tracked. Because this variable is used only by the SVM and must only be changed when a thread is moved to a running state or moved to the ready set, it cannot be accessed directly by the programmer. Second, the current ready set and the thread that is running must be maintained by the SVM process.

The rest of this section discusses the execution of the concurrent program shown in Exhibit 13. The steps involved in running this program are given in Exhibit 14 and are covered in the following discussion. As in Exhibit 10, the steps in Exhibit 14 are after the step or as completed, in this case including the choice of the next thread to be run. So, the running thread and PC represent the situation that will be run on the next step.

1. The program begins execution. The SVM creates the heap and thread context for main, initializing them to null. It also creates

the method area and loads the methods for the CExec class into the method area. Finally, it creates a PC. Because the program is still starting up, the PC exists and might even be used, but its value for now is undefined.

2. The SVM pushes an activation record for the main method on the stack. As part of this activation record, a reference to the CExec object is created; however, this object is not yet created so the reference is null. We will represent this reference using a convention similar to that in C: *ce. The SVM at this point also assigns the process PC and the thread PC to the first executable line in the main method (line 10).
3. The SVM now executes the code at line 10, which creates an instance of the CExec class in the heap. The *ce reference points to this object in the heap, and the SVM updates the PC in this context and the process PC to point to the next executable line in the program (line 11).
4. The SVM executes the code at line 11, which creates an instance of the Thread class in the heap. When the thread object is created, a context for the thread is also created, but the status is born, and this thread is not yet executable. To actually be eligible to run, a thread must be ready or running; therefore, only one thread, the main thread, can be run and execution continues in the main thread.
5. Line 12 is executed, which puts the t1 thread in the ready set and sets the status of the t1 queue to ready. The SVM is now free to choose either the main thread or the t1 thread to run. In this example, the t1 thread is chosen, but the choice of t1 is completely arbitrary. Because t1 has been chosen, a context switch from the main thread to the t1 thread is necessary. The process PC is set to the PC from the context of the t1 thread, and the current process PC is saved in the context of the main thread. Finally, the state of the two threads is updated.
6. Line 5 in the t1 thread is executed, which produces a line of output, part of which is the value of the local variable counter. The SVM now chooses which thread to run. In this example, thread t1 is chosen to be run again, but, again, this is completely arbitrary.
7. Line 4 in the t1 thread is executed, which adds the local variable counter, located in the stack of thread t1. The SVM now chooses to run the main thread again and performs a context switch.
8. Line 13 in the main thread is executed and produces a line of output. The SVM chooses to continue to run in the main thread, updating the PC to line 14.
9. Line 14 is executed, which completes the main thread. This thread is now dead, and it cannot be executed; however, it can also not finish. A thread that creates another thread is called a *parent thread*, and a parent thread must remain until all of its children are dead. Therefore, this thread is moved to state dead and sits idle until all

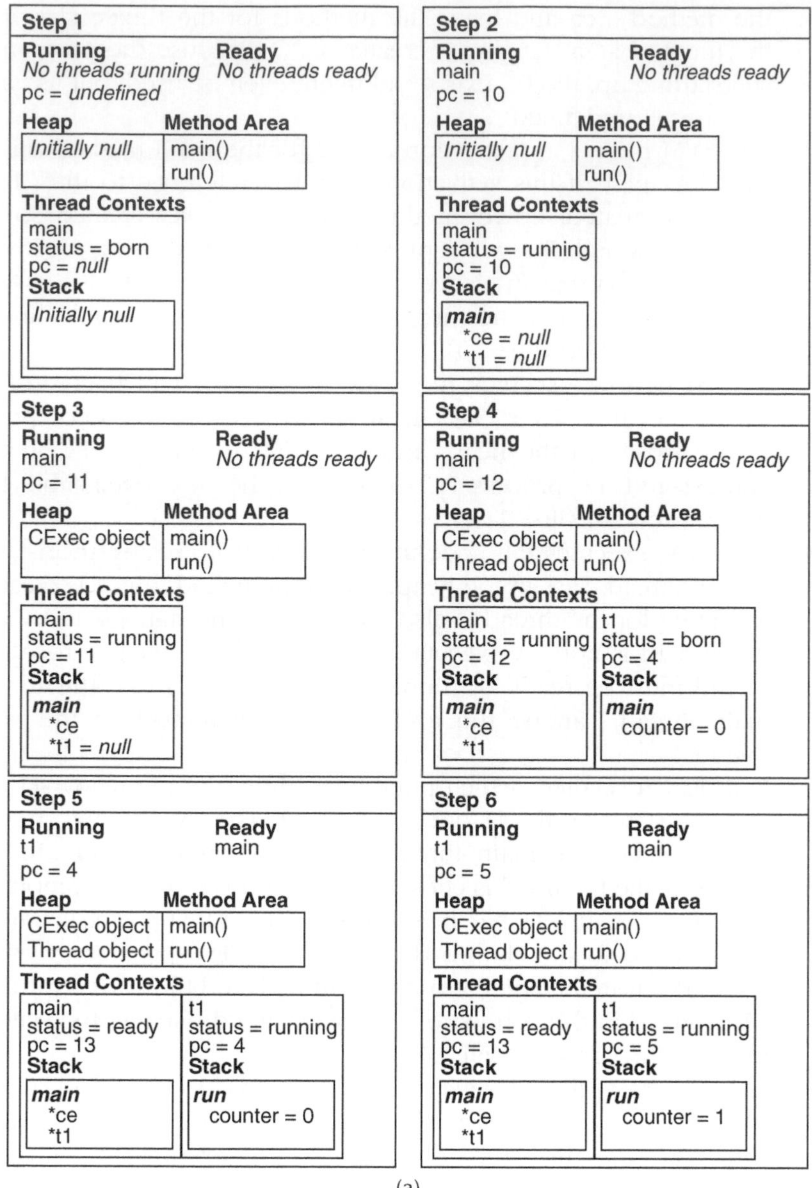

(a)

Exhibit 14. Steps in Executing a Concurrent Program

of its children also die. Only one thread can be run now (thread t1), so the SVM must select it to run.

10. Line 6 in thread t1 is executed and produces an output. The SVM continues to execute in thread t1, updating the PC to line 7.
11. Line 7 is executed, which completes thread t1. Thread t1 changes to state dead; because it has no children, it can complete and its context is deleted. The main thread now has no children, and its context is also deleted. The program is now free to exit.

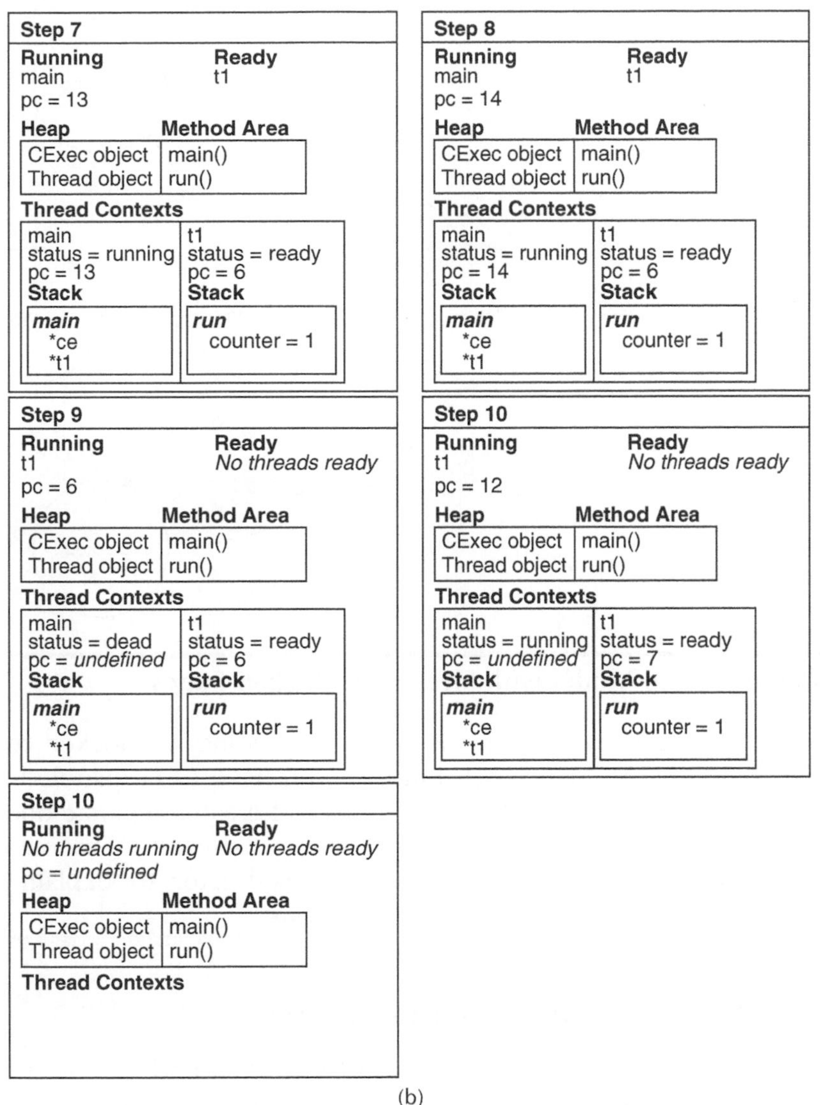

Exhibit 14. (Continued)

2.4.5 Sleeping and Blocking

This model is good enough to explain a program where all the threads are always either ready or running. However, often a thread will be suspended for some period of time, such as when a call is made to Thread.sleep or an I/O is requested. When this occurs, the thread is moved into a sleeping or blocked state until the condition that moved it to this state has been satisfied, as shown in Exhibit 15. When a thread is in a sleeping or blocked state, it cannot be run, so it would be a waste of time to have the CPU check whether or not to run it

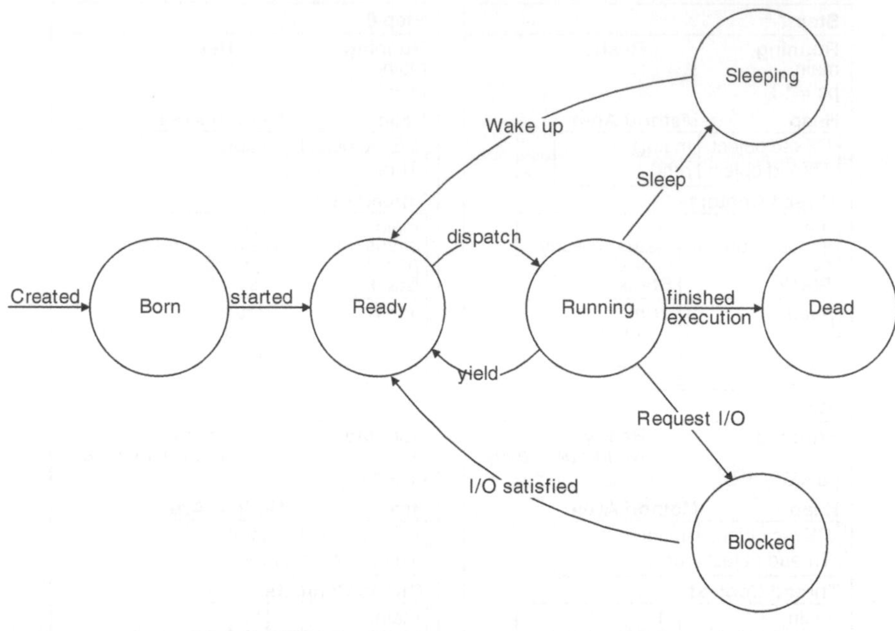

Exhibit 15. State Model with Sleep and Blocked States

in each execution cycle. Threads that are sleeping or blocked really do not belong in the ready set, but they still have to be handled and accounted for by the SVM. Therefore, the SVM creates separate queues for threads that are in these states, as shown in Exhibit 16. This method of handling suspended threads will be used later to explain the behavior of the Java wait and notify methods.

2.4.6 Nondeterminism and Concurrency

As shown by the output of Program2.5 (Exhibit 6) and the discussion in Section 2.4.4, because the SVM (and the JVM and most concurrent execution environments) can choose the thread to run at each step in the program execution, it is possible to have more than one possible valid output from a concurrent program. As shown in the discussion of Program2.5 (Exhibit 6), the number of different possible execution paths in a program can be very large even for very simple programs with a very small number of threads. This property of a program being able to produce a number of different execution paths not completely controlled by the programmer is referred to as *nondeterminism* because the programmer cannot determine the absolute order of the statements.

Programmers who have never programmed with concurrency would not be familiar with nondeterministic behavior in a program. If a procedural program is run a million times, it will always produce the same answer. However, a concurrent program that runs correctly a

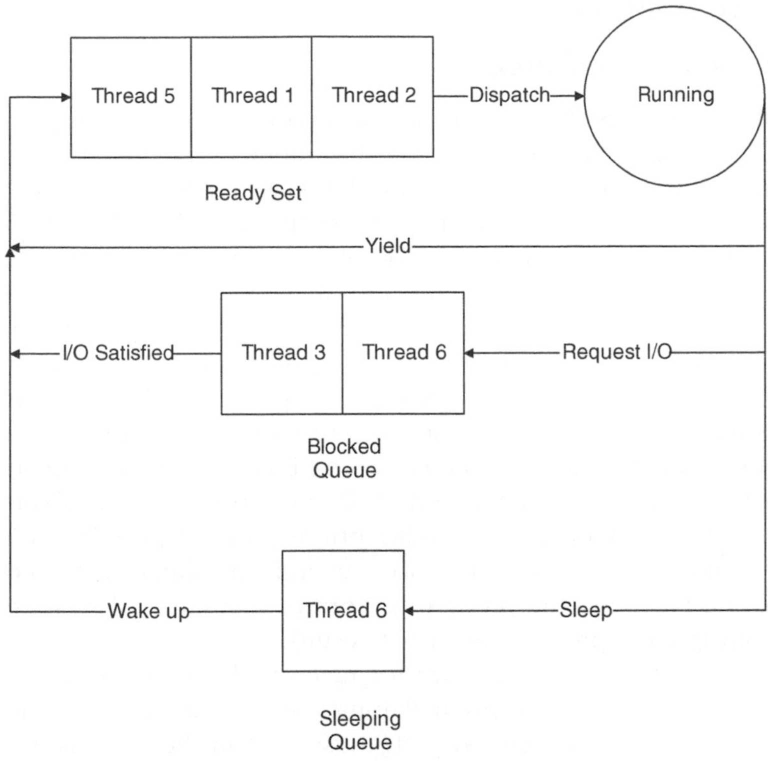

Exhibit 16. SVM with Sleep and Blocked Queues

million times could produce an error on the millionth and first run. This is the problem with nondeterminism; a programmer cannot test to show that a program is correct even for a limited subset of input. The only way to show a program is correct is to execute all possible paths through the program, and hence produce all results that can be produced by any possible interleaving of threads. While this is theoretically possible, it is completely impractical because of the large number of possible ways the threads can interleave. And, if even one of these ways to interleave is invalid, the possibility exists that the program will produce an invalid answer. The need to have a program always produce a correct answer for a given set of input is referred to as *program safety*.

Maintaining program safety is difficult because problems can become more prevalent as the number of interacting threads is increased. Normally, when a program is tested, a test suite is developed that is more limited than the environment in which the program will actually be run, so some problems occur only when the program is put into production and often can only be repeated in production environments. The problem of unsafe programs is one of the central issues in concurrent programming and is examined in more detail in Section 2.5.

2.5 Program Safety

2.5.1 Race Conditions

As pointed out in Section 2.3, problems unique to concurrent programs occur because of the nondeterministic interactions between threads. At the heart of most of these problems is a *race condition*. Race conditions occur when one activity, such as a thread, produces a correct answer as long as it can complete a task without interruption; however, if another activity interrupts it while it is in the middle of the task, the answer produced will be in error. A simple example of a race condition would be two threads printing a report to a printer. If both threads are allowed to access the printer at the same time, it is possible for the data for the two reports to be mixed together, obviously ruining both reports. However, if one report finishes before the next one begins, both reports will be correct. This problem can be seen as one where one thread printing one report is *racing* to finish printing the report before the second one starts. If it succeeds, it wins the race, and the program is correct. If it fails, it loses the race and both threads produce incorrect results.

Two conditions are necessary for race conditions to occur. First, a resource (in this case, a printer) must be shared between the two threads. Second, an execution path must exist in the threads where a resource is shared in an unsafe manner (in this case, the ability of the two threads to access the printer at the same time). If these two conditions exist, a race condition is present in the program even if the problem never actually occurs, because the fact is that the problem could happen. Even if a programmer is satisfied that the likelihood is extremely small, the program is dangerous because it is unstable. If a later change is made to the program that changes the assumptions that made the program appear safe, problems can begin to appear that cause the program to produce wrong answers. Often these problems are more difficult to solve because they will be intermittent and not consistently reproducible.

This is a problem for many programmers because they have a habit of "hacking" a program, which is writing the basic structure and tweaking it and testing the results until it produces the desired behavior. This strategy is not effective for concurrent programs, as the program cannot be shown to be correct by testing. So, if a concurrent program cannot be tested to show it is safe, how *can* the program be shown to be safe? Only two valid mechanisms are available. The first is to show a proof by induction that the program will satisfy any conditions necessary for the program to be safe. The second is to develop the program using strategies known to be safe in developing a program, which requires that implementation of the program is planned and implemented carefully.

What types of strategies can be applied to make a program safe? The necessary conditions for a race condition imply strategies to correct the problem. One strategy is to simply not share resources — for example, to have two printers and have each thread access its own printer. A program that does not share resources is obviously safe, and this strategy is often used as part of a concurrent program (for example, in the Java Event Model; see Chapter 7); however, such an approach is not always practical. Few computers will have a printer for every possible output that can be produced, thus some sharing is inevitable.

The second strategy for handling race conditions is to make sure that the shared resource is in a safe state before allowing another thread to access it. In the case of the printer, this means that a thread that wishes to use a printer must be guaranteed that it will have exclusive access to a printer until it has completed printing, and only then will a second thread be allowed to print. This strategy of isolating and locking a resource while it is in an unsafe state is the basis of most strategies for writing safe concurrent programs and is the topic of the rest of this section.

When doing concurrent programming, the shared resources that are most often subject to race conditions are program variables. The next section shows how race conditions can occur in a simple program that shares variables and shows the mechanisms built into Java for safely handling these shared variables.

2.5.2 Race Conditions in Programs

Just as in the printer example, race conditions exist in programs because multiple threads attempt to access a shared resource, often a program variable. Because concurrent threads interleave in a nondeterministic fashion, the variable can sometimes be changed so that it produces an incorrect result. For example, consider Program2.6 (Exhibit 17). This program simply swaps two numbers in two different threads. Obviously, two correct answers can be produced from this program when each thread swaps their numbers, as shown in Exhibit 18. However, this program can also produce two incorrect answers when the threads interleave and the second thread changes the value in the tmp variable being used by the first thread, also shown in Exhibit 18.

The reason this program can produce these incorrect results is that it is unsafe. It is sharing a resource, the SwapInt object and its variable tmp, and it uses that variable in an unsafe manner. The unsafe scenario is that one thread enters the swap method, saves its val1 to the variable tmp, and then calls Thread.sleep. Because its state is now sleeping, the SVM chooses the second thread to execute and does a context switch to the second thread. The second thread can then enter the

Exhibit 17. Program2.6: Program with a Race Condition

```
public class ShowRaceCondition implements Runnable {
    int val1, val2; // store the values to be swapped.
    static SwapInt so = new SwapInt(); // SwapInt object.
    Note that it is
                    // static so it is shared between all
                    // instances of this class.

    /**
     * Constructor. It just takes two integers and stores them
     * so that they can be swapped later.
     */
    public ShowRaceCondition(int i1, int i2){
        val1 = i1; val2 = i2;
    }

    /**
     *  Run method that simply swaps the integers and prints
     *  the result.
     */
    public void run() {
        so.swap(this);
   System.out.println("Val1 = " + val1 + " Val2 = " + val2);
    }

    /**
     *  main method that creates and starts the objects and
        threads
     */
    public static void main(String args[]) {

      (new Thread(new ShowRaceCondition(4,7))).start();
      (new Thread(new ShowRaceCondition(2,5))).start();
    }
}

/**
 *    Purpose: Provide an object that swaps integers.
 *        An object is needed so that an instance variable
 *        exists that can be shared.  If a method is used
 *        variable will be stored on the stack and not shared
 *       between threads, and no race condition would exist.
 */
class SwapInt {
    volatile private int tmp;

    public void swap(ShowRaceCondition s) {
        try {
            Thread.sleep((int) (Math.random() * 100));
            tmp = s.val1;
            s.val1 = s.val2;
            Thread.sleep((int) (Math.random() * 100));
            s.val2 = tmp;
        } catch (InterruptedException e) {
        }
    }
}
```

Exhibit 18. Possible Output from Program2.6 (Exhibit 17)

```
Correct Output

  Val1 = 5 Val2 = 2Val1 = 7 Val2 = 4
  Val1 = 7 Val2 = 4Val1 = 5 Val2 = 2

Incorrect Output

  Val1 = 5 Val2 = 4Val1 = 7 Val2 = 2
  Val1 = 7 Val2 = 4Val1 = 5 Val2 = 2
```

swap method and overwrite the value for tmp, thus losing the value from the first thread. This is an example of a race condition on a variable. Often, the first thread executes the swap method completely and the value in tmp has no meaning when the second thread enters the swap method, so the program produces a correct answer. However, if the first thread loses the race and does not finish the swap method before the second thread enters it, the value of tmp is changed which causes the first thread to incorrectly swap values.

One of the reasons that the program is unsafe is that the SwapInt object is shared. This object is shared because it is declared *static*, so there is only one copy of the object for the class, and that copy is shared by all the ShowRaceCondition objects. One way to make this program safe is to simply remove the static modifier, creating a SwapInt object for each ShowRaceCondition object. This same effect could be achieved by declaring the SwapInt object inside of the run method, making a SwapInt object for each thread. An object that is not shared is safe. However, as with printers, it is often necessary to share an object, so a method must be developed that will ensure that the data can be used safely. Because this program shows how a race condition can occur, it is also used to show how to solve it.

2.5.3 Locking Objects

The race condition in Program2.6 (Exhibit 17) occurred because the two threads could both be executing in the swap method at the same time. What is needed is a mechanism that locks the swap method when one thread enters it, preventing other threads from entering the method until the first thread has completed executing it. When the first thread leaves the method, it unlocks it, allowing another thread to obtain the lock and run in the method. This solution is shown in Program2.7 (Exhibits 19 and 20). Program2.7 is made up of two classes: a binary semaphore (as shown in Exhibit 19, Program2.7a) and a class that implements a safe solution to the problem in Program2.6 (Exhibit 17) (as shown in Exhibit 20, Program2.7b).

Exhibit 19. Program2.7a: Binary Semaphore

```
public class BinarySemaphore {
  private boolean locked = false;
  /**
   * Get the lock.
   */
  public synchronized void getLock() {
    while (locked) {
      try {
        wait();
      } catch(InterruptedException e) {
      }
    }
    locked = true;
  }
  /**
   * Release the lock.
   */
  public synchronized void releaseLock() {
    locked = false;
    notify();
  }
}
```

One way to implement locking is to use a binary semaphore, such as the one implemented in Exhibit 19 (Program2.7a), which is shown later to be correct; however, for now you should assume that this binary semaphore is indeed safe. To use this binary semaphore, a thread makes a call to the method getLock. If the variable locked is false, the semaphore is not locked, so the thread obtains the lock by setting the value of locked to true. Now, if another thread tries to get the lock by calling getLock, it finds that the lock is taken (i.e., the value of locked is true), and it must wait until the lock is free to continue.

The thread that obtained the lock is now free to run in the *critical section* of the program. A critical section is a portion of code where only one thread may be executing at a time to ensure the safety of the program. The thread running in the critical section now does the swap operation, and because no other thread can enter this section of code the swap is safe.

When the thread has finished executing in the critical section, it makes a call to the releaseLock method, which releases the lock by setting the value of locked to false and notifying any thread that is currently waiting for the lock that it may now try to obtain the lock and proceed. For now, do not worry about the syntax or how the synchronized, wait, and notify statements actually work; they are covered in detail later. Just understand that a lock can be used to suspend threads until the lock is freed, ensuring the safety of using a critical section.

Exhibit 20. Program2.7b: Program that Safely Swaps Values

```
public class SolveRaceCondition implements Runnable{
  int val1, val2;
  static SwapInt SO = new SwapInt();

  public SolveRaceCondition(int i1, int i2){
    val1 = i1; val2 = i2;
  }

  public void run() {
    SO.swap(this);
    System.out.println("Val1 = " + val1 + " Val2 = " + val2);
  }

  public static void main(String args[]) {
    (new Thread(new SolveRaceCondition(4,7))).start();
    (new Thread(new SolveRaceCondition(2,5))).start();
  }
}
/**
 *   Purpose: This SwapInt object shows how a lock can be
 *            used to prevent two threads from sharing a
 *            critical section, thus fixing a race condition.
 *
 * Procedure: 1 - Get the lock; 2 - Execute the Critical
 *            section; 3 - Release the lock.
 */

class SwapInt {
  private volatile int tmp;
  private BinarySemaphore mutex = new BinarySemaphore();

  public void swap(SolveRaceCondition s) {
    mutex.getLock();
    try {
      Thread.sleep((int) (Math.random() * 100));
      tmp = s.val1;
      s.val1 = s.val2;
      Thread.sleep((int) (Math.random() * 100));
      s.val2 = tmp;
    } catch (InterruptedException e) {
    }
    mutex.releaseLock();
  }
}
```

The binary semaphore has now been added to Exhibit 17 (Program2.6) to produce Exhibit 20 (Program2.7b). Note that the only difference is that in Exhibit 20 (Program2.7b) a locking variable, called *mutex* (for mutual exclusion), is created as part of the object to protect the critical section in the swap object. The lock for mutex is obtained when the thread enters the swap method, and the lock is released when the thread leaves the swap method. The program is now obviously safe, and it can be tested many times to show that it works; however, as was pointed out earlier, a concurrent program cannot be tested to show it is correct. The only valid way to show that a concurrent program is correct is to do an inductive proof of the program, which is done for Exhibit 20 (Program2.7b) in the next section.

Before continuing, the reader should note that the lock for the swap method is associated with the SwapInt object, not the swap method or SwapInt class. This is often confusing to programmers new to concurrent programming. Because of this, if more than one method in the SwapInt object uses the mutex lock, only one thread can be in any method for that object at any time. If there are multiple SwapInt objects, one thread can be in the swap method for each object at any time. This should become more clear when the details of the Binary-Semaphore class are discussed.

2.5.4 Proving Exhibit 20 (Program2.7b) Is Correct

As was pointed out earlier, a concurrent program cannot be tested to show it is correct; an inductive proof is necessary to show the program is correct. The technique for performing an inductive proof on a program is important to understand, even if the proof is rarely done, because the inductive proof provides the reasoning for showing a concurrent program is correct.

The inductive proof of Exhibit 20 (Program2.7b) starts with the assumption that the BinarySemaphore object is safe. Also, the variables used in the SwapInt class must be private so that they cannot be modified by a thread except by calling the getLock and releaseLock methods. The base case and inductive case are stated, and the inductive step is done to show that the program is indeed safe:

- *Base case:* The two threads start at the beginning of the run method.
- *Induction hypothesis:* One thread enters the swap method, while the other thread is still executing code prior to entering the swap method. Because neither thread has yet entered the swap method, we know it is safe to this point.
- *Inductive step:* Both threads execute after the swap method, and the variables are swapped correctly.

As proof, all we have to do is show that all paths from the inductive hypothesis to the inductive step result in a correct program. Assuming thread 1 has entered the swap method, the possibilities are as follows:

- Thread 1 executes to completion of the swap method before thread 2 executes again. Thread 1 will thus finish before thread 2 can enter the swap method, and is safe. Thread 2 will enter the swap method after thread 1 no longer uses it, and so it is safe. This path is safe.

- Thread 1 and thread 2 interleave execution, but thread 2 never tries to enter the swap method. This path is again safe.
- Thread 1 and thread 2 interleave, but thread 2 attempts to enter the swap method. Thread 2 is stopped on the lock, and thus thread 1 can complete safely, followed by thread 2. This path is also safe.

The second part of the proof would be to show that the program is safe if thread 2 enters the swap method before thread 1, and the proof is conducted the same as above, with the result that the program in Exhibit 20 (Program2.7b) is indeed shown to be safe.

2.5.5 The Synchronized Modifier

The proof in the previous section assumed that the BinarySemaphore object was safe. The next two sections show that this object is indeed safe and explain the workings of the *wait* and *notify* methods and the *synchronized* modifier. They also show how these methods can be used to implement a special type of object known as a *monitor*, of which the BinarySemaphore class is a good example.

The idea of protecting critical sections of programs using a lock is so useful that Java implemented it using the synchronized modifier. The synchronized modifier is placed at the beginning of a block of code, in this case an entire method. Associated with every instance of the Object class is a binary semaphore (which will be referred to as a lock). Because every object in Java extends the Object class, every object has a lock. The synchronized keyword automatically inserts the logic to obtain the lock on the object at the beginning of the block and inserts code for releasing the lock at the end of the block. When a thread attempts to enter a synchronized block of code, the lock for the object is checked, just as it was in the SwapInt object. If the lock is not taken, the thread obtains the lock, preventing any other thread from entering any other synchronized block in that object. When the thread leaves the block, the lock is released.

So the race condition in Exhibit 17 (Program2.6) could easily have been solved by adding the synchronized keyword to the swap method, as shown in Exhibit 21 (Program2.8), and the BinarySemaphore object is not needed. However, actually implementing the BinarySemaphore object is interesting for two reasons. First, it explains what happens when the synchronized modifier is used, and, second, implementation of the BinarySemaphore can be used to demonstrate the wait and notify methods.

Before explaining the use of wait and notify, however, one last point must be made about the synchronized modifier: It is associated with a block of code and an object. That block of code is often a method, and that object is often the "this" object. However, the block of code could be a part of the method, and the object could be any

Exhibit 21. Program2.8: Safe Swap Program Using the Synchronized Modifier

```
public class SolveRaceCondition_2 implements Runnable{
  private int val1, val2;
  static SwapInt so = new SwapInt();

  public SolveRaceCondition_2(int i1, int i2){
    val1 = i1; val2 = i2;
  }

  public void run() {
    so.swap(this);
    System.out.println("Val1 = " + val1 + " Val2 = " + val2);
  }

  public static void main(String args[]) {

    (new Thread(new SolveRaceCondition_2(4,7))).start();
    (new Thread(new SolveRaceCondition_2(2,5))).start();
  }
}

/**
 * Purpose: This class shows the use of the synchronized
 *          clause to lock the swap method.
 */
class SwapInt {
  private int tmp;

  synchronized public void swap(SolveRaceCondition_2 s) {
    Thread.sleep((int) (Math.random() * 100));
    try {
      Thread.sleep((int) (Math.random() * 100));
      tmp = s.val1;
      s.val1 = s.val2;
      Thread.sleep((int) (Math.random() * 100));
      s.val2 = tmp;
    } catch (InterruptedException e) {
    }
  }
}
```

object, not simply the "this" object. To specify the block of code to be synchronized, the synchronized statement is simply used at the start of the block. To synchronize on an object other than "this," the object is specified as a parameter to the synchronized modifier. For example, the synchronization of the swap method in Exhibit 13 was achieved by synchronizing the entire method:

```
synchronized public void swap(SolveRaceCondition_2 s) {
}
```

This could have been written equivalently as:

```
public void swap(SolveRaceCondition_2 s) {
```

```
    synchronized(this) {
    }
  }
```

Because the synchronized block uses the "this" object and contains the entire method, these two methods would be equivalent.

2.5.6 The Wait and Notify/NotifyAll Methods

Because Java has already implemented a locking mechanism for objects using the synchronized block, BinarySemaphore is not necessary to make the swap method correctly. But, the BinarySemaphore class is interesting in that it shows how to use the synchronized keyword and wait and notifyAll methods to implement what is called a *monitor*. Monitors are important data structures that form the basis for much of the material in Chapter 3, as well as the rest of the book. The BinarySemaphore class is a very good example of a monitor.

An easy way to understand a monitor is to think of it as an object in which all the data are private and all the methods are protected by a single lock so that only one thread may be executing in any method in this object at any time. Because the data of the object is private and all the methods that can access the data are synchronized, it is not possible for unintended interactions between the threads to cause a race condition. This is the simplest type of monitor using *complete synchronization*. This type of object is always *thread safe*, so it can always be used safely in a program that uses threads.

Using complete synchronization, while safe, is too restrictive for many objects — for example, the BinarySemaphore object. So, a slightly more complex monitor can be written that has a "state," or conditions under which the methods in the object can be run. In the case of BinarySemaphore, the getLock method can only be run when the locked variable is false. If the locked variable is true, the thread must wait until it has changed value to false before continuing to run that thread. This is accomplished by calling the wait method.

The wait method is a method in the Object class. It is matched with the notify or notifyAll method, also in the Object class. To understand how the wait and notify methods work, we need to refine the model of contexts. Earlier, we said that the SVM could choose any context that was ready or running to execute next. The SVM keeps a list of all the threads in the system that are ready to be run, called a ready set. Associated with each thread is its context, including the PC. The SVM chooses one thread from the ready set to run and begins to execute the code at the PC for that context. After the thread has executed for some time, where the time is as small as each line of code, the SVM takes the thread that is running and puts it back in the ready set. The SVM again chooses a thread to run from the ready set, possibly the same thread that it has just moved back to the list, and executes that thread. This cycle continues until all threads have completed and the program has finished running.

However, just as when a thread is waiting on an I/O or is sleeping, not all threads are always ready to run. The SVM has no reason to consider these threads when choosing a thread to run, as these threads are not ready; therefore, the SVM keeps a number of sets and moves the threads between the sets as the program executes. When something happens, such as when a thread wakes up from sleeping, the SVM moves the thread from the sleeping set to the ready set. This thread can then be selected to run the next time that the SVM chooses a new thread to move from the ready set to running.

Many such sets of threads not ready to run are managed by the SVM. The one of interest here is the one associated with the wait call on an object. When a thread makes a call to wait it is telling the SVM that it does not want to run again until a call to notify or notifyAll method is invoked on the object on which it did the wait. When the wait method is called, the SVM moves this thread to the wait set for the object that it is waiting on and only moves the object back to the ready set when a notify or notifyAll call is made on the object, as shown in Exhibit 22.

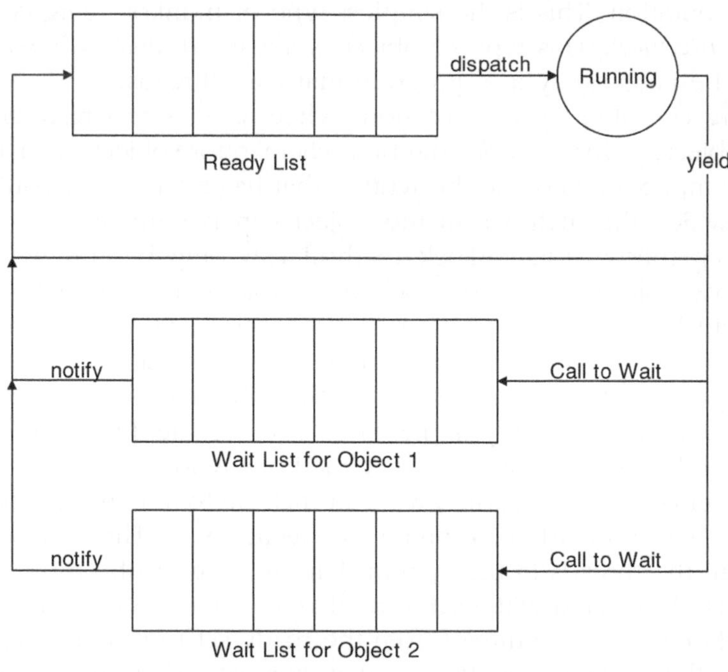

Exhibit 22. SVM with Wait Queue on an Object

The two forms of the notify call are notify and notifyAll. The notify call moves any one thread (the choice of the thread to move is nondeterministic, not the one waiting the longest) from the wait set for this specified object to the ready set. The notifyAll call moves all threads on the wait set for the object to the ready set. As will be seen in Chapter 3, the notifyAll call, while it has more overhead, will be used more frequently than the notify call.

2.5.7 Semantics of a Wait Call

Earlier it was said that only one thread can be executing inside of any synchronized method for an object. This condition was necessary to ensure that the safety of the object is maintained. However, if this is true, then we have a problem with the semantics of the wait call. Consider the BinarySemaphore object in Exhibit 19 (Program2.7a) and used in Exhibit 20 (Program2.7b). Thread 1 enters the synchronized block by calling getLock and obtains the lock for the BinarySemaphore object. It then sets the value of the locked variable to true and exits the getLock method, which releases the object's lock. Thread 2 then tries to use the BinarySemaphore by entering the getLock method. It can enter the method as the object is not locked, but it finds the variable locked to be true and so executes the wait method. If thread 2 continues to holds the object's lock on the BinarySemaphore object, then when thread 1 later tries to call the releaseLock method it finds that the BinarySemaphore object is locked, and it cannot continue. This results in thread 1 not being able to continue (because it cannot get the lock on the BinarySemaphore object held by thread 2), and thread 2 cannot continue because it is waiting for a notify call, which cannot happen because it continues to hold the BinarySemaphore object's lock. This is called *deadlock*, and is the subject of Section 2.6. Notice, though, that this problem would be an unavoidable consequence if this is actually how the wait and notify methods work.

In order to make the semantics of the wait method work they must be changed so that the wait method releases the object's lock when a thread is moved to the wait list. In the Java wait method, when thread 2 calls the wait method it releases the lock, allowing thread 1 to call the releaseLock method, which in turn calls the notify, allowing thread 2 to continue.

It should be noted that when thread 2 starts to run again, it does not hold the lock on the object as it was released when the thread called the wait method. This could be a problem. If another thread attempts to call getLock or releaseLock, the BinarySemaphore object is no longer locked, and this new thread could obtain the lock. If thread 2 continues to run as if it holds the lock, then the possibility exists for two threads running in a synchronized block on an object.

This problem can also occur if multiple threads are waiting on the same object and notifyAll is called, which releases all of them. Therefore, in order to ensure that the locking is maintained a thread that is moved to the ready set from a wait state must first regain the object lock before it can continue to run. This ensures that only one thread can execute in any synchronized block for an object at any time.

This also explains why notify and notifyAll cannot guarantee that the first thread to wait will be the first to execute when the object's lock becomes free. When a thread wakes up, it will be moved to the ready set. When it starts to execute, it must then try to obtain the object's lock. Because we already have said that the SVM is allowed to choose any thread from the ready set to execute, another thread may have obtained the lock between the time the thread was notified and when it can execute. Thus, the notify and notifyAll cannot guarantee which thread will execute first and obtain the lock. This is an important point that programmers need to keep in mind when using wait and notify/notifyAll in Java. The calls are not *fair* (i.e., the first thread to wait is not the first thread to begin execution after a notify/notifyAll) and cannot be made fair in Java. A programmer must build a mechanism to make the calls fair, if that is needed; such a mechanism is shown in Chapter 8.

From this discussion, we now have two ways to release a synchronized lock in Java. The first is to leave a synchronized block, which is safe, and the second is to call the wait method, which might not be safe. The second alternative is required in order to make the semantics of the wait and notify methods work correctly; however, a problem can occur if the call to wait is not used carefully. A wait call inside of a synchronized method means there is a possibility that the method will not run from start to end with no interference from other threads, leading to unsafe behavior by introducing race conditions back into the program. A programmer needs to be careful with how a wait call is used. Normally, wait is only called near the beginning of a synchronized block (as shown in Chapter 3) or by using very well-defined and carefully thought through semantics (such as notification objects, as discussed in Chapter 8).

Synchronization is very powerful but difficult to use correctly. If it is used incorrectly, it will result in either race conditions or deadlock; therefore, it is recommended that synchronization be implemented using standard patterns. In Chapter 3, the wait call is always used in a standard precondition block at the beginning of the method. Chapters 7 and 8 show other more complex but safe methods to do thread synchronization. If a programmer needs to use synchronization in a non-standard way, the only way to be sure that the program is correct is by supplying an inductive proof. So, the implementation of a concurrent program must be carefully considered.

2.6 Deadlock

2.6.1 Coordinating Threads

One problem that occurs frequently in concurrent programming is the need to allow the threads to coordinate. For example, a program may require two or more threads to take turns running. An example of two threads running but not taking turns is shown in Exhibit 23 (Program2.9). In this program, the two threads share a TurnPrinter component that is created in the main and saved in an instance variable for each UnsafeTurns objects. Even though these two threads share the TurnPrinter component, and the TurnPrinter component is completely synchronized, no mechanism for coordinating the two threads to take turns has been implemented, so they can run in any order. It is important to note that the solution to concurrent programming problems is not always simply synchronization, as shown here. Synchronization makes the object thread safe (it can be used safely with threads) but does not solve the problem of making the threads take turns.

One possible solution to this problem is given in Exhibit 24 (Program2.10). In this program, the first thread enters the printTurn method, prints its turn, and then waits for a notify call to occur. This can only happen when the second thread calls the printTurn method to print its turn, executes notify, and calls wait. In this way, each thread prints, calls notify, and waits, resulting in the threads taking turns.

Exhibit 24 (Program2.10) does correctly take turns, but the program never stops running. This problem occurs because, although the number of wait and notify calls are equal, the first notify call is lost because no thread is available to be moved from the wait set to the ready set. This means that one wait call will not be matched with a notify call, resulting in a thread that is permanently in the wait set and unable to finish. This situation is called *deadlock.*

2.6.2 Deadlock

Deadlock occurs when active threads are still in the system, but no thread can continue so the program cannot finish executing. In the case of Exhibit 24 (Program2.10), this is a result of the first notify being called before the second thread has called wait. As was said earlier, all a notify call does is move a thread from a wait list to a ready list. If no threads are in the wait set, then the notify is simply ignored. Because the first notify is ignored, an imbalance exists between the notify and wait calls in the program, with one wait not matched with a notify. This means that the second thread will always be left in a wait set that it cannot leave, and that thread can never complete. This

Exhibit 23. Program2.9: Two Cooperating Threads Not Taking Turns

```
import java.util.*;

public class UnsafeTurns implements Runnable {
  private static Random rand = new Random();
  private TurnPrinter tp;
  private int myNum;

  public UnsafeTurns(TurnPrinter tp, int myNum) {
    this.tp = tp;
    this.myNum = myNum;
  }

  public void run() {
    for (int i = 0; i < 10; i++) {
      tp.printTurn(myNum);
      try {
        Thread.sleep(rand.nextInt(100));
      } catch (InterruptedException e) {
      }
    }
  }

  public static void main(String args[]) {
    TurnPrinter tp = new TurnPrinter();
    (new Thread(new UnsafeTurns(tp, 1))).start();
    (new Thread(new UnsafeTurns(tp, 2))).start();
  }
}
/**
 *    Purpose: This TurnPrinter is intended to coordinate threads
 *             that want to take turns printing. It does not
 *             work.
 */
class TurnPrinter {
  public synchronized void printTurn(int turn) {
    System.out.println("turn is " + turn);
  }
}
```

example illustrates the need to be careful in implementing components, as even simple components can use locking schemes that can lead to deadlock.

One easy way to remove the deadlock in this program is shown in Exhibit 25 (Program2.11). The thread using the TurnPrinter component simply recognizes the presence of a bug in the TurnPrinter component (the extra wait) and compensates for it by putting a notify in the using programming after it is done using the component to print. While this solution is correct, it is a very bad way to program. A program that uses the TurnPrinter component should not have to compensate for programming errors in the component in order to work. In fact, any component that does not produce a valid result if

Exhibit 24. Program2.10: Two Cooperating Threads Taking Turns but Resulting in Deadlock

```
import java.util.Random;

public class SafeTurns implements Runnable {
  private static Random rand = new Random();
  private TurnPrinter tp;
  private int myNum;

  public SafeTurns(TurnPrinter tp, int myNum) {
    this.tp = tp;
    this.myNum = myNum;
  }

  public void run() {
    for (int i = 0; i < 10; i++) {
      tp.printTurn(myNum);
      try {
        Thread.sleep(rand.nextInt(100));
      } catch (InterruptedException e) {
      }
    }
  }

  public static void main(String args[]) {
    TurnPrinter tp = new TurnPrinter();
    (new Thread(new SafeTurns(tp, 0))).start();
    (new Thread(new SafeTurns(tp, 1))).start();
  }
}

/**
 *    Purpose: This TurnPrinter is intended to coordinate threads
 *             and make them take turns. It works; however, the
 *             first notify occurs before the first wait and is
 *             lost. Because the number of notifies matches the
 *             number of waits, one thread ends up stuck waiting
 *             for a notify that never occurs.
 */

class TurnPrinter {
  public synchronized void printTurn(int turn) {
    try {
      System.out.println("turn is " + turn);
      notify();
      wait();
    } catch (InterruptedException e) {
    }
  }
}
```

used correctly is wrong. It is the component writer's responsibility to make sure that a component works as advertised and to try to take into consideration as many errors that users will make as possible.

Exhibit 26 (Program2.12) provides a more appropriate solution to this problem, as it is solved entirely within the TurnPrinter object. Problems frequently arise due to a poorly designed component causing

Exhibit 25. Program2.11: Incorrect Usage of a Component to Compensate for an Error in Implementing the TurnPrinter Component

```
import java.util.Random;

public class SafeTurns1 implements Runnable {
  static private Random rand = new Random();
  private TurnPrinter tp;
  private int myNum;

  public SafeTurns1(TurnPrinter tp, int myNum) {
    this.tp = tp;
    this.myNum = myNum;
  }

  public void run() {
    for (int i = 0; i < 10; i++) {
      tp.printTurn(myNum);
      try {
        Thread.sleep(rand.nextInt(100));
      } catch (InterruptedException e) {
      }

      synchronized(tp) {
        tp.notify();
      }
    }
  }

  public static void main(String args[]) {
    TurnPrinter tp = new TurnPrinter();
    (new Thread(new SafeTurns1(tp, 0))).start();
    (new Thread(new SafeTurns1(tp, 1))).start();
  }
}
/**
 *    Purpose: This TurnPrinter is intended to coordinate threads
 *             and make them take turns. It works; however, the
 *             first notify occurs before the first wait and is
 *             lost. Because the number of notifies matches the
 *             number of waits, one thread ends up stuck waiting
 *             for a notify that never occurs. This is accounted
 *             for in the program using the component.
 */
class TurnPrinter {
  public synchronized void printTurn(int turn) {
    try {
      notify();
      System.out.println("turn is " + turn);
      wait();
    } catch (InterruptedException e) {
    }
  }
}
```

incorrect programs (an example is provided in Chapter 7). This is another reason why programs should rely on sound principles to implement concurrent programs and not try to implement them by reasoning about the program logic.

Exhibit 26. Program2.12: Correct TurnPrinter Component

```
import java.util.Random;

public class SafeTurns2 implements Runnable {
  static Random rand = new Random();
  TurnPrinter tp;
  int myNum;

  public SafeTurns2(TurnPrinter tp, int myNum) {
    this.tp = tp;
    this.myNum = myNum;
  }

  public void run() {
    for (int i = 0; i < 10; i++) {
      tp.printTurn(myNum);
      try {
        Thread.sleep(rand.nextInt(100));
      } catch (InterruptedException e) {
      }
    }
  }

  public static void main(String args[]) {
    TurnPrinter tp = new TurnPrinter();
    (new Thread(new SafeTurns2(tp, 0))).start();
    (new Thread(new SafeTurns2(tp, 1))).start();
  }
}

/**
 *   Purpose: This TurnPrinter coordinates threads so they
 *            take turns. It works by keeping track of whose
 *            turn it is to run the method and allowing only
 *            that thread to run.
 */
class TurnPrinter {
  int currentTurn = 0;
  public synchronized void printTurn(int turn) {
    try {
      if (currentTurn ! = turn)
        wait();
      System.out.println("turn is " + turn);
      currentTurn = (currentTurn + 1)% 2;
      notify();
    } catch (InterruptedException e) {
    }
  }
}
```

Deadlock is not only a problem when designing components; it can also occur in any concurrent program. One simple cause of deadlock is the use of circularity in locking objects. For example, consider Exhibit 27 (Program2.13), which is an example of deadlock that occurs with a race condition. The two threads lock Objects A and B in the opposite order. If thread_1 is able to lock both A and B, it is able to complete, and then thread_2 will be able to lock both B

Exhibit 27. Program2.13: Circular Deadlock Example

```
public class MakeDeadlock{
  public static void main(String args[]){
    Object a = new Object(), b = new Object();
    Thread thread_1 = new Thread(new LockAB(a,b));
    thread_1.start();
    Thread thread_2 = new Thread(new LockBA(a,b));
    thread_2.start();
  }
}

class LockAB implements Runnable {
  private Object a, b;
  public LockAB(Object a, Object b) {
    this.a = a; this.b = b;
  }

  public void run() {
    try {
      Thread.sleep((int)(Math.random() * 100));
      synchronized(a) {
        Thread.sleep((int)(Math.random() * 100));
        synchronized(b) {
          System.out.println("LockAB worked");
        }
      }
    } catch (InterruptedException e) {
    }
  }
}

class LockBA implements Runnable {
  private Object a, b;
  public LockBA(Object a, Object b) {
    this.a = a; this.b = b;
  }

  public void run() {
    try {
      Thread.sleep((int)(Math.random() * 100));
      synchronized(b) {
        Thread.sleep((int)(Math.random() * 100));
        synchronized(a) {
          System.out.println("LockBA worked");
        }
      }
    } catch (InterruptedException e) {
    }
  }
}
```

and A, thus avoiding the deadlock. However, thread_1 could lock object A before thread_2 and thread_2 could lock object B before thread_1, which leads to a situation where neither thread can proceed, and the system is deadlocked.

The deadlock example in Exhibit 27 (Program2.13) is probably the most common type of deadlock. It occurs because of circularity in the order in which the resources are locked. If both threads had locked them in the same order, a deadlock would not have occurred. This type of deadlock is very common in many systems; for example, it occurs frequently in database management systems. Deadlock can arise in many other ways, some of which are covered in subsequent chapters.

2.7 Conclusion

Thread-based programming in Java involves understanding how to create threads and how to control them with the synchronize keyword and wait and notify methods. This understanding is non-trivial, as the presence of threads produces nondeterministic behavior in the programs. To understand the effects of nondeterminism in a program it is necessary for the programmer to understand how a concurrent program executes and whether or not resources such as variables are actually shared. Understanding the context of each thread allows the programmer to reason about these issues. Race conditions and deadlock are two types of problems that can arise with thread programs and concurrent programs, in general, and that do not exist in procedural programming. The best way to deal with these problems is to use standard designs for components that are well understood and known to be correct. A programmer who implements solutions in any other manner needs to be very careful and should prove that the program is correct.

2.8 Further Reading

Because the idea of a program context is central to how asynchronous activities (threads, processes, etc.) are implemented on a computer, a good understanding of them is important in understanding the behavior of concurrent activities. The material in this chapter tries to give a basic understanding of these concepts. A more complete explanation of how program stacks are used and what is contained in them can be found in most books on programming languages, such as *Concepts of Programming Languages* by Sebesta [SEB99]. A more complete explanation of program contexts and how they are used is found in most books on operating systems, such as *Operating Systems*, fourth edition, by Stallings [STA01]. Finally, a detailed explanation of a simple computer architecture, one that can be used to understand how a subroutine call is executed, can be found in *Computer System Architecture* by Mano [MAN93]. For a more in-depth presentation of how stacks and threads are implemented specifically in the JVM, see *The Java Virtual Machine Specification*, second edition, by Lindehold and Yellin [LIN99], or *Java Threads*, by Oaks and Wong [OAK97], both of which give good details on the internals for Java.

2.9 Problems

1. Is it easier or more difficult to test and debug a concurrent program than a procedural program? Why?
2. Throw an exception in the run method for a program where the run method is called directly from the main. Throw an exception from the run method that is called by using the start method in a thread. What is the difference between the two programs? What does this say about the program stack for the two types of executions? How do you think your answer to this question will impact the programs you write that use threads?
3. Can a race condition ever occur when an automatic (or local) variable is shared between two threads? Why or why not? Consider where in memory automatic variables are stored. Assume the variable is declared and allocated in a single method.
4. What are all the possible program outputs if Exhibit 6 (Program2.5) is run with three threads instead of two? How many outputs are possible with four threads? With five threads? What if three lines are output for each thread instead of two? What does this say about the complexity of predicting the output of concurrent programs with multiple threads?
5. Make the Exhibit 16 (Program2.6) safe by creating separate, non-shared resources to do the swap. Show two ways to accomplish this.
6. Exhibit 17 (Program2.6) showed the existence of a race condition, and Exhibit 20 (Program2.7b) showed a solution to the problem. Run Exhibit 20 (Program2.7b) 100 times. Is the answer always correct? Because Exhibit 17 (Program2.6) failed occasionally when run, and Program2.7b did not, can we say that testing showed that Exhibit 20 (Program2.7b) is correct? Why or why not?
7. What happens if a call to wait occurs in the middle of a synchronized block? Are any variables that are accessed still safe, or can race conditions occur? Why?
8. Why do you think that Java did not specify notify/notifyAll to implement a fair (i.e., first-in, first-out, or FIFO) mechanism for notifying waiting objects? Could a fair mechanism have been used? If so, do you think it was a good decision not to implement a fair mechanism? Explain. Consider the behavior of thread priorities in your answer.
9. Do synchronized methods lock on all methods within an object, on one method across all objects for that class, or on all methods across all objects? Explain why or why not.
10. Can static methods be synchronized? If so, how? If not, why not?
11. Can Java synchronize on any block of code or only methods? Can you justify why this decision was made?
12. If no object is specified, what object is used in a Java synchronized statement? If synchronization can be specified, how is it done? Can

method synchronization (using the synchronize statement to modify the method declaration) specify the object to use?

13. The binary semaphore given in this chapter is a special case of a counting semaphore. In a counting semaphore, some positive numbers of resources are available. The counting semaphore has two methods: getResource and releaseResource. Each time a getResource call is made, the number of resources available is decremented by 1. As long as the number of resources is greater than or equal to (≥) zero, the thread requesting the resource can continue. If, however, the number of resources is less than 0, the thread requesting the resource must wait for a releaseResource call to occur, which increments the number of resources available. Implement a counting semaphore with a constructor that takes the initial number of resources available and the getResource and releaseResource methods. In what situations is a counting semaphore useful?
14. Implement a binary semaphore using the counting semaphore from Problem 13.
15. Implement the counting semaphore without a constructor that sets the initial number of resources available. How can you set the initial number of resources without setting it in the constructor?
16. Compare Java threads and tasks in Ada. What are the advantages and disadvantages of both?
17. Compare the locking strategies of Ada-protected types with synchronized blocks in Java. What are the advantages and disadvantages?
18. Compare threads and semaphores using Pthreads in C/C++ and Java synchronized blocks and threads. What are the advantages and disadvantages of each implementation?
19. What happens if a call to notify or notifyAll is made, and no threads are currently waiting? Why?
20. When a program calls Thread.sleep, is it guaranteed only to sleep for the length of time specified in the call? Can the sleep time be longer? Can the sleep time be shorter? Explain your answer.
21. Assume that the notifyAll call is fair in the sense that the first thread to wait on the object is the first one moved to the ready set. Is this thread guaranteed to get the object lock when notifyAll is called with more than one thread waiting? Why or why not? Consider thread priorities when answering the question.
22. Assume priorities are used in a program, and multiple threads are waiting on the same object. When a notify call is made, will the thread with the highest priority be the one that gets notified? Justify this decision by considering the Big-O of implementing a notify that chooses any thread vs. one that chooses the highest priority thread. *Note:* Also consider the interaction between the notify and the ready set.
23. Which of the following actions results in an object lock being dropped?

- Call to notify
- Call to notifyAll
- Call to yield
- Call to wait
- Call to Thread.sleep
- Leaving a synchronized block

24. A common programming mistake is to make a notify or wait call when you are not in a synchronized block. What error is produced if you try to do a notify or a wait on an object when you are not in a synchronized block? Is it a runtime or compile time error? Explain the error.
25. Is the TurnPrinter object in Exhibit 27 (Program2.13) a component by the definition in Chapter 1? Is the BinarySemaphore object? Why or why not?
26. How does the use of priorities for threads impact which thread will be executed when several are moved from an object's wait set to the ready set? Is Java effective when threads of differing priorities are used?
27. Explain why deadlock is common in database management systems. Do you think deadlock can be predicted and thus avoided? If not, how do you think database management systems handle deadlock?
28. What can be inferred about a program when no threads are in the ready or running state? If all of the threads are in wait states? If some threads are in the sleeping or blocked state?
29. How many ways are there to cause a thread to drop a synchronized lock?
30. For the program in Exhibit 28, consider the statements commented out of the swap method. Which, if any, of the statements if uncommented could result in a race condition? Why?
31. Consider the following program (Exhibit 29) that uses threads (threads are run one after the other). By the definition in Chapter 1, is this program concurrent? Why or why not?
32. Consider the following program (Exhibit 30) that uses threads (threads do not synchronize). By the definition in Chapter 1, is this program concurrent? Why or why not?,

Exhibit 28. SolveRaceConditon_2.java

```
class SwapInt {
  private int tmp;

  synchronized public void swap(SolveRaceCondition_2 s) {
  tmp = s.val1;
  s.val1 = s.val2;
    try {
      //Thread.yield();
      //Thread.sleep(1000);
      //Thread.notify();
      //Thread.notifyAll();
      //wait();
      //wait(1000);
      //wait(1);
      //wait(0);
    } catch (Exception e) {
      e.printStackTrace();
    }
  s.val2 = tmp;
  }
}

public class SolveRaceCondition_2 implements Runnable {
  int val1, val2;
  static SwapInt so = new SwapInt();

  public SolveRaceCondition_2(int i1, int i2){val1 = i1; val2
= i2;
}

  public void run() {
    so.swap(this);
  System.out.println("Val1 = " + val1 + " Val2 = " + val2);
  }

  public static void main(String args[]) {

    (new Thread(new SolveRaceCondition_2(4,7))).start();
    (new Thread(new SolveRaceCondition_2(2,5))).start();
  }
   }
```

Exhibit 29. Problem2_31

```
public class Problem2_31 implements Runnable {
     public void run() {
          System.out.println("Starting run");
          try {
               Thread.sleep((int)(1000 * Math.random()));
          } catch (InterruptedException ie) {
          }
     }

     public static void main(String args[]) {
          Thread t1 = new Thread(new Problem2_31());
          Thread t2 = new Thread(new Problem2_31());
          Thread t3 = new Thread(new Problem2_31());
          try {
               t1.start();
               t1.join();
               t2.start();
               t2.join();
               t3.start();
               t3.join();
          } catch (InterruptedException ie) {
          }
     }
}
```

Exhibit 30. Problem2_32

```
public class Problem2_32 implements Runnable {
     public void run() {
          System.out.println("Starting run");
          try {
               Thread.sleep((int)(1000 * Math.random()));
          } catch (InterruptedException ie) {
          }
     }

     public static void main(String args[]) {
          Thread t1 = new Thread(new Problem2_32());
          Thread t2 = new Thread(new Problem2_32());
          Thread t3 = new Thread(new Problem2_32());
          try {
               t1.start();
               t2.start();
               t3.start();
          } catch (InterruptedException ie) {
          }
     }
}
```

Chapter 3

Designing and Implementing Concurrent Programs with State Diagrams

3.1 Introduction

Chapter 2 introduced the facilities for dealing with concurrency in Java. In this chapter, you will learn how to use those facilities to implement solutions to problems. The problems studied in this chapter are simulation problems; however, the techniques that are used will apply to a number of different problem types, particularly when describing the behavior of components in concurrent and distributed systems. Sections 3.3 and 3.4 give an overview of the methodology to be used. Section 3.5 then applies the methodology to the bounded buffer problem, a classical synchronization problem found in many operating systems textbooks. Section 3.6 demonstrates that passive objects are actually components and how they satisfy the five criteria for components given in Chapter 1. Finally, an example of simulation of a gas station is provided to show how the techniques in this chapter can be used.

3.2 Chapter Goals

After reading this chapter you should know:

- How to specify an ensemble, or a collection of objects that cooperate to implement a solution to a problem

- The difference between an active object and a passive object, and why the difference between these two types of objects is important
- How to implement an active object
- How to design a passive object using a state diagram
- How to translate a state diagram into a working Java object
- How to define a controlling object and how to use the control object to link together all the objects in an ensemble
- How to use this method to solve a problem that has multiple different threads
- Why passive objects are components

3.3 Background

Chapter 2 gave an overview of the facilities in Java for implementing concurrency, as well as some of the common problems that are unique to concurrent programs; however, explaining the mechanisms of concurrency is not sufficient for many programmers learning concurrency. Most programmers have been taught to understand programs as procedural entities — programs start at the first line in main and proceed in a stepwise fashion through the program, executing each statement in its logical order. In addition, programmers are taught that a program is totally ordered, that the execution of the program is deterministic in regard to the order in which statements are executed, so that each time the program is run it produces exactly the same results. So, while some programmers might understand that concurrent programs do not behave procedurally, they do not understand how to structure a program effectively to take advantage of concurrency. This became apparent me when I first started teaching concurrent programming in Java, as many students would attempt to write programs that would control the threads using the suspend, stop, and resume methods, rather than allowing the interactions between the threads to solve the problem.

The purpose of this chapter is to help programmers experienced in procedural programming to understand how to structure and create a concurrent program. The reader should be warned that this is often a very difficult undertaking that may require changes in the way one reasons about a program. It is not uncommon for programmers to say that they could not understand how the methodology in this chapter worked, and they simply implemented programs according to the rules laid out in the chapter. But, once a program works, the material seems trivial and they cannot understand why they had a problem with it.

The techniques presented in this chapter involve creating *ensembles*, which are collections of objects that coordinate with each other to solve a problem. Creating ensembles involves breaking a problem down into two types of objects, active and passive. *Active objects* implement procedural code running in threads. *Passive* or *reactive* objects do not perform actions except as a result of a request from an active object, and they control the interactions between the active objects. Passive objects are designed using state diagrams, and then are mechanistically translated into Java code.

3.4 Steps to Create a Concurrent Program

The procedure for creating programs used in this chapter has eight steps:

1. Write a short description of the problem to be solved. This description should drive any choices of objects or functionality that must be made in subsequent steps.
2. Create an ensemble by defining the objects and relationships that will be used in this program. A general rule is that nouns in the problem statement represent objects and/or attributes of the objects, and verbs represent actions and/or methods. However, do not simply choose objects based on the nouns and verbs in the description; instead, choose entities that will be useful in solving the problem stated in step 1.
3. For each object, specify if that object should be active (executing actions and generating events) or passive (responding to events).
4. Design the active objects using the verbs in the problem statement to define the flow of actions in the object. Specification of the active objects can be done using any procedural design technique, such as flow charts, pseudo-code, or activity diagrams. For the simple problems in this chapter, active objects are designed as pseudo-code.
5. Design the passive objects using a state diagram. In the state diagram, the nodes are states that the object can be in and are represented by one or more instance variables in the object. Arcs are methods that can be executed when the object is in the correct state.
6. Implement the active objects as Java threads.
7. Implement the passive objects as monitors using the rules given in Section 3.7.
8. Write a controlling object that will create instances of all the objects.

To demonstrate these steps, a simple program to solve the producer/consumer problem is implemented in the next section, and each step is explained as it is applied to this problem.

3.5 The Producer/Consumer Problem

3.5.1 Problem Description

The producer/consumer problem can be stated as follows: A buffer with a finite number of slots for data is created to hold data created by a producer. In our problem, the buffer will be implemented using a circular array called a *bounded buffer*. The producer will simply create integers from 1 to 10 and send them to the buffer. The buffer will store them in the next empty slot. The consumer will retrieve the 10 integers from the buffer and print them to the screen. The buffer will have the ability to store only three items, so it is possible for the producer to create more items than the buffer can hold before the consumer can retrieve an item. When this happens, the producer must wait for the consumer to take an item from the buffer to create a free slot before sending another item. Likewise, the consumer could retrieve all the items already created by the producer, and there would be no items in the buffer to retrieve. When this happens, the consumer must wait until the producer creates another item and adds it to the buffer before continuing to retrieve items from the buffer.

3.5.2 Write a Short Description of the Problem

The first thing that needs to be done is to write a short description of the problem. This step is probably the most important, and the one most frequently overlooked. Often programmers start designing their programs before they have a good grasp of the problem to be solved. This leads to the creation of many objects and methods that have no relationship to the problem to be solved simply because they are somehow referred to or implied in the problem definition. In this example, the problem statement is obvious. Create a producer that creates data and a consumer that uses the data and have them coordinate using a bounded buffer.

3.5.3 Define the Objects and Relationships

Looking at the problem definition, we find that the nouns are a producer, a consumer, a buffer, and a circular array with three slots to hold data. The producer, consumer, and buffer are the obvious objects, with the circular array being an attribute of the buffer. Of these three objects, the producer and consumer do things (produce and consume data) and are active. The buffer simply stores and retrieves data requested by the producer and consumer and is passive. The next step is to look at the verbs that describe the active objects. The producer is described as creating a number and sending it the buffer. The consumer is described as retrieving a number from the buffer and printing it to the screen. This is sufficient detail to describe the activities of both of these objects. These objects simply implement "for loops" to send and retrieve the data. The buffer object responds to two requests. The first is to take an item from the producer and add it to the circular array. The second is to take an item from the buffer and give it to the consumer; therefore, the buffer will have two methods: an addToBuffer and a takeFromBuffer.

3.5.4 Design and Implement the Active Objects

The active objects, the producer and consumer, are now implemented. The pseudo-code for the producer is simply:

```
for (I = 1 to 10)
  Send an item to the buffer
```

The pseudo-code for the consumer is just the mirror of the producer code:

```
for (I = 1 to 10)
  Get an item from the buffer
```

The code for these is shown in Program3.1 (Exhibits 1 and 2). Note that in all the problems in this chapter, the active objects are always threads; therefore, the actions that define these objects are stated in the *run* method, which is where the thread begins running.

One additional comment must be made about these objects. Both of these active objects must share the BoundedBuffer object, so the BoundedBuffer must be created outside of these objects and somehow passed into the objects. The constructors for these objects are used to accomplish this. The BoundedBuffer will first be created in the controlling object and then passed to these objects and stored when the objects are created. This is discussed further in Section 3.5.7.

3.5.5 Design the Passive Object (Components)

The next step is to design the passive object, the buffer. The buffer has two methods that allow active objects to use its services. The first method, addToBuffer, allows an object to add items to this buffer, and the second method, takeFromBuffer, allows an object to remove items from this buffer. These methods do not simply perform tasks for the active objects when their methods are called, as is normally the case with function calls in procedural languages. Instead, passive objects maintain a state across the various invocations of their methods. This state allows them to maintain a flow of events as the methods of the object are used. In the producer/consumer problem, the buffer can

Exhibit 1. Program3.1a: Producer Class

```
public class Producer implements Runnable {
  private BoundedBuffer bb;//BoundedBuffer used to coordinate
            //with the consumer

  /**
   * Constructor that saves the shared BoundedBuffer object
   */
  public Producer(BoundedBuffer bb) {
    this.bb = bb;
  }

  /**
   * Producer thread, which creates values and passes
   * them to the BoundedBuffer
   */
  public void run() {
    int value;
    for (int i = 0; i < 10; ++i) {
      System.out.println("Producer adding value = " + i);
      bb.addToBuffer(i);
    }
  }
}
```

Exhibit 2. Program3.1b: Consumer Class

```
public class Consumer implements Runnable {
  private BoundedBuffer bb;//BoundedBuffer used to coordinate
            //with the producer
  /**
   * Constructor that saves the shared BoundedBuffer object
   */
  public Consumer(BoundedBuffer bb) {
    this.bb = bb;
  }
  /**
   * Producer thread, which creates values and passes
   * them to the BoundedBuffer
   */
  public void run() {
    for (int i = 0; i < 10; ++i) {
      System.out.println("Consumer got value = " +
        bb.takeFromBuffer());
    }
  }
}
```

be in one of three states: The buffer can be EMPTY, with no items in any of the slots; the buffer can be FULL, with items in all of the slots; or the buffer can be AVAILABLE, with some slots holding data and some slots being empty.

The flow within a passive object is controlled by the state of that object. In the producer/consumer problem, when the object is first

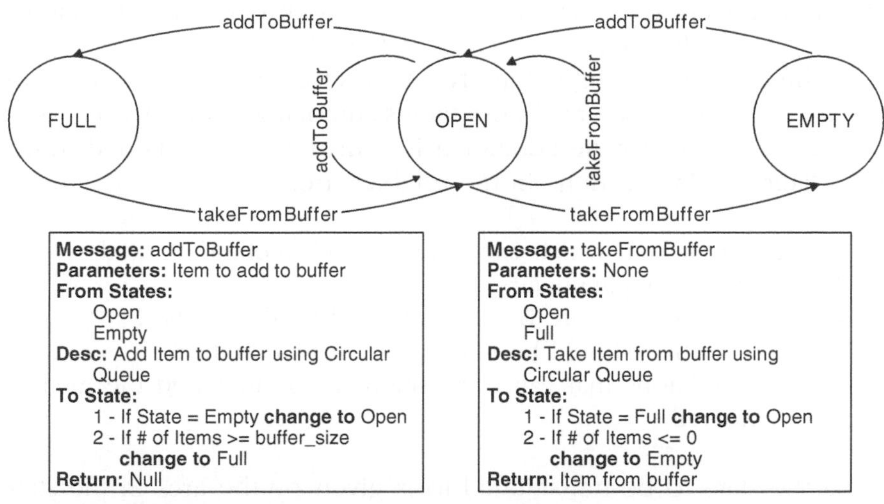

addToBuffer
addToBuffer
FULL
addToBuffer
OPEN
takeFromBuffer
EMPTY
takeFromBuffer
takeFromBuffer
Message: addToBuffer
Parameters: Item to add to buffer
From States:
Open
Empty
Desc: Add Item to buffer using Circular Queue
To State:
1 - If State = Empty change to Open
2 - If # of Items >= buffer_size change to Full
Return: Null
Message: takeFromBuffer
Parameters: None
From States:
Open
Full
Desc: Take Item from buffer using Circular Queue
To State:
1 - If State = Full change to Open
2 - If # of Items <= 0 change to Empty
Return: Item from buffer

Exhibit 3. State Diagram for Producer/Consumer Problem

created, the state of the object will be EMPTY, as no data has been added to the buffer. When the buffer is EMPTY, no calls to takeFromBuffer are allowed, as no data is available in the buffer to be removed. From the EMPTY state, a call to addToBuffer is allowed, which causes a change of state to AVAILABLE, thus allowing calls from both takeFromBuffer and addToBuffer. If two items are already in the buffer, adding a third item causes the buffer to be filled and changes the state of the buffer from AVAILABLE to FULL. A FULL buffer allows calls from takeFromBuffer, but not addToBuffer, as no more space is available to store an item.

It should be obvious that trying to describe the behavior of passive objects using prose, as above, is difficult. Because methods can only show procedural flow, the methods in a passive object are inadequate to represent the overall design of the passive object. Fortunately, passive objects are easy to design and represent using a technique called *state diagrams*. To model a passive object using a state diagram, the states are represented as nodes in the diagram and methods as transitions between those states. Exhibit 3 shows the design of the buffer as a state diagram. The reader should follow the logic and be convinced that the design does match the description provided here and implements the logic needed for the buffer.

State diagrams have been used for a long time to describe the behavior of programs. For example, they have been used in hardware design to describe the behavior of hardware components, and are part of the Unified Modeling Language (UML). The way that state diagrams are used to design the components does not differ greatly from the ways in which they are used for hardware design or Object Oriented Design (OOD), but the way they are actually implemented is different.

For more in-depth discussions of state diagrams, the reader should refer to the Further Reading section of this chapter.

At the bottom of Exhibit 3 are two tables that describe the methods that are used as transitions. These tables summarize information about the methods and provide additional information not contained in the state diagram. The sections in these tables are:

- The states from which execution of each method is valid
- The method's parameters
- The activity that is to be accomplished by the method
- Any data that should be returned from this method
- The conditions that cause transitions to occur when the method is executed

While the state to be transitioned to is given by the arcs in the state diagram, the conditions that cause this transition are not explicitly given in the diagram and so are specified here. From this summary, all the information needed to implement the passive objects is available, and the rules for implementing them are given in the next section.

3.5.6 Implementing Passive Objects

Implementing passive objects can be a daunting task for programmers who are new to concurrent programming, but, if a state diagram has been produced that describes the passive object, then the translation from the state diagram to an actual working implementation of the object is mechanistic. To implement passive objects we employ a data structure called a *monitor.* Monitors can be thought of as objects where only one thread can be executing inside of any method at any given time. Monitors can be created in Java by making all the methods of an object synchronized and putting in place guards (method preconditions) that allow entry to the methods to be controlled by the state of the object. Method post-conditions can then be implemented to model the transitions to other states. The rest of this section shows how to write methods to implement this behavior.

The first step in implementing the state diagram is to have some combination of one or more variables that are private to this object and represent the state of the object. In the simplest case, as in our producer/consumer problem, the state is represented by a single variable. Constants are defined that specify the valid values for that state variable. For example, in the bounded buffer we can define the states for the buffer using the following declarations:

```
private static final int EMPTY = 0;
private static final int AVAILABLE = 1;
private static final int FULL = 2;
private int state = EMPTY;
```

The second step in the translation of the state diagram involves dividing the method into sections of code corresponding to the sections in the tables at the bottom of the state diagram. Each method has the following: (1) a name and parameters corresponding to the first two sections in the tables; (2) a pre-condition, or guard, which prevents the method from being executed unless the object is in the correct state; (3) the code that performs any activities specified in the table; (4) any post-condition processing to check if the state of the object must be changed as a result of the execution of the method; and (5) return of any specified data.

Other than the sections of the method that do the pre-condition and post-condition processing, the implementation of the method is straightforward. Therefore, the only parts of the method that will be covered in more detail in this section are the pre-condition and post-condition processing.

Pre-conditions (or guards) protect the method from being executed when the object is not in a valid state. For example, if the buffer is EMPTY, the guard will force a thread calling addToBuffer to wait until another thread has completed a call to takeFromBuffer to create an open slot.

All pre-condition code has a similar format. The generic format for the pre-condition code used here is as follows:

```
while(! ((state = = validState1 ||
      state = = validState2))){
    wait();
 }
```

The values of validState1 and validState2 are states from which arcs emanate in the state diagram and are the states of the object from which this method can execute. If the object is in a correct state to execute this method, then the while statement is not executed and the thread continues to execute the method. If the object is not in a correct state, the wait statement is executed, and the thread calling this method will suspend, freeing the object to be used by other threads. To implement a pre-condition, a programmer need only place the valid states for executing the method in the "if" block above. Note the format of the pre-condition. The current state is compared with each valid state, and these comparisons are then "or'ed" together. The result of the "or'ed" statements is then negated.

Post-conditions work in conjunction with the pre-conditions to ensure that the monitor maintains a valid state. In post-condition processing, the method checks to see if some condition has been reached that causes the object to change to a new state. If the object does not change state, the method does nothing in the post-condition. However, if the state is changed (i.e., the state variable is set to a new value), then notifyAll must be called. This is done because another thread may be currently waiting on the monitor. If the state has not changed, the waiting threads do not need to check the status of the monitor as it will not have changed and the waiting threads will always have to do another wait. However, if the state has changed, it is possible that a thread waiting on the monitor will now be able to continue, so the notifyAll call allows all waiting threads to wake up and check the status of the monitor to determine if they can now continue.

The generic format of the post-condition process is:

```
if (condition1 = = true) {
  state = newState_1;
  notifyAll();
}
else if (condition2 = = true) {
  state = newState_2;
  notifyAll();
}
```

Note the lack of a final "else" condition; if no state change occurs, any waiting threads do not need to be notified.

The procedure for implementing each method in a monitor, given a state diagram, can be summarized as follows:

1. Define a variable or variables to represent the state of the monitor and possibly constants to represent each of the valid states of the monitor.
2. Write the declaration of the method, including the synchronized keyword as part of the declaration.
3. Implement any pre-conditions for the method using the procedure outlined above.
4. Implement the code to achieve the function defined for the method.
5. Implement any post-condition processing for the method using the procedure outlined above.
6. Return any indicated data from the method.

The implementation of the buffer monitor using these rules is shown in Exhibit 4 (Program3.1c).

3.5.7 Implementing the Controlling Object

Now that the pieces of the program are created, they need to be tied together to create a program. This is done in a *control object*. A control object is an object that controls the overall creation and linkage of the objects used in the program. It does not control the individual active or passive objects. For example, consider Exhibit 5 (Program3.1d). This program creates the passive BoundedBuffer object and then creates the objects for the threads, registering the shared BoundedBuffer

Exhibit 4. Program3.1c: Implementation of the BoundedBuffer Object

```
public class BoundedBuffer {

  //Variables need to define the circular queue used as the
  //buffer.
  private int values[];
  private int firstItem = 0;
  private int lastItem = 0;
  private int numberOfItems = 0;
  private int bufferSize;

  //Variables to maintain the monitor state
  public static final int EMPTY = 0;
  public static final int OPEN = 1;
  public static final int FULL = 2;
  private int bufferState = EMPTY;

  //Constructor for the BoundedBuffer. Note that the size of the
  //buffer is set here based on the parameter bufferSize.
  public BoundedBuffer(int bufferSize) {
    this.bufferSize = bufferSize;
    values = new int[bufferSize];
  }

  /**
   * addToBuffer adds the item in the parameter to the buffer.
   */
  public synchronized void addToBuffer(int value) {

    //Pre-condition processing (method guard)
    while(! ((bufferState = = EMPTY) ||
        (bufferState = = OPEN))) {
      try {
        wait();
      } catch (InterruptedException e) {
      }
    }

    //Processing done to add item to buffer
    System.out.println("item " + value + " added to buffer");
    values[lastItem] = value;
    lastItem = (lastItem + 1)% bufferSize;
    numberOfItems = numberOfItems + 1;

    //Post-condition processing to change states
    if ((bufferState = = OPEN) && (numberOfItems > = bufferSize)) {
      bufferState = FULL;
      notifyAll();
    }
    else if (bufferState = = EMPTY) {
      bufferState = OPEN;
      notifyAll();
    }
  }
```

(continued)

Exhibit 4. Program3.1c (Continued)

```
/**
 * takeFromBuffer retrieves and removes an item from the buffer.
 */
public synchronized int takeFromBuffer() {
  int value;

  //Pre-condition processing (method guard)
  while(! ((bufferState = = FULL) ||
      (bufferState = = OPEN))) {
    try {
      wait();
    } catch (InterruptedException e) {
    }
  }

  //Processing done to take item from buffer
  value = values[firstItem];
  System.out.println("item " + value + " taken from buffer");
  firstItem = (firstItem + 1)% bufferSize;
  numberOfItems = numberOfItems - 1;

  //Post-condition processing to change states
  if ((bufferState = = OPEN) && (numberOfItems < = 0)) {
    bufferState = EMPTY;
    notifyAll();
  }
  else if (bufferState = = FULL) {
    bufferState = OPEN;
    notifyAll();
  }

  //Return the value taken from the buffer.
  return value;
  }
}
```

Exhibit 5. Program3.1d: Implementation of the Producer Consumer Control Object

```
public class ProducerConsumer {
  public static void main(String args[]) {
    BoundedBuffer bb = new BoundedBuffer(3);
    (new Thread(new Producer(bb))).start();
    (new Thread(new Consumer(bb))).start();
  }
}
```

objects with each of these active objects by passing the passive object to their constructors. Threads are then created and started for each of the active objects. The most interesting feature of the controlling object is that it does not really contain any procedural code. All of the code in this object involves declaring object and threads or starting a thread. The control for the program resides entirely in the run methods of the active objects.

3.6 Why Passive Objects Are Components

The BoundedBuffer object in the previous program is obviously a component because it provides a service for and coordinates between the producer and consumer thread. In Chapter 1, five characteristics of a component were given. The following looks at how the bounded buffer meets all of these criteria.

1. The bounded buffer object is not created in the producer or the consumer thread but is created in the controlling objects and is registered with those objects through a parameter passed in the constructor for the thread object.
2. The bounded buffer communicates with the other objects through a standard method call procedure.
3. The bounded buffer coordinates between the producer and consumer threads by implementing a state inside the bounded buffer and allowing transitions according to the rules in the state diagram used to design the bounded buffer.
4. Race conditions are controlled for in the bounded buffer by using the monitor techniques described for the BinarySemaphore class in Chapter 2. Only one object can execute inside any BoundedBuffer method at any time. Because all the wait calls are part of the precondition processing and do not occur once the program begins to modify the object data (the object state and circular queue variables), the state of the buffer is guaranteed and will be safe. This shows the advantage of separating the pre-condition processing from the rest of the program. Often, programmers who build passive objects by reasoning about their behavior are tempted to put processing inside of the pre-condition, but a wait exists in the pre-condition. If internal variables and the state can be changed in the pre-condition, then dropping the object lock causes a race condition and the program is unsafe. Using the precondition only to check to see when the method can be run ensures that a wait condition will not drop a lock, causing a possible race condition.
5. The absence of deadlock if the bounded buffer component is used correctly can be easily demonstrated by examining the state diagram and its properties. This state diagram has the property that it is strongly connected; that is, every node can be reached by some path from every other node. Therefore, no states can be entered into where an active object will be stuck. The two possibilities of deadlock are (1) having the component permanently enter a FULL or EMPTY state, and (2) using this component with another component in such a manner as to produce a circular deadlock situation. Both of these conditions could only be caused by an error in the program using the component (i.e., have more takeFromBuffer calls than putToBuffer calls), so the component is safe if used properly.

3.7 Gas Station Simulation Problem

A program using threads will now be implemented in a domain that is very much amenable to the techniques in this chapter: simulation problems. The problem presented here is to simulate a gas station. Section 3.7.1 introduces the problem and it is solved in Section 3.7.2.

3.7.1 Problem Statement

A gas station is to be modeled to calculate the average time a driver spends getting gas. The time starts when the driver begins waiting for a pump and ends when the car leaves the pump. The simulation starts with 50 cars arriving at the gas station randomly between 0 and 30 seconds after the simulation begins. The driver in each car will first check to see if the pump is free. If the pump is not free, the driver will wait until the pump is free. Once the pump is free, the driver will pull the car up to the pump and shut off the engine. For this simulation, this will take .5 second. After the engine has been turned off, the driver will unlock the door of the car and open the door, which takes an additional .5 second. The driver will then close the car door, which will take a negligible amount of time. The driver then walks to the pump, turns the pump on, and selects a grade of gas. This also takes .5 second.

The possible grades of gas that can be selected are low octane (87 octane), medium octane (89 octane), and high octane (91 octane), where the octane number is the average of the motor octane number and the research octane number. Motor octane is calculated by running the gasoline in a standard engine, and research octane is calculated by doing a weighted sum of the components in the gasoline. The octane number on the pump is always the average of the two.

When the driver has turned on the pump and selected the grade of gasoline, he will put the gas nozzle in the fuel intake for the gas tank for the car. Once again, this will take .5 second in this simulation. Also in this simulation, filling the tank with gasoline will take 2.5 seconds. The driver then puts the nozzle back in the pump (which takes another .5 second), opens the car door, and leaves the pump, taking a final .5 second. So the total time that the driver is at the pump is 6 seconds. Once the driver leaves the pump, the pump is free and another driver may use the pump. Write a simulation of this gas station.

3.7.2 Gas Station Simulation

This gas station simulation is instructive in that it is more like real-world problems. In this problem, programmers are not given too little information; rather, they are given too much information, most of it totally irrelevant. For example, the simulation has nothing to do with octane, so the entire paragraph about the octane number can be disregarded. But what other information is important?

Programmers who attempt to use object-oriented programming (OOP) on this problem will be faced with many red herrings. They will be creating objects for doors with locks, nozzles, and fuel tanks because they are in the problem statement. They may start creating dials on the pumps, because the pumps they have seen in the real world have dials to show how much gas is sold, or may try to address the issue of payment, because gas is not free. Left to their own devices, programmers can become very creative in finding ways to obfuscate a simple problem.

Programmers should not be interested in objects just because they may exist in the problem statement or possibly in the real world. They should be concentrating on objects that are actually needed to solve the problem. Do we need to model the doors on the car? Or even the driver? What is missing is a concise statement of the problem, one which can then drive the decisions of the objects required to solve the problem. That is why writing a description of the problem is always the first step in writing a program.

This problem is simple because programmers can simply take a few sentence fragments from the description given and come up with a valid statement of the problem. Doing this, we see that the problem can actually be described as:

> A gas station is to be modeled to calculate the average time a driver spends getting gas. The time starts when the driver begins waiting for a pump and ends when the car leaves the pump. The simulation starts with 50 cars arriving at the gas station randomly between 0 and 30 seconds after the simulation begins. ...Once the pump is free, the driver will pull the car up to the pump. ...The total time that the driver is at the pump is 6 seconds. When the driver leaves the pump, the pump is free and another driver may use the pump.

In the real world, defining the actual problem is seldom this easy, but it is extremely important. Programmers who begin to create a program without first describing what they are doing are bound to create useless objects and other artifacts that will only create confusion.

Given the description of the problem, one active object is necessary. This object will be modeled in this program as a car object. The car is active and has the following behavior: It waits a random amount of time between 0 and 30 seconds. It then tries to use the pump, and when the pump is free it pulls up to the pump, pumps gas, and leaves the pump. To match the car object we now need a pump object. This object will have two states: The pump is BUSY or the pump is FREE.

The state diagram for the pump is given in Exhibit 6. Implementation of these car and customer objects is shown in Program3.2a and Program3.2b (Exhibits 7 and 8).

All that remains is to implement the controlling object, the GasStation, which is shown in Exhibit 9 (Program3.2c). This will create the objects, run the simulation, and create the answer. Note that some method of notifying the main thread when all the cars have finished running has to be implemented. In this case, the main thread is "joined" with all the child threads. This task can be accomplished in many ways, and some of the problems at the end of this chapter explore those options.

Many programmers who see this solution do not like it. After all, a car does not literally pump gas, and many of the objects in the original problem are missing. This bothers many programmers, particularly

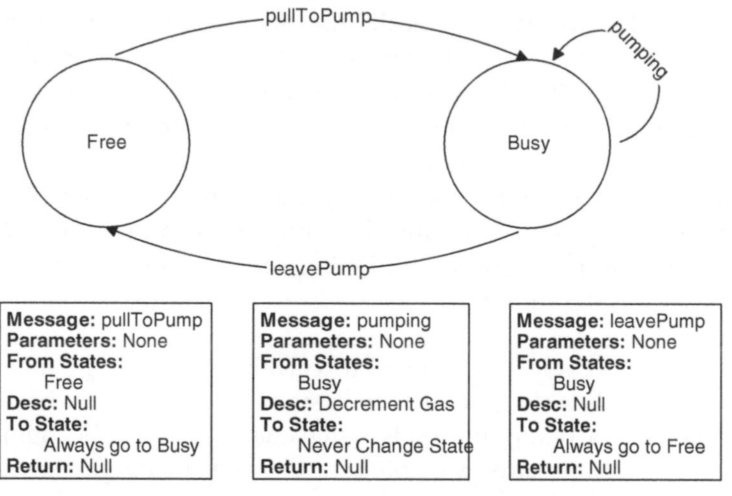

Message: pullToPump	Message: pumping	Message: leavePump
Parameters: None	Parameters: None	Parameters: None
From States: Free	From States: Busy	From States: Busy
Desc: Null	Desc: Decrement Gas	Desc: Null
To State: Always go to Busy	To State: Never Change State	To State: Always go to Free
Return: Null	Return: Null	Return: Null

Exhibit 6. State Diagram for Gas Pump Problem

Exhibit 7. Program3.2a: Car Class

```
import java.util.*;

class Car implements Runnable {
  private static int totalTime = 0,//Total time spent by all
                                   //cars
       totalCars = 0;              //Total number of cars
  private int customerNumber;      //The customer number to set
                                   //Random value, and for
                                   //intermediate output
  private Pump myPump;             //The pump the customer
                                   //should use
  /**
   * Constructor: Set the customerNumber and pump.
   */
```

(continued)

Exhibit 7. Program3.2a (Continued)

```
  public Car(int customerNumber, Pump pump) {
    this.myPump = pump;
    this.customerNumber = customerNumber;
  }

  /**
   * Static function to calculate average at the end of
   * simulation.
   */
  public static float calcAverage() {
    return totalTime/totalCars;
  }

  /**
   * Thread that implements the pump.
   */
  public void run() {
    //Declare variables needed for simulation.
    final int WAIT_TIME = 30000;
    long startTime, endTime;
    Random random = new Random(customerNumber);
    int waitTime = random.nextInt(WAIT_TIME);
    //Wait a random amount of time before coming to pump.
    try {
      Thread.sleep(waitTime);
    } catch (InterruptedException e) {
    }

    //use the pump, pump the gas, and leave.
    System.out.println("Customer " + customerNumber +
              " arrives at pump");
    startTime = (new Date()).getTime();
    myPump.usePump();
    System.out.println("Customer " + customerNumber +
              " pumps gas");
    myPump.pumpGas();

    System.out.println("Customer " + customerNumber +
              " leaves pump");
    myPump.leave();
    endTime = (new Date()).getTime();
    System.out.println("Time = " + (endTime - startTime));

    //Update the variables to calculate the average. If this is
    //the last car, let the main() finish and print the average.
    //Note that to use the static variables we need to get the
    //lock on the class.
    synchronized(Car.class) {
      totalTime + = (endTime - startTime);
      totalCars++;
    }
  }
}
```

Exhibit 8. Program3.2b: Pump Class

```
class Pump {
  private static final int FREE = 0;
  private static final int BUSY = 1;
  private int state = FREE;

  /**
   * Method to call when a car first wishes to use a pump. It
   * adds a 1/2 second to the simulated time in the problem.
   */
  synchronized public void usePump() {
    try {
      //Pre-condition processing (guard)
      while(true) {
        if (state = = FREE)
          break;
        wait();
      }

      //Simulate pulling to the pump by waiting 1/2 second.
      Thread.sleep(500);
      //Post-condition processing, change state.
      state = BUSY;
      notifyAll();
    } catch (InterruptedException e) {
    }
  }

  /**
   * Simulate pumping the gas by waiting 5 seconds.
   */
  synchronized public void pumpGas() {
    try {
      //Pre-condition processing (guard)
      while(true) {
        if (state = = BUSY)
          break;
        wait();
      }
      //Simulate pumping gas by waiting 5 seconds.
      Thread.sleep(5000);

      //Post-condition processing, no change state needed.
    } catch (InterruptedException e) {
    }
  }

  /**
   * Leave the pump, freeing it for the next customer.
   */
  synchronized public void leave() {
    try {
      //Pre-condition processing (guard)
      while(true) {
        if (state = = BUSY)
          break;
        wait();
      }
```

(continued)

Exhibit 8. Program3.2b (Continued)

```
        //Simulate leaving the pump by waiting 1/2 second.
        Thread.sleep(500);

        //Post-condition processing, change state
        state = FREE;
        notifyAll();
      } catch (InterruptedException e) {
      }
    }
  }
```

Exhibit 9. Program3.2c: Gas Station Class

```
public class GasStation {
  static final int TOTAL_CARS = 10;

  public static void main(String args[]) {
    Thread carThreads[] = new Thread[TOTAL_CARS];
    try {
      //Create the monitor (passive object).
      Pump pump1 = new Pump();

      //Start all the Car threads
      for (int i = 0; i < TOTAL_CARS; i++) {
        Car car = new Car(i, pump1);
        (carThreads[i] = new Thread(car)).start();
      }

      //Now suspend and wait for simulation to finish.
      for (int i = 0; i < TOTAL_CARS; i++) {
        carThreads[i].join();
      }
    } catch (InterruptedException e) {
    }

    //Print average time at the end of the simulation.
    System.out.println("Average time to get gas = " +
      Car.calcAverage());
  }
}
```

programmers just learning object-oriented programming. They have come to believe that somehow the real world can be represented in the computer. The real world has cars, pumps, doors, drivers, etc., and if these can be abstracted and put into a program then the problem can be magically solved. But, a computer does not have cars and pumps; it has 1's and 0's. You cannot represent the real world in a computer; you can simply create an abstract model of it. When an attempt is made to represent the real world in a computer, the problems become hopelessly complex because the real world is hopelessly complex. What parts of the real world are actually built into the abstract model depends on the problem to be solved. What are the boundaries and constraints of the problem? What is the result to be produced? These are the important questions, not what objects can be found (or imagined to be present) in the real world.

3.8 Conclusion

Concurrent programs can often be effectively implemented using active and passive objects. This is true of many types of concurrent programs, including distributed programs. In these models, the most interesting part will be the passive object, which is a component. It is the most interesting because it is used to implement the coordination that allows the concurrent program to do useful work. One very powerful way to implement passive objects is through the use of state diagrams. State diagrams allow a programmer to reason about the behavior of the passive object. These state diagrams can then easily be translated into working Java programs. The reader should note that state diagrams are easily translated into Java objects because of the language constructs, such as synchronization, wait, and notify, so the design of these objects makes sense in languages that support the design of monitors, such as Java and Ada, but are difficult to implement in languages such as C/C++ that do not.

3.9 Further Reading

State diagrams are used to design a large number of different systems in computer science. The basic theory of state diagrams and their application to computing can be found in any textbook on formal models of computing such as [SAV98]. These books use state diagrams as part of larger computing machines to implement finite-state automata (FSA) and then use FSA to design more general computational models, such as random-access computers and Turing machines. State diagrams have also been widely used in hardware design, and most books on computer architecture (see, for example, [MAN93] or [CAR01]) have a section on how to use state diagrams to design hardware components. The use of state diagrams in the design of software is found in a number of design methodologies, such as Rumbaugh et al. [RUM91] or Booch [BOO91] and has been included in the Unified Modeling Language (UML) (see Booch [BOO99]). State diagrams to design concurrent programs have been proposed by a number of authors, such as Sanden [SAN94] and Magee and Kramer [MAG99].

State diagrams in this chapter were implemented as monitors. Hoare [HOA74] originally introduced monitors. The version of a monitor used in Java is based on the Lampson and Redell [LAM80] extensions to this monitor model. The implementation of monitors using program guards can be found in Lea [LEA00], and a number of design books (notably [BOO91]) use state diagrams to represent passive objects and map them to program guards. The monitors used in this chapter map very nicely to Ada Protected Types, as defined in [ADA95], where the use of a "when" clause removes the necessity for implementing the program guards.

Finally, many of the problems solved in this chapter or given as problems at the end of the chapter are classical problems in computer science (such as the producer/consumer, barber shop, dining philosophers, and Santa Clause simulations) and can be found in a number of books on operating systems or concurrent programming (see, for example, [STA01]).

3.10 Problems

1. Modify the producer/consumer problem to include a random wait in the active objects (producer and consumer) between the times they place items in the buffer or take items from the buffer. How does this impact the program?
2. Modify the producer/consumer program in Problem 1 to have five producers and one consumer. How difficult is this? How does this impact the program? Now change size of the buffer to ten items. How does this affect the program? Create two consumers. How is the program affected?
3. Modify the BoundedBuffer object to use the relationship between the bufferSize and numberOfItems variables to specify the state of the object. For example, instead of the buffer having a FULL state, it would have a state where "numberOfItems = = bufferSize." What does this say about how the state can be specified in a passive object?
4. Modify the gas station problem to include two pumps where a customer chooses a pump upon arrival at the station and gets in the line for that pump. Run the simulation where customers randomly choose a pump. Rerun the simulation so that customers can choose a pump based on how many customers are already waiting at each pump. Does the checking of the lines affect the overall wait time? What about the maximum wait time for a customer?
5. This program is a simulation of an elevator in a building with 6 floors. In this simulation, the elevator is always moving between floors, arriving at a floor, allowing passengers to get on or off the elevator if anyone is waiting for that floor, and then leaving the floor. The elevator takes 1.0 seconds to travel between the floors, and when it reaches the top or bottom floor it reverses direction and continues to run. The 50 passengers will choose floors to get on and get off. The passengers sleep a random amount of time up to 2 minutes and then wait for the elevator to arrive. Once

Exhibit 10. Pseudo-Code for the Elevator and the Passenger

```
Pseudo-Code for the Elevator
floorNumber = 1
increment = 1
forever {
  floors[floorNumber].elevatorArrives()
  floors[floorNumber].elevatorLeaves()
  Sleep for 1 second.
  if (floorNumber = = 1)
    increment = 1;
  else if (floorNumber = = MAX_FLOORS)
    increment = -1
  floorNumber = floorNumber + increment
  }

Pseudo-Code for the Passenger
Sleep a random amount of time < 2 minutes.
Choose a floorNumber to start at.
floors[floorNumber].waitForElevator()
floors[floorNumber].getOnOffElevator()
Choose a destination floorNumber.
floors[floorNumber].waitForElevator()
floors[floorNumber].getOnOffElevator()
```

the elevator arrives at the floors they are leaving, they get on and wait for the elevator to arrive at the floors they are going to. When the elevator gets to their destination floors, they get off, and these passengers are no longer considered in the simulation. The design for the elevator is as follows: Of the three types of objects, two objects are active (the elevator and the passenger) and one object is passive (a floor). Because the building has 6 floors, an array of 6 floors must be included in this simulation. The pseudo-code for the elevator and the passenger is given in Exhibit 10, as well as the state diagram for the elevator in Exhibit 11. Implement this elevator simulation.

6. Can a waitForElevator transition from state Loading to state Loading be added safely to the state diagram in Exhibit 11? How does this change the semantics of the program?
7. The design for the floor object shown in Exhibit 12 uses the same elevator and passenger objects described in pseudo-code in Problem 5. Critique the following elevator design. Can any problems be identified? If so, enumerate them.
8. Critique the elevator design described in Exhibit 13 and shown in Exhibit 14. Can any problems be identified? If so, enumerate them.
9. The design for the floor object shown in Exhibit 15 uses the same elevator and passenger objects described in pseudo-code in Exhibit 13. Critique the elevator design. Can any problems be identified? If so, enumerate them.
10. Modify the elevator simulation in Problem 5 so that the passenger is more realistic. All passengers enter the building at floor 1 and then randomly choose floors to ride between until they come back

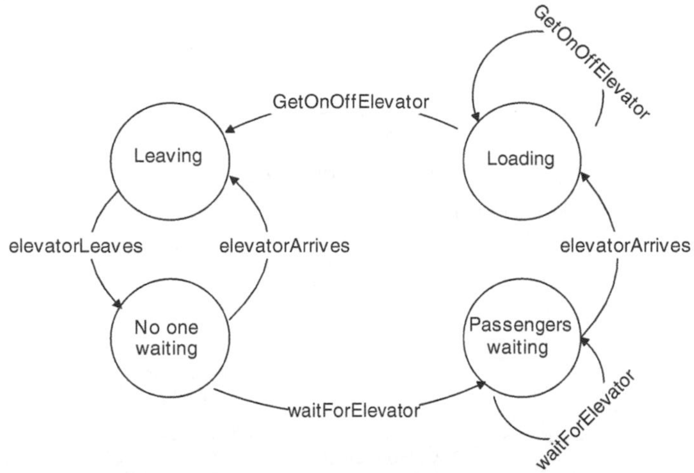

Message: waitForElevator
Parameters: None
From States:
NoOneWaiting
PassengersWaiting
Desc: Increment passengersWaiting
To State:
if current state = No one waiting
goto state Passengers waiting
Return: Null

Message: getOnOffElevator
Parameters: None
From States:
Loading
Desc: Decrement passengersWaiting
To State:
if numberWaiting = 0
goto state Leaving
Return: Null

Message: Elevator Arrives
Parameters: None
From States:
NoOneWaiting
PassengersWaiting
Desc: Null
To State:
if current state = Passengers Waiting
goto state Loading
Return: Null

Message: Elevator Leaves
Parameters: None
From States:
Leaving
Desc: Null
To State:
goto state NoOneWaiting
Return: Null

Exhibit 11. Problem 6: State Diagram for the Floor Object

to floor 1 and leave the building. Make the simulation more realistic by having the passengers all arrive between 8:30 and 9:30 in the morning and leave between 4:30 and 5:30 in the afternoon.

11. Modify the design in Problem 5 to include two elevators and five elevators. If this is done well, the design using five elevators should require changing only the number of elevators declared and started compared to the design for two elevators.
12. The barber shop problem is a famous problem in concurrency. This problem models a barber shop with the following characteristics: The barber shop has a single chair. If the barber finds a customer in the chair, the barber cuts the person's hair, which takes some fixed amount of time (5 seconds for this simulation). Customers who come to the barber shop and find the chair taken can wait on a bench in the shop. The next customer to use the barber's chair must be a customer already waiting on the bench. Finally, if a customer comes and finds no room on the bench, he

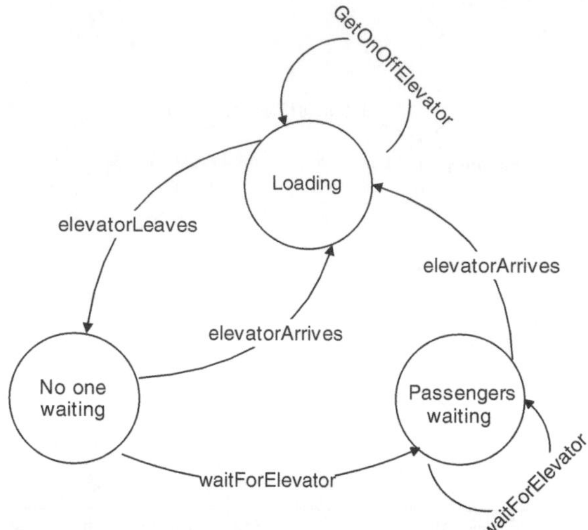

Message: waitForElevator
Parameters: None
From States:
NoOneWaiting
PassengersWaiting
Desc: Increment passengersWaiting
To State:
if current state = No one waiting
goto state Passengers waiting
Return: Null

Message: getOnOffElevator
Parameters: None
From States:
Loading
Desc: Decrement passengersWaiting
To State:
if numberWaiting = 0
goto state Leaving
Return: Null

Message: Elevator Arrives
Parameters: None
From States:
NoOneWaiting
PassengersWaiting
Desc: Null
To State:
if current state = Passengers Waiting
goto state Loading
Return: Null

Message: Elevator Leaves
Parameters: None
From States:
Leaving
Desc: Null
To State:
goto state NoOneWaiting
Return: Null

Exhibit 12. Problem 7: State Diagram for the Floor Object

must wait outside the barber shop until a seat on the bench opens up. Run a simulation of this barber shop when 30 customers come in randomly over the course of 2 minutes, and report the average wait time. Then run the simulation with 40 customers randomly arriving over the course of 2 minutes. What is the difference in the result?

13. Run the barber shop problem with two barbers. What is the result of the simulation?
14. The dining philosophers problem is a classic problem in concurrency that shows how deadlock can occur. The problem involves five philosophers who are eating Chinese food, and five chopsticks are available. The philosophers sit in a circle, each with one chopstick on the left and one chopstick on the right (they share the chopsticks with each other). To eat, each philosopher picks

Exhibit 13. New Pseudo-Code for the Elevator and the Passenger

```
Pseudo-Code for the Elevator
floorNumber = 1
increment = 1
forever {
  floors[floorNumber].elevatorLeaves()
  floorNumber = floorNumber + increment
  Sleep for 1 second
  floors[floorNumber].ElevatorArrives()
  if (floorNumber = = 1)
  increment = 1;
  else if (floorNumber = = MAX_FLOORS)
  increment = -1
}

Pseudo-Code for the Passenger
Sleep a random amount of time < 2 minutes.
Choose a floorNumber to start at.
floors[floorNumber].getOnOffElevator()
Choose a destination floorNumber.
floors[floorNumber].getOnOffElevator()
```

up the chopstick on the left and then the chopstick on the right, eats, and then puts the chopsticks back down. Write a simulation of this problem.

15. The dining philosophers is a classic illustration of deadlock. If all the philosophers pick up the chopstick on the left, no one can pick up the chopstick on the right, and they all starve. One way to solve this problem is to create a philosopher who picks up the right chopstick first. Change the simulation in problem 9 to implement this deadlock-free solution. Why is deadlock avoided here?
16. Another way to solve the dining philosophers problem is to allow only four philosophers to sit at the table at a time, making one wait if the table already has four diners. Write a solution to the dining philosophers problem that uses this design. Why is deadlock avoided?
17. By reviewing the state transitions in the state diagram, and the possible actions that are taken by the active objects, do you think it is possible to predict the possibility of deadlock before a program is run? Describe an algorithm that would do this.
18. Explain how deadlock could occur if two passive objects are in an ensemble.
19. The problem illustrated in Exhibit 16 models Santa Claus at the North Pole. Santa Claus is a very busy man, and he only has time for three things: sleeping, answering elves, or delivering toys. To get his rest, he only wakes up when one of two things is true: (1) at least three elves have questions, or (2) all nine reindeer have been gathered together and hitched to the sleigh so Santa can deliver toys. If Santa is awake and any elves are waiting with questions, then Santa will answer their questions before going back

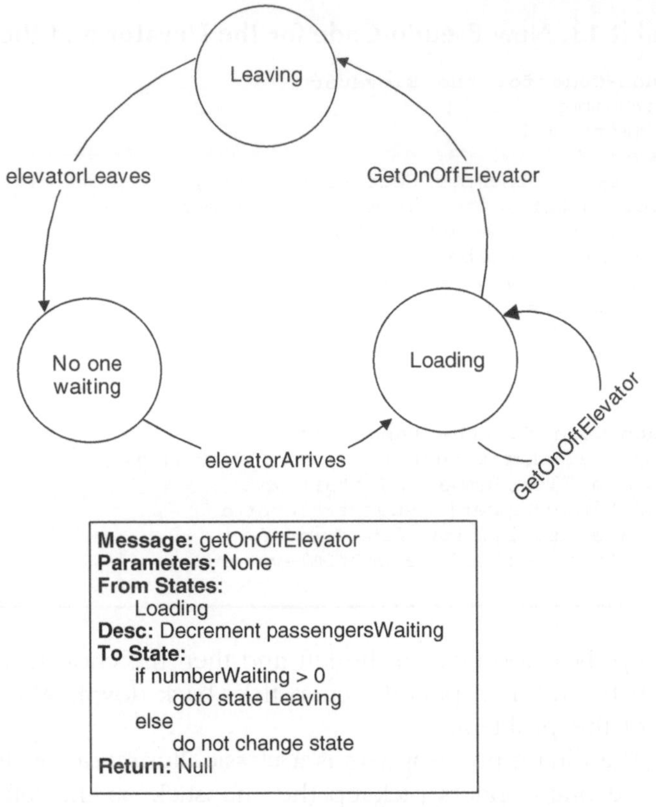

Message: Elevator Arrives
Parameters: None
From States:
NoOneWaiting
Desc: Null
To State:
goto state Loading
Return: Null

Message: Elevator Leaves
Parameters: None
From States:
Leaving
Desc: Null
To State:
goto state NoOneWaiting
Return: Null

Exhibit 14. Problem 8: State Diagram for the Floor Object

to sleep. If Santa is awake and answering questions when all nine reindeer are ready to leave, it is more important to deliver toys than answer questions, so Santa will deliver the toys and then go back to answering questions from the elves. To simulate the elves, assume that 15 elves are working and they will work a random amount of time between 0 and 100 seconds before answering a question. Assume that the reindeer all wait 200 seconds for a Christmas to arrive and then are made ready to deliver gifts in an additional 0 to 30 seconds. Santa takes 5 seconds to answer each question and 30 seconds to deliver the gifts.

20. Show a state diagram for the BinarySemaphore class in Chapter 2.

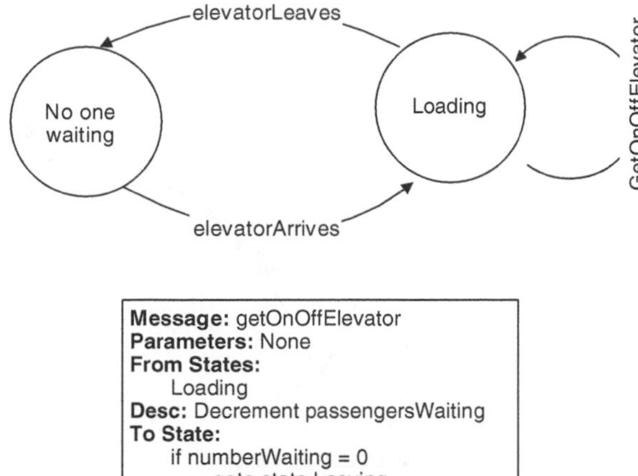

Message: getOnOffElevator
Parameters: None
From States:
Loading
Desc: Decrement passengersWaiting
To State:
if numberWaiting = 0
goto state Leaving
Return: Null

Message: Elevator Arrives
Parameters: None
From States:
NoOneWaiting
PassengersWaiting
Desc: Null
To State:
if current state = Passengers Waiting
goto state Loading
Return: Null

Message: Elevator Leaves
Parameters: None
From States:
Leaving
Desc: Null
To State:
goto state NoOneWaiting
Return: Null

Exhibit 15. Problem 9: State Diagram for the Floor Object

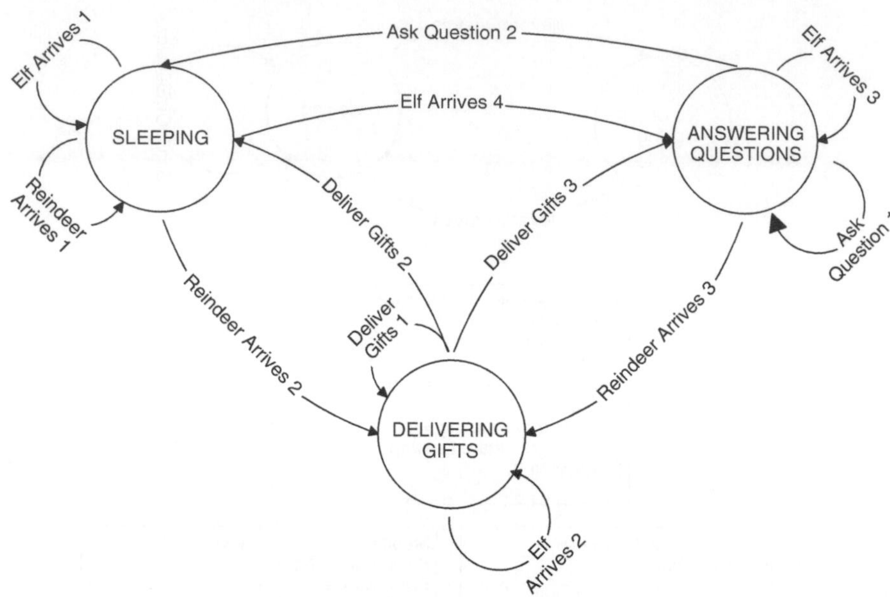

Message: Elf Arrives 1
From State: SLEEPING
Return: Null
Desc: Increment Elves Waiting
To State: SLEEPING
Condition: Same State

Message: Elf Arrives 2
From State: DELIVERING GIFTS
Return: Null
Desc: Increment Elves Waiting
To State: DELIVERING GIFTS
Condition: Same State

Message: Elf Arrives 3
From State: ANSWERING QUESTIONS
Return: Null
Desc: Increment Elves Waiting
To State: ANSWERING QUESTIONS
Condition: Same State

Message: Elf Arrives 4
From State: SLEEPING
Return: Null
Desc: Increment Elves Waiting
To State: ANSWERING QUESTIONS
Condition: Elves Waiting <= 3

Exhibit 16. Problem 19: Santa Claus at the North Pole

Chapter 4

Identifiers, Variables, Objects, and Collection Classes

4.1 Introduction

The purpose of this chapter is to cover the concept of identifiers and variables in Java. The distinction between identifiers and variables is one of the biggest differences between languages that implement data types for runtime objects (such as Smalltalk and Java) and those that only use data types at compile time to generate runtime executable code to manipulate those objects (such as C/C++ and Ada). This distinction helps to account for the fact that, although the syntax of Java and C++ are similar, programming in the two languages feels very different. Objects are handled very differently at runtime, which impacts how objects are manipulated in the language in general. Understanding how Java treats objects will be important in subsequent chapters, when objects are passed between other objects or even around a network using tools such as RMI. Being aware of the nature of objects at compile time and runtime is also important in understanding the concept of an interface, which does not define any data or behavior for an object but simply what messages an object must accept.

This chapter first introduces identifiers and variables by showing how not understanding their differences can lead to incorrect programs. The way in which Java implements variables for objects is then covered, and it is shown how this approach is an improvement over languages that do not maintain the type with the variable. The implementation of arrays in Java is then addressed, and the special case of an array of objects is introduced to discuss the concept of a collection class. Finally, the Java Vector class is used to demonstrate a simple collection class built into Java.

4.2 Chapter Goals

When you have finished this chapter you will know the following:

- The difference between a variable and identifier, and why this distinction matters, particularly in Java
- What a data type is and how data type mismatch between identifiers and variables can cause program errors
- How Java makes sure primitive data types are safe
- How Java stores runtime data types with tags and why these tags are useful
- How Java can manage memory to ensure it is correctly used
- What a container class is and how it can be used

4.3 Identifiers and Variables

Many programmers confuse *identifiers* and *variables*. This is probably because many programming languages, particularly languages as they are used in introductory programming classes, make no practical distinction between variables and identifiers. Even introductory textbooks that do make a distinction between identifiers and variables do not make it sufficient to be practically applied to objects in Java.

A first step to understanding Java, then, is to understand what identifiers and variables are. An identifier is the name and associated data type that identify a variable in a program source file. Except in interpreted languages, an identifier is generally only available when a program is compiled. A variable is the actual instantiation of the data at runtime or simply the memory that stores the data values being manipulated in the program. These are two very different things, and the failure to understand this distinction hinders the ability of a programmer to learn Java, particularly the object model as it is used in Java.

The purpose of this chapter is to clarify this difference between a variable and identifier. The discussion begins by defining data type, which is what defines the attributes (data values) and behavior (operations) of identifiers and variables:

> *Data type: A set of data values and operations on those data values.*

An integer is a data type because it has a set of values, the two's complement representation of integer values, and operations such as

Exhibit 1. Program4.1: Simple C Program That Treats a Variable and Identifier Data Types As If They Are the Same

```
main()
{
  int nt;
  nt = 1;
  nt = nt + 1;
  printf("nt = %d\n," nt);
}
```

"+," "–," etc. Objects are also data types because they have a set of data values, represented by the values of the *instance variables* for an object, and operations that are the instance methods for those objects.

Identifiers and variables are realizations of a data type. The difference is that an identifier is the *reference* to the data type that is contained in the source code and maintained in a symbol table by the compiler, and the variable is the *realization* of that data type in memory when the program runs. The following defines these terms:

> *Identifier: The name of the variable that is in the source code for the program.*
>
> *Variable: The actual memory that is allocated at runtime.*

Many programmers confuse these definitions and combine these two very different concepts, referring to both as a variable. Again, the reason for this confusion between an identifier and a variable is that often variables and identifiers are treated as the same concept in many languages. For example, consider Program4.1 (Exhibit 1).* In this program, the identifier intVar and the variable created at runtime are both of the same int data type. When the compiler generates the object code to be executed, it knows the data type for the identifier and generates machine code that does integer addition, correctly incrementing the variable. The data type of the variable is only known at compile time, when the code to manipulate it is created. But, because the generated code works correctly for an int type, it appears that considering the identifier and variable as the same data type makes no difference. Indeed, for simple programs such as this the difference between the identifier and the variable is irrelevant.

The distinction between an identifier and variable, however, quickly becomes a problem even in simple C programs such as Program4.2 (Exhibit 2). Here, the *union* statement allows the compiler to choose between two different data types for the variable. In this program, the compiler generates machine code to store the variable using the integer

* Program4.1 and Program4.2 are written in C.

Exhibit 2. Program4.2: Operation on an Incorrect Data Type in C

```
main()
{
  typedef union {
    int intVar;
    float floatVar;
  } NumType;

  NumType nt;
  nt.intVar = 1;
  nt.floatVar = nt.floatVar + 1;
  printf("nt.floatVar = %d\n," nt.floatVar);
}
```

identifier, and then generates floating-point machine code to increment the variable. Because the operation of adding 1 to an integer is very different from adding 1 to a float, the code to increment the variable is incorrect and a wrong answer is produced when the program is run. This problem is caused by the data type of the variable (integer) not matching the data type of the identifier (float) and shows why it is important to always make sure data types match.

The problem of an identifier having a different type than the variable it represents has been carried forward to instances of structures and classes (objects) in C++. The data types for an object are maintained only at compile time in C++. At runtime, the object becomes simply a reference to memory in the heap, with most of its identifying information being lost. Because only one data type is known (the one from the compiler), the compiler must generate any code to manipulate the object. Thus, the data type for the object identifier that the programmer encoded at compile time is used to manipulate the object variable at runtime. Nothing in the language or program execution model can be used to check that the compile time and runtime data types match.

Because C/C++ allows the use of many other unsafe referencing mechanisms, such as pointers, and also allows the programmer to assign a compile time identifier of nearly any data type to any object, it is the programmer's responsibility to ensure that the data type used for the variable is correct. Therefore, it is impossible to identify and use the type difference between the identifier and variable, and many C/C++ programmers simply lose the distinction and refer to both identifiers and variables as the variables. This makes directly referencing memory unsafe, and we have no good way to fix this problem.

The problem with invalid memory accesses is one of the main reasons why constructs such as union and pointers were not allowed in Java. Java recognizes that bifurcation of the data type can occur between the compile time and runtime data types, and it implements two mechanisms to ensure type matching between compile time identifiers and runtime variables. The first method is used to ensure that primitives are always of the correct type at runtime and is explained in Section 4.4. The second method uses a different model for storage of its runtime objects, a model in which the data type of the object is maintained throughout the life of the object, for both compile time and runtime, to ensure that the correct type is maintained (see Section 4.5).

4.4 Java Identifiers and Variables

Java deals with the possibility of the identifiers and variables having different types by using two different mechanisms, one for primitive data types and one for objects. Because these two mechanisms are very different, they are addressed in separate sections.

4.5 Primitives

Primitive data types are built directly into the Java virtual machine (JVM). For example, an *int* is a primitive, but an *Integer* is an object that *wrappers* an int primitive. You can always tell the primitives in the Java language because they start with a lower-case character; for example, *float* is a primitive, but *Float* is an object.

Because the Java language has no union constructs or pointers,* the data type of the variable referenced by the identifiers for primitives cannot be changed in Java. When a variable of a different data type is used in an assignment statement for a primitive, it always involves copying the variable and converting the copy to the correct type. For example, when setting an int variable to a float variable, the float variable is copied to another variable that has a data type of int, so the reference cannot change the data type it represents. And, because both the Java compiler and the JVM share the same representations and operations for primitive data types, they can agree that the compiler can generate the code to manipulate these variables, and their data types can be safely forgotten after the compilation step. This saves space, makes operations on primitives faster than operations on objects, and is similar to the mechanisms employed by the C/C++ compiler. However, these primitives are safe in Java because no mechanism is included to change the data type of any identifier or the referenced variable once it is created. In Java, then, the programmer can always rely on the fact that the data type of the identifier is the same data type of the variable it references. Thus, for Java primitives, while it is

---

* This statement is often misinterpreted to mean that Java has no pointers. Pointers are always used when running a program. The point here is that the Java language does not allow a programmer to access a pointer directly. This ensures that a programmer cannot make a reference to an invalid type when accessing a variable.

Exhibit 3. Program4.3: Compiler Error in Referencing an Object of Data Type Object with a Variable Data Type of Person

```
class Person {
  String name;
  public Person(String name) {
    this.name = name;
  }

  public String getName() {
    return name;
  }
}

public class ReferenceError {
  public static void main(String args[]) {
    Object o1 = new Person("Chuck");
    o1.getName();
  }
}
```

strictly incorrect to refer to the identifier and the variable as being the same, not making the distinction has no serious consequence; however, the mechanism for ensuring safe access of objects is very different than that for primitives in Java.

4.6 Objects

The mechanism for ensuring that objects are safe in Java recognizes the difference between the identifier in the program source file and the actual runtime variable it represents; therefore, to represent the data types properly, information about the data type for both the identifier (compile time) and the variable (runtime) must be maintained. To accomplish this, in Java every object carries with it a runtime data type tag. This is simply a data item, hidden from the programmer, that contains information about the actual data type of the variable. This runtime data type tag keeps information about not only the current type of the object but also any interface or extends clause that applies to this variable.

A number of example programs are now presented to show how Java uses the compile time and runtime types to make sure a program is correct. The first is Program4.3 (Exhibit 3), which illustrates how the data type of the compiler identifier can be different than the data type of the runtime variable. In this example, the program creates an identifier of type Object, named o1, that references a variable of type Person. In the program, a call is made to the method o1.getName. Even though the runtime object has a type of Person, the compiler only knows it as an object; hence, the call to the method fails to compile.

Exhibit 4. Program4.4: Runtime Error Casting a Variable to a Non-Matching Data Type

```
class Person {
}

class Car {
}

public class RuntimeError {
  public static void main(String args[]) {
    Object o1 = new Person();
    Object o2 = new Car();
    Person p1 = (Person) o1;
    Person p2 = (Person) o2;
  }
}
```

Program4.4 (Exhibit 4) illustrates that Java has a compile time data type and a runtime data type, and that information can be used to ensure that the type assumed at compile time is the type that actually exists at runtime. In this example, two identifiers, o1 and o2, with an identifier data type of Object are created. The first references a Person variable, and the second a Car variable. The compiler only knows that the identifiers are of data type Object, but the runtime maintains their types. When the program is run, it attempts to cast both variables to a Person. This works in the first case, because the variable object is actually a Person. It fails in the second case, because the variable is not a Person, but a Car. When the generated machine code to do the cast to a Person is executed, it realizes that the type is incorrect, and the program throws a runtime ClassCastException. Note that the error even prints out the true data type of the variable, in this case a Car. This shows that a data type is maintained at both runtime and compile time.

The existence of a runtime data tag is an important feature in Java. While the use of runtime data tags does not remove the possibility of data type mismatch between the identifiers and the variables (as was achieved with primitives), it does make any mismatch explicit, which is useful to the programmer, compiler, and the JVM. Having the runtime data type tags offers at least four big advantages over systems that do not use them:

- Being able to verify that the runtime data types match the data types expected when the program was compiled produces safer systems.
- Knowing the runtime data types allows the VM to manage the memory, which is error prone and easier to implement than having the programmer do it.

- Knowing the runtime data types allows the objects to be effectively written to other systems or persistent storage (such as a disk or database).
- Standard classes, called *collection classes*, can be developed to safely store and retrieve objects.

The first three of these points are covered in the next three sections; point 4 is the subject of Section 4.7.

4.6.1 Using Runtime Data Type Tags Results in Safer Programs

One of the main advantages of using runtime data type tags is that doing so makes programs safer for two reasons: First, the data type of the variable can be checked when the variable is being used to be sure that it matches the type that the compiler expected. If the type does not match, the JVM will immediately throw an error at the point where the mismatch occurs, as shown in Exhibit 4 (Program4.4). Languages that do not have this runtime check often allow a program to access data in memory that is outside of the variable currently being operated on. When this happens, often the program does not immediately fail, as the reference itself is not invalid, but what the reference does to memory that it does not own is invalid. Most often this results in corrupting memory used by some other variable or method in the program. The program continues to execute until a statement is reached that is affected by the corrupted memory, and the program fails, often with a strange and cryptic message. The statement that fails is normally perfectly valid, and it is only the existence of the corrupted memory that causes it to fail. In fact, the statement that fails normally has no logical connection, from the point of view of the source program, to the statement where the program memory was corrupted.

This problem is actually worse than a program simply failing. If the memory that was corrupted is persistent (i.e., stored in a file or database), then the failure of the program could occur days or weeks after the actual execution of the statement that caused it. This makes finding these types of bugs exceedingly difficult to find and fix and can result in very far-reaching effects if the errors are allowed to exist over time. Having the program fail when an invalid casting error is encountered does not guarantee that the error will not happen, but it does protect against the knock-on effects of allowing a corrupted program to continue to run. It also makes the bug easier to find and fix because the reason for the error and the exact location of the error are known.

The second reason why runtime data type tags improve the safety of a program is that they allow the programmer to control the behavior

Exhibit 5. Program4.5: Catching a ClassCastException

```
class Person {
}

class Car{
}

public class CatchCast {
  public static void main(String args[]) {
    try {
      Object o1 = new Person();
      Car c1 = (Car)o1;
    } catch (ClassCastException cce) {
      System.out.println("The program produced a class cast
        exception.");
      System.out.println("Please call your software
        representative.");
    }
  }
}
```

of the program when a mismatched data type is encountered. This can be done in two ways: First, a programmer can control for casting errors by catching them if they occur and acting on them in a manner consistent with the error-handling strategy in the program. Exception handling in Java is the topic of Chapter 6, but a simple try/catch block that catches ClassCastException is shown in Exhibit 5 (Program4.5). This program shows that when an invalid cast is made the programmer can control how the program reacts to the problem. Even if recovery from the error is not possible, the program can gracefully handle any necessary cleanup of data, as well as generate user-friendly messages before exiting (not the generally useless "bus error — core dumped" or "segmentation fault" errors produced when C/C++ has corrupted memory). The second way a programmer can handle casting errors is to make sure they do not happen by using the instanceof* operator. The instanceof operator checks the runtime data type tag of the object to make sure that it matches the type specified in the second operand. It returns true if they match, false otherwise. Note that the instanceof not only checks the class of the object but also can be used to check any superclass or interface that the class for this object extends or implements. Exhibit 6 (Program4.6) shows how the instanceof operator can be used to make sure that a cast is correct. If the object is an instanceof a Person, it is cast to a Person; if it is an instanceof a Car, it is cast to a Car. The cast is guaranteed to be correct as the runtime data type tag is checked before the cast is performed.

* Note that instanceof is an operator, like "+," "–," etc. It is not a method; hence, the somewhat strange syntax.

Exhibit 6. Program4.6: Using the Instanceof Operator to Check the Runtime Data Type before Casting

```
class Person {
}

class Car {
}

public class CorrectCast {
  public static void main(String args[]) {
    Object object;

    //Randomly choose to create a Car or
    //Person object.
    int flag = (int)(2.0 * Math.random());
    if (flag = = 0)
      object = new Car();
    else
      object = new Person();

    //Cast to the correct object
    if (object instanceof Person) {
      Person person = (Person)object;
    }
    else if (object instanceof Car) {
      Car car = (Car)object;
    }
  }
}
```

Because the use of runtime data type tags forces a Java programmer to cast to a correct type, the Java compiler also helps ensure that the use of objects is correct by forcing the programmer to consciously define the expected result when a potentially unsafe cast is to be made. To understand what type of cast is potentially unsafe, consider the casting done in Program4.7 (Exhibit 7). In this program, an object of class Person is first cast to an object of class Object. Because all Person objects are also instances of Object, this cast is guaranteed to be 100% safe, so the compiler makes an implicit cast to Object. However, a cast made from an object of type Object to a Person or a Car is not always safe. In Exhibit 7 (Program4.7), it is obvious that objects can be instances of classes other than Person as they can also be instances of class Car. The compiler forces the programmer to acknowledge this by explicitly casting the object to a Person. Because the compiler could not ensure the safety of this cast, it put the onus of making sure that the cast was legal on the programmer, which the programmer acknowledges by doing an explicit cast.

Finally, the Java compiler will check to make sure that a cast is correct, if it can. For example, Java will not compile a cast that cannot

Exhibit 7. Program4.7: Implicit and Explicit Casting in Java

```
class Person {
  String Name;
}

class Car {
  int EngineSize;
}

public class CastError1 {
  public static void main(String args[]) {
    Person person = new Person();
    Object object = person;
    Car car = (Car)object;
  }
}
```

Exhibit 8. Program4.8: Casting Error Example

```
class Person {
  String Name;
}

class Car {
  int EngineSize;
}

public class CastError2 {
  public static void main(String args[]) {
    Person person = new Person();
    Car car = (Car)person;
  }
}
```

be correct, as shown in Program4.8 (Exhibit 8). Here, there is no way a valid cast can be made from a Car object to a Person object, and so the compiler simply does not allow the cast to be written.

Programmers coming from other languages often complain about the amount of casting that must be done in a Java program; however, a Java program that compiles will generally run or produce an understandable error. Often, in other languages, casts are made that the programmer has not considered carefully, and sometimes the language will make an implicit cast that is not even understood by the programmer. Considering the number of major problems in software caused by improper casting in these languages, it is difficult to understand why these programmers feel so strongly about not enforcing rules that ensure safe casting.

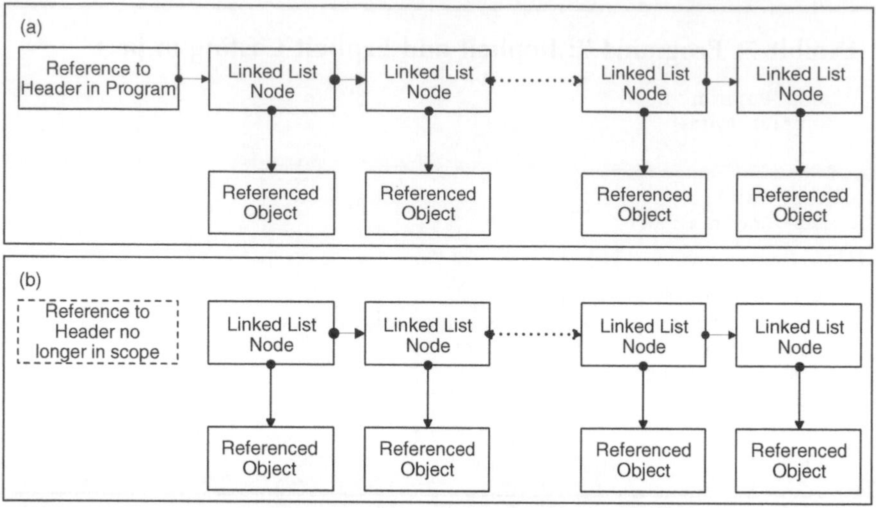

Exhibit 9. Memory Leak with a Linked List

4.6.2 Memory Allocation is Simpler and Safer

A second advantage of using runtime data type tags is that memory can be managed by the JVM and is not the responsibility of the programmer. Because Java keeps the runtime data type tags and class definitions during runtime, the JVM knows how the objects are constructed. Using a relatively straightforward *garbage collection* algorithm, the JVM can therefore allocate and deallocate memory for objects. In languages that do not have runtime data type tags, the information about the data that makes up the object is lost after the program is compiled. Therefore, the methods to create and recover memory used by an object must be supplied by the programmer. Giving the programmer control over the allocation and deallocation of memory can lead to the problems of dangling pointers and memory leaks. Having the VM do this job removes these two possible problems.

A simple linked-list example is used here to illustrate how a programmer implementing memory management can create both memory leaks and dangling pointers. This same linked-list example is then used to show how Java can simply and safely deal with allocating and deallocating memory. This example also demonstrates that when a programmer implements memory management it can be a daunting task to get it correct.

First, consider a memory leak. A memory leak occurs when memory is allocated in a program and not returned to the system after it is no longer being used. This memory is no longer used but is inaccessible, so the amount of available memory slowly leaks away. This situation is illustrated in Exhibit 9. In Exhibit 9(a), a linked list has been allocated with a number of nodes. The only access to each subsequent node is from a pointer from the previous node. If at some point the head of the list is no longer available (for example, the variable referring to the head of the list goes out of program scope), then all the nodes remain allocated but none can be accessed, as shown in Exhibit 9(b). To solve this problem, the programmer must create a method, often called a *destructor*, that is called when the variable is destroyed. The purpose of the destructor is to go through the list of nodes in Exhibit 9(b) and call a method that deallocates each node. This scheme poses a number of problems. First, the programmer must properly code the destructor, which is a non-trivial task, as shown later in this section. Second, it is often the responsibility of the programmer who uses the linked list to explicitly call the destructor, and this is sometimes forgotten. Even if good managerial controls are in place to ensure that programmers follow acceptable standards, they are not as effective as rules that are automatically enforced by the compiler and JVM.

The second problem that occurs when programmers must handle memory management is dangling pointers. Dangling pointers occur when a variable is deallocated while it is still referenced. To see how this can happen, consider the case of an object that is stored in two separate linked lists, as in Exhibit 10(a). This could happen if employees for each department in a company are stored in a linked list. If the entire department is sold to another company, the entire linked list for that department would be deallocated. However, suppose an employee is assigned to two departments, one that leaves and one that stays. An employee staying with the company in the second department would now be referenced in the linked list for the second department, but the record of this employee would have been deleted when the first list was deleted to prevent a memory leak. The employee record is deallocated, but it is still referenced, so the reference is called a *dangling reference* because it points to an object that no longer exists.

So what should programmers do? If they do not free the memory for the employees when they delete the department, they have a memory leak; however, if they do free the memory, the second list is invalid because one employee pointer is a dangling reference. This problem arises because it is not possible in most languages to easily figure out if an object is still being used, so it is a complex task for a programmer to handle this situation correctly. Some scheme such as reference counting must be implemented, but this, too, is fraught with difficulties. It is hoped that this discussion has convinced the reader that correctly allocating and deallocating memory is not an easy task even for a programmer who is properly motivated to do it carefully.

This type of problem cannot happen in Java. In Java, information about the data types of all objects is maintained at runtime. This information can be used to reconstruct all the variables that are part of the objects. For example, the JVM knows if a data value stored in

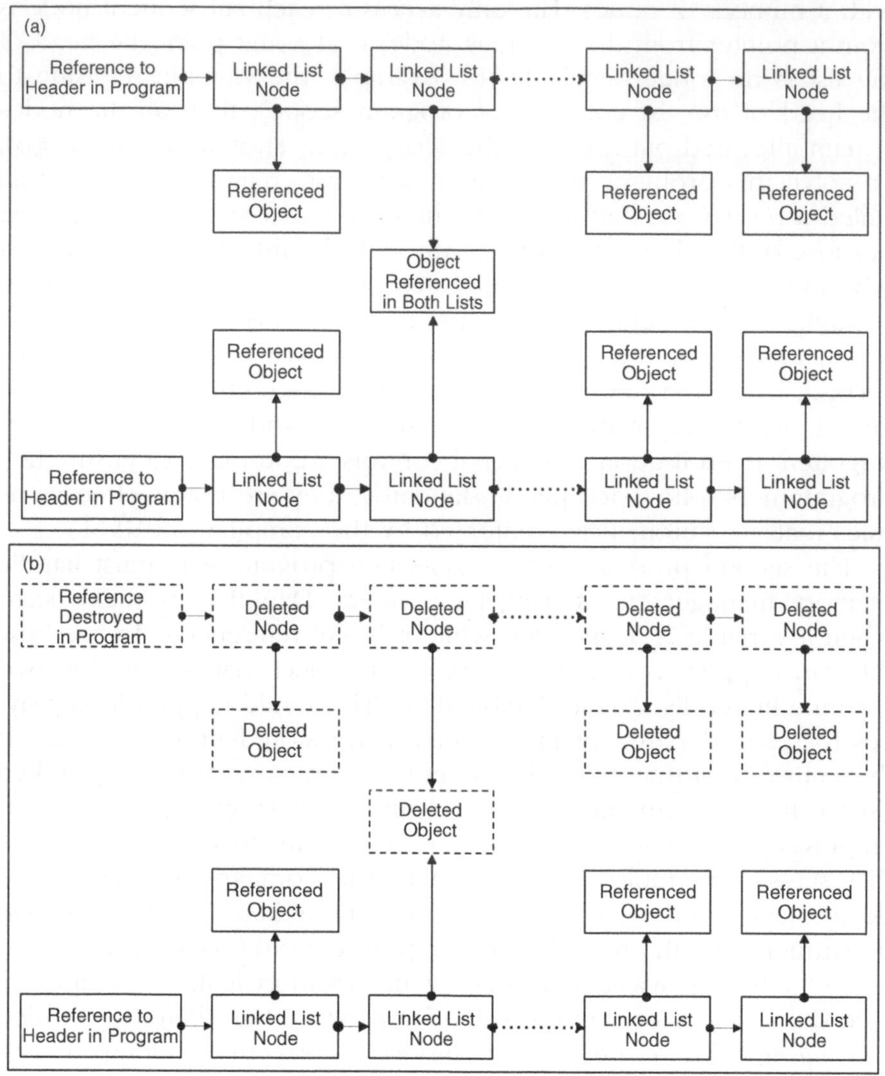

Exhibit 10. Dangling Reference with a Linked List

an object is a primitive (e.g., an int) or a reference to another object. Knowing this, Java can build a list of all objects that are currently active. Having this information, Java can safely deallocate objects no longer used, called *garbage collection*, which provides the memory management for the programmer.

Exhibit 11 provides a brief example of how a JVM can handle garbage collection. When an object goes out of scope in a program, the JVM does not immediately attempt to reclaim the space; instead, it allows that space to remain allocated, as shown in Exhibit 11(a). When Java runs low on memory to allocate for new objects, the JVM begins garbage collection. It first marks all unreferenced objects that

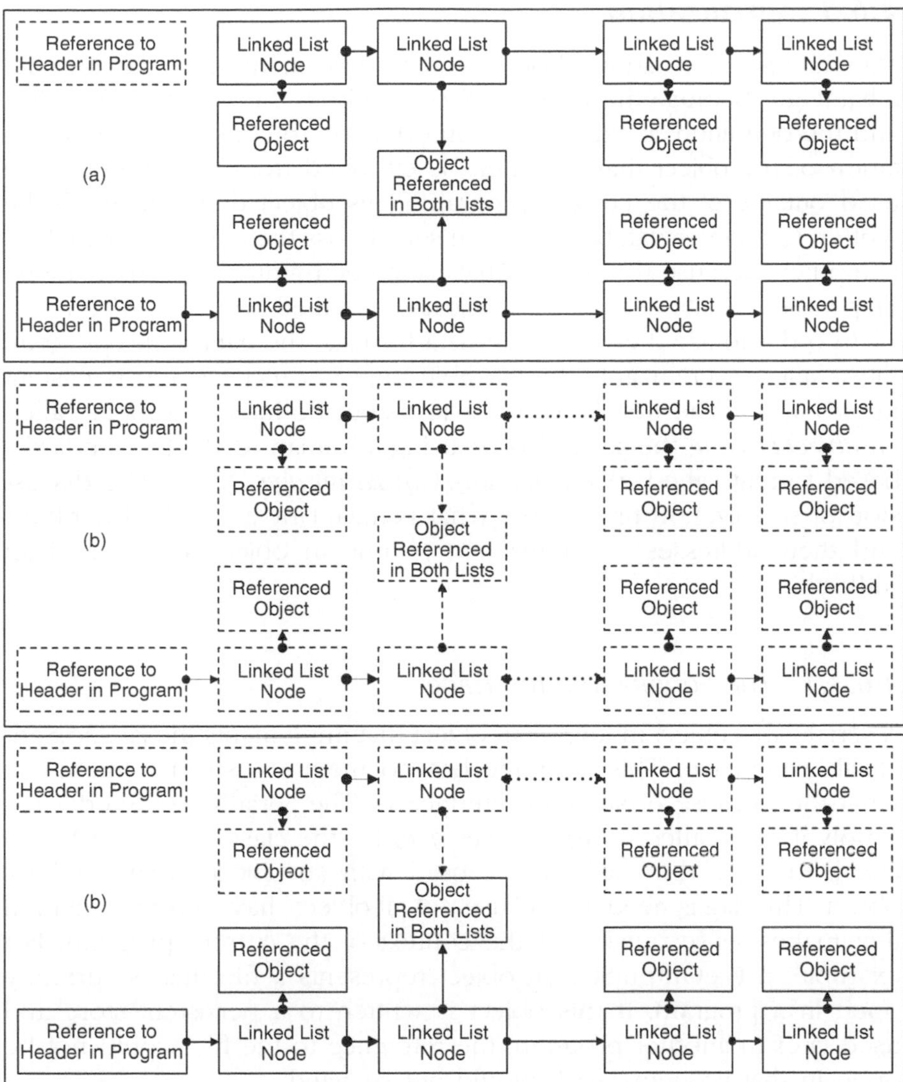

Exhibit 11. Proper Memory Collection with a Doubly Linked List

can be collected as garbage, as shown in Exhibit 11(b). Next, all objects currently in scope are unmarked, as they are currently referenced. Then, because Java can distinguish between objects that are referenced from unmarked objects (because it has kept the data type tag and object definition), it can continue to unmark all the objects that it references. It does this until all objects that are currently referenced are unmarked. Any objects left marked are not currently referenced, and can be collected as garbage and the memory can be returned to the system, as shown in Exhibit 11(c). This mechanism ensures that memory leaks and dangling pointers cannot occur.

4.6.3 Serialization

Maintaining information about the data type at runtime has another advantage. Because the JVM has access to both the data for the object and the definition, it can use that information to construct a representation of the object that can then be exported from the program and used outside of the current program. This object then can easily be written to a file or database or even sent across the network to another computer. Because the objects that have been written to a permanent, or persistent, data store, these objects are called *persistent objects*.

In order to use these external data formats, the data in the program must first be serializable. Serializable objects can be made persistent in two ways. The first is to use a Java-specific internal format called an *object stream*; the second is by using a human-readable, standards-based format called *eXtensible Markup Language* (XML). The discussion of serialization first covers what is meant by a serializable object and then addresses programs that output an object stream and an XML object.

4.6.3.1 The Serializable Interface

A serializable object in Java is an object that implements the java.io.Serializable interface. This interface has no methods, so one might ask what the purpose of such an interface is. The Serializable interface is simply a flag (called a *tagged interface*) for the class that the JVM can check to see if the class can be used with an object stream or XML object. This flag is needed because not all objects have a representation that makes sense outside of the context of the current program. For example, a FileOutputStream object represents a file that is currently open in a program. If this object is written to a persistent store and used later in another program, the reference to the file would not be open in that program, so it would not be valid.

Another example is a Graphics object. A Graphics object is an object created by a Frame that allows a programmer to draw on the current window. If the Frame that created the Graphics object no longer exists, that Graphics object is not valid, so the Graphics object cannot be made persistent. FileOutputStream and Graphics are two examples of objects that are not serializable. Most objects that a programmer creates in Java contain only data comprised of serializable objects or primitives; therefore, most objects that are created can implement the Serializable interface.

The JVM checks the objects being written to see if they implement the Serializable interface. If an attempt is ever made to write a non-serializable object to an output that expects serialized objects, such as an object stream or an XMLEncoder, a runtime error is generated.

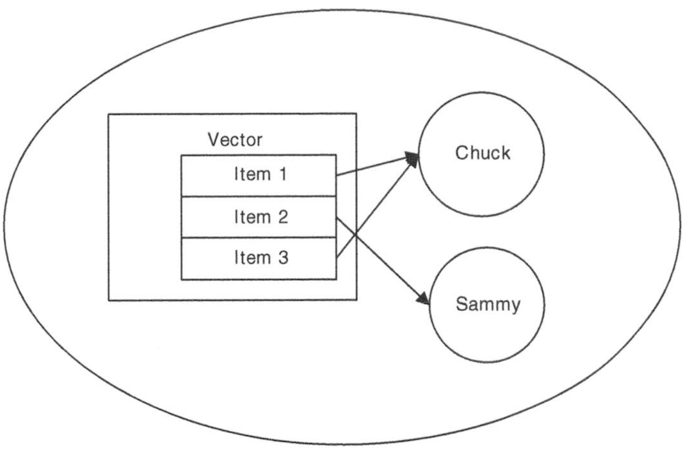

Exhibit 12. Vector Object for Exhibit 13 (Program4.9) as Stored in Memory

Another option for creating serializable objects arises when not all of the data fields have valid external representations. Programmers can choose to write their own serialization for such an object by making the object implement java.io.Externalizable, or the fields that are not serializable can be marked with the Java keyword *transient*, which indicates that the data field should not be written to a stream.

4.6.3.2 Serializing Data

Once it is known that the data in the object has an external representation, the JVM must be able to transform that data into a format that allows it to be written to a file or other persistent store. To understand how this is done, you must first know how the data is stored in memory when the program is running. Consider Exhibit 12, which represents the heap memory used by a Vector object containing two Person objects, as shown in Exhibit 13 (Program4.9). Note that the heap memory to store this element is not organized but follows pointers to each of the objects that are stored. This memory cannot simply be copied, as the program memory used when this object is created almost certainly will not be free to take these values when the object is read in.

To write this data to an external source, the data represented in this vector object must be "flattened" or serialized into a series of bytes. All references to objects must be made in this flattened representation. To do this, the object doing the serialization (e.g., an object stream) must have knowledge of all the objects stored as part of the aggregate stored object. Fortunately, in Java this knowledge is obtained through the runtime data type tag. Each data value making up the object can

Exhibit 13. Program4.9: Program to Create a Vector Object

```
import java.util.Vector;

class Person {
  String name;
  public Person(String name) {
  }
}

public class VectorMemory {
  public static void main(String args[]){
    Vector People = new Vector();
    Person Chuck = new Person("Chuck"));
    People.addElement(Chuck);
    People.addElement(new Person("Cindy"));
    People.addElement(Chuck);
  }
}
```

be matched to its definition and then each referenced object to its definition until only primitive data remains.

While serialization in Java is achievable, it is not trivial, as shown in Exhibit 12, which has two references to a single object that has the name "Chuck" stored. If this object is simply written to the external stream twice, when the vector is reconstructed later it would not be the same vector, as it would now reference two different objects. Serialization must take this into account. It is also possible for objects to reference each other, in effect creating a "loop" in the object graph. To see how serialization does indeed take this into account, an example of the serialized XML format of the Vector object in Exhibit 13 (Program4.9) is written in Exhibit 14 (Program4.10). The XML representation is shown in Exhibit 15. Note that the XML representation makes it clear that only one "Chuck" object is referenced twice.

4.6.3.3 Writing External Data

Once the data is serialized, it can be treated as any other stream of data and written externally from the program. For example, Exhibit 14 (Program4.10) writes a Vector object to a simple file output stream. Note that in this program the entire Vector object is serialized so that it can be written to and read from a file. Because a number of different types of objects are written to the file (in this case, the Vector object and the Person objects), the JVM must maintain the data type tag with the objects in the files so that the objects can be properly reconstructed. This is done using metadata tags in the case of XML and with an internal, binary format with object streams that is more compact than XML but not easily readable by people.

Exhibit 14. Program4.10: Program to Write XML Definition of Exhibit 15

```
import java.util.Vector;
import java.io.BufferedOutputStream;
import java.io.FileOutputStream;
import java.beans.XMLEncoder;
import java.io.Serializable;

public class Person implements Serializable {
  private String name;

  public Person() {
  }

  public Person(String name) {
    this.name = name;
}
  public String getName() {
    return name;
  }

  public void setName(String name) {
    this.name = name;
  }

  public static void main(String args[]){
    try {
      Vector People = new Vector();
      Person chuck = new Person("Chuck");
      People.addElement(chuck);
      People.addElement(new Person("Sam"));
      People.addElement(chuck);
      XMLEncoder e = new XMLEncoder(
                          new BufferedOutputStream(
                      new FileOutputStream("out.xml")));
      e.writeObject(People);
      e.close();
    } catch (Exception e) {
      e.printStackTrace();
    }
  }
}
```

Serializable data is not intended only to be written to persistent output such as files and databases. Because the data has a representation external to the program, it can be used on computers other than the one on which it was created. Thus, serializable data is the basis for passing data in a number of distributed programming schemes, such as RMI (Chapter 13) or other protocols, such as the simple object access protocol (SOAP), or even as simple objects using sockets.

Exhibit 15. XML Output for Vector in Exhibit 13 (Program4.9)

```
<?xml version = "1.0" encoding = "UTF-8"?>
<java version = "1.4.0" class = "java.beans.XMLDecoder">
  <object class = "java.util.Vector">
    <void method = "add">
      <object id = "Person0" class = "Person">
        <void property = "name">
          <string>Chuck</string>
        </void>
      </object>
    </void>
    <void method = "add">
      <object class = "Person">
        <void property = "name">
          <string>Sam</string>
        </void>
      </object>
    </void>
    <void method = "add">
      <object idref = "Person0"/>
    </void>
  </object>
</java>
```

4.6.4 Performance Considerations

If runtime data type tags are so useful, why are they not used in languages such as C/C++? One reason is that they were not used when such languages were defined, and the languages that did not include them cannot be easily retrofitted to take advantage of them. Also, one can argue that runtime data type tags do not come without a price and that the overhead involved in using them is too costly in terms of memory and computing time. However, two points must be considered when discussing these tags. The first is whether the amount of program safety achieved with the runtime data type tags is worth the cost to implement them. The answer for most managers would be *yes*. One successful hack attack using a simple buffer overflow from the Web is likely to be far more costly than the extra hardware required for efficiently executing a Java program, and debugging one instance of corrupted memory from a miscast object is much more expensive than the computing power required to implement runtime checking as in Java. These types of problems, which are all too common, are impossible to guard against without the use of runtime data type checking built into the language.

The second point is whether or not using runtime data type tags is actually more expensive than not using them. This question is problematic because, while the tags do incur overhead, the presence of the information they provide allows the JVM to make optimizations of the programs that would otherwise be impossible. Whether or not these optimizations can actually make up for, or even exceed, the overhead necessary to implement and use the tags is still an open question. It may turn out that runtime data tags are indeed free (or nearly so). Regardless, with the current generation of JIT compilers, the extra cost is small, and the benefits normally far outweigh the costs.

4.7 Collection Classes in Java

4.7.1 Arrays in Java

Arrays in Java are very different than arrays in C/C++. In C/C++, arrays are little more than pointers to a block of memory, and the operations to access them are defined at compilation time. In that way, arrays in C/C++ are very much like primitive data types. In Java, arrays have some primitive support to access members using the "[ ]" operators, but are different in that they are more like first-class objects with some extra syntax built into the language to manipulate them. Thus, using arrays in Java is different than using arrays in C/C++.

Arrays in any language are contiguous pieces of memory that hold a set of values. The size of the data types stored in an array must be constant to allow the individual members of the array to be directly accessed. Because the data in the array must be a constant size, arrays in Java are most useful for primitive data. This is true, first, because with primitive data, the size of each data item is fixed, so the actual data items can be created when the array is created. Also, because the data items are stored in the array, arrays are useful with primitives because they can be directly accessed by normal array-addressing mechanisms of calculating a base address and an offset. Neither of these two advantages holds for arrays of objects.

Note that, while an array of primitives is a list of data values, the array itself still behaves largely as an object. For example, consider Exhibit 16 (Program4.11), which allocates an array of primitives, in this case ints, and writes the array to a file using an ObjectOutput-Stream. This program shows that arrays are like objects in Java in the following ways:

- The memory (or variable) for the array cannot be allocated at the same time that the identifier for the array is declared. Just as with objects, memory for the array must be allocated with a "new" statement, and is stored in the heap.
- Arrays are stored with information about the number of elements in the array, and that information can be accessed and used at runtime. The loop in this program gets its range by querying the "length" variable of the array. Accesses to members of the array are checked, as shown when an OutOfBoundsException is generated.

Exhibit 16. Program4.11: Allocating an Array of Primitives

```
import java.io.*;

public class ArrayOfPrimitives {
  public static void main(String args[]) {
    try {
      int array[] = new int[10];
      ObjectOutputStream oos = new ObjectOutputStream (
      new FileOutputStream("temp.dat"));
      oos.writeObject(array);
    } catch (IOException ioe) {
      ioe.printStackTrace();
    }
  }
}
```

- As with objects, all elements in the array are initialized to 0 or null. In the case of arrays of primitives, all elements are initialized to 0.
- Arrays can be serialized. This shows that the memory allocation properties that were true of other objects also apply to arrays.

So, arrays in Java take on the properties of objects, even when they store primitives. In fact, other than to store arrays of primitives, which cannot be achieved with container classes, using arrays as opposed to container classes in Java offers few advantages.

4.7.2 Arrays of Objects

In Java, because any class (except a class that is declared final) can be overridden, the size of an object to be stored at runtime cannot be guaranteed by the type; thus, it is not possible to store objects directly in an array. Instead, arrays of objects in Java store references (normally addresses) to the individual objects, so the array and objects must be allocated separately, as shown in Exhibit 17 (Program4.12). This makes arrays less useful for objects, and means that collection classes, such as Vector, are normally used when storing collections of objects. Using collection classes will remove any ambiguity that surrounds arrays as to whether they are objects or not because collection classes will be first-class objects. Arrays in Java can be used to store either primitives or objects. For primitives, arrays are a useful construct; however, arrays of objects are less useful and have largely been replaced by collection classes, which are covered in Section 4.7.3. This section explains arrays of objects and why collection classes were developed.

When arrays of objects are allocated, only the references for the objects are created; no objects are actually created. The actual objects to be stored must be allocated individually at runtime. While this might

Exhibit 17. Program4.12: Allocating an array of objects

```
class Person {
}

class Car {
}

public class ArrayOfObjects {
  public static void main(String args[]) {
    Object array[] = new Object[10];
    array[0] = new Person();
    array[1] = new Car();
    array[2] = new Object();
    //array[3..9] is unallocated.
  }
}
```

appear to be a negative, it allows objects of any type to be stored in an array of objects. One significant problem with storing arrays of amorphous objects in some languages other than Java is that the compiler needs to know the type of the object in order to generate the machine code required to manipulate it at runtime. If objects are stored in an array, it is not possible to determine the type of the object when it is taken from the array. The best that can be done is that the programmer can *guess* what the object will be and cast the object so that the compiler can generate code for the data type that the programmer thinks is stored. Thus, many languages do not include classes for containers of generic objects. However, thanks once again to the runtime data type tag, using object arrays is perfectly safe because the runtime data tag allows the JVM to identify the type of object stored when it is accessed at runtime.

For example, Exhibit 18 (Program4.13) shows an example of an array of objects in which a Person object and a Car object are stored and retrieved. Despite the apparent simplicity of this program, what is happening is really quite amazing. First, the array of objects is created and all of the objects are initialized to null. This array can take objects of any type and will correctly handle them. Next, several objects of different data types (in this case, an object, a Person, and a Car) are added to the array in an order that can only be determined at runtime. The compiler cannot determine which objects are stored in the array because the order in which they are stored is completely determined by the random variable at runtime. Later, the elements in the array are retrieved and their toString methods are called. The correct toString method is called for each object, including the null elements, because the runtime data type tag allows the JVM to select the correct data type for each object and to dispatch the correct function for that type. This process of calling correct methods at runtime based on the runtime data type is discussed in more detail in Chapter 5; however, this

Exhibit 18. Program4.13: Array of Objects

```
class Person {
}

class Car {
}

public class RandomCreate {
  public static void main(String args[]) {
    Object object;

    //Randomly choose to create a Car or
    //Person Object.
    int flag = (int)(2.0 * Math.random());
    if (flag = = 0)
      object = new Car();
    else
      object = new Person();

    //Cast to the correct Object
    if (object instanceof Person) {
      Person person = (Person)object;
    }
    else if (object instanceof Car) {
      Car car = (Car)object;
    }
  }
}
```

example demonstrates that knowing the data types at runtime is a very powerful mechanism that allows storage of objects of unknown data types.

Because arrays are already almost objects, it would be handy to add a number of operations to their definition. For example, it would be nice to be able to find any element by its value, not just its position. It would also be nice to be able to insert an element into an array without having to include logic to move all the other elements to make room for the new one. A programmer might want the array to be sorted or have keys to look up objects. The developers of Java recognized that the limited capabilities of an array could be greatly improved in these ways and so included in the language a number of classes that enhance the ability of an array to handle collections of objects. In the next section, we look at one of these classes, a collection class called a *Vector*.

4.7.3 Collection Classes

A collection class is simply a class that allows collections of disparate object types to be stored inside a single object. It is very similar to an array of objects, except that collection classes generally have more functionality included in the class than can be included in an array.

For example, one specific type of a collection is the class Vector. A Java Vector is an array that grows as needed to make sure there is always space when an element is added. It also incorporates additional functionality, such as allowing elements to be added at any place in the array, and allows the elements to be manipulated by the object rather than the index. Exhibit 19 (Program4.14) shows an example of using the Vector to store and retrieve objects. Two special functions have been included from the Vector class for this program. The first inserts a record into the table and uses the Vector's add method to add an element in the second component in the Vector, causing all other elements in the Vector to be moved one position forward one position. The second function finds the object in the Vector using the indexOf method, taking advantage of the searching capability of the Vector to find the item.

The many different types of collections allow for special functionality in the collection. For example, maps allow objects to be accessed by a key, and sets ensure that no duplicate elements are in a collection. Many different predefined collection classes implement these types of collections, and each implements the collection in ways that help with the problem. When using the predefined collections classes in Java, specific methods have to be defined. These override methods in class Object, such as equals and hashcode, or implement interfaces, such as Comparable. For example, in Exhibit 19 (Program4.14) the Person class has to implement an equals method to allow the program to work correctly. If the equals method had not been implemented, the Vector class would have used the Object's equals method to compare the two Person objects; however, because they are equivalent but not the same object, it would have failed to have found the object.

4.8 Further Reading

Data types are central to every introductory text on computer science, such as [DEI02] or [LEW03]. The concepts involved in memory management in Java can be found in several disciplines in computer science. For example, books on programming languages, such as Sebesta [SEB99], cover many of the basic concepts of objects, as well as overviews of basic garbage collection. A more detailed analysis of garbage collection algorithms can be found in many books on data structures and algorithms, such as Aho et al. [AHO93]. Details on serialization can be found in the Java specification for serialization [SUN02b] and reflection [SUN02a], as well as the Java Beans specification [SUN96]. Finally, the best place to find information on the many different types of collection classes in Java is the tutorial provided by Sun [MAG02], as well as the javadoc for the java.util package. Eckle [ECK98] also has a good section that describes these classes.

Exhibit 19. Program4.14: Example of Using a Vector Class

```
import java.util.Vector;

class Person {
  private String name;

  public Person() {
  }

  public Person(String name) {
    this.name = name;
  }

  public boolean equals(Object object) {
    return this.name.equals(((Person)object).name);
  }

  public String toString() {
    return name;
  }

  public String getName() {
    return name;
  }

  public void setName(String name) {
    this.name = name;
  }
}

public class ShowVector {
  private static Vector People = new Vector();

  public static void main(String args[]) {
    people.add(new Person("Chuck"));
    people.add(new Person("Patty"));
    people.add(new Person("Linda"));

    //Note that this line puts the new record in at
    //component 2 in the vector and moves everything
    //else down one place in the vector.
    people.add(1, new Person("Cindy"));

    //Print the vector to show that the add worked.

    for (int i = 0; i < people.size(); i++) {
      System.out.println("Person = " + people.elementAt(i));
    }

    //Now find the record "Chuck"

    int elementNo = people.indexOf(new Person("Chuck"));
    System.out.println("Chuck at " + elementNo);
  }
}
```

4.9 Problems

1. What is the difference between a runtime and a compile time data type? Does the distinction make any practical difference in a program?
2. Why does Java not allow pointers? If they are unsafe, what (if anything) can be done to make them safe?
3. At what time (compile time or runtime) is the data type of an interface checked?
4. Given the following code, how many "int" primitives are created?

   ```
   int array[] = new int[10];
   ```

   If the array is changed from an int array to an object array, how many are created?

   ```
   Object array[] = new Object[10];
   ```

5. Write a program that saves integer values from 1 to 100 in a Java array. What must be true of these integers? Use an object output stream to write these values to an Object output file. Read the Vector back into another program.
6. Write a program that saves integer values from 1 to 100 in a java.util.Vector. What must be true of these integers? Use an object output stream to write these values to an Object output file. Read the Vector back into another program.
7. Explain how the finalize method works. When is it called? How is it invoked when memory is recovered?
8. Consider the four swap methods provided in Exhibit 20. Which (if any) work? Explain the behavior of each method.
9. For each numbered line in Exhibit 21, what is the output of the program? Explain how Java called the methods to create this result.
10. What objects are eligible for garbage collection at each of the identified points in the program shown in Exhibit 22? Why?
11. Persistent objects are objects that persist (continue to exist) outside of a program. For example, objects that are written to a database or a file could be created in one program and used in another. Could the JVM be modified to manage persistent objects? Consider when these objects come into and go out of scope. What types of changes would have to be made to the JVM to allow it to handle persistent objects automatically?
12. Can constructors and finalize methods be used to implement persistent objects? What would be some of the problems with using these methods?
13. Create a memory leak and a dangling reference in Java. Describe any difficulties encountered when doing this.
14. Does the instanceof operator check type of the identifier or the variable? Why?

Exhibit 20. Four Swap Methods

```
a.
int swap(int a, int b) {
    int tmp = a;
    int a = b;
  int b = tmp;
}

b.
int swap(Integer a, Integer b) {
  int tmp = a.intValue();
  a = b;
  b = new Integer(tmp);
}

c.
int array[] = new int{1,2};
int swap(array, int a, int b) {
  int tmp = array[a];
  array[a] = array[b];
  array[b] = tmp;
}

d.
class SwapClass {int a, int b};
SwapClass sc = new SwapClass(); sc.a = 1; sc.b = 2;
int swap(SwapClass sc) {
  int tmp = sc.a;
  sc.a = sc.b;
  sc.b = tmp;
}
```

15. Explain why, in the following code fragment, the thread is not simply de-referenced and thus allowed to be garbage collected as soon as the call to start finishes.

```
class MyRunnable implements Runnable {
  public void run() {
    //Do something in the thread
  }
}
(new Thread(new MyRunnable())).start();
```

16. Would concepts such as C/C++ templates or Ada generics be useful in Java? If not, why not? If so, give specific instances where they could be used. Would the usage be the same as in C/C++ or Ada?
17. The Serializable interface in Java is referred to as a "tagged" interface because it simply provides a tag to the runtime that the object has some specific behavior. What other tagged interfaces can be found in the Java API?
18. In the program shown in Exhibit 23, if the equals method in class Person is removed, the program does not work correctly. What is the problem? Why does this occur?
19. What could be the reason for a runtime error (not a compile time error) being generated when attempting to write a non-serializable

object to an object stream? Could the error be trapped at compile time? If so, is it not always preferable to trap errors at compile time rather than runtime?

20. What is the difference between the instanceof operator and the getClass method of class Object? Can the two be used interchangeably?
21. Some collection classes, specifically the Vector and the Hashtable class, synchronize all of their methods. This ensures that only one thread can be executing inside of the object at any time, thus eliminating the possibility of a race condition. An object with all of its methods synchronized is referred to as *thread safe*. When accessing all elements in a Vector or a Hashtable, either an Enumeration or Iterator type is used. Consider the following code fragment for accessing a Vector using an Enumeration. Is this code fragment safe if used in a concurrent program, given that the Vector class is thread safe? Why or why not?

```
Vector v = new Vector;
v.add("1");
v.add("2");

Enumeration e = vector.elements();
while (e.hasMoreElements()) {
  System.out.println(e.nextElement());
}
```

22. When Iterators are used in the place of Enumeration types, they are *fail fast*. Fail fast is described in the Java Application Programming Interface (API) for any collection class (Vector, LinkedList, etc.). What does fail fast mean? Does it provide protection for the collection class when it is run in a concurrent program?
23. Consider the following code fragment. Explain why it is not safe, even though the Vector class methods are all fully synchronized.

```
Vector table = new Vector();
if (!table.isEmpty()) {
  Object o = table.elementAt(0);
}
```

24. Collection classes are not synchronized; instead, the application that uses it must provide the synchronization to make it safe. Consider the safe example shown below of the program in Problem 4.23. What unnecessary overhead is present? Based on the explanation of the unnecessary overhead, explain why synchronization was omitted from collection classes.

```
Vector table = new Vector();
synchronized (table) {
  if (!table.isEmpty()) {
  Object o = table.elementAt(0);
  }
}
```

25. Describe a method to safely access the Enumeration or Iterator for a collection class.
26. Consider the program shown in Exhibit 24. What is the result of running it? Explain the result.
27. For each numbered line in the program shown in Exhibit 25, state whether the line is valid or will result in a runtime or a compile time error.

Exhibit 21. Program with Numbered Lines

```
class Parent {
  String Name;

  public void function_1() {
    System.out.println("In Parent - function 1");
  }

  public void function_2() {
    System.out.println("In Parent - function 2");
    function_1();
  }
}

class Child extends Parent {
  String Name;

  public void function_1() {
    super.Name = "Childs Name";
    System.out.println("In Child - function 1");
  }
}

public class Question1 {
  public static void main(String args[]) {
    Parent parent = new Parent();
    Child child = new Child();

    parent.function_1();                    //Part 1
    parent.function_2();                    //Part 2
    child.function_1();                     //Part 3
    child.function_2();                     //Part 4
    ((Parent)child).function_1();           //Part 5
    ((Parent)child).function_2();           //Part 6
  }
}
```

Exhibit 22. Garbage Collection Program

```
class LinkedLetter {
  char letter;
  LinkedLetter nextLetter;

  public LinkedLetter(char letter, LinkedLetter nextLetter) {
    this.letter = letter;
    this.nextLetter = nextLetter;
  }

  public LinkedLetter(char letter) {
    this.letter = letter;
    this.nextLetter = null;
  }
}

public class GarbageCollect {
  public static void main(String args[]) {
    LinkedLetter A, B;
    {
      LinkedLetter C, D, E;
      B = new LinkedLetter('B');
      E = new LinkedLetter('E', B);
      C = new LinkedLetter('C', E);
      D = new LinkedLetter('E');
      A = new LinkedLetter('A', D);
    }                                         //Point 1
    B = new LinkedLetter('B');                //Point 2
  }                                           //Point 3
}
```

Exhibit 23. Equals Method in Class Person

```
import java.util.*;
class Name {
  String firstName;
  String lastName;

  public Name(String firstName, String lastName) {
    this.firstName = firstName;
    this.lastName = lastName;
  }

  public boolean equals(Object name) {
    if (! (name instanceof Name))
      return false;
    if ((((Name) name).firstName.equals(firstName)) &&
      (((Name) name).lastName.equals(lastName)))
      return true;
    return false;
  }

  public int hashCode() {
    String buffer = new String(firstName + lastName);
    return buffer.hashCode();
  }
}

class Person {
  Name name;
  int age;
  char sex;

  public Person(Name name, int age, char sex) {
    this.name = name;
    this.age = age;
    this.sex = sex;
  }

  public String toString() {
    return("Name = " + name.firstName
                                " " + name.lastName
                                " age = " + age
                                " sex = " + sex);
  }
}

public class HashcodeExample {
  public static void main(String argv[]) {
    Hashtable myTable = new Hashtable();
    myTable.put(new Name("Chuck," "Kann"),
      new Person(new Name("Chuck," "Kann"), 42, 'M'));
    Person P = (Person) myTable.get(new Name("Chuck," "Kann"));
    System.out.println(P);
  }
}
```

Exhibit 24. Program for Problem 26

```
import java.util.*;

class MyObject {
  int value;

  public MyObject(int input) {
    this.value = input;
  }

  public String toString() {
    return “”+ value;
  }
}

public class Question4 {
  public static void main(String args[]) {
    Hashtable ht = new Hashtable();
    ht.put(“3,” new MyObject(3));
    MyObject mo = (MyObject)ht.get(“3”);
    Enumeration e = ht.elements();
    while (e.hasMoreElements()) {
      System.out.println(e.nextElement());
    }
  }
}
```

Exhibit 25. Program with Numbered Lines

```
class Person {
  String Name;
  public Person(String Name) {this.Name = Name;}
  public String getName() {return Name;}
}

class Car {
  String Name;
  public Car(String Name) {this.Name = Name;}
  public String getName() {return Name;}
}

class ques8 {
  public static void main(String args[]) {
    Object table[] = new Object[10];

    table[0] = new Person(“Chuck”);
    table[1] = new Car(“BMW”);
    table[2] = new Object();

    System.out.println(table[0].getName());                  //1
    System.out.println(table[2].getName());                  //2
    System.out.println(((Person)table[0]).getName());        //3
    System.out.println(((Car)table[1]).getName());           //4
    System.out.println(((Car)table[2]).getName());           //5
    System.out.println(table[3].getName());                  //6
    System.out.println(((Car)table[3]).getName());           //7
  }
}
```

Chapter 5

Programming to an Interface

5.1 Introduction

This chapter introduces the concept of a Java interface. An interface in Java is a definition of behavior to be implemented by objects. Once an interface is defined, components can then be written to take advantage of the behavior promised in the interface. These components can then be reused, as they work with any object that implements the behavior of the interface. This is a type of reuse that we will call *generic reuse*.* Note that an interface is not a data type, which is a collection of data values and operations on those values. An interface is simply a definition of behavior an object must implement to work correctly with an algorithm, collection class, or component. However, like a data type, an interface is checked at compile time to ensure that the objects are valid to be used with the component.

Interfaces are important, as they are basic building blocks for many paradigms, such as many design patterns, algorithm reuse (such as generic sort methods), Java collection classes, and the Java Event Model (Chapter 7). All of these make use of interfaces so that they can work with multiple data types. Interfaces are also important in a number of distributed object technologies, such as RMI (Chapter 13), Enterprise Java Beans (EJB), and the Common Object Request Broker Architecture

* Normally, generic reuse is done through parameterized types, such as templates in C++ or generics in Ada. Java does not, at this time, have parameterized types, but they are proposed in JSR 14 [SUN02f].

(CORBA), for which a language called the Interface Definition Language (IDL) was written to specify interfaces.

This chapter presents the topic of interfaces by using two examples. The first creates a special type of collection class, called a SortedPrintTable, which stores sorted data and prints that data in order. This SortedPrintTable class is used to store objects of two different types, Person objects and Car objects, and shows how both can even be stored in the same table. The purpose is to demonstrate that using interfaces allows the programmer to separate the data type from the definition of the behavior of the object. The second example of an interface develops a program that can be used to do simple arithmetic. This program uses a special collection class, called an *expression tree*, to store arithmetic expressions and to solve them by doing a simple inorder tree walk. This expression tree example is revisited in Chapter 11, where an alternative solution using classification is presented.

5.2 Chapter Goals

When you finish this chapter you will know:

- How to achieve reuse of components using Java interfaces
- How to use Java interfaces and implement clauses to implement polymorphism
- How to define and use multiple interfaces in a Java program
- How to implement an expression tree using Java interfaces

5.3 Reuse with Interfaces

Reuse is the principle that some parts of a program that have already been developed can be applied to new problems in the current program or even to an entirely different program. Usually, when programmers think of reuse they think of code that can either be copied or abstracted into a method that can then be applied in a different situation. For example, one of the most common ways to reuse code is to take an existing function or object, copy it, and modify it to make it work to solve a new problem. This is referred to as *reuse by copy* and is perhaps the most common form of reuse. This type of reuse where existing code is applied to new situations is covered in Chapters 10 and 11.

Another less common way to think about reuse in programming is to write algorithms, collection classes, and components so that they can be applied to a number of different data types. These data types, called *generic data types*, are data types for which the operations are

Exhibit 1. Program5.1a: Class Template for Generic Stack

```
template<class ItemType> class Stack
{
  public:
    Stack();
    void push(ItemType item);
    ItemType pop();
  private:
    int top;
    ItemType items[10];
};

template<class ItemType>
Stack<ItemType>::Stack() {
  top = 0;
}

template<class ItemType>
void Stack<ItemType>::push(ItemType item) {
  items[top] = item;
  top++;
}

template<class ItemType>
ItemType Stack<ItemType>::pop() {
  top -- ;
  return items[top] = item;
}
```

defined but the actual types are not. Components that are implemented using generic data types are called *generic components*. When implementing a generic component, the implementation details of an object (such as the object's methods) are not being reused; rather, the way the algorithm or component acts on an object is being reused. A simple example of this type of reuse is the Vector class from Chapter 4, where the Vector could be used to store any object regardless of its data type.

Generic objects* can be implemented in two ways. One is to allow class, such as a collection class, to be defined with a dummy placeholder data type. This data type will be substituted with a real data type when the class is compiled, and a new class will actually be created for that specific data type at compile time. This type of reuse does not exist in Java, so an example using templates in C++ is shown in Exhibit 1 (Program5.1a). In this program, a class template is defined for a stack collection object. This stack will store items with a data type of ItemType, but the statement in the definition "template<class ItemType>" tells the compiler that this type is not a real type, but one that will be substituted for when the program is compiled.

---

* The term *generic object* will be used throughout the rest of this chapter to refer to to algorithms, collection classes, or components that are built around an interface.

Exhibit 2. Program5.1b: Main Program Creating Two Stack Template Classes

```
int main() {
  Stack<int> intStack;
  Stack<float> floatStack;
}
```

In the main method in Exhibit 2 (Program5.1b), the template class is used to define two new Stack classes, one that stores ints and the other that stores floats. When the program is compiled, it is as if the compiler replaces everywhere the occurrence of the ItemType string in the Stack class template with the actual type (int or float), and then the new template class with the correct type is compiled. This means that two stack classes are created, one class for each object. Nothing like templates currently exists in Java.

The second way to write generic objects is to use interfaces. Unlike a template, only one component class is ever defined for generic objects that use interfaces, but that one class can handle any data type that implements the interface. This allows the component classes using interfaces to be used with many actual data types. How this is accomplished is the subject of the rest of this chapter.

According to Gamma et al. [GAM95, p. 18], "Program to an interface, not an implementation." The reason is that components and algorithms written to apply to objects with a given behavior can be used with any object that implements that behavior. Designing components around interfaces rather than specific data types allows those components to be used in a wide variety of situations and separates the definition of the object from implementation of the object, which decouples the objects in the program and tends to make the program more robust.

5.4 Programming to a Promise

5.4.1 Programming to a Fact

Most programs written by novice programmers are developed with all the classes necessary for the program completely developed. We will call this *programming to a fact* because all the objects are facts; they exist when the program is written. For example, the Person class defined in Exhibit 3 (Program5.2) is used in the PersonTable class as the type for the array that stores the objects in the table, as well as for the type of parameters for the add method to make sure that only Person objects are added to the table. Because all objects stored in the table are Person objects, and all Person objects have a function

Exhibit 3. Program5.2: PersonTable Object That Stores Only Person Records

```
class Person
{
  private String name;
  public Person(String name){
    this.name = name;
  }

  public void print(){
    System.out.println("My Name is " + name);
  }
}

public class PersonTable
{

  private Person people[];
  private int currentSize;

  public PersonTable(int size) {
    people = new Person[size];
    currentSize = 0;
  }

  public void add(Person person) {
    people[currentSize] = person;
    currentSize = currentSize + 1;
  }

  public void printAll(){
    for (int i = 0; i < currentSize; ++i)
      people[i].print();
    }

  public static void main(String args[]) {
    PersonTable table = new PersonTable(10);
    table.add(new Person("Benoit"));
    table.add(new Person("Roget"));
    table.printAll();
  }
}
```

"print," the programmer can program the loop in the printAll method that calls the print method for each object.

Because all of the objects and code exist when the PersonTable and Person objects are created, the programmer can follow the exe cution through every line of code from the start of the program until it finishes. However, this advantage comes at the price of flexibility. The table that is created can only store Person objects, which is fine when everything for the program is written specifically for that program and is used only once in that program.

At some point, another instance of the table might be needed where objects of type Car will be stored instead of objects of type Person. The easiest and perhaps most common way in which the new program can be created is through reuse by copying, which involves copying the old program and modifying it to create a new program. For instance, a CarsTable program can be created by changing the references to Persons to Cars.

While this works, it has a number of disadvantages:

- It leads to a large number of classes (and source programs) that must be stored, tracked, and maintained.
- It is error prone, as a error could be introduced while changing the program to work for Cars.
- If at a later time an error is found in a table, that change must be migrated to all the other copies of that table.
- Only objects of one class (e.g., either Persons or Cars) can be stored in any one table; this is both a disadvantage and advantage, as we shall see later.

Generic objects can be developed to work in a number of different programs and to use multiple types of objects. What the generic object does and how it does it remain the same, but the component is able to do these operations on a number of different types of objects. In the case of the PersonTable, a more generic form would allow the table to store objects of any type, as long as they have a print method.

5.4.2 Implementing and Using Promises

One way to improve reuse by copying is to abstract out the behavior of the objects we wish to store (in this case, the ability to be printed) and write the generic object so that it can store any object as long as it contains the abstracted behavior. This can be thought of as the objects stored in the table making a promise to implement a method and the component then writing its methods to take advantage of the promises that will be made, referred to as *programming to a promise.*

The concept of programming to a promise is illustrated using the PrintTable class in Program5.3 (Exhibits 4 through 8). The first step is to define the promise, which is that the objects stored will have a print method. The actual classes for the objects that are stored are not defined when the PrintTable is written. These objects and their print methods are totally separate from the PrintTable and could be many different actual types as long as they make the promise to implement a print method. The promise to define a method in Java is called an *interface.* An example of the interface used to implement the Printable promise used by the PrintTable is shown in Exhibit 4 (Program5.3a).

Applying the suffix "-able" to the verb that describes their functionality often generates names for interfaces. Here, the name *Printable* implies that the objects implementing the interface have a print method.

Exhibit 4. Program5.3a: Printable Interface

```
public interface Printable
{
  public void print();
}
```

Exhibit 5. Program5.3b: PrintTable Class

```
public class PrintTable
{
  private Printable printableArray[];
  private int currentSize;
  /**
   * Public constructor. The size of the array to allocate
   * (table size) must be passed in, as there is no default
   * table size.
   */
  public PrintTable(int size) {
  printableArray = new Printable[size];
  currentSize = 0;
  }

  /**
   * Add a Printable object to the table.
   */
  public void add(Printable a) {
  printableArray[currentSize] = a;
  currentSize = currentSize + 1;
  }

  /**
   * Print all objects stored in the table. Note that we know
   * that they are all Printable, so we know that a Print
   * method will be associated with each object.
   */
  public void printAll(){
    for (int i = 0; i < currentSize; ++i)
    printableArray[i].print();
  }
}
```

This convention applies to many, but not all, of the interfaces in the Java API, such the interfaces Runnable and Serializable.

The PrintTable class is now implemented, as shown in Exhibit 5 (Program5.3b). It is almost the same as the PersonTable in Exhibit 3 (Program5.2), except that the PrintTable is not defined for a particular data type, but for any data type that is a Printable. So, everywhere that the Person data type was used in Exhibit 3 (Program5.2), the Printable interface is used. This tells the compiler to enforce the following rules:

Exhibit 6. Program5.3c: Table That Stores Person Objects

```
public class Person implements Printable
{
  private String name;
  public Person(String name){
    this.name = name;
  }

  public void print(){
    System.out.println("My Name is " + name);
  }

  public static void main(String args[]) {
    PrintTable T1 = new PrintTable(10);
    T1.add(new Person("Benoit"));
    T1.add(new Person("Roget"));
    T1.printAll();
  }
}
```

- Any object parameter passed to the add method is an instance of a class that has implemented the Printable interface.
- An object stored in the printableArray is an instance of class that has implemented the Printable interface.

Because any object stored in the printableArray is an instance of a class that has implemented Printable, the objects stored will have to make a promise to have a print method to be stored in that array, and that promise can be enforced by the compiler, as we will see later. Thus, a loop can now be written in the printAll method that calls the print method on objects stored in the printableArray. What are the data types of these objects? It is not known at this time, only that the data types will be classes that implement Printable. So where are the print methods? Once again, they will only be known when the objects are defined. The next step in this process of programming to a promise will define those objects.

The objects to be stored in the PrintTable can now be defined. These objects have only two requirements: (1) the class implements the Printable interface, and (2) a print method is included in the class. Because these requirements can be true for many different types of objects, the PrintTable itself can be used in many different programs to store objects of different types. Two example programs are given here. Exhibit 6 (Program5.3c) uses the PrintTable to store objects of type Person, and Exhibit 7 (Program5.3d) uses it to store objects of type Cars.

An important advantage of these interfaces is that they ensure that the program is safe. The PrintTable class can be checked to verify that it does not call methods that do not exist, as only methods defined in the Printable interface can be used. There is no need at this point

Exhibit 7. Program5.3d: Table That Stores Car Objects

```
public class Car implements Printable
{
  private int engineSize;
  public Car(int engineSize){
    this.engineSize = engineSize;
  }
  public void print(){
    System.out.println("My engine size is " + engineSize);
  }

  public static void main(String args[]) {
    PrintTable T1 = new PrintTable(10);
    T1.add(new Car(320));
    T1.add(new Car(150));
    T1.printAll();
  }
}
```

to know what the actual data types of the stored objects are because the PrintTable is written to work with the Printable interface. Later, when the objects to be stored are created, they must implement the Printable interface, which ensures that they have a print method. That the class for the object implements the Printable interface and that the print method is defined for classes that implement the Printable interface can be checked by the compiler.

5.4.3 Some Notes on Interfaces

It is important to note that interfaces do not define any data or implement methods. If the design requires that some data or methods must be defined, this can be accomplished using abstract classes, which are covered in Chapter 11. The reason for this is twofold, the first is practical and the second is semantic. The first reason why Java does not allow interfaces to define data or implement methods is that a class can implement multiple interfaces. If a method is defined in more than one implemented interface, it does not cause any problems, as the class that implements the interfaces implements that method once and it satisfies the requirement for all the interfaces. However, if multiple classes have been extended that define data with the same identifier or implement methods with the same signature, then the compiler must have a way to choose which identifier or method is meant when the identifier or method is accessed. This is a complex problem in languages that allow multiple inheritance and one that Java avoided.

The second problem with defining data or implementing methods in an interface is semantics. An interface is simply a "promise" that an implementing class will implement some behavior via method calls. It does not, and should not, put any constraints on that class as long as it provides a valid method call to satisfy its promise. Any functionality built into an interface forces the implementing class to do something in a specific manner, which violates the principal of the interface simply providing a promise.

One result of interfaces not defining data or implementing methods is that it does not make sense to try to instantiate an interface. For example, the following code would be invalid:

```
Printable p = new Printable();
p.print();
```

Because Printable does not define a print method, only a promise that an object implementing Printable will create a print method, there would be no print method to call if an interface could be instantiated. If the "object" p is added to the printArray, a call to its print method would obviously be invalid. This violates the safety guaranteed by the interface. Thus, it does not make sense to allow interfaces to be instantiated, and it is not allowed in Java.

This example shows what we mean by programming to a promise, or more appropriately *programming to an interface.* If we write a component (in this case, an object that stores and prints a table of objects) using interfaces instead of classes, it can be used for any objects that will implement that interface. This principle of using interfaces to define components is used throughout the rest of the book and forms the basis for the Java Event Model used in the AWT, and for most distributed programming paradigms. It also provides the basis for isolating classes in a program and producing more robust and reusable objects.

5.5 Dynamic Polymorphism

Up until now all the tables we have created have stored only Car objects or Person objects. Because both types of objects implement the Printable interface, what is to prevent storing both Car objects and Person objects in the same table? The answer is nothing prevents it, and in fact it is easily done, as shown in Exhibit 8 (Program5.3e). When running Exhibit 8 (Program5.3e), the reader will note that both Person and Car objects are properly stored in the table and accessed at runtime. What is interesting is that when the print method of the Printable object is called it references the print method in the correct object; a Person object calls the print method in the Person class, and the Car object calls the print method in the Car class. Because the program does not know until runtime what type of object will be stored at each location in the table, the JVM must be determining the object type and thus the correct method to call at runtime, which is

Exhibit 8. Program5.3e: Implementing a PrintTable that Stores Both Person and Car Objects

```
public class Polymorphism
{
  public static void main(String args[]) {
    PrintTable T1 = new PrintTable(10);
      T1.add(new Person("Benoit"));
      T1.add(new Car(340));
      T1.add(new Person("Roget"));
      T1.add(new Car(200));
      T1.printAll();
  }
}
```

referred to as *dynamic polymorphism*. The term *polymorphism* comes from the Greek terms *poly* ("many") and *morphous* ("forms" or "shapes"). In object-oriented programming (OOP), dynamic polymorphism means that the object used and hence the method called from a component can actually change as the algorithm is running.

The implementation of dynamic polymorphism in Java is easy to explain, given the explanation in the previous chapter that all objects in Java have a runtime data type tag, and the runtime data type is kept in a tag associated with the actual object variable. When the program is running, the JVM simply looks at the data type tag and finds the actual class (not the interface) that this object represents. Because the class for the object implements the Printable interface, we know that it must have implemented the print method. The JVM finds the object's class and calls the print method associated with that object. The important point here is that the method that is called is determined when the program is running, not when it is compiled.

It should be noted that the interface really plays no part in determining which print method is actually called at runtime. It is simply a compile time check to make sure the object obeys the rules of the interface promise. The promise is actually fulfilled by an object that implements the print method; hence, the calling of the methods for an interface is dynamic at runtime.

5.6 Using Multiple Interfaces

The PrintTable class can store objects of any class that implements the Printable interface. Now we will develop a table that can store these objects in some order. This table will add, delete, and print objects in the table. (Note that the example implements only the add method; the delete method is left for an exercise.) In order to add and delete sorted records, two methods must be available in the objects that will be stored. We will use *gt* for a method that returns true if the current record is greater than the record with which it is compared, and *eq* for a method that returns true if the two objects are equal.* We can now define an interface promise for our new SortedPrintTable. This interface would be:

```
interface PrintableSortable {
  public void print();
  boolean equals(PrintableSortable ps);
  boolean gt(PrintableSortable ps);
}
```

Note that this interface is completely separate from the Printable interface. The Person class can now be written as implementing only a PrintableSortable interface as follows:

```
class Person implements PrintableSortable {
}
```

This definition has a problem in that the Person object is no longer Printable, and so is no longer usable in the PrintTable. Just because an object implements a method (in this case, print) does not mean that it implements an interface. It must also implement the correct interface. To make the Person object both Printable and PrintableSortable, it would have to be defined as follows:

```
class Person implements Printable, PrintableSortable {
}
```

This definition tells the components that use the Printable interface and the PrintableSortable interface that a print method is available for this object. A useful alternative defining a class with multiple overlapping interfaces is to create an interface that is a combination of other interfaces. For example, Exhibit 9 (Program5.4a) shows the definition for the PrintableSortable interface. Here, the PrintableSortable interface is a combination of the Printable and Sortable interfaces. Any class that implements this PrintableSortable interface also implements the Printable and Sortable interfaces. So, now the Person class must only implement the PrintableSortable interface to be used by components that require the Printable, Sortable, or PrintableSortable interface.

Note that the interfaces are combined using an extends clause, not an implements clause. This is sometimes confusing to programmers the first time they try creating interfaces from other interfaces; however, this is not an example of multiple inheritance in Java, as the definitions of the interfaces are combined and not really extended. Also, note that

* Java has an equals function from class Object that is generally overridden to check for equals and a Comparable interface with a compareTo function to compare the ordering of two objects. However, the functions here were chosen to illustrate the behavior of interfaces, not to follow Java conventions.

Exhibit 9. Program5.4a: PrintableSortable Definition

```
interface Printable {
  public void print();
}

interface Sortable {
  public boolean gt(Sortable s);
  public boolean eq(Sortable s);
}

public interface PrintableSortable extends Printable, Sortable
{
}
```

the gt and eq methods take parameters of type Sortable. This is one of the advantages of defining the interface using the extends clause. Because a PrintableSortable object is both Printable and Sortable, only the relevant part of the interface needs to be used. If the PrintableSortable was defined with the gt, eq, and print methods, the gt and eq methods would have to use the PrintableSortable interface, and two distinct and different gt and eq methods defined, one for Sortables and one for PrintableSortables.

5.7 Implementing the SortedPrintTable

The SortedPrintTable can now be written using the promises contained in the PrintableSortable interface. The printAll method does not need to be changed, and the delete method is left for an exercise, so only the add method is different from the PrintTable class. The PrintTable class is implemented in Exhibit 10 (Program5.4b).

The code for the add method is as follows. Before looking to see where to insert the record, two special cases are handled: (1) when the table is empty and no comparisons need to be made, the record is simply put in the first place in the table; and (2) when the table is full, for now the method simply returns. Obviously, it is incorrect behavior not to do something when the table is full, but to define the proper behavior requires the use of exceptions, which are covered in Chapter 6; no errors or exceptions are handled in this chapter.

Once the special cases are handled, the add method starts to process the array from the end and moves each item one place forward until it finds the correct place to put the item (this assumes that duplicates are allowed in the table). The point at which to insert the record is found by using the gt method on the PrintableSortable object to be inserted and the object in the array at the current position. As long as the object to be inserted is greater than the current array object, the array object is moved down one space in the list. When the object to be inserted is no longer greater than the current array object, the spot

Exhibit 10. Program5.4b: The PrintTable Class

```
public class SortedPrintTable {
  private PrintableSortable psArray[];
  private int currentSize;

  /**
   * Constructor method. Create the table and set the
   * currentSize to 0 to indicate the table is empty.
   */
  public SortedPrintTable(int size) {
    psArray = new PrintableSortable[size];
    currentSize = 0;
  }

  /**
   * Delete method. Remove an object from the table. Note that
   * implementing this has been left as an exercise.
   */
  public void delete(PrintableSortable p) {
  }

  /**
   * Add method. Add an object to the table. Note that the gt
   * method from the Sortable interface is used to find the
   * place to insert this object.
   */
  public void add(PrintableSortable p) {

    //To handle an empty table
    if (currentSize = = 0)
    {
      psArray[0] = p;
      currentSize = 1;
      return;
    }

    //To handle a full table
    if (currentSize = = psArray.length) {
      return;
    }

    //Start from the bottom of the table, and move items out
    //of the way until we find the place to insert.
    for (int i = currentSize-1 ; i > = 0; — i) {
      if (psArray[i].gt(p)) {
        psArray[i+1] = psArray[i];
        //Special Case to handle insertion at the start
        //of the table.
        if (i = = 0)
          psArray[0] = p;
      }
      else {
        //We have the right spot, so insert and stop the loop.
        psArray[i+1] = p;
        break;
      }
    }
    currentSize = currentSize + 1;
  }
```

(continued)

Exhibit 10. Program5.4b (Continued)

```
  /**
   * printTable method. Go through the array and call the print
   * method for each object stored.
   */
  public void printTable(){
    for (int i = 0; i < currentSize; ++i)
      psArray[i].print();
  }
}
```

at which to insert the object has been found and the object is placed in the list. The question now raised is where is the gt method implemented? The answer is that it is not yet implemented. The SortedPrintTable knows that an object stored in the table and the parameter to the add method will have a gt method, but it does not know what that method is. Until an actual object is in the table and its runtime data type tag can be queried to find out what method to call, all that is known is that any object used will have a gt method. Finally it might seem counterintuitive to start at the end of the list rather than at the beginning of the list to find the position at which to insert the item; however, on average this algorithm takes half as long, assuming that duplicates are allowed, so that the item will always be inserted.

5.8 Using the SortedPrintTable

Now, to store a Person object in the SortedPrintTable, the Person class must implement the PrintableSortable interface (the promise to implement the gt, eq, and print methods). These methods must be defined in the Person class. This is done in Exhibit 11 (Program5.4c), which implements the Person class and a program tocreate a Person Table. Note that, while we want Person records passed to the gt and eq methods, the interface specifies that the objects that will be passed are Sortable. Because a Person object is Sortable, the parameter passed can be a person, but it is not guaranteed that the parameter is a Person object. It could be an object of any data type that is Sortable. Because we need to cast the parameter object to a Person object, the possibility exists that a ClassCastException will be raised. To prevent this, the instanceof operation is used to make sure the object is a Person; however, the behavior if the object is not a Person is incorrect, in that it just returns false. How to properly handle this situation is demonstrated using exceptions in Chapter 6.

The SortedPrintTable, like the PrintTable, can be used to store objects of any data type that implements PrintableSortable. This means that the SortedPrintTable can handle polymorphic data. As we pointed

Exhibit 11. Program5.4c: Program to Store Person Objects

```
import java.io.*;
public class Person implements PrintableSortable {
  private String name;

  /**
   * Public constructor.
   */
  public Person(String name){
    this.name = new String(name);
}

/**
 * Method to satisfy the Printable interface. Just prints the
 * name to system.out.
 */
public void print(){
  System.out.println("My Name is " + name);
}

/**
 *  Greater than (gt) method, which simply compares two name
 *  strings and returns true if this name string is lexically
 *  greater than the one for the person to compare it to;
 *  otherwise, false
 */
public boolean gt(Sortable P) {

  //Note that we have to type cast here.
  if (name.compareTo(((Person)P).name) > 0)
    return true;
  else
    return false;
  }

  /**
   * eq method. Note that it is stubbed out and is to be completed
   * as an exercise.
   */
  public boolean eq(Sortable P) {
    return true;
  }

  /**
   * A simple main to test running the program.
   */
  public static void main(String args[]) {
    SortedPrintTable t1 = new SortedPrintTable(10);


    t1.add(new Person("Cindy");
    t1.add(new Person("Chuck");
    t1.add(New Person("Linda");
    t1.add(new Person("Frieda");
    t1.add(new Person("Patty");

    t1.printTable();
  }
}
```

out earlier, polymorphism is a great idea in many cases, and the SortedPrintTable suggests how this table can be used generically with multiple data types; however, this feature comes at a price. In the add method of the SortedPrintTable, the PrintableSortable parameter did not have to be cast to call the correct gt method because the method was the one for that object. Thus, if the parameter was a Person object, the Person gt method was called; if the parameter was a Car object, the Car gt method was called. There is no guarantee, however, that if a Person gt method is called that the object in the array to be compared to it is a Person and not a Car. In fact, nothing in this program prevents a programmer from inserting into this table objects that are not the correct data type for that table. All that is guaranteed is that the object will be PrintableSortable and have a gt method. That the gt method will work properly with the parameters it is passed is not assured. In fact, if an attempt is made to insert both Car and Person objects in the table, an error will occur. This is dealt with further in Chapter 6.

To complete the SortedPrintTable class, the delete method must be implemented, which means that the correct behavior must be put into the eq methods for the Person and Car classes. This is left as an exercise.

5.9 Expression Trees

As was pointed out earlier, interfaces can also be used in algorithms to abstract out the objects acted on when executing an algorithm. For example, consider the use of an interface in representing an expression tree. An expression tree is a binary tree representing an arithmetic expression. It has two types of nodes. Internal nodes are operators, such as "+" or "–." Leaf nodes are operands, in this case constant. These trees can be used to represent arithmetic equations. Exhibits 12 and 13 are examples of expression trees. Exhibit 12 represents the expression "((5 – 3) + 1)" and Exhibit 13 represents the expression "(5 – (3 + 1))." As the fully parenthesized expressions infer, these expression trees are different and will yield different results. The problem with this tree is that the internal operator nodes do not know what type of node its left or right children are. The children of an operator node could be either another operator node or an operand node. This makes building and evaluating the tree difficult.

However, if each operator node in the expression tree could simply call an evaluate method on its children's nodes, which would return the result of the operation to its parent, it would not matter if the node was an operator or an operand node. The equation could be calculated by simply calling evaluate on the root node of the tree, and the answer would simply be returned as each node is evaluated. The problem is that obviously the two types of nodes for this tree are very

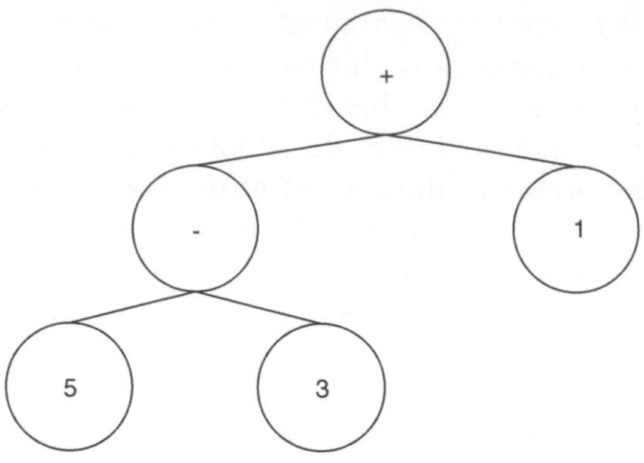

Exhibit 12. Tree Map #1

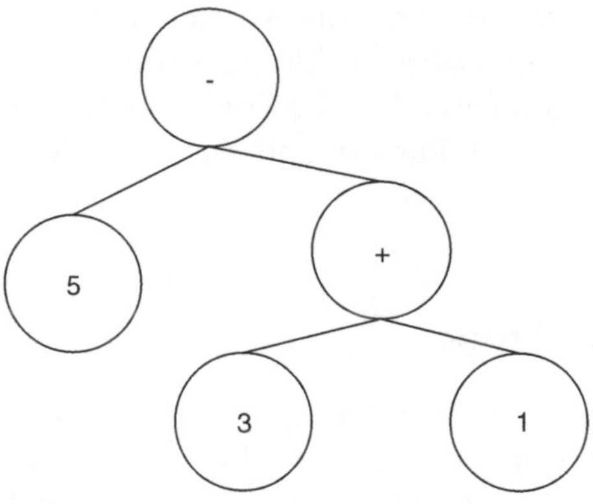

Exhibit 13. Tree Map #2

different. The operand nodes store a constant value and have no children, whereas the operator nodes have an operator and left and right children, the children being either operator or operand nodes. Somehow the operator node needs to reference its children in such a way that whether they are operator nodes or operand nodes does not matter.

The solution here is to realize that all the evaluate method in the operator node cares about is that the left and right children are evaluated and an answer is returned; therefore, an interface can be created that simply specifies that a node is something that can be evaluated via a call to its evaluate method, and the OperatorNode and OperandNode classes can implement this interface. This Node interface is shown in Exhibit 14 (Program5.5). The operator class is now defined so that its left and right children are nodes; however, it really does not matter what type of node the children are. The expression tree can then be built of nodes, which are either OperatorNode or OperandNode

Exhibit 14. Program5.5: Expression Tree

```
interface Node {
  public void printTree();
  public float evaluate();
}

/**
 *  An OperatorNode is a tree node that stores an operator. An
 *  operator needs both left and right children (all operators
 *  are binary). When printing or evaluating the node, the
 *  printTree or evaluate methods are called on the children,
 *  and the result is handed back to the calling method.
 */
class OperatorNode implements Node {
  char operator;
  Node left, right;
  public OperatorNode(char operator, Node left, Node right) {
    this.operator = operator;
    this.left = left;
    this.right = right;
  }

  public void printTree() {
    System.out.print(" (");
    left.printTree();
    System.out.print(" " + operator);
    right.printTree();
    System.out.print(")");
  }

  public float evaluate() {
    if (operator = = '+')
      return left.evaluate() + right.evaluate();
    else if (operator = = '-')
      return left.evaluate() - right.evaluate();
    else
      return 0;//Invalid condition
    }
  }

  /**
   *  An OperandNode is a leaf node that stores a value. It has
   *  no children, thus the printTree and evaluate methods
   *  simply return or print the value currently stored in the
   *  node.
   */
  class OperandNode implements Node {
    float value;
    public OperandNode(float value) {
      this.value = value;
    }

    public void printTree() {
      System.out.print(" " + value);
    }

    public float evaluate() {
      return value;
    }
  }
```

(continued)

Exhibit 14. Program5.5 (Continued)

```
/**
 *  ExpressTree is the driver program that shows how the
 *  expression tree program works. It builds trees of operator
 *  and operand nodes and then prints and evaluates those
 *  trees.
 */
public class ExpressionTree {
  public static void main(String args[]) {
    Node root;

   //((5 - 3)+1)
   root = new OperatorNode('+',
          new OperatorNode('-',
          new OperandNode(5), new OperandNode(3)),
          new OperandNode(1));
   root.printTree();
   System.out.println(" = " + root.evaluate());

   //(5 - (3+1))
   root = new OperatorNode('-',
          new OperandNode(5),
          new OperatorNode('+',
          new OperandNode(3), new OperandNode(1)));
   root.printTree();
   System.out.println(" = " + root.evaluate());
  }
}
```

type, and when the evaluate method on the root is called the expression tree is processed. The value returned from the root is the value calculated by the arithmetic expression represented in the tree.

5.10 Further Reading

Most introductory books on Java include a section on how to use interfaces (see, for example, [DIE02] or [LEW03]). Also, the books by Eckel [ECK98], Budd [BUD00], Flannagan [FLA02], and Jia [JIA00] all do a very good job of presenting interfaces, how they work in Java, and specific problems that can be encountered in using them. However, the book that best captures how to use interfaces is [MAY99]. Readers who have never been exposed to binary expression trees can find more information about them in any basic data structures book, such as those by Weiss [WEI99] or Dale [DAL99].

5.11 Problems

1. What happens if a class implements an interface but does not define the methods specified? What happens if it defines the methods but does not implement the interface?

Exhibit 15. Interface Example

```
interface ExampleInterface {
  public void method1();
}

class Class1 implements ExampleInterface {
  public void method1() {}
  public void method2() {}
}

class Class2 {
  public void method1() {}
  public void method2() {}
}

public class Problem52 {
  public static void main(String args[]) {
    Class1 c1 = new Class1();
    Class2 c2 = new Class2();
    Object o1;
    ExampleInterface ei1;
    ExampleInterface ei2 = new ExampleInterface();

    o1 = c1;
    o1.method1();
    ei1 = c1;
    ei1 = o1;
    ei1 = (ExampleInterface) o1;
    ei1.method1();

    o1 = c2;
    o1.method1();
    ei1 = c2;
    ei1 = o1;
    ei1 = (ExampleInterface) o1;
    ei1.method1();
  }
}
```

2. Identify all of the errors in the program in Exhibit 15. Are the problems occurring at compile time or runtime?
3. Explain how Java implements polymorphism with interfaces; that is, how does Java determine the method in the correct class to call when an interface is used?
4. Complete the implementation of the SortedPrintTable in Exhibit 10 (Program5.4b) by including the delete method. Modify the Person class in Program in Exhibit 11 (Program5.4c) to test your program.
5. Show that the SortedPrintTable is usable by different types of objects by implementing a table of cars using the Car class in Exhibit 7 (Program5.3d). Note that you will have to implement PrintableSortable in the Car class to make it work.
6. While instance variables cannot be defined for an interface, it is possible to define static and final variables. Why do interfaces allow static and final variables to be defined? What are some examples of defining static or final variables in an interface?

7. What methods are in the java.lang.Comparable interface? How is the Comparable interfaced used with the Java collection classes?
8. A *tagged interface* is an interface in Java that does not have any methods defined. One example of a tagged interface is java.io.Serializable. What are some other examples of tagged interfaces? Why does Java have tagged interfaces?
9. Change the ExpressionTree program to include nodes that have variables. To implement a variable, store an object of type Float in a Hashtable. For the key to the Hashtable, use a string that names the variable. Now create a new type of node called a VariableNode, which stores the name of the variable and whose evaluate method looks up the value for the node.
10. Write a simple calculator that can be used to do simple arithmetic. The calculator should be able to do "+," "–," "*," and "/." It should also be able to use either numbers or variables in equations and be able to store and retrieve variables. To do this from a command prompt, read in the line of text and use the StringTokenizer to break the string down into tokens and delimiters (make sure the StringTokenizer is set to return delimiters as well as tokens and does not require spaces between all tokens). Then, assume that the first token is either a variable to store the result into or the word "output", which will write the result using System.out. A simple example of using the calculator would be:

    ```
    A1 = 2.0
    B2 = 4.0 * A1
    output A1 B2
    ```

    This would produce the result:

    ```
    A1 = 2.0, B2 = 8.0
    ```

    You can tell if a token is an operator, number, or variable as follows. First check if it is an operator. If not, then see if the first character is a number (digit). If it is, the token is a number, else it is a variable.
11. A Bubble Sort is implemented by comparing two adjacent elements and swapping them if they are not in the correct order. The program in Exhibit 16 implements a Bubble Sort for an integer array. Implement the Bubble Sort so that it can be used with the compareTo method from the java.lang.Comparable interface. Create a Person class that implements the java.lang.Comparable interface, and implement an array that contains several Person objects. Show that your Bubble Sort works by sorting this array of Person objects in ascending order. Change the compareTo method so that the array is sorted in descending order.

Exhibit 16. Implementing a Bubble Sort for an Integer Array

```
public class Problem511 {
  public static void swap(int array[], int i, int j) {
    int temp = array[i];
    array[i] = array[j];
    array[j] = temp;
  }

  public static void bubbleSort(int array[]) {
    boolean swapMade = false;
    for (int i = 0; i < (array.length-1); i++) {
      swapMade = false;
      for (int j = (i+1); j < array.length; j++) {
        if (array[i] > array[j]) {
          swapMade = true;
          swap(array, i, j);
        }
      }
      if (!swapMade)
        break;
    }
  }

  public static void main(String args[]) {
    int array[] = {5, 8, 1, 4, 9, 6, 2, 3, 7};
    bubbleSort(array);
    for (int i = 0; i < array.length; i++) {
      System.out.println(array[i]);
    }
  }
}
```

12. Explain why the definition below for the class Problem5.6 is incorrect. Why does Java implement this check?

```
public class Problem56 implements PrintableSortable {
  boolean eq(Sortable s) {
  }

  boolean gt(Sortable s) {
  }

  void print() {
  }
}
```

Exhibit 16. Implementing a Bubble Sort for an Integer Array

```
public class [illegible]
  public static void [illegible] (int[] array) [illegible]
    int [illegible]
      array[j] = array[j + 1];
      array[j + 1] = temp;
[illegible]
    boolean [illegible] = true;
[illegible]
    [illegible] = false;
[illegible]
      if [illegible]
        [illegible]
[illegible]
  public static void main(String args[]) {
    int[] array = { [illegible] };
    [illegible](array);
    for (int i = 0; i < array.length; i++)
      System.out.println(array[i]);
[illegible]
```

12. Explain [illegible] the [illegible] definition [illegible] the [illegible] the array. [illegible] implement this check.

[illegible]

Chapter 6

Exceptions in Java

6.1 Introduction

Exceptions occur when a part of a program, such as a method, encounters a problem that it cannot handle correctly. These problems are not necessarily bugs; they could be such situations as a user entering invalid input that cannot be handled in the current method. Often the programmer has made allowances for these problems, but to keep the methods in the program as generic as possible, programs are designed so that these problems are handled outside of the method where they occur.

Developing a good strategy for handling exceptions in a normal, non-concurrent program is not an easy or straightforward task. A number of decisions must be made when deciding on how to handle exceptions and errors. What problems should a method handle, and what problems should be referred to the calling method? What should the program do when an error is encountered? What strategies can be employed to try to correct errors, and which errors should the program try to correct? These are difficult questions that should be addressed before beginning to write a program, as a poorly designed or incorrectly implemented strategy for handling exceptions can destroy an otherwise well implemented component. Developing a strategy for handling and reporting exception is as important to implementing a component correctly as any other part of the design.

Developing an exception handling strategy for components is much more difficult. Propagating exceptions out of a component is not the same as propagating an exception out of an ordinary object because many threads share components; therefore, the exceptions and actions to handle them must be consistent with the various ways a thread might use a component. Also, exception handling is done on a per-thread basis, so unlike a procedural program that can use the default exception handling mechanism and simply die if an exception is raised, an unhandled exception in a concurrent program could cause a single thread to die but leave others running, resulting in safety and liveness problems in the other threads.

Unfortunately, exception handling is often something even experienced programmers add to a program or component as an afterthought. When a problem is encountered, the programmer simply does something to ameliorate the situation with little or no thought as to how it will impact the eventual usability of the component. Error handling, like all other aspects of programming, is something that must be planned and is not something that can be hacked into the system after it is implemented.

This chapter explains why it is important to consider carefully how error handling and reporting will be done in a program. It begins by showing some less robust error handling strategies that are often used and often are all that a programmer has available to use. The drawbacks of these mechanisms are pointed out, and the chapter then shows how exceptions are used in Java and how they can be applied to the construction of a component.

6.2 Chapter Goals

When you have completed this chapter, you should be able to:

- Identify several different types of exception handling techniques and their limitations.
- Use try-catch blocks in Java to handle exceptions that are raised, particularly when multiple catch statements and finally statements are used.
- Understand what is meant by unwinding the stack when an exception is raised and be able to predict the behavior of an exception when it is raised.
- Understand the Java exception hierarchy, the difference between *checked* and *unchecked exceptions*, and how to determine if an exception is checked or unchecked.
- Define your own exceptions that are specific for the component you are writing and why you cannot always use predefined exceptions.

6.3 How to Handle Errors Incorrectly

An important part of implementing components is effectively handling errors that inevitably will occur. Using exceptions to handle program errors at runtime is probably the best way to implement an error-handling strategy. The use of exceptions allows a program to implement a consistent and flexible strategy for dealing with errors and is very useful in keeping generic objects generic. Most books seem to assume that the reader understands error-handling strategies and why strategies such as the try-catch blocks and exceptions in Java are powerful. These books then proceed to explain how to do exception handling in Java. Most students, however, tend to build programs around getting the program to work and then paste in error handling as an afterthought when problems occur. In larger, real-world systems, this is a recipe for inconsistent and improper error handling. In these systems, inconsistent and even improper handling of errors can result in failure of an otherwise well-designed and well-written program. Correct error handling cannot be added to a program after it is completed; it must be built into a program from its inception to ensure that it is implemented in a coherent and consistent manner; when it is done in an *ad hoc* fashion, it will probably never be correct.

To help the reader understand why exceptions are included in the Java language to handle errors correctly and why correct error handling is important, this chapter first looks at two bad strategies for handling errors. This should help the reader understand the power of exception handling and provide a basis for understanding the Java implementation of exceptions. The chapter then explains how try-catch blocks can be used in Java to handle exceptions properly and provides rules for how to use exceptions.

6.3.1 Handle an Error When It Occurs

The first error-handling strategy programmers often employ is dealing with the error when it occurs. In this strategy, after the programmer has written the program, a problem is found during testing and debugging (or even later, when the program is in production). The programmer corrects this problem by adding logic to the program for handling that error, often without considering the overall impact of that change. For example, in Program 5.4c, a ClassCastException can occur if an object stored in the table and passed as a parameter to the gt method is not a Person object. A programmer who encounters this problem sees that the easiest way to fix this problem is to have the method print out an error message and return false, reasoning that the user has been notified of the problem and if the object is not of the right type the method should return false as it did not work correctly. This modification to the program is shown in Exhibit 1 (Program6.1).

Now, when an object of incorrect type is sent to the method, the program will give an error message to the programmer that says that an object of an incorrect type was used. This is an example of a

Exhibit 1. Program6.1: Modification to the Person Class to Handle ClassCastException

```
public class Person implements PrintableSortable
{
  private String name;
  public Person1(String name){
    this.name = new String(name);
  }

  public void print(){
    System.out.println("My Name is " + name);
  }

  public boolean gt(Sortable p) {
    //We check here to make sure that the object
    //passed in is indeed of the correct type.
    if (! (p instanceof Person)) {
      System.out.println("Invalid object type; must be a
        Person.");
    return false;
    }
    else if (name.compareTo(((Person1)p).name) > 0)
      return true;
    else
      return false;
  }

  public boolean eq(Sortable P) {
    return true;
  }
}
```

"handle it when it occurs" strategy. A problem is identified (an object of the incorrect type has been sent to the gt method), and the program generates an error message that incompatible object types have been entered into the table. This approach solves the programmer's immediate problem, that the logic used to insert records into the table is flawed, and as long as printing this error message provides a meaningful result (in this case, allowing the programmer identify a logic problem), it is a valid error strategy.

We can identify at least three problems with this strategy. First, this message works fine as long as the only person who can possibly get this error is the programmer who wrote the program, as the message that is produced is understandable only to the programmer working on debugging the program. However, the purpose of a program is not to allow a programmer to write and debug code; rather, it is to solve a problem for an end user. If a message does not make sense to users or help them decide what actions to take in response to the message, the system has failed. This is particularly a problem with generic objects such as the SortedPrintTable. The programmer who implements a generic object does not know anything about the application using the generic object; therefore, it is nearly impossible to make informed decisions about how to handle an exception in a generic object. The exception can almost never be handled when it occurs and should be reported back to the application that called the method.

Second, the SortedPrintTable class that is calling this method in the Person class is meant to be generic, and it can be used in any number of programs, which is why so much care was taken to design the SortedPrintTable class around interfaces. But, writing the message to System.out implies that the Person class is only to be used with programs using a terminal-based interface, which has broken the generic nature of the object. If the SortedPrintTable is now to be used by a program that will use a GUI or Web-based interface, the program will not even show the user that an error has occurred. For a Web-based program, the error will likely appear on the operator's console, with the operator unable to identify the objects or program generating the error. Meanwhile, the user, who does not receive any indication that the program has any problems, assumes that the data is being correctly stored in the table. This type of problem is all too common in real-world server programs, even supposedly robust programs developed by experienced programmers.

Finally, handling an error in this way is not only unhelpful, it is wrong. Because the compare could not work, and the gt method could not make a valid decision as to the rank of the object, it simply returns a value of false. This might seem a reasonable thing to do in the context of the Person object, particularly to a programmer attempting to quickly debug the program, but this false return value is interpreted by the table as meaning that the new object is smaller than the previous object, and, rather than the object not being inserted, it is simply inserted at the beginning of the table. This error handling is completely inappropriate for the program but is typical of "handle it when it occurs" strategies for error handling.

Once a "handle it when it occurs" strategy for handling errors has been initiated, the problems begin to multiply. Because the fix for the class cast problem incorrectly inserts the data at the beginning of the table, the programmer may decide to fix the SortedPrintTable so that it will not add a record of the wrong type. To do this, the add method is modified as in Exhibit 2 (Program6.2) so that if the gt method returns false the object in the psArray is checked to see if it is a Person object. It is inserted into the psArray only if it is a Person object. Now the program is correct for a Person object, but the generic SortedPrintTable is no longer generic, as it will only work for a Person object. Other programs that use it will now have to modify this generic table so that it works with their data types, and the SortedPrintTable is sliding down a slippery slope to becoming completely tied to systems that implement it, each implementation having a lot of code specifically for each program that implements it. Because it now has to be modified for each new data type, all systems that use it must be retested when

Exhibit 2. Program6.2: Modification of SortedPrintTable to Stop Invalid Person Objects from Being Stored in a Person Table

```
public class SortedPrintTable {
  private PrintableSortable psArray[];
  private int currentSize;

  public SortedPrintTable(int size) {
    psArray = new PrintableSortable[size];
    currentSize = 0;
  }

  //Method: delete
  //Purpose:
  public void delete(PrintableSortable p) {
  }

  public void add(PrintableSortable p) {

    //To handle an empty table
    if (currentSize = = 0)
    {
      psArray[0] = p;
      currentSize = 1;
      return;
    }
    //To handle a full table
    if (currentSize = = psArray.length) {
      return;
    }
    //Start from the bottom of the table, and move items
    //out of the way until we find the place to insert.
    for (int i = currentSize-1 ; i > = 0; – i) {
      if (psArray[i].gt(p)) {
        psArray[i+1] = psArray[i];
        //Special Case to handle insertion at the start
        //of the table.
        if (i = = 0)
          psArray[0] = p;
        }
        else {
          //Check to see if we have the right object type.
          //If the object is of the wrong type, the gt method
          //returns false. If this false is because the
          //object is the wrong type, we should just return,
          //as the gt method already printed out an error.
          if (p instanceof Person1)
            return;

          //We have the right spot, so insert and stop the
          //loop.
          psArray[i+1] = p;
          break;
        }
    }
    currentSize = currentSize + 1;
  }

  public void printTable(){
    for (int i = 0; i < currentSize; ++i)
      psArray[i].print();
  }
}
```

changes are made; otherwise, currently working systems could be broken when the new changes are implemented. In short, the advantages of being generic are completely destroyed, and the SortedPrintTable is well on its way to becoming a mess. By the time this is caught by a lead programmer or architect it is possible that the changes will have gone so deep and become so embedded that the component will never be able to be fixed. Anyone who thinks this scenario is farfetched probably has not worked long enough as a programmer to see systems that have been modified by literally dozens of programmers over many years.

This example shows that to be effective error handling must be built into the initial design of the system. Poor error handling can destroy even a well-designed program. The next section looks at another, widely used error-handling method using return values.

6.3.2 Use Return Values

Another poor error-handling strategy uses method return values to signal whether or not the method executed correctly. Adopting this error-handling strategy is not limited to students; in fact, some languages, such as C, rely on this method of handling errors. For example, Exhibit 3 (Program6.3) shows how a typical C program might handle opening and reading from a file. In this program, the user opens a file and gets a file handle. If the value is non-negative, the file is successfully opened. The program then starts reading records from the file until the program reaches the end of file and prints each record out to the terminal.

A number of problems with this strategy to handle errors are apparent from this program. Generally, data values should not have overloaded meanings. For example, in Exhibit 3 (Program6.3), the return from the open can either be a file handle or a flag indicating whether or not the file was opened correctly. This is often problematic. At best, delineating valid and invalid data based on the value of the field can be difficult; at worst, it can affect the meaning of the program. For example, the gt method of the Person class could be changed so that a return value of 0 means that the object is greater, 1 means the object was equal or less, and –1 means that the comparison was invalid. However, having the method return an int makes the function less intuitive and more difficult to use than the simple return of a boolean value.

Nothing in the strategy forces the programmer to handle the case of a file not being opened correctly. In fact, in Exhibit 3 (Program6.3), an improperly opened file will cause an error when an attempt is made to use the file with the fgets function call. This error will simply shut the program down with a cryptic message, "bus error — core dumped." C programmers argue that a good C program will check all

Exhibit 3. Program6.3: An Example of Error Handling in a Simple C Program

```
#include <stdio.h>

main()
{
  FILE *fp;
  char buf[80];
  fp = fopen("temp.dat," "r");
  while(fgets(buf, 80,fp))
  {
    printf("%s\n," buf);
  }
}
```

conditions where a program can fail, but errors such as this still occur frequently in C programs, indicating that many C programmers are not checking these problems. The truth is that no management mandate, programming standards document, or code walk-through can ensure that a program will check all possible error conditions or that it will even check the obvious ones a programmer knows can and will happen. Unless the handling of errors is automated and enforced by a compiler or similar mechanism, many, if not most, errors will go unchecked.

Similar to the problem just discussed is the situation when, even if errors are checked, a programmer might not check for the *right* errors. Consider the loop fgets call in Exhibit 3 (Program6.3). Here, the programmer is relying on the fact that, when the fgets call returns a null pointer, the end of file (EOF) has been reached, terminating the loop; however, any error-reading data can cause the fgets to return a null. In order to find the actual meaning of the error, the error indicator for the file must be checked. This is often not done; in fact many C/C++ programmers do not even know how to check this value.

Even if errors are properly checked for, the impact of those errors might be such that the error could propagate up the call stack to the invoking method, possibly all the way to the main method for the program. This means that all methods must check the return values from all the functions to ensure that the functions are working correctly. Making sure return values are always set and checked requires a disciplined approach to implementing error handling that, despite the best of intentions, is often not implemented.

Often a number of errors can be generated that will all cause the same behavior. For example, in a program that opens many files, if any one file cannot be opened, then the error processing might print out an error message and stop the program. Ideally, this should be achievable in a single error-handling block; however, if return values are used, the return value must be checked for every method call that opens a file. This forces the programmer to insert similar code around every file opened to check for a problem. This is referred to as *micromanaging an error* and ideally should be avoided.

Because of the drawbacks of handling errors where they occur and return codes, Java implements error handling using a "try-catch" mechanism, similar to the "try-catch" mechanisms in C++ or Exception blocks in Ada. However, unlike C++ (which, unfortunately, was built on top of C and has a mixed mode for exception handling of try-catch and return values), the exception handling in Java is consistently built around using these try-catch blocks. And, unlike Ada and C++, Java implements checked exceptions that can validate that a program does in fact handle errors that are likely to occur. The rest of this chapter explains how exception handling is implemented in Java.

6.4 Java Exception Handling

This section covers the basic mechanism for handling Java exceptions. Generation and handling of exceptions is shown through the use of try-catch blocks. First, simple try-catch blocks and the actions that can be taken in a catch block are shown, then more complicated behaviors of try-catch blocks, such as exception propagation, finally blocks, and re-throwing of exceptions, are discussed. The basic structure of exceptions handling demonstrated in this section is used in subsequent discussion regarding the uses of exceptions in designing components.

6.4.1 Try-Catch Blocks

The basic mechanism in Java for handling problems that occur at run time is to try to run a section of code. If it completes normally, then the program proceeds to the next statement after all associated catch blocks. However, if a problem is encountered, the program immediately *throws* the error. The program then looks at each enclosing try block to see if any mechanism to *catch* the error has been defined. If a try block can catch the exception, the program branches to that catch block, executes it, and then continues executing at the next statement after all the associated catch blocks. If the try block does not have a catch block that can handle the exception, it is sent to the next enclosing try block to check to see if it can be handled. This continues until the exception is caught or the exception has propagated out of the current context (for procedural programs, this is the main method; for threads, it is the run method where the thread started) and has been caught by the Java virtual machine (JVM), which will by default print a stack trace.

Some examples of try-catch blocks are given here. Exhibit 4 (Program6.4a) illustrates a try-catch block that completes normally. The

Exhibit 4. Program6.4a: Try-Catch Block with No Exception Thrown

```
public class TryCatch1 {
  public static void main(String args[]) {
    int i = 3, j = 7, k;

    try {
      //This division results in a zero divide
      //and immediately branches to the catch block.
      k = j/i;

      System.out.println("Statement is executed normally");
    } catch(ArithmeticException e) {
      System.out.println("Zero divide occurred - This does not
        happen.");
    }

    //The exception was handled, so we continue.
    System.out.println("This is after the exception is
      handled.");
  }
}
```

flow of the program can be followed by the messages that are output. In this case, the program executes all the statements in the try block, and because no problem was encountered it skips the catch block and continues executing after the catch block, ending the program.

In Exhibit 5 (Program6.4b) the program enters the block and attempts to do a division when the denominator is 0. This causes an ArithmeticException (specifically, a divide by zero) to be thrown which is caught by a catch for the enclosing try block. The catch block handles the error and prints a message and then continues executing the program at the end of all catch blocks for this try block, printing out the answer. Note that any lines of code after the exception is thrown in the try block are not executed.

Exhibit 6 (Program6.4c) shows what happens if the exception is not handled in the program. In this case, a ClassCastException is caught, not a ArithmeticException, so the zero divide is not caught. The program will now start to look to other enclosing catch blocks to see if one catches the exception. None does, so the Java VM finally catches the exception, printing out an error and a stack trace.

Finally, a try block can catch more than one exception, as shown in Exhibit 7 (Program6.4d). When this happens, the catch blocks are evaluated in the order in which they appear in the program until one is found that catches the exception. That catch block is executed, the exception is reset, and the program continues executing after the last catch associated with the try block where the exception was raised.

Once an exception is caught, what you do with it depends on the overall exception handling strategy for the program. Some examples

Exhibit 5. Program6.4b: Catch Block Handling the ArithmeticException

```
public class TryCatch2 {
  public static void main(String args[]) {
    int i = 0, j = 7, k;

    try {
      //This division results in a zero divide
      //and immediately branches to the catch block.
      k = j/i;

      System.out.println("Statement is not executed.");
    } catch(ArithmeticException e) {
      System.out.println("Zero divide occurred.");
    }

    //The exception was handled, so we continue.
    System.out.println("This is after the exception is
      handled.");
  }
}
```

Exhibit 6. Program6.4c: Unhandled ArithmeticException

```
public class TryCatch3 {
  public static void main(String args[]) {
    int i = 0, j = 7, k;

    try {
      //This division results in a zero divide
      //and immediately branches to the catch block.
      k = j/i;

      System.out.println("Statement is not executed.");
    } catch(ClassCastException e) {
      System.out.println("This is not an Arithmetic Exception,
        so this is not executed.");
    }

    //The exception was handled, so we continue.
    System.out.println("This statement is never reached.");
  }
}
```

of the things that can be done are shown in Exhibit 8 (Program6.4e). If the program is a simple student program, often the best strategy is to call the printStackTrace method to print out the reason for the exception, the line of code that failed, and the program stack at the time of the call. This can be very useful in debugging the program; however, if this is meant to be a production program, a stack trace will be less than useful. Because it will most likely confuse the person using the system and because it will provide no suggestions for fixing

Exhibit 7. Program6.4d: Multiple Catch Statements

```
public class MultiCatch {
  public static void main(String args[]) {
    int i = 0, j = 7, k;

    try {
      //This division results in a zero divide
      //and immediately branches to the catch block.
      k = j/i;

      System.out.println("Statement is not executed.");
    } catch(ArithmeticException e) {
      System.out.println("Arithmetic Exception caught.");
    } catch(ArrayIndexOutOfBoundsException e) {
      System.out.println("Array Index Out Of Bounds Exception
        caught.");
    } catch(Exception e) {
      System.out.println("Any other Exception was caught.");
    }
  }
}
```

Exhibit 8. Program6.4e: Actions That Can Be Taken on Exceptions

```
import java.io.*;

public class ExceptionActions {
  public static void main(String args[]) {
    int i = 0, j = 7, k;

    try {
      k = j/i;
    } catch(Exception e) {
      try {
        System.out.println("e.toString = " + e.toString());
        System.out.println("e.getMessage = " + e.getMessage());
        e.printStackTrace();
        PrintStream ps = new PrintStream(
          new FileOutputStream("temp.dbg"));
        e.printStackTrace(ps);
      } catch (IOException e1) {
        System.out.println("File write failed.");
      }
    }
  }
}
```

the problem, it is likely to lead to worry and frustration. Further, if the user is running a GUI interface, the stack trace might not even be accessible to the user. In production programs, a catch block should provide the user with a message on which the user can act, even if it is only to call a program support number. The message should follow any conventions that have been established for the project in regard to how to report the error. If the programmer would like to see a stack trace for debugging purposes, it should be written to a file that the user could later send to the programmer.

In a production program, even if the stack trace is written to a file, the user must be informed as to what has happened. It might be enough to know the type of exception, in which case the catch clause that is executed could provide enough information to give the user an error message. However, sometimes the catch clause could be used for a number of different exceptions; for example, an ArithmeticException catches both "zero divide" and "underflow" exceptions. In these cases, more information about the message can be obtained by calling the *toString* or *getMessage* methods on the exception. The information from these methods can be used to give the user a more specific error message. These methods are defined in the Throwable object* and thus are available for every exception and error. Exception handling is relatively easy as long as only a single method and try-catch block are used; however, it becomes more complicated for multiple method calls and try-catch blocks, as will be shown in the next section.

6.4.2 Exception Propagation: Unwinding the Stack

In the preceding example, the error was handled immediately in the block in which it occurred, but what happens when an error occurs in a block that is contained inside of a try block? With Java exception handling, when an exception occurs in a block enclosed in another block, the exception is passed up the blocks until a catch is found that can handle this error. This is called *propagating an exception*. How this works is important, but the details can be somewhat confusing.

To understand exception propagation, remember that anything between a set of "{ }" is a block in Java. Thus if a method is called from within a try block, that method is an enclosed block in the try block. A method called from a method in the try block is still in the try block. For example, in Exhibit 9 (Program6.5), the statement "k = j/i;" in the try block in f2 is also in the block for method f2, which is in the try block in method f1, which is in the block for the method f1, etc.

The rule for try blocks is that when an exception occurs the program immediately branches to the end of each enclosing block until it reaches a try-catch block that can handle that exception. So, when an exception occurs in a try block, the program immediately goes to the

* JDK 1.4 has extended the Throwable to include a cause and to allow the programmer access to parts of the stack trace. The reader should read the Java API for the latest extensions to the Throwable class.

Exhibit 9. Program6.5: Exception Propagation

```
public class ErrorPropagation {
  public void f1() {
    try {
      f2();
    } catch (ArithmeticException e) {
      System.out.println("Error is handled here.");
    }
    System.out.println("Error has been handled in f1.");
  }

  public void f2() {
    int i = 0, j = 7, k;

    try {
      //This division results in a zero divide
      //and immediately branches to the catch block.
      k = j/i;

      System.out.println("Statement is not executed.");
    } catch(ClassCastException e) {
      System.out.println("This does not catch the zero
divide.");
    }
    System.out.println("Error was not handled, so we skip
      this.");
  }

  public static void main(String args[]) {
    ErrorPropagation ep = new ErrorPropagation();
    try {
      ep.f1();
    } catch (ArithmeticException e) {
      System.out.println("Exception was already handled");
      System.out.println("so we skip this statement.");
    }

    //The exception was handled, so we continue.
    System.out.println("This is after the exception is
      handled.");
  }
}
```

end of that try block to find a catch block that can handle this exception. If the program does not find an applicable catch block, then it immediately goes to the end of the block enclosing the try block. It continues to do this until either the exception can be handled in a catch block or the main method is exited. Because some of these blocks can be methods, it appears that an immediate return from the method is executed when the exception occurs and that the program is returning from the methods. Thus, this behavior is referred to as *unwinding the stack*.

How this works is illustrated in Exhibit 9 (Program6.5), where the exception occurs in a method call two levels deeper than the try block that catches it. In this program the main method calls method f1, which in turn calls method f2. In method f2, an ArithmeticException (zero divide) exception occurs. When this happens, the first enclosing try block, the one in f2, is checked to see if it can handle the exception. Because it does not handle the ArithmeticException, the exception is propagated to the try block in method f1. This try block handles the exception and then resets the exception and continues executing at the next statement in the method after the catch block. The catch for ArithmeticException is not executed in the main method, as it was handled and reset in method f1.

If an exception is not caught in any try block in the program, it is propagated to the JVM, which has an implicit try-catch block. If an exception propagates to the JVM, the default behavior is to print the exception and a program trace and then to end the program.

6.4.3 Finally Blocks

Often, some code needs to be executed regardless of whether or not an exception occurs or, if one does occur, whether or not it is caught. For example, a program using a socket for network communication might want to shut the socket down cleanly so that the process on the remote computer knows that it is going away. The program will always want to do this clean shut down, regardless of any exceptions that might occur. The code to handle this shutdown cannot be at the end of the try block, because if an exception occurs then this code will not be executed. It cannot be after the try block, because if the exception is not caught in this try block then the code will again be skipped. It cannot be in the catch block, because if the exception does not occur then the code will never be executed. This situation is not easily handled simply by using try-catch blocks; therefore, an additional block, a finally block, is used.

A try-catch-finally block works by making the finally block always execute. Exhibit 10 (Program6.6) shows how this is done. If no exception occurs, the code in the finally block is executed. If an exception occurs and is caught, the code in the finally block is executed. If an exception occurs but is not caught, the code in the finally block is executed. Even if an attempt is made to get around the finally block by using a return statement, the finally block is executed. The finally block is always executed.

6.5 Checked and Unchecked Exceptions

In Java programs some exceptions have to be explicitly handled and some exceptions do not have to be explicitly handled. This is often confusing to programmers unfamiliar with Java exceptions. The rationale for this behavior is that some exceptions and errors can almost

Exhibit 10. Program6.6: Finally Block

```
public class FinallyExample {
  public void f1() {
    try {
      f2();
    } catch (ArithmeticException e) {

      System.out.println("Error is handled here.");
      return;
      //Note that even though there is a return
      //statement here, the finally block is executed.
    } finally {

      System.out.println("Error is handled and finally block
        executed.");
    }
  }

  public void f2() {
    int i = 0, j = 7, k;
    try {
      //This division results in a zero divide
      //and immediately branches to the catch block.
      k = j/i;

      System.out.println("Statement is not executed.");
    } catch(ClassCastException e) {
      System.out.println("This does not catch the zero
divide.");
    } finally {

      System.out.println("Error is not handled but finally
        is executed.");
    }
  }

  public static void main(String args[]) {
    FinallyExample ep = new FinallyExample();
    try {
      ep.f1();
    } catch (ArithmeticException e) {

      System.out.println("Exception was already handled");
      System.out.println("so we skip this statement.");
    } finally {
      System.out.println("No error, but finally still
        executed.");
    }
  }
}
```

always occur, and when programmers acknowledge this reality in the code the program becomes unwieldy without producing any positive effect. However, some errors, such as trying to open a nonexistent file, are sufficiently limited in scope and important enough to require the programmer to acknowledge that they might occur and to make allowances for them.

The tradeoff between programmers acknowledging and specifically handling *all* errors or handling only a limited number of important

Exhibit 11. Program6.7: Java Program Equivalent to C Exhibit 3 (Program6.3)

```
import java.io.FileReader;
import java.io.BufferedReader;
import java.io.IOException;

public class PrintFile {
  public static void main(String args[]) {
    try {
      FileReader fr = new FileReader("tmp.dat");
      BufferedReader br = new BufferedReader(fr);

      String s = br.readLine();
      while (s ! = null) {
        System.out.println(s);
        s = br.readLine();
      }
    } catch(IOException ioe) {
      ioe.printStackTrace();
    }
  }
}
```

errors is a very nice feature of Java. Some programmers react badly to a language forcing them to acknowledge anything, and they often write programs such the one shown in Exhibit 3 (Program6.3) out of ignorance, haste, or a simple refusal to handle errors. Java programs are much safer because the types of errors that occur in Exhibit 3 (Program6.3) must be explicitly handled or propagated, or their not being handled must at least be acknowledged. This is shown in Exhibit 11 (Program6.7), which shows the Java program equivalent to Exhibit 3 (Program6.3). Note that the exceptions for opening and writing to a file cannot simply be ignored in the program, so the program will produce a correct error if any problems are encountered.

6.5.1 Exception Hierarchy

Exceptions that are limited as to where they can occur and thus are handled in a program are referred to as *checked exceptions*. Exceptions that do not have to be handled are called *unchecked exceptions*. To understand the difference between checked and unchecked exceptions it is necessary to understand how Java groups exceptions and errors. Exhibit 12 provides a hierarchy chart of some of the exceptions in Java. In Java, all exceptions are objects and extend from a base class Throwable, which provides the basic functions such as printStackTrace and getMessage. The hierarchy is then broken down into three categories: Error, RuntimeException, and Exception. Each of these is described in more detail below.

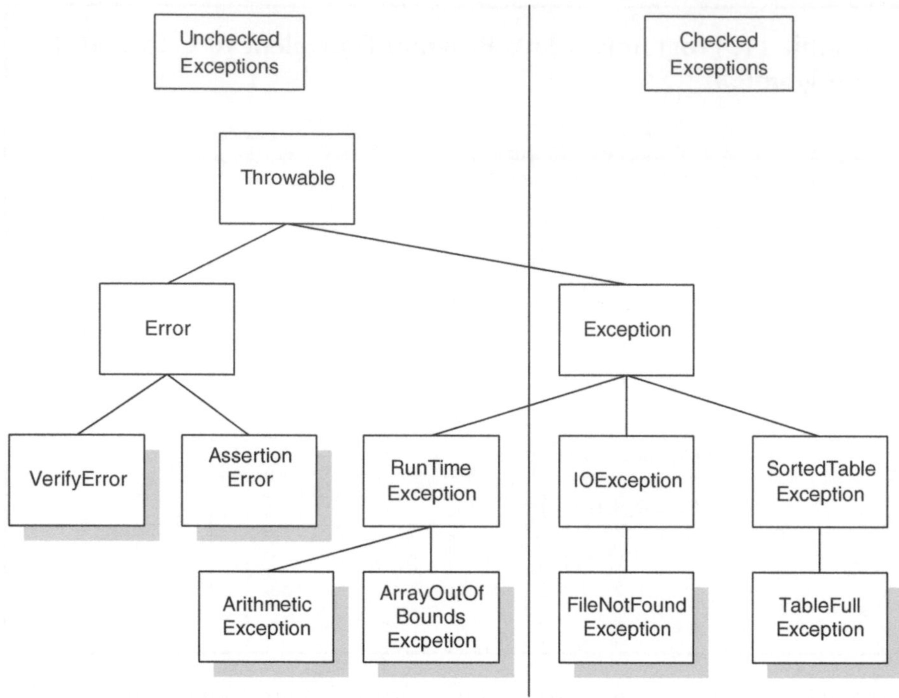

Exhibit 12. Java Exception Hierarchy

- *Errors* are normally problems in the JVM that are outside of the programmer's control and would probably cause the program to quit running. They can occur anywhere in the program. For example, an OutOfMemoryError occurs in the JVM if for any reason it cannot satisfy a memory request. This could mean that a program on the computer has a memory leak, all the memory on the system has been used up, and the computer must be rebooted; this situation is something the programmer cannot do anything about. Another problem is a VerifyError that says that the ".class" file being read has some type of internal inconsistency such as an invalid check sum. This could mean that the file has been hacked and malicious code inserted so it should not be run.
- *RuntimeExceptions* are problems that are the result of the logic or implementation of a program and potentially can occur anywhere in a program. For example, an ArrayIndexOutOfBoundsException occurs when a program attempts to read or write an array position not in the array. This error is the result of the program not properly handling the array indexing and could be fixed by the programmer either by correcting the code or possibly in a catch block in the program.
- *Exceptions* are problems in the program caused by the logic or implementation of the program but are generally limited in scope. For example, a FileNotFoundException is thrown when an attempt

is made to open a file that does not exist. This type of error occurs only when a call is made to a method to open a file, so it is generated by an explicit action in the program and is limited to the open method call.

Any exception or error class that is an ancestor of another class can be used to catch an exception. For example, IOException is the parent of both the FileNotFoundException and the EOFException and therefore can be used as a surrogate in a catch block for either of these exceptions. Further, Exception is the parent of IOException, so it can be used as a surrogate for any IOException, as well as any other exception for which it is an ancestor. So, when creating a file, a FileNotFoundException must be caught, which can be achieved by a FileNotFoundException, an IOException, or simply an Exception.

6.5.2 Checked and Unchecked Exceptions

Checked exceptions are exceptions that must be either explicitly caught or thrown. These are the exceptions that cause the message "exception must be explicitly caught or thrown" when compiling a program. Errors or exceptions that are descendants of class Error or RuntimeException are unchecked, and they do not have to be explicitly caught or thrown. Any other exceptions must be handled.

A checked exception can be handled in two ways. The first is to use a catch block to handle the exception, and the second is to explicitly propagate the exception to the calling method. Exhibits 13 and 14 (Program6.8 and Program6.9) illustrate both of these points. In Exhibits 13 and 14 (Program6.8 and Program6.9), the constructor for the FileInputStream throws a check exception, FileNotFoundException. In Exhibit 13 (Program6.8), this exception is caught in a try block that encloses the constructor class. Note that, because a FileNotFound-

Exhibit 13. Program6.8: Catching a Checked Exception

```
import java.io.FileInputStream;
import java.io.FileNotFoundException;

public class CatchImmediate {
  public FileInputStream openFile(String fileName) {
    FileInputStream fis = null;
    try {
      fis = (new FileInputStream(fileName));
    } catch(FileNotFoundException fnfe) {
      fnfe.printStackTrace();
    }
    return fis;
  }
}
```

Exhibit 14. Program6.9: Throwing a Checked Exception

```
import java.io.FileInputStream;
import java.io.IOException;
/**
 *  There are two ways to handle a checked exception. The second
 *  is to explicitly propagate it. This program shows
 *  propagating the FileNotFoundException by having the method
 *  throw the exception rather than handle it. Note that the
 *  method throws an IOException, not a FileNotFoundException.
 *  But, because the IOException is the parent of the
 *  FileNotFoundException, it can be used as a proxy for the
 *  exception. Note that only the FileNotFoundException can ever
 *  be thrown, but by using the IOException the calling method
 *  must now handle the IOException.
 */

public class Propagate {
  public FileInputStream openFile(String fileName) throws
      IOException {
    return new FileInputStream(fileName);
  }
}
```

Exception is also an IOException, an Exception, and a Throwable, catching any of these would handle this exception. In Exhibit 14 (Program6.9), the FileNotFoundException is handled by explicitly throwing an IOException. Once again, because the FileNotFoundException extends the IOException, this statement explicitly allows the IOException to be thrown.

Checked and unchecked exceptions confuse many programmers. If an unchecked exception can occur or even if it is explicitly thrown, it does not have be explicitly handled. Exhibit 15 (Program6.10) shows that even though an ArithmeticException is explicitly thrown by the method f1 it does not have to be caught in the main method. This is because it is not the presence of an exception in a throws clause that determines if the exception must be checked or not, but the type of exception.

Checked exceptions must be declared with a throws clause as part of the method signature for a method, so it is easy to check the Javadoc to see what exceptions are thrown and must be handled. However, often the easiest way to figure out if an exception needs to be caught in a program is simply to code the function up and see if the compiler generates any messages or to use an Integrated Development Environment (IDE) that automatically inserts the necessary catch clause.

6.6 Writing Exceptions

In order to design an effective error-handling strategy, the implementer of a component must be able to implement his own exceptions. In

Exhibit 15. Program6.10: Explicit ArithmeticException That Does Not Have to Be Handled

```
public class NotChecked {
  public static void throwUnchecked() throws ArithmeticExcep-
tion
      {
    int i = 0, j = 7, k;
    k = j/i;
  }

  public static void main(String args[]) {
    //Note that no try block is needed to call method.
    throwUnchecked();
  }
}
```

order to do this, knowledge of how to create and implement Java exceptions is necessary. This section goes through the steps of creating and implementing an exception. Section 6.6.1 explains how to create a new exception, Section 6.6.2 shows how to advertise the exception to let other classes know it will be thrown, and Section 6.6.3 shows how to throw this exception at runtime.

6.6.1 Writing the Exception Class

To create a new exception, all that a programmer has to do is create a class that extends Exception. This class can now be used as an exception. However, if this is all that is done, then when the programmer later tries to call getMessage to find out something about the exception, no message will have been set and a null string results. Therefore, it always best to define two constructors: a default constructor that takes no parameters and does not set the exception message and a constructor that takes a String of the message as a parameter. Also, a programmer will often want to define special information that will be available with the exception. For example suppose the programmer would like to create an exception for when a user types in a number that is out of range of the expected values. A NumberOutOfBoundsException can be created for this exception. Associated with this exception is a variable Number, which is the actual number that was entered. This Number would be stored as part of the exception and set when the exception is created. Because this Number would be immutable, it will be set only in the constructor and a method to retrieve its value defined so that users of the exception have access to it. The NumberOutOfBoundsException is shown in Exhibit 16 (Program6.11a). Note the four constructors with this exception, one for each of the four possible ways in which the exception could be

Exhibit 16. Program6.11a: Creating a User-Defined Exception

```
public class NumberOutOfBoundsException extends Exception {
  private int number;

  public NumberOutOfBoundsException() {
    number = 0;
  }

  public NumberOutOfBoundsException(String Message) {
    super(Message);
  }

  public NumberOutOfBoundsException(int number) {
    this.number = number;
  }

  public NumberOutOfBoundsException(String Message, int number)
      {
    super(Message);
    this.number = number;
  }

  public int getNumber() {
    return number;
  }
}
```

created. Once the exception class has been created, any methods that use it must advertise that they are using it.

6.6.2 Advertise the Exception

Because the exception that is created extends Exception, it is a checked exception. This means that to use it the exception must be advertised so that the calling method knows it is responsible for handling it. An exception is advertised by using the *throws* clause in the method signature. This is shown in the getNumber method of Exhibit 17 (Program6.11b). Note that a program does not have to actually throw the exception to advertise it in the throws clause. A programmer could put a throws clause for an exception in the signature in order to reserve the right of this method to throw the exception if it chooses. This is particularly useful in interfaces, where an exception could be thrown by some objects that are instances of that object and not by others.

6.6.3 Throw the Exception

Once the exception has been created and advertised, the program needs to throw it when it occurs. Creating a new instance of the object and using the throw statement does this. Exhibit 17 (Program6.11b)

Exhibit 17. Program6.11b: Using the NumberOutOfBoundsException

```
import java.io.*;

public class NumberTest {
  public int getNumber() throws NumberOutOfBoundsException {
    int number = 0;

    try {
      StreamTokenizer st = new StreamTokenizer(
            new BufferedReader(
            new InputStreamReader(System.in)));
      st.nextToken();
      number = (int)st.nval;
      if (! (number > 0 && number < 100))
        throw new NumberOutOfBoundsException(
          "Invalid Number," number);
    } catch (IOException e) {
      e.printStackTrace();
    }
    return number;
  }

  public static void main(String args[]) {
    NumberTest nt = new NumberTest();
    int number = 0;
    while(true) {
      try {
        System.out.println("Enter a number from 1 to 100");
        number = nt.getNumber();
        break;
      } catch(NumberOutOfBoundsException e) {
        System.out.println("Invalid Number " + e.getNumber() +
          " try again\n");
      }
    }

    System.out.println("number = "+ number);
  }
}
```

illustrates a complete method that advertises and throws an exception, as well as the main program that handles the exception. This is all there is to creating and using programmer-defined exceptions. These exceptions behave exactly as exceptions that are built into the Java API because they are implemented in the same way as exceptions in the Java API. This is nice because classes that are defined by programmers do not have to have a second-class status with respect to their implementation of exception handling.

6.7 Further Reading

The basic topic of exceptions can be found in any basic Java text book (see, for example, [DEI02] or [LEW03]). Most books that are study aids for the Java Certified Programmer Exam (such as [HEL99]) contain very good sections on exceptions. Eckel [ECK98] presents a more in-depth view of exceptions as well as giving anomalies that can occur when using them. Finally, a number of Web sites contain tutorials on using exceptions (see, for example, [VEN98]).

6.8 Problems

1. Because an ArithmeticException is unchecked, it does not have to be caught in a try block or explicitly thrown. The program below catches the ArithmeticException, a zero divide, in the program using an ancestor of the ArithmeticException, class Exception. However, when the ArithmeticException is re-thrown, it must now be caught. Explain the behavior of this program.

```
public class Problem61 {
  public static void method1() {
    try {
      int i = 0, j = 7, k;
      k = j/i;
    } catch(Exception e) {
      if (e instanceof ArithmeticException) {
        System.out.println("Arithmetic Exception raised");
        throw e;
      }
    }
  }
}
```

2. Can a constructor throw an exception? If the constructor can throw an exception, what must be true of the default constructors of any class that extends it?
3. This program continues the thought in Problem 2. In this case, the Person object can throw an AgeNotValidException. Using the Java extends clause, extend this class into an Employee class. What happens when you use the default constructor in your Employee class?

```
class AgeNotValidException extends Exception {
}

class Person {
  int age;
  public Person(int age) {
    if (age < 0 || age > 120)
      throw new AgeNotValidException();
    this.age = age;
  }
}
```

4. In the following program, an interface is defined that specifies that an exception can be thrown from this method, but the method as implemented does not throw the method or include it in its

signature. Is this valid or invalid in Java? Why was it defined this way in Java?

```
interface HasAge {
  public void setAge(int age) throws AgeNotValidException;
}

class Person implements HasAge {
  int age;
  public void setAge(int age) {
    this.age = age
  }
}
```

5. In the following program an interface is defined. The class that implements the interface now tries to throw an exception that is not defined in the interface. Is this valid or invalid in Java? Why do you think Java implemented this behavior?

```
interface HasAge {
  public void setAge(int age);
}

class Person implements HasAge {
  int age;
  public void setAge(int age) throws AgeNotValidException {
    if (age < 0 || age > 120)
      throw new AgeNotValidException();
    this.age = age
  }
}
```

6. Implement the program from Problem 5.4 with exceptions. The exceptions needed for this problem are defined here:
   - *TableException* is the parent of all other exceptions.
   - *TableFullException* should be thrown from the add method when an insert is attempted on a table that is full.
   - *ObjectNotFoundException* should be thrown when a delete is attempted on an object that is not in the current table.
   - *UnmatchedTypesException* should be thrown from the eq and gt methods of the class that implements the Sortable interface. It should be thrown if the type of object passed as a parameter to this method is not compatible with the current object. While this object is generated from the eq and gt methods, it should be propagated out of the add and delete methods.

Note: You must also redefine the Sortable interface as follows:

```
interface Sortable {
  public boolean gt(Sortable s) throws
    UnmatchedTypesException;
  public boolean eq(Sortable s) throws
    UnmatchedTypesException;
}
```

7. In Problem 6, if an UnmatchedType exception is not needed and if the types do not match, an attempt could be made to cast the object and a ClassCastException allowed to be raised if the objects are not of compatible types. What is the advantage of defining an exception specifically for this case in our program? (*Hint:* Consider what exceptions each of these extends.)
8. The text mentioned that exception handling was expensive and you should not use an exception when a simple test would be sufficient. You should prove this. To do so, notice that the java.util.Stack object has an empty method and throws an EmptyStackException if a pop is attempted when no items are on the stack. This means that a pop operation on a stack can be handled in two ways:

   (a)

   ```
   if (! stack.empty())
     stack.pop();
   ```

   (b)

   ```
   try {
     stack.pop();
   } catch(EmptyStackException) {
   }
   ```

   Use the System.currentTimeMillis method to time both of these ways of popping a stack by pushing and popping 1,000,000 objects. Which method takes longer? How much longer? Explain why one takes longer than the other.
9. What is the result of running the program shown in Exhibit 18?

Exhibit 18. Program to Problem 6.9

```
class Except1 extends Exception {
}

public class TE {
  public static void method2() throws Except1 {
    throw new Except1();
  }

  public static void method1() {
    try {
      method2();
      System.out.println("After method 2");
    } catch(Except1 e) {
      System.out.println("Caught Except1 in method 1");
    } catch(Exception e) {
      System.out.println("Caught Exception in method 1");
    } finally {
      System.out.println("Finally in method 1");
    }
      System.out.println("Leaving method1");
    }

  public static void main(String args[]) {
    try {
      method1();
    } catch(Exception e) {
      System.out.println("Caught Exception in main");
    } finally {
      System.out.println("Finally in main");
    }
    System.out.println("Leaving main");
  }
}
```

Chapter 7

Implementing an Animator Component Using the Java Event Model

7.1 Introduction

The Java Event Model is a ubiquitous way to handle communications between asynchronous activities. This model is used to implement the Java AWT but is also designed to be a generic method of passing events between asynchronous activities, such as threads. Because the Java Event Model was designed as a generic component, it has wide applicability for asynchronous activities that must be coordinated. Because it was designed to take advantage of the Java programming language, it integrates well with the Java language, and it is particularly useful when combined with other facilities in Java (such as RMI) to write programs distributed across a number of computers, such as chat programs, multiplayer games, or even Web servers.

This chapter explains the Java Event Model by creating a visual animator component. The process of building this animator component begins with a very simple animation program to show how animation can be achieved using the Java AWT and Swing Components. This simple animator is then converted into a generic component that can be used to handle a number of different animation tasks. The code for this generic component is refined to handle potential race and deadlock conditions until it implements the complete Java Event Model, which is safe and deadlock free if used correctly.

The animator is an example of a generic component in that it uses a Java interface so that it can work with objects of any type, including objects that are asynchronous activities such as threads. How to use the animator in procedural programs is also addressed in this chapter. Applying the animator to concurrent objects requires a better understanding of the nature of the interaction between the animator and other asynchronous activities and is covered further in Chapter 8.

The Java Event model that is presented in this chapter occurs frequently throughout the remainder of the book. It will prove especially useful in situations when passive objects must be linked with active objects at runtime — for example, when ActionListeners need to be associated with Buttons. It is also useful when combined with other techniques (presented in later chapters), creating powerful paradigms that can be used to implement concurrent programs.

7.2 Chapter Goals

After completing this chapter you should be able to:

- Do simple animations in Java.
- Explain the concepts behind the Java Event Model, why it is important, and how to use it.
- Correctly implement the Java Event Model.
- Describe some of the problems that can occur when writing concurrent programs and how to avoid those problems using a standard model such as the Java Event Model.
- Explain how the Java Event Model is used in the Java AWT and how AWT components work.
- See how interfaces can be used to create programs where the objects are loosely coupled and only interact through services provided in the interface.

7.3 A Very Simple Animator

Animation is a technique where pictures are changed slightly and displayed on a terminal in succession so quickly that the eye perceives movement. It is a nice way to explain a number of topics; the results of running a program are visual, so problems in a program are readily apparent. Once the problem is seen, it is much easier to figure out why it occurred and how to correct it.

This chapter uses animation to illustrate how to implement the Java Event Model and provides a rationale for why it is implemented the way it is. A generic animator component is developed through a number of steps, each step illustrating and solving a problem in the previous animator, until a final animator that implements a correct animation component is created. The authoritative description of the Java Event Model is given in the Java Beans Specification [SUN96] and is available from Sun's Web site as part of the Java documentation; the final animator component provided here follows the rules and conventions found in this specification. The reader should note that the Java Beans Specification shows that the Vector and Hashtable classes, while fully synchronized, are not thread safe. For that reason, it is probably better to use the Collection classes such as Lists and Maps that do not impose the penalty of synchronization on the methods. This topic is explored further in the problems at the end of the chapter.

To begin the discussion, a basic understanding of animation in general is needed. Computer animation is achieved by using a flip-card analogy. Children's game cards often have pictures on the back. These cards are numbered, and the pictures on adjacent cards vary slightly from each other. When the cards are placed in order, rapidly flipping from one card to the next gives the impression of motion. This process of flipping through pictures is also the way a movie works. Frames are displayed at a rate faster than the eye can process them. The pictures on these discrete frames changing slightly from one frame to the next gives the illusion of continuous motion.

The same effect can be accomplished with a computer. The computer simply generates pictures that are slightly different and displays them on the screen. If these images are displayed fast enough, they appear to have a continuous motion. Program7.1 (Exhibits 1 through 3) is an example of this effect. Here, a ball is moved back and forth from the top left of the screen to the bottom right. Because the ball is redrawn slightly as we move through each frame, it appears that the ball is moving across the screen.

Exhibit 1. Program7.1a: Path Class

```
import java.awt.Point;

public interface Path {

  /**
   * Check to see if the path has MoreSteps.
   */
  public boolean hasMoreSteps();

  /**
   * Get the next position. If the path has no more steps,
   * return the current position.
   */
  public Point nextPosition();
}
```

Exhibit 2. Program7.1b: Straight Line Path Class

```
import java.awt.Point;

public class StraightLinePath implements Path {
  int startX, startY, endX, endY, steps;
  int currentStep = -1;// This makes the first step 0
  double deltaX, deltaY;

  /**
   *  Constructor stores the points and builds the information
   *  needed to construct the next point. Note that for a path
   *  we need the initial point for the path (X1, Y1), the final
   *  point for the path (X2, Y2), and the number of steps in
   *  the path (numSteps).
   */
  public StraightLinePath(int X1, int Y1, int X2, int Y2, int
      numSteps) {
    startX = X1;
    startY = Y1;
    endX = X2;
    endY = Y2;
    steps = numSteps;
    deltaX = ((double)(X2 - X1))/steps;
    deltaY = ((double)(Y2 - Y1))/steps;
  }

  /**
   * Check to see if the path has MoreSteps.
   */
  public boolean hasMoreSteps() {
    if (currentStep > steps)
      return false;
    return true;
  }

  /**
   * Get the next position. If the path has no more steps,
   * return the current position.
   */
  public Point nextPosition() {
    currentStep++;
    if (currentStep > steps)
      return new Point(endX, endY);
    return new Point((int)(startX + (deltaX * currentStep)),
        (int)(startY + (deltaY * currentStep)));
  }
}
```

7.3.1 The Path Class

How Program7.1 (Exhibits 1 through 3) works can be explained by first examining how the program figures out where to draw an object using the Path interface. The Path interface is shown in Exhibit 1 (Program7.1a). A path is simply an ordered set of points indicating where an object will be drawn. The points are obtained by calling the hasMoreSteps and nextPosition methods. So, each time an object is to be drawn, the path is queried to obtain the next position to draw the object.

How the Path object determines how to get to the next position is not determined by the interface. Some real object needs to be implemented that will determine the actual behavior. Any object that defines this behavior and implements the Path interface can be used. Thus, the path could be a straight line, a spline curve, or a set of points stored in an array. The actual implementation of the path can be easily changed. In the programs in this directory, a simple straight line is used to generate the path, as shown in Exhibit 2 (Program7.1b). The Path object takes a starting position, an ending position, and a number of steps and by using a straight line calculates the positions at which to draw the object. An object to be animated must give the Path the points at which to start and end and the number of steps it should take to get from the starting point to the ending point. Then, the object can use the path in a loop by checking to see if there are more steps in the path and, if so, asking the path for the next position in the path.

For example, to move a circle from a position of 10,10 to 100,100 in 10 steps, the program could do the following:

```
Graphics g = new Graphics();
Path path = new StraightLinePath(10, 10, 100, 100, 10);
while (path.hasMoreSteps()) {
  Point point = path.nextStep();
  g.drawOval((int)pos.getX(), (int)pos.getY(), 15, 15);
}
```

Using a path is something that will be done frequently in animation in order to calculate the positions of objects as they move on a screen. By creating a Path interface and the StraightLinePath class, this behavior has been abstracted and must be implemented only once. Now objects that need to move can create a Path object and allow that Path object to implement the logic behind calculating the points where the object should be drawn. This approach offers three advantages. First, the logic for implementing the path is not part of the paint method for the object to be animated; thus, the paint method is more cohesive, as it is responsible only for drawing the object and not for calculating its position which can make these objects significantly less complex, easier to understand, and easier to implement and debug. The second advantage is related to the first. Because the ability to calculate the position given a path is encapsulated inside of the Path class, the programmer for the object to be drawn does not need to worry about the details of how a path is calculated. This means that the algorithm to generate points in a path only needs to be developed, tested, and supported once, instead of in each and every object that requires a path.

The third advantage to using a path interface is that it also makes the object less tightly coupled to a particular behavior. For example, assume that at some point in the future the application no longer requires a straight line but must implement a Bessel function to calculate the positions for drawing the object. If the path was defined as part of the paint method in the animated object, the animated object would have to be changed in order to implement this new behavior; thus, the behavior of the path is tightly coupled with this object. However, by using a path interface, the definition for the path can be changed by changing the type of path object that is used. Rather than making the path a StraightLinePath, a BesselPath object could be created, and only the actual object instantiated would have to be changed. This decoupling of the animated object from the specific path it will use allows greater flexibility in implementing new ways to animate the object.

7.3.2 A Simple Animator

Now that we have examined the method of calculating where to draw an object, we will now take a look at the way that the Java AWT and Java Swing handle drawing by using a simple animator with a ball, as shown in Exhibit 3 (Program7.1c). This animator consists of two parts: a SimpleAnimator class, which is also a JFrame because it extends

Exhibit 3. Program7.1c: Simple Animator and Ball Classes

```
import java.awt.*;
import javax.swing.*;

public class SimpleAnimator extends JFrame {

  Ball ball = new Ball(Color.red, 20, 20, 450, 450);

  /**
   * Constructor that adds the ball and then sets the size
   * of the frame and shows it on the screen.
   */
  public SimpleAnimator() {
    Container con = this.getContentPane();
    con.add(ball);
  }

  /**
   * This method simply dispatches paint events to the ball
   * object, waits for 0.1 seconds, and does it again.
   */
  public void paint(Graphics g) {
    super.paint(g);
    try {
      Thread.sleep(100);
      repaint();
    } catch(InterruptedException e) {
    }
  }
```

(continued)

Exhibit 3. Program7.1c (Continued)

```
  /**
   * Start the program.
   */
  public static void main(String args[]) {
    SimpleAnimator sa = new SimpleAnimator();
    sa.setSize(500,500);
    sa.show();
  }
}

/**
 *  Purpose: This class implements a ball JPanel on which
 *           it can draw a ball to be displayed on the JFrame to
 *           which it has been added. It animates the ball by moving
 *           it on the screen a little each time the paint method
 *           is called.
 */
class Ball extends JPanel {
  Color ballColor;
  int xStart, yStart, xLimit, yLimit;
  Path myPath;

  /**
   *  Constructor sets the ball up to run and sets the limits
   *  for the size of the screen area on which it is to run.
   *  It also sets the initial path by which to move the ball.
   */
  public Ball(Color ballColor, int xStart, int yStart,
      int xLimit, int yLimit) {
    this.ballColor = ballColor;
    this.xStart = xStart;
    this.yStart = yStart;
    this.xLimit = xLimit;
    this.yLimit = yLimit;

    myPath = new StraightLinePath(xStart, yStart, xLimit,
      yLimit, 50);
  }

  /**
   *  This method draws the ball at the correct position on
   *  the screen given by the path. When the end of path is
   *  reached, a new path is created to move the ball in the
   *  opposite direction.
   */
  public void paint(Graphics g) {
    super.paint(g);
    Point pos = myPath.nextPosition();

    g.setColor(ballColor);
    g.fillOval((int)pos.getX(), (int)pos.getY(), 15, 15);
    if (! myPath.hasMoreSteps()) {
      if (pos.getX() = = xStart)
        myPath = new StraightLinePath(xStart, yStart, xLimit,
          yLimit, 50);
      else
        myPath = new StraightLinePath(xLimit, yLimit, xStart,
          yStart, 50);
    }
  }
}
```

JFrame, and a Ball class, which is also a JPanel because it extends JPanel. The discussion begins by describing the JFrame and then covers how it works with the JPanel.

A JFrame is simply a frame displayed on the computer screen that is responsible for displaying the graphics generated in paint methods and for sending *events* to any components added to it. For example, when a JButton is added to a JFrame object, the JFrame is responsible for displaying the button by calling the paint method in the button. It is also responsible for making sure that any time the mouse is clicked when the cursor is inside of the button that the button is informed so that it can call the actionPerformed method for any ActionListeners registered with that button (this topic should become clear by the end of this chapter). In this section, the only events that the JFrame will handle are messages to "repaint" the screen, or repaint events.

When a repaint event is received by the JFrame, its paint method and the paint methods of all of the components added to it are called. Repaint events are generated when the Frame needs to be redrawn or redisplayed — for example, when the application first comes up and needs to be drawn or when the screen is resized. A programmer can also force a repaint event by calling the repaint method on the JFrame object. This is what is done in the paint method in the SimpleAnimator class. The paint method for the SimpleAnimator first executes any code, sleeps for 0.1 seconds, and then calls repaint, which schedules the JFrame to call paint again. The paint method then exits, and the JFrame processes the repaint event, calling the paint method again. This creates a JFrame object that is redrawn every 0.1 seconds and so can be used to implement an animation where the pictures are redrawn every 0.1 seconds.

We now turn our attention to the behavior of the JPanel object, the Ball object. As discussed earlier, a JFrame not only draws itself on a screen, but it also extends a Container, so it can have any number of Component* objects added to it. When the repaint event is generated for a JFrame, the paint methods for all of the objects that have been added to this JFrame are also called. Because class Ball extends JPanel, which in turn extends Component, this Ball object can be added to the JFrame and have its paint method called every 0.1 seconds. The default paint method for the JPanel is then redefined for class Ball, which allows it to draw a filled oval, or ball, on the JFrame on the computer screen. Because it checks with the path variable each time it is drawn, it moves the ball a little every 0.1 seconds, which produces the appearance of a ball moving across the screen. When it reaches

* The term *Component* here specifically means the class "java.awt.Component," not generic components. This is the only place in the book that uses the term to mean this specific class.

the end of a path, it simply creates a new path to reverse direction, so the ball moves back and forth across the screen.

This SimpleAnimator is effective, but to make it more usable it would be nice to add a ScrollBar to control the speed of the animation (which we will do in the next section). Before starting to add control components, an important aspect of this animator should be discussed. Although it might appear otherwise, the repaint call in the SimpleAnimator does not call the paint method. If the repaint were to call the paint method, it would represent a recursive call, and the mechanism would eventually cause the program stack to overflow. This stack overflow would occur fairly quickly, so the design of the Java AWT and Swing components would be very unstable. Instead, the GUI thread that was talked about in Chapter 1 is started when a JFrame is started. This GUI thread runs as long as the JFrame is displayed and is responsible for calling the paint method in the JFrame object (in this case, the SimpleAnimator object) each time a repaint event is scheduled. So, when repaint is called from the paint method, a flag is set for the GUI thread that tells the GUI thread to call paint again. The GUI thread then exits the paint method, finds this flag set, and again calls paint. This distinction between repaint calling paint and setting a repaint event is very significant, and as shown in the next section. If it is not understood, it can cause an application to be implemented in such a way as to perform very badly or possibly not work at all.

7.4 Adding a Speed Control to the Animator

The animator as given in Exhibit 3 (Program7.1c) appears to work fine; however, the speed is fixed and cannot be changed without recompiling the program. An enhanced animator with a scrollbar to control the speed and an exit button is shown in Exhibit 4 (Program7.2). This program differs from Exhibit 3 (Program7.1c) only in that the control panel has now been added to the SimpleAnimator constructor, and the amount of time the animator waits between redrawing the frame is now controlled by the variable sleepTime. When the scrollbar is all the way to the left, the scrollbar sets the sleepTime to 10,000 and the JFrame is redrawn every 10 seconds. When it is all the way to the right the sleepTime is set to 10 and the JFrame is redrawn every 1/100 of a second.

While this seems to be a nice improvement, the animator exhibits a very disturbing behavior when the scrollbar is pulled all the way to the left to allow the redraw to occur every 10 seconds. When this happens, the scrollbar and button appear to handle user requests incorrectly. For example, if the user pulls the scrollbar all the way to the left and then tries to immediately pull it all the way to the right,

Exhibit 4. Program7.2: Simple Animator with a Speed Control

```
import java.awt.*;
import java.awt.event.*;
import javax.swing.*;

public class SimpleAnimator1 extends JFrame {

  private Ball ball = new Ball(Color.red, 20, 20, 450, 450);
  private int sleepTime = 100;

  /**
   * Constructor that builds the simple GUI with a scrollbar to
   * keep track of speed and an exit button. The ball object is
   * then added to the Frame to be animated.
   */
  public SimpleAnimator1() {
    Container con = this.getContentPane();

    // = = = = = = = = = = = = = = = = = = = = = = = =
    // Control Panel. It consists of the button
    // and scrollbar defined below.
    JPanel controlPanel = new JPanel();

    JButton exitButton = new JButton("Exit");
    exitButton.addActionListener(new ActionListener() {
      public void actionPerformed(ActionEvent e) {
        System.exit(0);
      }
    });
    controlPanel.add(exitButton);

    controlPanel.add(new JLabel("Animator Speed"));
    final JScrollBar speedControl = new JScrollBar(JScrollBar.
        HORIZONTAL, 4900, 10, 50, 5000);
    speedControl.addAdjustmentListener(new AdjustmentListener()
        {
      public void adjustmentValueChanged(AdjustmentEvent e) {
      sleepTime = 5000 - e.getValue();
    }
  });
  controlPanel.add(speedControl);

    con.add(controlPanel, BorderLayout.SOUTH);
    // = = = = = = = = = = = = = = = = = = = = = = = = = =
    // Add the ball to the JFrame.
    con.add(ball, BorderLayout.CENTER);

  }

  /**
   * This method simply dispatches paint events to the ball
   * object, waits for 0.1 seconds, and does it again.
   */
  public void paint(Graphics g) {
    super.paint(g);
    try {
      Thread.sleep(sleepTime);
      repaint();
    } catch(InterruptedException e) {
    }
  }
```

(continued)

Exhibit 4. Program7.2 (Continued)

```
  /**
   *  Start the program.
   */

  public static void main(String args[]) {
    // Display the Frame.
    SimpleAnimator1 sa = new SimpleAnimator1();
    sa.setSize(500,500);
    sa.show();
  }
}

/**
 *  Purpose: This class implements a ball JPanel on which it
 *           can draw a ball to displayed on the JFrame it has
 *           been added to. It animates the ball by moving it
 *           on the screen a little each time the paint method
 *           is called.
 */
class Ball extends JPanel {
  Color ballColor;
  int xStart, yStart, xLimit, yLimit;
  Path myPath;

  /**
   *  Constructor that sets the ball up to run and sets the
   *  limits for the size of the screen area on which it is to run.
   *  It also sets the initial path over which to move the ball.
   */
  public Ball(Color ballColor, int xStart, int yStart,
      int xLimit, int yLimit) {
    this.ballColor = ballColor;
    this.xStart = xStart;
    this.yStart = yStart;
    this.xLimit = xLimit;
    this.yLimit = yLimit;

    myPath = new StraightLinePath(xStart, yStart, xLimit,
      yLimit, 50);
  }

  /**
   *  This method draws the ball at the correct position on
   *  the screen given by the path. When the end of path is
   *  reached, a new path is created to move the ball in the
   *  opposite direction.
   */
  public void paint(Graphics g) {
    super.paint(g);
    Point pos = myPath.nextPosition();

    g.setColor(ballColor);
    g.fillOval((int)pos.getX(), (int)pos.getY(), 15, 15);

    if (! myPath.hasMoreSteps()) {
      if (pos.getX() = = xStart)
        myPath = new StraightLinePath(xStart, yStart, xLimit,
          yLimit, 50);
      else
        myPath = new StraightLinePath(xLimit, yLimit, xStart,
          yStart, 50);
    }
  }
}
```

it appears to be "jammed" at the left-most position for 10 seconds and then suddenly moves to the right. Similarly, if the scrollbar is moved all the way to the left and the exit button is pressed, the program waits 10 seconds before exiting the program. It is almost as if the GUI components are improperly implemented.

This reveals the fallacy of trying to understand how to program by looking only at the external behavior of a component. Many programmers develop mental models of the behavior of components that work in a number of limited instances but eventually fail because they contain errors in understanding. In this case, a programmer might be led to believe that a bug in the GUI components needs to be fixed, when in fact the GUI components are being properly implemented. The problem here is the presence of a systemic bug in the design of the animator, which only a complete redesign can correct.

The animator is using the threads in the program incorrectly. As explained in Section 7.3, the GUI thread for this frame is responsible for calling the paint method when a repaint event occurs. The GUI thread is also responsible for handling other events, such as an ActionEvent when the button is pressed or an AdjustmentEvent when the scrollbar is moved. What is happening is that in the paint method the programmer has put a call to Thread.sleep, and that call is suspending the current thread (in this case, the GUI thread) for the length of time requested in the sleep call. When the GUI thread enters the paint method and sleeps for 10 seconds, the ActionEvent and AdjustmentEvent are only processed every 10 seconds, at which point the GUI thread can run again. This in effect creates a time delay of up to 10 seconds between when an event is generated and when it is handled. When this is understood, the behavior of the Button and Scrollbar makes sense, but they are still very frustrating to use.

Exhibit 4 (Program7.2) points out a very important rule in using the GUI thread: Never do anything that is time intensive in the GUI thread. Actions such as sleeping or RMI calls are seldom appropriate actions when running the GUI thread and should not be used when a program is running in a GUI thread as they will impact all the other components added to the JFrame. The number of methods that can possibly run in the GUI thread is large, but they are relatively limited in scope, so it is less of a problem than might be imagined. Obviously, all the methods defined as listeners in the AWT (such as actionPeformed for the ActionListener, or adjustmentValueChanged for an AdjustmentListener) run in a GUI thread. The paint method runs in the GUI thread, as does the "init" and most of the other methods in an applet. Other than these, programmers are unlikely to use methods running in the GUI thread unless they are writing GUI components.

As was pointed out, the problem with the animator in Exhibit 4 (Program7.2) is systemic; there is no way to fix Exhibit 4 (Program7.2) to make it work correctly. The loop running the sleep and repaint must be moved out of the GUI thread and a separate thread created to specifically handle the delay using sleep. In the next section, we implement an improved version of the animator that has a control interface but does not have the problem of the GUI components not responding. This new animator is further improved in that it is not tied to a single object, such as the Ball object in the SimpleAnimator, but can be used to animate many different types of objects.

7.5 Implementing a Generic Animator

The animator in Exhibit 4 (Program7.2) has two basic problems. The first is that it caused the GUI components, such as buttons, to behave poorly because it called Thread.sleep inside of the paint method in the GUI thread. The second problem is that the animator is specific to the Ball program. To use it in another program it must be copied and modified to work with the new program. A better way to develop the animator would be using the techniques in Chapter 5 to create a generic component that can be used with many different types of objects and in many different programs.

The animator presented in Exhibit 5 (Program7.4) solves both of these problems. The changes to make it generic and to add a separate thread to handle delays are limited in number but involve interactions between three threads and so are somewhat complex. The changes to implement the control panel are a relatively straightforward implementation of a Java GUI; however, as with most GUI components, they require a fair amount of code. Therefore, the generic animator is developed here in two steps. The first step, shown in Exhibit 6 (Program7.3a) and used in Exhibit 7 (Program7.3b), implements the basic generic animator that allows objects of nearly any type to be animated; however, it does have a fixed time delay, like that shown Exhibit 2 (Program7.1b), so that the complexity of the control panel does not have to be considered (see Sections 7.5.1 and 7.5.2). Section 7.5.1 explains the basic design of the animator and how interfaces can be used to implement a generic solution to make the animator able to handle many objects of different types. Section 7.5.2 explains how the threads that are present interact to make the animator work.

The second stage of the animator involves adding the ControlPanel. This is done in Exhibit 5 (Program7.4), and explained in Section 7.5.3. It will allow a user to control the speed of an animation, stop the animation, or single step the animation. The change to the animator itself is minor, but implementing the ControlPanel requires a lot of standard Java GUI code, and would have been confusing in the amount of detail if presented with Exhibit 6 (Program7.3a).

The animator produced in Exhibit 5 (Program7.4) is a large improvement over the one in Exhibit 9, but unfortunately it is not a final

Exhibit 5. Program7.4: Generic Animator with Control Panel

```
import java.awt.*;
import java.awt.event.*;
import java.util.*;
import javax.swing.*;

public class Animator extends JPanel implements Runnable {
  private Vector elementsToDraw = new Vector();
  private long sleepTime = 100;
  private boolean animatorStopped = true, firstTime = true;
  private ControlFrame controlFrame;
  private JFrame animFrame;

  /**
   * Constructor that creates the JFrame for the animator. Note
   * that the JFrame is shown in the show() method because this
   * starts the GUI thread. Starting the thread in the
   * constructor can lead to a race condition.
   */
  public Animator() {
    // Create the control Frame.
    controlFrame = new ControlFrame(this);

    // set up the frame to draw in.
    animFrame = new JFrame("Generic Animator");
    Container animContainer = animFrame.getContentPane();
    animContainer.add(this);
    animFrame.setSize(700, 450);
    animFrame.setLocation(0,100);
  }

  /**
   * setVisible is called to display or hide the animator. Note
   * that only display = true is implemented, and this function
   * only works at this point if it is called once. It is left
   * as an exercise to implement it correctly. If display =
   * false, the Control Thread must be suspended. If
   * display = true, the control thread should be started only
   * the first time; after that it should be unsuspended. This
   * can be accomplished by using control variables in the
   * paint method for Program7.4 and after and should not be
   * done using the suspend and resume methods.
   */
  public void setVisible(boolean display) {
    if (display = = true) {
      if (firstTime) {
        firstTime = false;

        // Show the control Frame
        controlFrame.setVisible(true);

        // Show the animator. This starts the GUI thread.
        animFrame.setVisible(true);

        // Put the animator in another thread so that the
        // calling object can continue.
        (new Thread(this)).start();
      }
    }
  }
```

(continued)

Exhibit 5. Program7.4 (Continued)

```
/**
 *  Thread that runs the animator. This thread sleeps for some
 *  amount of time specified by sleepTime, then calls repaint,
 *  which forces a call to the paint method, but in the GUI
 *  thread. Note that the animatorStopped button allows the
 *  animator to single step and pause the animation. The
 *  notify is done in the control frame from the button.
 */
public void run() {
  while (true) {
    try {
      synchronized(this) {
        if (animatorStopped = = true) {
          wait();
        }
      }
      if (animatorStopped ! = true)
        Thread.sleep(sleepTime);
    } catch (InterruptedException e) {
      System.out.println("Program Interrupted");
      System.exit(0);
    }
    repaint();
  }
}

/**
 *  The paint method redraws all the objects registered with
 *  this animator. It is run in the GUI thread. The repaint
 *  command causes this method to be called, and it passes the
 *  graphics object g to each of the registered objects to
 *  have them draw themselves.
 */
public void paint(Graphics g) {
  super.paint(g);
  Enumeration e = elementsToDraw.elements();
  while (e.hasMoreElements())
    ((Drawable) e.nextElement()).draw(g);
}

/**
 * addElement adds each drawable to the vector for use by the
 * DrawElements method.
 */
public void addDrawable(Drawable d) {
  elementsToDraw.addElement(d);
}

/**
 *  removeElement is used to remove drawables from the vector.
 */
public void removeDrawable(Drawable d) {
  elementsToDraw.removeElement(d);
}

/**
 *  This is an inner class which implements the control panel
 *  for the application. It is not important to the behavior
 *  of the animator component, which can be understood without
 *  understanding this control panel.
 *
```

(continued)

Exhibit 5. Program7.4 (Continued)

```
   * Note that we do not need to synchronize any of these
   * methods because the values they change can only be changed
   * in the GUI thread and are read only elsewhere, so no race
   * conditions exist.
   */
  private class ControlFrame {
    Animator ca;
    static final int RUNNING = 0;
    static final int WAITING = 1;
    int state = WAITING;
    JFrame controlFrame;

    public ControlFrame(Animator Parent) {
      ca = Parent;
      controlFrame = new JFrame("Controller");
      Container controlContainer = controlFrame.getContentPane
          ();
      controlContainer.setLayout(new FlowLayout());

      final JButton startButton = new JButton("Start");
        startButton.addActionListener(new ActionListener() {
        public void actionPerformed(ActionEvent e) {
          if (state = = RUNNING) {
            state = WAITING;
            startButton.setText("Start");
            ca.animatorStopped = true;
          }
          else {
            state = RUNNING;
            startButton.setText("Stop");
            synchronized (ca) {
              ca.animatorStopped = false;
              ca.notify();
            }
          }
        }
      });

      controlContainer.add(startButton);

      final JButton stepButton = new JButton("Step");
      stepButton.addActionListener(new ActionListener() {
        public void actionPerformed(ActionEvent e) {
          if (state = = RUNNING) {
            state = WAITING;
            startButton.setText("Start");
            ca.animatorStopped = true;

          }
          synchronized (ca) {
            ca.notify();
          }
        }
      });
      controlContainer.add(stepButton);
      JButton exitButton = new JButton("Exit");
      exitButton.addActionListener(new ActionListener() {
        public void actionPerformed(ActionEvent e) {
          System.exit(0);
        }
      });
      controlContainer.add(exitButton);
```

(continued)

Exhibit 5. Program7.4 (Continued)

```
      controlContainer.add(new Label("Animator Speed"));

      final JScrollBar speedControl = new JScrollBar(JScrollBar.
          HORIZONTAL, 500, 25, 100, 1000);
      speedControl.addAdjustmentListener(new AdjustmentListener
          () {
        public void adjustmentValueChanged(AdjustmentEvent e) {
          ca.sleepTime = 1000 - e.getValue();
        }
      });
      controlContainer.add(speedControl);

      controlFrame.setSize(500, 100);
    }

    public void setVisible(boolean show) {
      controlFrame.setVisible(show);
    }
  }
}
```

Exhibit 6. Program7.3a: The Drawable Interface

```
import java.awt.*;

/**
 *  Purpose: The Drawable interface allows objects to register
 *           with the animator. It defines one method, a draw
 *           method, that takes a single parameter, a Graphics
 *           object.
 */
interface Drawable {
  public void draw(Graphics g);
}
```

product because a race condition arises when adding or removing objects from the animator. This problem is explained in Section 7.5.4, and solved by implementing the Java Event Model for this animator in Section 7.6.

7.5.1 The Basic Design of the Animator

The first problem to be solved is creating a generic animator that can animate many objects of many different types. Chapter 5 showed that the correct way to do this in Java is to write components using interfaces; then an algorithm or component (in this case, an animator) can operate on any object that implements this interface. So, the first step in this process of writing a generic animator is to create an interface. For the animator, the interface created will be a Drawable,

Exhibit 7. Program7.3b: The Generic Animator

```
import java.awt.*;
import java.awt.event.*;
import java.util.*;
import javax.swing.*;

public final class Animator extends JPanel implements Runnable
{

  Vector elementsToDraw = new Vector();
  long sleepTime = 100;
  boolean animatorStopped = true, firstTime = true;
  JFrame animFrame;

  /**
   * Constructor that creates the JFrame for the animator. Note
   * that the JFrame is shown in the show() method because this
   * starts the GUI thread. Starting the thread in the
   * constructor can lead to a race condition.
   */
  public Animator() {
    animFrame = new JFrame("Generic Animator");
    Container animContainer = animFrame.getContentPane();
    animContainer.add(this);
    animFrame.setSize(700, 450);
    animFrame.setLocation(0,100);
  }

  /**
   * setVisible is called to display or hide the animator. Note
   * that only display = true is implemented, and this function
   * only works at this point if it is called once. It is left
   * as an exercise to implement it correctly. If display =
   * false, the Control Thread must be suspended. If
   * display = true, the control thread should be started only
   * the first time; after that it should be unsuspended. This
   * can be accomplished as using control variables in the
   * paint method for Program7.4 and after and should not be
   * done using the suspend and resume methods.
   */
  public void setVisible(boolean display) {
    if (display = = true) {
      if (firstTime) {
        firstTime = false;
        // Show the animator. This starts the GUI thread.
        animFrame.setVisible(true);

        // Put the animator in another thread so that the
        // calling object can continue.
        (new Thread(this)).start();
      }
    }
  }

  /** Thread that runs the animator. This thread sleeps for some
   * amount of time specified by sleepTime, then calls repaint,
   * which forces a call to the paint method, but in the GUI
   * thread. Note that the animatorStopped button allows the
   * animator to single step and pause the animation. The
   * notify is done in the control frame from the button.
   */
```

(continued)

Exhibit 7. Program7.3b (Continued)

```
  public void run() {
    while (true) {
      try {
        Thread.sleep(100);
      } catch (InterruptedException e) {
        System.out.println("Program Interrupted");
        System.exit(0);
      }
      repaint();
    }
  }

  /**
   * The paint method redraws all the objects registered with
   * this animator. It is run in the GUI thread. The repaint
   * command causes this to be called, and it passes the
   * graphics object g to each of the registered objects to
   * have them draw themselves.
   */
  public void paint(Graphics g) {
    super.paint(g);
    Enumeration e = elementsToDraw.elements();
    while (e.hasMoreElements())
      ((Drawable) e.nextElement()).draw(g);
  }

  /**
   * addElement adds each drawable to the vector for use by the
   * DrawElements method.
   */
  public void addDrawable(Drawable d) {
    elementsToDraw.addElement(d);
  }

  /**
   * removeElement is used to remove drawables from the vector.
   */
  public void removeDrawable(Drawable d) {
    elementsToDraw.removeElement(d);
  }
}
```

as shown in Exhibit 6 (Program7.3a). It has a single method, draw, which takes as a parameter an object of type Graphics.

This definition of the draw method is called with the Graphic object from the paint method in the animator. The animator is only responsible for handling repaint events and calling this draw method. Determining what to draw and where to draw it is the responsibility of the object being animated. So, if the Drawable implements a path and draws an image at the points given by the path on the Graphic object passed from the animator's paint method, it will in effect be animated by the animator.

The animator that uses this Drawable interface is shown in Exhibit 7 (Program7.3b). This animator is different from the animator in Exhibit 4 (Program7.2) in that it is not designed to implement as part of a single

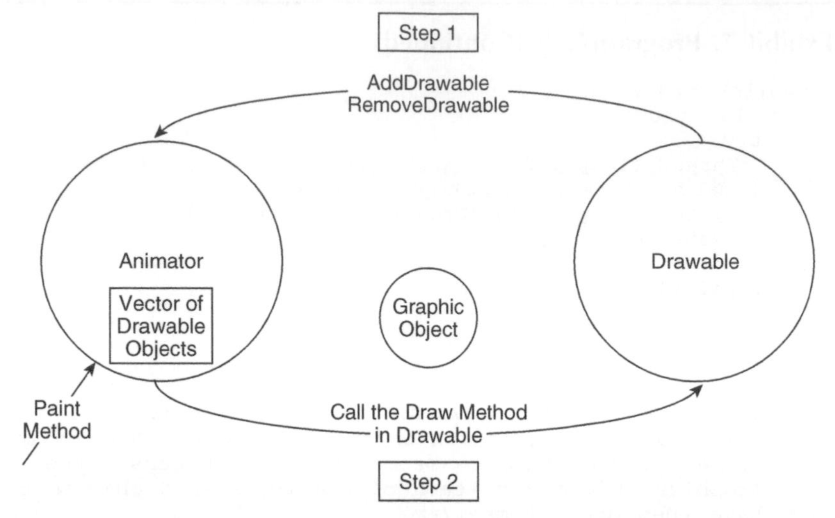

Exhibit 8. Deadlock in an Animator

program but is to be used generically in many different programs. The basic design is that objects that are to be animated declare that they are Drawable, or they have a draw method and can be drawn and used in the animation. These objects then register with the animator using the addDrawable method in the animator. If an object no longer wishes to be a part of the animation, it is passed to the removeDrawable method (see step 1 in Exhibit 8). The animator then has repaint events generated (see Section 7.5.2). When these repaint events occur, the animator calls the draw method in all the registered objects passing the Graphic object (see step 2 in Exhibit 8).

The animator implements the design in Exhibit 8 as follows. The animator contains a vector, called ElementsToDraw, which keeps track of objects that are to be drawn with the animator. When the addDrawable method is called, the Drawable object passed to it is added to the ElementsToDraw (thus being added to the animation), and when the removeDrawable method is called the object is removed (thus being removed from the animation). Each time a repaint event is scheduled, the paint method in the animator is called, and the paint method in turn calls the draw methods of all the objects that are registered with the animator (all objects in the ElementsToDraw vector). Each object draws on the Graphic object, and the result is that all the registered objects are displayed in the animator. The part of the paint method that allows Drawable objects to draw on the Graphics object is given below:

```
Enumeration e = elementsToDraw.elements();
while (e.hasMoreElements())
  ((Drawable) e.nextElement()).draw(g);
```

Note that each time paint is called (each 0.1 seconds) the draw methods of all registered elements are called.

To better understand how this works, consider Exhibit 9 (Program7.3c), which uses this animator. To use the animator, an instance of the Animator is first created, then the objects to be drawn as part of the animator are created and added to the animator. This is shown in the following five lines of code, which implement the heart of the MoveObjects program in Program7.3 (Exhibits 6 , 7, and 9):

```
Animator animator = new Animator();
MoveBall mb = new MoveBall(animator, MoveBall.UP, 1);
animator.add(mb);
MoveRect mr = new MoveRect(animator, MoveRect.DOWN, 2);
animator.add(mr);
```

The specific classes MoveBall and MoveRect implement the Drawable interface. So, when added to the animator (via the animator.add method), they are contained in the elementsToDraw vector and will have their draw methods called every 0.1 seconds. In their draw methods, they define a path to keep track of what to draw at what positions. Thus, every 0.1 seconds they draw on the animator's Graphics object, which is displayed on the terminal, giving the appearance of movement.

Exhibit 9 (Program7.3c) shows that the animator is generic in two ways. First, the animator is separated from the types of objects that can be used, as any object that implements Drawable can be used by the animator. Program7.3 (Exhibits 6, 7, and 9) could animate both Ball and Rect objects. Second, the animator is separate from the program that uses it, as any program can create an animator object and then add Drawable objects to it. This is a big advantage over Exhibit 4 (Program7.2), where the animator could only animate specific objects and need to be copied and modified to be used in other programs.

7.5.1.1 Extending the Class Vector

One final point must be considered in regard to the design of the generic animator shown in Exhibit 7 (Program7.3b). Some programmers would feel that the addDrawable and removeDrawable methods are redundant, as all they do is call the addElement and removeElement methods in the Vector class, and it would be better for the animator to extend the Vector class, thus allowing for reuse of all the methods in the Vector. However, the Java AWT indicates that this is not the way the implementers of the AWT chose to implement AWT components, such as Button with addActionListener or Textfields with addTextListener, which should make these programmers wonder why not. The reasons that extending class Vector is a bad idea are covered in more detail in Chapter 10; however, it can be pointed out here that one

Exhibit 9. Program7.3c: Program That Uses the Generic Animator

```
import java.awt.*;

public class MoveObjects {

  public static void main(String args[]) {
    Animator animator = new Animator();
    MoveBall mb = new MoveBall(MoveBall.UP, 1);
    animator.addDrawable(mb);
    MoveRect mr = new MoveRect(MoveRect.DOWN, 2);
    animator.addDrawable(mr);
    animator.setVisible(true);
  }
}

/**
 *  Purpose: This class implements a ball that moves itself on
 *           subsequent call to the draw method.
 */
class MoveBall implements Drawable {

  static final int UP = 1;
  static final int DOWN = 0;
  private int direction = DOWN;

  private Path myPath;
  private Point myPosition = new Point(10,10);
  private int myNumber;

  /**
   *  Constructor, simply save the initial values.
   */
  public MoveBall(int direction, int myNumber) {
    this.direction = direction;
    this.myNumber = myNumber;
  }

  /** Draw is called each time through the animator loop to draw
   *  the object. It uses the path to calculate the position of
   *  this object and then draws the object at that position.
   */
  public void draw(Graphics g) {
    if (myPath ! = null && myPath.hasMoreSteps())
      myPosition = myPath.nextPosition();
    else {
      // Get a random number of steps to make the balls move
      // at different speeds. Note there has to be at least
      // one step in each path, but for appearances we used at
      // least ten steps.
      int numberOfSteps = (int) (10.0 + (Math.random() * 100.0));

      if (direction = = DOWN) {
        myPath = new StraightLinePath(410, 410, 10, 10,
          numberOfSteps);
        myPosition = myPath.nextPosition();
        direction = UP;
      }
      else {
        myPath = new StraightLinePath(10, 10, 410, 410,
          numberOfSteps);
```

(continued)

Exhibit 9. Program7.3c (Continued)

```
        myPosition = myPath.nextPosition();
        direction = DOWN;
      }
    }
    g.setColor(Color.RED);
    g.fillOval((int)myPosition.getX(), (int)myPosition.getY(),
      15, 15);
    g.setColor(Color.BLACK);
    g.drawString("" + myNumber,
      (int)myPosition.getX()+3, (int)myPosition.getY()+12);
  }
}

/**
 * Purpose: This class implements a rectangle that moves
 *          itself on subsequent call to the draw method.
 */
class MoveRect implements Drawable {

  static final int UP = 1;
  static final int DOWN = 0;
  private int direction = DOWN;

  private Path myPath;
  private Point myPosition = new Point(10,10);
  private int myNumber;

  /**
   *Constructor simply saves the initial values.
   */
  public MoveRect(int direction, int myNumber) {
    this.direction = direction;
    this.myNumber = myNumber;
  }
  /**
   * Draw is called each time through the animator loop to draw
   * the object. It uses the path to calculate the position of
   * this object and then draws the object at that position.
   */
  public void draw(Graphics g) {
    if (myPath ! = null && myPath.hasMoreSteps())
      myPosition = myPath.nextPosition();
    else {

      // Get a random number of steps to make the balls move
      // at different speeds. Note there has to be at least
      // 1 step in each path, but for appearances we used at
      // least 10 steps.
      int numberOfSteps = (int) (10.0 + (Math.random() * 100.0));
      if (direction = = DOWN) {
        myPath = new StraightLinePath(410, 410, 10, 10,
            numberOfSteps);
        myPosition = myPath.nextPosition();
        direction = UP;
      }
      else {
        myPath = new StraightLinePath(10, 10, 410, 410,
            numberOfSteps);
```

(continued)

Exhibit 9. Program7.3c (Continued)

```
          myPosition = myPath.nextPosition();
          direction = DOWN;
        }
      }
      g.setColor(Color.YELLOW);
      g.fillRect((int)myPosition.getX(), (int)myPosition.getY(),
          15, 15);
      g.setColor(Color.BLACK);
      g.drawString("" + myNumber,
        (int)myPosition.getX()+3, (int)myPosition.getY()+12);
    }
  }
```

problem that makes this strategy unworkable is if class Vector is extended then the addElement call can take objects of any type, not just objects of classes implementing Drawable. Using the animator in Exhibit 7 (Program7.3b), if a programmer attempted to add an object that was not a Drawable, a compiler error would be generated. If, instead, the class Vector was extended, the adding of a non-Drawable object would not be caught until runtime when the JVM was attempting to cast the object in the paint method. Given a choice, it is always better to catch an error at compile time than runtime, so making the animator extend the class Vector is a bad solution.

7.5.2 How the Repaint Events Are Generated

This section explains in detail how the animator in Exhibit 7 (Program7.3b) actually generates the repaint events, thus creating the animation. This requires only about 25 lines of code but involves coordinating between three threads, two of them implicit, so it is important that the interactions be carefully considered and understood. The three threads are the main thread, which is started when the program is started; a GUI thread, which is started when the JFrame is created; and a thread started when the animator's setVisible method is called, which controls the repaint event and is called the control thread.

The Animator object is short but very complex because at some point in time each of the three threads can be executing in methods in the object. For example, the main thread runs the animator constructor when it first creates the animator. Once the animator is created, the main thread adds and removes objects from the animator by calling the addDrawable and removeDrawable methods, thus these methods are also run from the main thread. The GUI thread is running once the JFrame is created and made visible, and each time the JFrame is repainted the paint method of the animator is called by the GUI thread.

This is as expected because the paint method and any listener methods are always run in the GUI thread. Finally, the control thread started in the setVisible method starts in the run method for the animator object. Because it consists entirely of an infinite loop calling the Thread.sleep and repaint methods, it is always running in a method in the animator. So, at some point in time all three threads are executing in methods in the animator object.

The reason the control thread was added to the design is that it moves the sleep out of the paint method (thus, out of the GUI thread) and into a completely separate thread, thus allowing the GUI thread to still run and process events while the control loop is sleeping. Now the animator will work correctly when a control panel with scroll bar and buttons is added, because the control thread is sleeping and generating the repaint events, which allows the GUI thread to run and process events from the buttons and scrollbar in an expeditious manner.

The fact that multiple threads are running in the animator object can cause many problems to programmers who do not carefully consider how the threads in the program interact. For example, some programmers are so afraid of race conditions that they automatically synchronize all methods in an object. Doing so creates an immediate problem in this object, as synchronizing the run method causes the control thread to keep the object locked and does not allow the GUI thread or the main thread to ever execute calls in the animator. So, the question of which methods, or parts of methods, really must be synchronized must be examined carefully. As pointed out in Section 7.5.4, a race condition does exist in this component, and some form of locking needs to be added; however, unlike the programs in Chapter 3, the required synchronization must be more carefully considered and can become quite complex. That is why it is important for programmers to understand the issues involved and to choose the simplest means to coordinate programs that works effectively.

7.5.3 Adding the Component Controls

Now that the basic animator is in place, a control frame can be created to do such things as single stepping through the animation or controlling the animation speed. Because the entire control of the animator is in the run method for the Animator class, a controller can be created so that only two methods in the Animator class require minor modifications from Program7.5 (Exhibits 12 through 15). These modifications are in the constructor and the run method. The actual creation of the controls is put in a separate class named ControlFrame, and except for the variables animatorStopped and sleepTime it is completely isolated from the Animator Class.

The ControlFrame class is a standard Java GUI, so the issues involved in writing it are not really germane to the creation of the component. A more detailed explanation of how to implement a Java GUI can be found in any number of books on programming in Java. The only results from the ControlFrame are to set the sleepTime and animatorStopped variables. The sleepTime is the amount of time to wait between calls to repaint when the animator is running and thus controls how quickly the animation runs. The animatorStopped works by having the control thread call wait if animatorStopped is true, and the animation only continues when the ControlFrame calls notify to wake up the control thread. This allows the animation to be started and stopped, as well as single stepped.

The changes that need to be made in the Animator class are shown in Exhibit 5 (Program7.4). In the animator's constructor a Control Frame object is created. Also, in the run method the amount of time to sleep has been changed from a constant to a variable that can be set in the Control Frame. Also, a wait condition if the animatorStopped variable is true has been added; otherwise, the Animator class and the basic animator design are unchanged from the version shown in Exhibit 7 (Program7.3b). This version of the animator has the same external interface as Exhibit 7 (Program7.3b), so the same MoveObject program in Exhibit 9 (Program7.3c) can be run in the new version of the animator.

7.5.4 Minimalist Approach to Design

The design of the animator is minimalist in that the animator only creates and propagates the paint events. It does not include all the behavior needed to draw object and images nor is this behavior necessary to calculate and move objects contained in the animator. The fact that the behavior will be available is guaranteed by the Drawable interface; however, exactly how to implement that behavior is left up to the object to be drawn.

By using an interface and making the objects responsible for what and where to draw, the animator allows Drawable objects to do anything in their draw methods, from drawing stick figures using circles and lines to generating and displaying complex images; indeed, anything that can be done with a Graphics object can be displayed with this animator. The animator does not have to be extended to provide this functionality. This makes the animator move cohesive.

The use of the Drawable interface also allows the animated object to decide how to move. This means that if the object chooses not to use a path, or to use a complex path with a Bessel function or Spline Curve, the animator does not have to be modified to allow for this new movement behavior. Even complex behaviors, like balls bouncing off of each other or off the sides of the screen, can be implemented in the animated objects, and would not cause the animator to be modified in any way. This reduces the coupling between the animator and the objects that implement it.

This minimalist approach to implementing the animator is what makes it more cohesive and less tightly coupled to the program. This is important because it allows applications that use the animator to be designed to solve the problems they are intended to solve and not to follow rules imposed by the animator. In fact, entire applications written without considering how to animate them can have animation added as a feature, as shown in Chapter 8 when programs from Chapter 3 are animated. The animator can even be used, unmodified, with objects distributed on a network. Because all of the behavior of the objects is part of the application that uses the animator, and not built into the animator itself, the animator can be used with a wide variety of applications, making it a much more powerful component than its simple design might imply.

This is an important aspect of this design. Often programmers are tempted to make a component such as an animator a single, monolithic entity that implements all the behavior that is possible using that component. In this case, this would mean that the animator would not call draw methods in the objects that are animated, but instead would implement the mechanisms to draw the objects in the animator itself. Any other type of behavior, such as how the objects move or interact, would also be built into the animator. When this happens, large, complex components are created. A simple argument would suggest that these components are tightly coupled with the applications that use them, as much of the behavior required by the application is contained in the animator and not in the objects. Also, the cohesion of the animator is lost, as it now has to perform many duties other than calling draw methods in the using objects. So, a cursory argument would say a monolithic animator is not as good an option as the generic animator in Program7.4 (Exhibit 5). That said, anyone who has dealt with a large, complex system that tries to do anything should be able to appreciate the simplicity of the animator given in Exhibit 5 (Program7.4).

Not making the Animator a single, monolithic entity has a number of other advantages as well. First, the Animator is simple and thus easier to use, and it probably contains fewer errors. This is particularly important when using concurrency because programming with concurrency can have a number of unanticipated consequences. Second, the animator is more likely to be usable by other programs because much of the behavior is provided by the user program and not enforced by the animator, so an application can be written to the constraints of the application and the concurrency added as a separate feature by implementing a draw method in the object. Finally, because the Animator provides only the minimum functionality, new functionality (such as drawing shapes or images not originally envisioned when the animator was created) does not involve modifying a large, complex animator with all the version control, debugging, testing, and distribution problems doing so would entail. This allows the animator to be extended and used in situations beyond those it was originally envisioned to handle.

7.5.5 Race Condition in the Generic Animator

The generic animator in Exhibit 5 (Program7.4) is a big improvement over the animator in Exhibit 4 (Program7.2); however, it still has a problem that needs to be fixed: a race condition in the interaction between adding and removing objects from the elementsToDraw vector and the walking of elementsToDraw in the paint method to call each object's draw method. This race condition exists in spite of the fact that the Vector class that the elementsToDraw instantiates is synchronized completely (the results of running any method that modifies or uses data in the Vector will be in a synchronized block). In fact, each call to a method in the Vector is safe in that a call to addElement cannot be run at the same time as another call to removeElement. The possible race condition occurs when the Vector is assumed to be safe between calls, as when it is used in an enumeration in the paint method.

To see this race condition, assume that the paint method is currently calling each of the objects in the elementsToDraw. In the middle of the list, the GUI thread is suspended, and the main thread runs and adds or removes an object from the elementsToDraw. When the GUI thread later resumes, the item added or removed has shifted the elements in the elementsToDraw, and this can cause one of two problems. If the items are shifted down one element, it is possible that an object whose draw method has already been called will be called a second time. If the items have been shifted up, it is possible to skip the call to the draw method for an object. In either case, the result is incorrect. If an Iterator is used instead of an Enumeration, the program would throw a ConcurrentModificationException when this situation occurs; however, as stated in the API for an Iterator, this exception cannot be relied on, and even if it could be relied on it does nothing to help fix the problem that a Drawable object could be drawn twice or not at all. The animator has to be fixed to deal correctly with this problem.

One simple fix would be to simply synchronize all the methods that have access to the elementsToDraw vector. This would require that the addDrawable, removeDrawable, and paint methods be synchronized, which has two drawbacks. The first is that an addDrawable

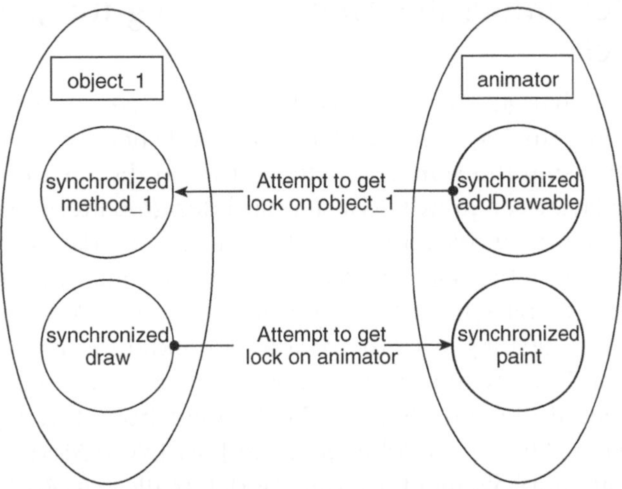

Exhibit 10. Design of the Generic Animator

or removeDrawable call should be quick, but if the calls to the draw methods of the elementsToDraw objects from the paint method are slow (for example, if the objects were to exist in a distributed computing environment), then the addDrawable and removeDrawable methods would have to wait, which would result in poor performance.

A more serious problem, however, is the possibility of deadlock. Exhibit 10 shows how this could occur. Assume that a Drawable object named object_1 exists, and it has two methods, method_1 and draw, both of which are synchronized. At some point earlier in the program, object_1 has registered with the animator using the addDrawable method and now wishes to remove itself from the animation by calling removeDrawable. The thread running in object_1's method_1 now has the lock on object_1 and is attempting to obtain the lock on the animator. At the same time, a repaint event has occurred, and the paint method in the animator is being run. The GUI thread in paint now has the lock on the animator and is attempting to obtain the lock on object_1's draw method. Obviously, neither can proceed, and deadlock has occurred.

Because the time scale for the animator is so large, on the order of milliseconds, it is likely that it will run for a very long time before this problem occurs, but the problem is still there and could arise at any time, often at a most unfortunate time. These types of problems are extremely subtle and difficult to reason through, and nearly impossible to test for and debug after the fact; therefore, it is important to use a pattern to implement the type of event dispatching that is known to be correct. This can be done using the Java Event Model, which is applied to the animator in Section 7.6 to produce an animator that is correct.

7.6 Implementing the Animator Using the Java Event Model

We will now change the Animator to fix the race condition error in Exhibit 5 (Program7.4). This will be accomplished by implementing the Animator using the standard pattern used in the Java Event Model. Because the Java Event Model is a standard design pattern, the animator can be rewritten to work and to conform to its standards. Most of the changes are cosmetic, such as naming conventions and conventions on the objects to pass from the component to the interface; however, the approach to dealing with the deadlock condition introduced at the end of Section 7.5.4, while short, is substantive. Section 7.6.1 introduces the Java Event Model, and Section 7.6.2 shows how it is implemented in the animator. After the workings of the Java Event Model have been presented, an improvement to the model (called a *MultiCaster*) is provided in Section 7.7.

7.6.1 Java Event Model

The Java Event Model is a standard pattern used to implement dispatching of events. It is used in the Java AWT to implement components such as Buttons, and TextFields to connect the component with the objects that process the events for those components. Most programmers have used the Java Event Model at some point. For example, every time an ActionListener is added to a Button the Java Event Model is used to call the actionPerformed method when that Button is pressed. But, while most programmers have used the Java Event Model, many do not know how it works. This chapter explains how to implement it.

The Java Event Model is shown in Exhibit 11. What is striking is how similar diagrams in Figures 7.1 and 7.3 are. This similarity is intentional, as the Java Event Model is very similar to the structure of calling Drawable objects in the animator of Exhibit 5 (Program7.4). In fact, the only major differences between the Java Event Model and the animator in Exhibit 5 (Program7.4) are that the Java Event Model has a much more formal definition and the loop that sends the events to the listening objects in the Java Event Model fixes the race condition that exists in the animator. The Java Event Model is described in this section, using the JButton class to describe how it works. Section 7.6.2 then shows how to use it to implement the animator.

The Java Event consists of three parts: (1) an event source, which generates the events based on some stimulus from an external source; (2) a listener, which registers to receive the events when they occur; and (3) an event state object, which passes information about the event from the Event Source to the Listener. This relationship is illustrated in Exhibit 11.

One important aspect of the Java Event Model is the strict conventions for naming of the parts of the model. The type of event (for

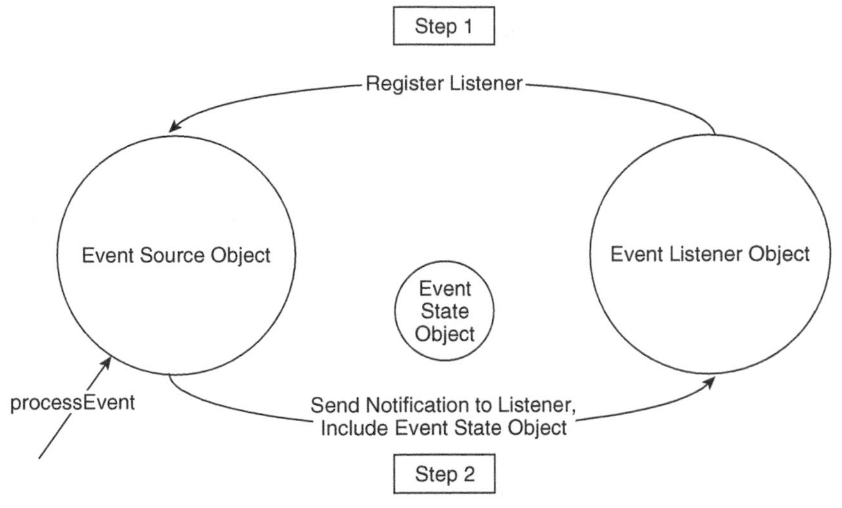

Exhibit 11. Java Event Model

example, an action for the JButton) forms the basis for names of the parts of the model. The source of the events would be the JButton and is called the *event source object*. The *listener* interface that will receive the event must be named for the type of event followed by the qualifier "Listener." The JButton uses action events, so the listener is named "ActionListener." Objects that implement the listener interface are called *event listener objects*. When an event source sends an event to the listener by calling the listener's method, it sends an object containing information about the event, called an *event state object*. The event state object passed from the event source to the Listener objects must be named for the type of event followed by the qualifier "Event" — for the JButton, an "ActionEvent."

The methods in the event source (JButton) that add and remove the listeners must be the name of the listener with the prefixes "add" and "remove," as in addActionListener and removeActionListener for the JButton. If you look at the Java AWT, you will find that these conventions are followed and allow a programmer to quickly identify the purpose of each of these classes.

The parts of the Java Event model for the JButton are shown in the following code fragments. First, the listener and even class are defined, as shown in step 1.

- *Step 1.* Definition of listener interface and event object:

```
public class ActionEvent extend java.util.Event {
  public ActionEvent(Object source) {
    super(source);
  }
}
```

```
public interface ActionListener extends java.util.EventListener {
  public void actionPerformed(ActionEvent e) {
  }
}
```

Note that other fields and information are defined in ActionEvent, but the information shown in step 1 is the basic information needed to define an event. Once the listener interface and event class are defined, the event source can be written. There are two parts to the event source object. The first allows listeners objects to register with the source object using add and remove methods. For an ActionListener, the code would look as follows:

- *Step 2.* Registering objects with the event source:

```
Private Vector actionListeners;
public synchronized void addActionListener(ActionListener al) {
  actionListeners.addElement(al);
}
public synchronized void removeActionListener(ActionListener al) {
  actionListeners.removeElement(al);
}
```

Note that both of these routines are synchronized and so protect access to the ActionListeners Vector.

When an event occurs, normally from an external source, the processEvent method of the event source is called. The processEvent method creates an event state object and sends the event to all registered listeners by calling the appropriate method in the listener (step 2). For the JButton, this occurs when the mouse is clicked while in the button, causing the GUI thread to call the processEvent method for the JButton. The code to perform this dispatching action is given below.

- *Step 3.* Dispatching the event:

```
public void processEvent() {
  ActionEvent ae = new ActionEvent(this);// create event
  synchronized {// clone Vector
    Vector v = actionListeners.clone();
  }
  Enumeration e = v.elements();
  // dispatch event
  while(e.hasMoreElements()) {
    ((ActionListener)(e.nextElement())).actionPerformed(ae);
  }
}
```

This is very similar to the animator paint method except that the addActionListener and removeActionListener calls are synchronized, and the vector of objects to send the event to has been cloned. This cloning of the vector is significant because it provides the mechanism for ensuring that the dispatching of events is safe and cannot result in deadlock.

Remember that the original problem with dispatching events is that the vector of listeners can be modified while the events are being dispatched. A simple solution to prevent the vector from being modified while the events are being dispatched is to synchronize all the methods that access the vector of listeners, but this solution can result in deadlock. In fact, any solution that tries to synchronize all the methods will never work.

Fortunately, trying to find a way to synchronize all the methods accessing the vector of listeners is not the problem that has to be solved; rather, we want to provide the dispatching function with a vector that cannot be changed (i.e., is *immutable*) while it is dispatching the events. The Java Event Model does this by creating a local copy of the vector in variable *v* that is not accessible outside of this method (because it is on the program stack, it is unique to this thread). This vector is never changed in the method and hence is immutable. Because this vector never changes it cannot result in a listener being called twice or not at all. Further, this thread must be synchronized only for the length of time it takes to clone the vector to ensure that an add or remove is not running while the copy is being made. Now the thread processing the event does not hold the lock on the event source object when calling the listener object and circular deadlock is not possible, so the solution is safe.

It should be noted that the code to process an event presented here is from the Java Beans Specification; however, the actual solution implemented in the Java AWT to make an immutable collection of listeners is not the same as presented here. The actual solution that is used (a MultiCaster object) still relies on the fact that an immutable collection used in dispatching the events is separate from the collection used when adding and removing items, thus building on the ideas presented here (see Section 7.7). The animator presented here is correct, however, and is much easier to understand, so it is used throughout the remainder of the text.

7.6.2 Implementing the Corrected Animator Component

The Java Event Model just explained is now used to implement the animator as a component that obeys all of the rules of the Java Event Model. First, the interface Drawable does not follow the standards and is renamed a DrawListener. The name of the method that is called (the draw method) is fine, but the parameter to it must be an Event. Finally, any listeners defined in the Java Event Model must extend the java.util.EventListener interface; therefore, the DrawListener interface is created to extend java.util.EventListener and has a draw method that takes a parameter of a DrawEvent. Exhibit 12 (Program7.5a) shows

Exhibit 12. Program7.5a: DrawListener Class

```
import java.util.EventListener;

public interface DrawListener extends java.util.EventListener {
  public void draw(DrawEvent e);
}
```

the DrawListener class. Note that java.util.EventListener is a tag interface and does not have any methods, much like the Serializable interface.

Next in the Java Event Model, all event classes must extend the class java.util.Event and must have a constructor that takes an object as a parameter and passes that object to its super class. The object that is passed is the event source object, so when an event is created its constructor must be called with the "this" object as a parameter. In the case of the DrawEvent object, another variable is also needed, the Graphics object, so it is included in the object and set from a parameter in the constructor. Because this Graphics object is now a part of the event, a getGraphics method is included to retrieve the object in the DrawListeners draw method. Note that no setGraphics method is included because the Graphics object can only be set in the constructor and cannot be changed after the DrawEvent is constructed (the event object is immutable). Because the Graphic object is no longer a parameter to the draw method in the DrawListeners, the draw methods must retrieve it before they can use it. So, the start of all draw methods will now have code to retrieve the Graphic:

```
public void draw(DrawEvent de) {
  Graphics g = de.getGraphics();
}
```

The last changes to the animator to implement the Java Event Model are to synchronize the addDrawListener and removeDrawListener methods and to implement the correct the logic in the paint method given in Section 7.6.1. This results in the final Animator code given in Program7.5 (Exhibits 12 through 15).

Exhibit 15 (Program7.5d) uses this animator. Note that it is similar to Exhibit 15 (Program7.5d), except for such things as naming conventions and the need to get the Graphics object from the event and not the parameter. Often, programmers are intimidated by high concepts such as the Java Event Model and feel that they are unapproachable; however, if you can understand the operation of the animator you should be able to understand the Java Event Model.

One other caveat must be noted regarding the objects that are to be added to the animator. As is shown in Chapter 8, it is often necessary to save the animator with the object to be animated so that it can add and remove itself as the animation is run. This is particularly useful when using threads or other concurrent programming techniques where

Exhibit 13. Program7.5b: DrawEvent Class

```
import java.util.*;
import java.awt.*;

public class DrawEvent extends EventObject {
  Graphics myGraphics;

  public DrawEvent(Object source, Graphics graphics) {
    super(source);
    myGraphics = graphics;
  }

  public Graphics getGraphics() {
    return myGraphics;
  }
}
```

the object is responsible for its own behavior. When doing this, one might be tempted to allow the object to register itself with the animator in the constructor, such as in the following MoveBall constructor:

```
public MoveBall(Animator animator, int direction, int myNumber) {
  this.animator = animator;
  animator.addDrawListener(this);
  this.direction = direction;
  this.myNumber = myNumber;
}
```

The code in this constructor is unsafe as it contains a race condition. The race condition exists because the object is added to the animator at the beginning of the constructor, allowing the GUI thread to possibly call the draw method on this object before the constructor for the object has completed the constructor code. Information that might be needed by the animator, such as the variable's direction or myNumber, might not at that point be initialized, which could cause the program to fail. This problem becomes even more buried if the class is extended, in which case the child's constructor will have called the parent's constructor and been added to the animator without the child even being aware of the possible race condition. This situation is dangerous and will lead to a general rule that anything that can start or use external threads should be avoided in constructors. In the case of the animator, it is always better if the object is added to the animator outside of the constructor, either in the main, as shown in Exhibit 15 (Program7.5d), or in the run method in a thread.

7.7 Event Multicaster

The animator implemented in Exhibit 14 (Program7.5c) is correct but can be optimized greatly. The cloning of a vector is a potentially expensive operation, and being called in the dispatch method ensures

Exhibit 14. Program7.5c: Animator Class

```
import java.awt.*;
import java.awt.event.*;
import java.util.*;
import javax.swing.*;

/**
 * Animator simply creates all the objects in this project, and
 * then goes into an infinite loop (here only to 300) that
 * waits some small period of time and then redraws all of
 * the objects that have registered themselves with the
 * DrawTable.
 */

public class Animator extends JPanel implements Runnable {
  private Vector elementsToDraw = new Vector();
  private long sleepTime = 100;
  boolean animatorStopped = true, firstTime = true;
  ControlFrame controlFrame;
  JFrame animFrame;
  /**
   * Constructor that creates the JFrame for the animator. Note
   * that the JFrame is shown in the show() method because this
   * starts the GUI thread. Starting the thread in the
   * constructor can lead to a race condition.
   */
  public Animator() {
    // Create the control Frame.
  controlFrame = new ControlFrame(this);

    // set up the frame to draw in.
    animFrame = new JFrame("Generic Animator");
    Container animContainer = animFrame.getContentPane();
    animContainer.add(this);
    animFrame.setSize(700, 450);
    animFrame.setLocation(0,100);
  }

  /**
   * setVisible is called to display or hide the animator. Note
   * that only display = true is implemented, and this function
   * only works at this point if it is called once. It is left
   * as an exercise to implement it correctly. If display =
   * false, the Control Thread must be suspended. If
   * display = true, the control thread should be started only
   * the first time; after that it should be unsuspended. This
   * can be accomplished by using control variables in the
   * paint method for Program7.4 and after and should not be
   * done using the suspend and resume methods.
   */
  public void setVisible(boolean display) {
    if (display = = true) {
      if (firstTime) {
        firstTime = false;

        // Show the control Frame
        controlFrame.setVisible(true);
        // Show the animator. This starts the GUI thread.
        animFrame.setVisible(true);
```

(continued)

Exhibit 14. Program7.5c (Continued)

```
      // Put the animator in another thread so that the
      // calling object can continue.
      (new Thread(this)).start();
    }
  }
}

/**
 *  Thread that runs the animator. This thread sleeps for some
 *  amount of time specified by sleepTime, then calls repaint,
 *  which forces a call to the paint method, but in the GUI
 *  thread. Note that the animatorStopped button allows the
 *  animator to single step and pause the animation. The
 *  notify is done in the control frame from the button.
 */

public void run() {
  while (true) {
    try {
      synchronized(this) {
        if (animatorStopped = = true) {
          wait();
        }
      }
      if (animatorStopped ! = true)
        Thread.sleep(sleepTime);
    } catch (InterruptedException e) {
      System.out.println("Program Interrupted");
      System.exit(0);
    }
    repaint();
  }
}

/**
 *  The paint method is run in the GUI thread. The repaint
// command causes this to be called, and it passes the
// graphics object g to each of the registered objects to
// have them draw themselves.
 */
public void paint(Graphics g) {
  Vector v;
  synchronized(this) {
    v = (Vector) elementsToDraw.clone();
  }

  super.paint(g);
  DrawEvent de = new DrawEvent(this, g);
  Enumeration e - v.elements();
  while (e.hasMoreElements())
    ((DrawListener) e.nextElement()).draw(de);
}

/**
 *  addElement adds each drawable to the vector for use by
 *  the DrawElements method. You need to write this method.
 */
```

(continued)

Exhibit 14. Program7.5c (Continued)

```
public synchronized void addDrawListener(DrawListener d) {
  elementsToDraw.addElement(d);
}

/**
 *  removeElement is used to remove drawables from the vector.
 *  While not needed to make the animator work, you need to
 *  implement this method for the project.
 */
public synchronized void removeDrawListener(DrawListener d) {
  elementsToDraw.removeElement(d);
}

/**
 *  This is an inner class that implements the control panel
 *  for the application. It is not important to the behavior
 *  of the animator component, which can be understood without
 *  understanding this control panel.
 *
 *  Note that we do not need to synchronize any of these
 *  methods because the values they change can only be changed
 *  in the GUI thread and are read only elsewhere, so no race
 *  conditions exist.
 */
private class ControlFrame {
  Animator ca;
  static final int RUNNING = 0;
  static final int WAITING = 1;
  int state = WAITING;
  JFrame controlFrame = new JFrame("Controller");

  public ControlFrame(Animator Parent) {
    ca = Parent;
    controlFrame = new JFrame("Controller");
    Container controlContainer = controlFrame.getContentPane
        ();

    controlContainer.setLayout(new FlowLayout());
    final JButton startButton = new JButton("Start");
      startButton.addActionListener(new ActionListener() {
      public void actionPerformed(ActionEvent e) {
        if (state = = RUNNING) {
          state = WAITING;
          startButton.setText("Start");
          ca.animatorStopped = true;
        }
        else {
          state = RUNNING;
          startButton.setText("Stop");
          synchronized (ca) {
            ca.animatorStopped = false;
            ca.notify();
          }
        }
      }
    });
    controlContainer.add(startButton);

    final JButton stepButton = new JButton("Step");
```

(continued)

Exhibit 14. Program7.5c (Continued)

```
      stepButton.addActionListener(new ActionListener() {
        public void actionPerformed(ActionEvent e) {
          if (state = = RUNNING) {
            state = WAITING;
            startButton.setText("Start");
            ca.animatorStopped = true;
          }
          synchronized (ca) {
            ca.notify();
          }
        }
      });
      controlContainer.add(stepButton);

      JButton exitButton = new JButton("Exit");
      exitButton.addActionListener(new ActionListener() {
        public void actionPerformed(ActionEvent e) {
          System.exit(0);
        }
      });
      controlContainer.add(exitButton);

      controlContainer.add(new Label("Animator Speed"));

      final JScrollBar speedControl = new JScrollBar(JScrollBar.
          HORIZONTAL, 500, 25, 100, 1000);
      speedControl.addAdjustmentListener(new AdjustmentListener
          () {
        public void adjustmentValueChanged(AdjustmentEvent e) {
          ca.sleepTime = 1000 - e.getValue();
        }
      });
      controlContainer.add(speedControl);

      controlFrame.setSize(500, 100);
    }

    public void setVisible(boolean show) {
      controlFrame.setVisible(show);
    }
  }
}
```

that it is called often. Also, the use of the vector requires the vector object's lock to be obtained on each call to a vector method, even though the vector is encapsulated in the source object and so is safe even without holding the object lock. It would be much faster if we had some way to decrease the number of times the vector needed to be cloned and handled. The key to doing this is to remember that the reason for the vector being cloned was to create an immutable vector for the dispatcher method to use. So, what is needed is to create the immutable vector in the add and remove methods when an object is added or removed from the vector and not in the dispatch method, where it is created each time an event is dispatched. Because objects are added and removed much less frequently than they are dispatched, the potential savings in computer resources could be quite large.

Exhibit 15. Program7.5d: MoveObjects Program with the Corrected Animator Component

```
import java.awt.*;

public class MoveObjects {

  public static void main(String args[]) {
    Animator animator = new Animator();
    MoveBall mb = new MoveBall(MoveBall.UP, 1);
    animator.addDrawListener(mb);
    MoveRect mr = new MoveRect(MoveRect.DOWN, 2);
    animator.addDrawListener(mr);
    animator.setVisible(true);
  }
}

// Two classes, MoveBall and MoveRect, are almost exactly the same.
// The constructor adds them to the animator, and the draw handles
// the path on which to move them and the drawing of them.
//

class MoveBall implements DrawListener {

  static final int UP = 1;
  static final int DOWN = 0;
  private int direction = DOWN;

  private Path myPath;
  private Point myPosition = new Point(10,10);
  private int myNumber;

  /**
   * Constructor - Simply register myself with the animator.
   */
  public MoveBall(int direction, int myNumber) {
    this.direction = direction;
    this.myNumber = myNumber;
  }

  /**
   *  Draw is called each time through the animator loop to draw
   *  the object. It simply uses the path to calculate the
   *  position of this object and then draws itself at that
   *  position.
   */

  public void draw(DrawEvent de) {
    Graphics g = de.getGraphics();
    if (myPath ! = null && myPath.hasMoreSteps())
      myPosition = myPath.nextPosition();
    else {
      // Get a random number of steps to make the balls move at
      // different speeds. Note that there has to be at least one
      // step in each path, but for appearances we used at least
      // ten steps.
      int numberOfSteps = (int) (10.0 + (Math.random() * 100.0));

      if (direction = = DOWN) {
        myPath = new StraightLinePath(410, 410, 10, 10,
            numberOfSteps);
```

(continued)

Exhibit 15. Program7.5d (Continued)

```
        myPosition = myPath.nextPosition();
        direction = UP;
      }
      else {
        myPath = new StraightLinePath(10, 10, 410, 410,
            numberOfSteps);
        myPosition = myPath.nextPosition();
        direction = DOWN;
      }
    }
    g.setColor(Color.RED);
    g.fillOval((int)myPosition.getX(), (int)myPosition.getY(),
        15, 15);
    g.setColor(Color.BLACK);
    g.drawString("" + myNumber,
      (int)myPosition.getX()+3, (int)myPosition.getY()+12);
  }
}

class MoveRect implements DrawListener {

  static final int UP = 1;
  static final int DOWN = 0;
  private int direction = DOWN;

  private Path myPath;
  private Point myPosition = new Point(10,10);
  private int myNumber;

  /**
   * Constructor - Simply register myself with the animator.
   */
  public MoveRect(int direction, int myNumber) {
    this.direction = direction;
    this.myNumber = myNumber;
  }
  /**
   *  Draw is called each time through the animator loop to draw
   *  the object. It simply uses the path to calculate the
   *  position of this object and then draws itself at that
   *  position.
   */
  public void draw(DrawEvent de) {
    Graphics g = de.getGraphics();
    if (myPath ! = null && myPath.hasMoreSteps())
      myPosition = myPath.nextPosition();
    else {
      // Get a random number of steps to make the balls move at
      // different speeds. Note that there has to be at least one step
      // step in each path, but for appearances we used at least
      // ten steps.
      int numberOfSteps = (int) (10.0 + (Math.random() *
          100.0));

      if (direction = = DOWN) {
        myPath = new StraightLinePath(410, 410, 10, 10,
            numberOfSteps);
        myPosition = myPath.nextPosition();
        direction = UP;
      }
```

(continued)

Exhibit 15. Program7.5d (Continued)

```
        else {
          myPath = new StraightLinePath(10, 10, 410, 410,
            numberOfSteps);
          myPosition = myPath.nextPosition();
          direction = DOWN;
        }
      }
      g.setColor(Color.YELLOW);
      g.fillRect((int)myPosition.getX(), (int)myPosition.getY(),
         15, 15);
      g.setColor(Color.BLACK);
      g.drawString("" + myNumber,
        (int)myPosition.getX()+3, (int)myPosition.getY()+12);
    }
  }
```

The way this is done in the Java AWT is through a class called AWTEventMulticaster, so the generic application of this technique will be called a Multicaster in this discussion. An example of a DrawEventMulticaster in the animator is given in Exhibit 16 (Program7.6a) and is used in Exhibit 17 (Program7.6b). It works because the addDrawListener and removeDrawListener methods no longer modify the elementsToDraw vector, but instead replace the DrawListener DrawEventMulticaster each time an element is added or removed. The Iterator created in the animator's paint method points to the original DrawEventMulticaster, not the new one, so a change to the DrawListener variable does not change the Iterator used and so does not affect the dispatching of events. This programming is now safe and much more efficient than the event dispatching in Exhibit 14 (Program7.5c).

7.8 Further Reading

For readers who are not familiar with programming using the Java GUI, any number of good books are available on the subject (see, for example, [VAN01] or [HOR02]). A trip to the local book store or visiting a Web bookseller will turn up many good books on GUI programming in Java. For more information on animation, most books on OOP (such as [BUD00]) include sections on animation. For readers who are interested in problems associated with using GUI threads, the article by Kann [KAN01] looks at some of the problems. For more information about the Java Event Model, and Java Beans in general, the Java Beans Specification [SUN96] is probably the best source. Readers who want more specific information should consult, for example, the books by Englander [ENG97] or van der Veer [VAN97]. Information on the Java AWT and Java Collection classes is available at the Sun Web site [SUN02c].

Exhibit 16. Program7.6a: DrawEventMulticaster

```
import java.util.*;
public class DrawEventMulticaster implements DrawListener {
  ArrayList elementsToDraw = new ArrayList();
  protected DrawEventMulticaster(DrawListener a, DrawListener b)
      {
    if (a ! = null) {
      if (a instanceof DrawEventMulticaster) {
        elementsToDraw.addAll(((DrawEventMulticaster)a).
          elementsToDraw);
      }
      else {
        elementsToDraw.add(a);
      }
    }

    if (b ! = null) {
      if (b instanceof Collection) {
        elementsToDraw.addAll((Collection)b);
      }
      else {
        elementsToDraw.add(b);
      }
    }
  }

  public static DrawListener add(DrawListener a, DrawListener b)
      {
    return new DrawEventMulticaster(a,b);
  }

  public static DrawListener remove(DrawListener a, DrawListener b)
      {
    DrawEventMulticaster dem = new DrawEventMulticaster(a,
      null);
    (dem.elementsToDraw).remove(b);
    return dem;
  }

  public void draw(DrawEvent e) {
    if (elementsToDraw ! = null) {
      Iterator i = elementsToDraw.iterator();
      while (i.hasNext()) {
        DrawListener dl = (DrawListener)i.next();
        dl.draw(e);
      }
    }
  }
}
```

Exhibit 17. Program7.6b: Animator Using the DrawEventMulticaster

```
import java.awt.*;
import java.awt.event.*;
import java.util.*;
import javax.swing.*;

/**
 * Animator simply creates all the objects in this project and
 * then goes into an infinite loop (here only to 300) that
 * waits some small period of time and then redraws all of the
 * objects that have registered themselves with the DrawTable.
 */

public class Animator extends JPanel implements Runnable {

  DrawListener drawListener = null;
  long sleepTime = 100;
  boolean animatorStopped = true, firstTime = true;
  ControlFrame controlFrame;
  JFrame animFrame;

  /**
   * Constructor that creates the JFrame for the animator. Note
   * that the JFrame is shown in the show() method because this
   * starts the GUI thread. Starting the thread in the
   * constructor can lead to a race condition.
   */
  public Animator() {
    // Create the control Frame.
    controlFrame = new ControlFrame(this);

    // Set up the frame to draw in.
    animFrame = new JFrame("Generic Animator");
    Container animContainer = animFrame.getContentPane();
    animContainer.add(this);
    animFrame.setSize(700, 450);
    animFrame.setLocation(0,100);
  }

  /**
   * setVisible is called to display or hide the animator. Note
   * that only display = true is implemented, and this function
   * only works at this point if it is called once. It is left
   * as an exercise to implement it correctly. If display =
   * false, the Control Thread must be suspended. If
   * display = true, the control thread should be started only
   * the first time; after that it should be unsuspended. This
   * can be accomplished as using control variables in the
   * paint method for Program7.4 and after and should not be
   * done using the suspend and resume methods.
   */
  public void setVisible(boolean display) {
    if (display = = true) {
      if (firstTime) {
        firstTime = false;
```

(continued)

Exhibit 17. Program7.6b (Continued)

```
      // Show the control Frame
      controlFrame.setVisible(true);
      // Show the animator. This starts the GUI thread.
      animFrame.setVisible(true);
      // Put the animator in another thread so that the
      // calling object can continue.
      (new Thread(this)).start();
    }
  }
}

/**
 * Thread that runs the animator. This thread sleeps for some
 * amount of time specified by sleepTime, then calls repaint,
 * which forces a call to the paint method, but in the GUI
 * thread. Note that the animatorStopped button allows the
 * animator to single step and pause the animation. The
 * notify is done in the control frame from the button.
 */

public void run() {
  while (true) {
    try {
      synchronized(this) {
        if (animatorStopped = = true) {
          wait();
        }
      }
      if (animatorStopped ! = true)
        Thread.sleep(sleepTime);
    } catch (InterruptedException e) {
      System.out.println("Program Interrupted");
      System.exit(0);
    }
    repaint();
  }
}

/** The paint method is run in the GUI thread. The repaint
// command causes this to be called, and it passes the
// graphics object g to each of the registered objects to
// have them draw themselves.
*/
public void paint(Graphics g) {
  super.paint(g);
  DrawEvent de = new DrawEvent(this, g);
  if (drawListener ! = null)
    drawListener.draw(de);
}

/**
 * addElement adds each drawable to the vector for use by the
 * DrawElements method. You need to write this method.
 */
public synchronized void addDrawListener(DrawListener d) {
  drawListener = DrawEventMulticaster.add(drawListener, d) ;
}
```

(continued)

Exhibit 17. Program7.6b (Continued)

```
  /**
   * removeElement is used to remove drawables from the vector.
   * While not needed to make the animator work, you need to
   * implement this method for the project.
   */
  public synchronized void removeDrawListener(DrawListener d) {
    drawListener = DrawEventMulticaster.remove(drawListener, d)
        ;
  }

  /**
   * This is an inner class that implements the control panel
   * for the application. It is not important to the behavior
   * of the animator component, which can be understood without
   * understanding this control panel.
   */
  private class ControlFrame {
    Animator ca;
    static final int RUNNING = 0;
    static final int WAITING = 1;
    int state = WAITING;
    JFrame controlFrame;

    public ControlFrame(Animator Parent) {
      ca = Parent;
      controlFrame = new JFrame("Controller");
      Container controlContainer = controlFrame.getContent-
Pane();

      controlContainer.setLayout(new FlowLayout());

      final JButton startButton = new JButton("Start");
        startButton.addActionListener(new ActionListener() {
        public void actionPerformed(ActionEvent e) {
          if (state = = RUNNING) {
            state = WAITING;
            startButton.setText("Start");
            ca.animatorStopped = true;
          }
          else {
            state = RUNNING;
            startButton.setText("Stop");
            synchronized (ca) {
              ca.animatorStopped = false;
              ca.notify();
            }
          }
        }
      });
      controlContainer.add(startButton);

      final JButton stepButton = new JButton("Step");
      stepButton.addActionListener(new ActionListener() {
        public void actionPerformed(ActionEvent e) {
          if (state = = RUNNING) {
            state = WAITING;
            startButton.setText("Start");
            ca.animatorStopped = true;
          }
```

(continued)

Exhibit 17. Program7.6b (Continued)

```
          synchronized(ca) {
            ca.notify();
          }
        }
      });
      controlContainer.add(stepButton);

      JButton exitButton = new JButton("Exit");
      exitButton.addActionListener(new ActionListener() {
        public void actionPerformed(ActionEvent e) {
          System.exit(0);
        }
      });
      controlContainer.add(exitButton);

      controlContainer.add(new Label("Animator Speed"));

      final JScrollBar speedControl = new JScrollBar(JScroll-
Bar.
          HORIZONTAL, 500, 25, 100, 1000);
      speedControl.addAdjustmentListener(new AdjustmentLis-
tener
          () {
        public void adjustmentValueChanged(AdjustmentEvent e) {
          ca.sleepTime = 1000 - e.getValue();
        }
      });
      controlContainer.add(speedControl);

      controlFrame.setSize(500, 100);
    }

    public void setVisible(boolean show) {
      controlFrame.setVisible(show);
    }
  }
}
```

7.9 Problems

1. Use the animator of Program7.5 (Exhibits 12 through 15) to animate an image such as a ".tiff" file. To do this, get an instance of the Toolkit and use the getImage method of the Toolkit class to read the image from a file. Use the Graphic drawImage method to draw it to the screen.
2. Use the Generic Animator of Program7.5 (Exhibits 12 through 15) to draw an image of a person. Create the impression of a person walking by cycling through images of a person in different stages of walking.
3. Change the MoveBall program so that the two balls bounce off each other when they meet. This would cause Ball 1 to stay in the upper left of the screen and Ball 2 to stay in the lower right.

Add more balls and have them interact. You do not need to (and should not) modify the Animator to do this.

4. Prove by induction that the interactions between the buttons in the ControlFrame and the Animator control loop are safe. What anomalies in the behavior exist? Do you think they would affect the animator?
5. Modify the animator component so that if either the control frame or animation frame is closed the program exits.
6. Can the paint method in the animator ever be running twice at the same time? Why or why not?
7. Write a program that creates two different animators to animate the balls in different frames. Are these two animations concurrent?
8. Write a program that puts five balls on the screen and moves them.
9. Extend the Path class so that it will handle Bessel functions and Spline Curves.
10. Explain why a race condition exists in Exhibit 5 (Program7.4).
11. Explain why synchronizing the add<Listener>, remove<Listener>, and processEvent methods to remove the race condition can result in deadlock.
12. The collection classes that were introduced in JDK1.2 (the classes that implement java.util.Collection) are specifically not synchronized because the synchronization of such classes as Vector does not make them thread safe and adds overhead. Explain why a Vector is not thread safe and account for the extra overhead generated by its use in the examples in this chapter, as compared to an unsynchronized collection.
13. Explain why the AWTMulticaster was used in the Java AWT and not the method of cloning the vector as in Program7.5 (Exhibits 12 through 15). Should a Multicaster always be used?
14. Is there any difference between using an Enumeration and an Iterator in Program7.3 (Exhibits 6 through 8)? If so, how and when would the difference become apparent?
15. Does it matter where the sleep method is called in the paint method of the SimpleAnimator in Program7.1 (Exhibits 1 through 3)? Why or why not?
16. Using the immutable object of Listeners in the processEvent method, can a Listener receive an event after it has successfully called remove<Listener> in the event source? How?
17. The following program is incorrect because a thread can be running in the object before the constructor has completed. Why does this occur? Change this program to correct this problem.

```
import java.awt.*;
public class MyClass extends Frame {
  public MyClass() {
    setSize(300,300);
    setVisible(true);
  }

  public static void main(String args[]) {
    MyClass mc = new MyClass();
  }
}
```

18. Create a race condition in a constructor by starting a thread in that constructor and then allocating an instance variable for that object in the run method and the constructor. What does this say about starting threads in a constructor?
19. Replace the "startAnimator" method with a "setVisible" method. This method should make the animator and control panel visible or hidden. When it is hidden, the control thread should stop running.
20. Using the class in Exhibit 18 and the documentation in the AWTEventMulticaster API, discuss in detail the methods that are in class Component. How is a button implemented? Implement your own Button class.

Exhibit 18. Program for Problem 20

```
import java.awt.*;

public class MyComponent extends Component {

  // contains checks to see if the mouse is in the current
  // component. If it is, the event is sent to the component.
  // Otherwise the event is not sent to the component.
  public boolean contains(int x, int y) {
    System.out.println("In contains " + x + " " + y);
    // return false;// If false is returned, the
          // processEvent is never called.
    return true;//Tell the container to send events to
          // this Component.
  }

  // processEvent is called when an event occurs. This is what
  // causes the Event Source to call all its listeners.
  public void processEvent(AWTEvent e) {
    System.out.println("In Event");
  }

  // Paint is always called on a repaint event. This is where
  // the Component is drawn.
  public void paint(Graphics g) {
    System.out.println("In Paint");
  }

  public static void main(String args[]) {
    MyComponent my_c1 = new MyComponent();

    // Set the event mask to some event; otherwise, processEvent
    // is never called.
    my_c1.enableEvents(AWTEvent.MOUSE_EVENT_MASK);

    // Put it all together in a Frame.
    Frame f1 = new Frame();
    f1.add(my_c1);
    f1.setSize(200,200);
    f1.show();
  }
}
```

Chapter 8

Cooperative Synchronization

8.1 Introduction

Synchronization is used to coordinate asynchronous activities, such as threads. Up to this point in the book, synchronization of asynchronous activities has always been on shared resources; this is called *competitive synchronization*, because the activities are always competing for the shared resource. However, at times activities must synchronize on an event that must occur before all threads can continue; this type of synchronization is called *cooperative synchronization*. This chapter explains what cooperative synchronization is and why it is important, as well as some of the pitfalls that can occur when implementing it.

The animator presented in Chapter 7 is used to demonstrate visually cooperative synchronization. All of the examples using the animator in Chapter 7 had objects that were created in the main thread, and then the animator simply called draw methods in these objects. The objects did not run in threads themselves but allowed their draw methods to be called in the GUI thread; therefore, they could only implement actions in the GUI thread and could not run independently from the GUI thread. In the examples in this chapter, the objects that are animated will implement threads, which requires that the threads cooperate with the GUI thread to implement the correct behavior.

A number of the same problems encountered in competitive synchronization will also be present in cooperative synchronization. Too little synchronization will result in race conditions and activities that do not cooperate correctly, while too much synchronization will result in activities that either deadlock or have performance problems. As always, care must be taken to implement an adequate amount of synchronization to solve the problem safely, but not so much that it causes liveness concerns.

8.2 Chapter Goals

After completing this chapter, you should know the following:

- The difference between cooperative synchronization and competitive synchronization
- What can happen if threads are not coordinated and how to use the synchronization with wait and notify methods to achieve cooperative synchronization
- Why it is invalid to use sleep times to achieve cooperative synchronization
- How to protect against race conditions when using the animator to move an object in a thread
- What is a notification object and how it can be implemented

8.3 Cooperative and Competitive Synchronization

Synchronization is used in a program for two reasons: allow threads to compete for a resource or allow them to coordinate activities. These two concepts were introduced in Chapter 1 in terms of baking a pie. Competitive synchronization in this case occurred when a shared resource (the bowl in which the pie crust and filling were to be mixed) was used. Cooperative synchronization occurred when two or more asynchronous activities had to wait for each other for a specific event to occur. So far in the text, only competitive synchronization has been covered, but this chapter introduces cooperative synchronization.

To understand how cooperative synchronization can occur in a problem we will use the animator from Chapter 7. The problem that illustrates cooperative synchronization is when a thread wishes to wait until the animator has finished moving an object before continuing to execute. To see how this problem occurs, consider Exhibit 1 (Program8.1),* which implements a simple animation of two threads that wait a random amount of time and then move a ball across the screen. The logic in the run method simply creates a path for the ball to travel, to the EAST if it was previously going WEST, to the NORTH if it was going SOUTH, etc. The thread then goes to sleep while the

* Note that the animations in this chapter all use the animator component developed in Chapter 8 and stored in the animator package that is available with this book. The useAnimator.bat file will correctly set up all the directories needed to run these programs.

Exhibit 1. Program8.1: Thread Animation with No Coordination

```
import java.awt.*;
import java.util.*;
import animator.*;

/**
 *  This class animates a ball in a thread using the animator
 *  component but fails because the thread is not coordinated
 *  with the GUI thread calling the draw method.
 */

public class ConcurrentBall implements DrawListener, Runnable {

  static final int EAST = 0;
  static final int WEST = 1;
  static final int NORTH = 2;
  static final int SOUTH = 3;
  int direction;
  Path myPath;
  Random random;
  Animator animator;

  /**
   *  Constructor. Just save information for this ball.
   */
  public ConcurrentBall(Animator animator, int direction) {
    this.direction = direction;
    random = new Random(direction);
    this.animator = animator;
  }

  /**
   *  The run method simulates an asynchronous ball. The
   *  myPath variable is set here and used in the draw method
   *  and is intended to coordinate the ball thread running in
   *  this method and the GUI thread (from the animator)
   *  running in the draw method. But, no coordination is in
   *  place, and this approach fails.
   */
  public void run() {
    animator.addDrawListener(this);
    try {
      while(true) {
        if (direction = = SOUTH) {
          myPath = new StraightLinePath(410, 205, 10, 205, 50);
          direction = NORTH;
        }
        else if (direction = = NORTH) {
          myPath = new StraightLinePath(10, 205, 410, 205, 50);
          direction = SOUTH;
        }
        else if (direction = = EAST) {
          myPath = new StraightLinePath(205, 410, 205, 10, 50);
          direction = WEST;
        }
        else if (direction = = WEST) {
          myPath = new StraightLinePath(205, 10, 205, 410, 50);
          direction = EAST;
        }
      Thread.sleep(random.nextInt(10000));
      }
    } catch (InterruptedException e) {
    }
  }
```

(continued)

Exhibit 1. Program8.1 (Continued)

```
  /**
   *  Draw is called each time through the animator loop to draw
   *  the object. It simply uses the path to calculate the
   *  position of this object and then draws itself at that
   *  position.
   */

  public void draw(DrawEvent de) {
    Point p = myPath.nextPosition();
    Graphics g = de.getGraphics();
    g.setColor(Color.red);
    g.fillOval((int)p.getX(), (int)p.getY(), 15, 15);
  }
  /**
   *  The main method just creates the animator and
   *  the ball threads and starts them running.
   */
  public static void main(String args[]) {
    Animator animator = new Animator();

    ConcurrentBall cb1 = new ConcurrentBall(animator, WEST);
    (new Thread(cb1)).start();

    ConcurrentBall cb2 = new ConcurrentBall(animator, NORTH);
    (new Thread(cb2)).start();

    animator.setVisible(true);
  }
}
```

GUI thread calls the draw method for the ball, which moves the ball. The draw method uses the Path variable that was created in the run method to control the steps in the animation. When the ball reaches its destination, when the path has no more steps, it will then simply wait until the thread is done sleeping and reverse its direction and move again.

Threads were used to make this program sleep a random amount of time between movement, as the sleep could be made part of the steps in the activity. This behavior of inserting a random sleep into the thread cannot be easily accomplished unless the balls are in threads. (A more complex example using the gas station simulation from Chapter 3 is presented later; utilizing sleep as part of the problem solution is easy to implement, as the cars will be in separate threads.)

When this program is run and the balls are moving quickly, the solution in Exhibit 1 (Program8.1) appears to be correct; however, as with everything else regarding asynchronous activities, we cannot test the program to prove it is correct. Care must be taken to implement the program correctly or the results may not be as expected. To see this, run the animation and pull the speed control all the way to the left, causing the program to go at its slowest speed. A disturbing behavior then becomes apparent. The ball moves some portion of the way across the screen, suddenly jumps to the far side of the screen, and begins moving in the opposite direction.

The reason the ball jumps to the other side of the screen is that the ball thread wakes up before the GUI thread has finished moving the ball to the other side of the screen. When the ball thread wakes up it creates a new path object and the draw method now uses this new path object immediately, thus moving the ball to the other side of the screen where this new path begins. This is not the intended behavior. The problem here is that the GUI thread and the ball thread are uncoordinated. The ball thread should actually suspend until the GUI thread has completed moving the ball across the screen and then should begin its sleep.

Making the program behave so that the ball thread does not start to sleep until the movement of the ball is completed is an example of cooperative synchronization. Somehow these two threads must be coordinated. How to coordinate these threads (i.e., how to achieve cooperative synchronization) is the topic of the remainder of this chapter. Once these techniques have been covered, they are combined in Chapter 9 with the competitive synchronization techniques already discussed. As will be seen, combining these techniques allows for the development of very powerful and extensible programs.

8.4 Coordinating Threads Using Long Sleep Times

The first way to try to fix the problem of the ball jumping across the screen is to fix the sleep time in the thread at some value that is always larger than the time it could possibly take to move the ball across the screen. For example, if the sleep time is greater than 100 seconds, the ball should always finish moving across the screen before the sleep is finished. This solution is not something I would have ever thought of; it comes from looking at a number of students' programs as they try to solve this problem. Even when given a correct methodology for solving the problem, many students will still try to make a solution by timing the threads. There appears to be something comforting about controlling the threads through some external mechanism, such as long sleeps, or by starting, stopping, and suspending the threads, even if doing so results in incomprehensible and incorrect programs. Solutions developed using these types of strategies are almost always a bad idea and seldom result in a correct program. In fact, the suspend, resume, stop, and destroy methods were so frequently used incorrectly that they have been deprecated in the Java API.*

* For more information, read the Java API for class Thread.

Why does using a large value of sleep time result in incorrect programs? The first problem with using a large value of sleep time is that it is not really possible to define a large enough sleep time. This is not as obvious as it may seem. I once worked on a program that was getting strings back from a server and processing them. It had been modified by a programmer who did not understand cooperative synchronization but needed to find a string from the server. Rather than try to coordinate threads, he set a sleep time that always worked for him. Over time, however, the server became more bogged down until this sleep time was occasionally exceeded, causing an error in the program. Because the error was very intermittent it was extremely difficult to reproduce and find, requiring weeks of debug statements, trial and error, and sleepless nights. Once I discovered the problem, however, a correct solution that did not rely on waiting a long enough time was easily implemented. The moral here is that one cannot test a concurrent program to prove that it is correct; one can only show that it works under the given assumptions. Unless a sleep time is set to an outrageously large value, the programmer can never be certain that external circumstances will not at some point make the value too small. And, when the program starts experiencing problems resulting from bugs in the wait times (and bugs will eventually occur), they most likely will be very difficult to find.

The second problem with creating a large value for the sleep time is that it might not be appropriate for the problem. For example, in the animation the value of the sleep time might be tied to some external constraint where the movement of the ball being used is part of the overall calculation of an average time in a simulation. Increasing the sleep time simply invalidates the entire simulation. An even worst case would be if a very large sleep time were used by a thread in a server. This could cause the server to suspend processing every request for an inappropriately long time, as happened in the GUI thread in Chapter 7, causing the server to have very poor response times and throughput. It is nearly always a bad idea to randomly sleep in a program, particularly to use sleep to coordinate threads.

The final reason why arbitrary sleep times is a bad idea is that it does not even solve the problem we are trying to address. In the animation in Exhibit 1 (Program8.1), we have no guarantee that movement of the object will finish before the sleep is complete. Unless the sleep time is infinite, there is always a non-zero possibility that the sleep will complete before the move; therefore, using sleep times cannot ever be guaranteed to be correct and will likely result in bugs at some point. Using statistics to demonstrate that the likelihood of a bug is so low as to be acceptable is sometimes used, even in hard real-time programming, and can occasionally be used when a problem cannot be solved in another way. But, doing so requires the use of statistical analysis to predict the possibility that the timing of the program avoids a problem to a sufficiently low probability, which is not an easy task. Also, because most types of problems have correct solutions that are easy to implement, all of these tricks using sleep times are really unnecessary. So, as a rule sleep time should not be used to coordinate threads.

8.5 Using Wait and Notify to Coordinate Threads

Chapter 2 showed that the best way to synchronize threads for competitive synchronization is by using wait and notify. These methods are also the best way to handle cooperative synchronization; however, as has already been shown, a notify and a wait call must be inside of a synchronized block, and deciding how to implement that synchronized block cannot be done in a haphazard manner.

Consider Exhibit 2 (Program8.2), which attempts to fix the problem of coordinating the ball thread and the GUI thread by putting a wait call in the run method of the Ball object (and thus in the ball thread) and a notify call in the draw method of the Ball object (and thus in the GUI thread). The two threads then cooperate through the use of the path variable. While the GUI thread is moving the ball on the screen in the draw method, the ball thread waits. The movement of the ball is completed when the end of the path is reached (it has no more steps), and the GUI thread then calls notify on the Ball object, freeing the ball thread to continue. The ball thread can now call the sleep method and create another Path object to move the ball back.

Because the wait and notify calls must be in a synchronized block, the simplest way to accomplish this is to synchronize the entire run and draw methods. This is done in Exhibit 2 (Program8.2). Now when the program runs, it completes the movement of the ball from one end of the screen to the other, so the problem with the ball moving while the ball thread is sleeping has been fixed. The ball waits while it is being moved and then sleeps, which is the behavior that is expected. If only one thread is running, the results do, indeed, appear to be correct. However, when two balls are displayed, the results are again disturbing. Now, rather than the balls sleeping different amounts of time, the balls move at the same time on the screen. This is obviously wrong behavior. The application has other problems, as well. For example, if you try to press any buttons or adjust the scrollbar you will find that the GUI thread is locked up, just as in Program7.2. Obviously, this is not what we wanted from the program, but at least the results indicate that whatever is wrong is also affecting the ability of the GUI thread to run.

The problem is a result of the Thread.sleep occurring in the synchronized block for the Ball object. Remember that Thread.sleep does not drop an object lock, so if a sleep occurs in a synchronized block

Exhibit 2. Program8.2: Thread Animation with the Run Method Synchronized

```
import java.awt.*;
import java.util.*;
import animator.*;

/**
 *    This class animates a ball in a thread using the animator
 *    component but fails because the run method is
 *    completely synchronized.
 */

public class ConcurrentBall implements DrawListener, Runnable {

  static final int EAST = 0;
  static final int WEST = 1;
  static final int NORTH = 2;
  static final int SOUTH = 3;
  int direction;

  Path myPath;
  Random random;
  Animator animator;

  /**
   *    Constructor. Just save information for this ball.
   */
  public ConcurrentBall(Animator animator, int direction) {
    this.animator = animator;
    this.direction = direction;
    random = new Random(direction);
  }

  /**
   *    The run method simulates an asynchronous ball. The
   *    myPath variable is set here and used in the draw method
   *    and is intended to coordinate the ball thread running in
   *    this method and the GUI thread (from the animator)
   *    running in the draw method. But, the complete
   *    synchronization of methods forces the GUI thread to
   *    suspend while it sleeps.
   */
  public synchronized void run() {
    animator.addDrawListener(this);
    try {
      while(true) {
        if (direction = = SOUTH) {
          myPath = new StraightLinePath(410, 205, 10, 205, 50);
          direction = NORTH;
        }

        else if (direction = = NORTH) {
          myPath = new StraightLinePath(10, 205, 410, 205, 50);
          direction = SOUTH;
        }
        else if (direction = = EAST) {
          myPath = new StraightLinePath(205, 410, 205, 10, 50);
          direction = WEST;
        }
```

(continued)

Exhibit 2. Program8.2 (Continued)

```
        else if (direction = = WEST) {
          myPath = new StraightLinePath(205, 10, 205, 410, 50);
          direction = EAST;
        }

      wait();
      Thread.sleep(random.nextInt(10000));
      }
    } catch (InterruptedException e) {
    }
  }

  /**
   *  Draw is called each time through the animator loop to draw
   *  the object. It simply uses the path to calculate the
   *  position of this object and then draws itself at that
   *  position. When the end of the path is reached, it notifies
   *  the ball thread.
   */

  public synchronized void draw(DrawEvent de) {
    Point p = myPath.nextPosition();
    Graphics g = de.getGraphics();
    g.setColor(Color.red);
    g.fillOval((int)p.getX(), (int)p.getY(), 15, 15);

    if (! myPath.hasMoreSteps()) {
      notify();
    }
  }

  /**
   *  The main method just creates the animator and
   *  the ball threads and starts them running.
   */
  public static void main(String args[]) {
    Animator animator = new Animator();

    ConcurrentBall cb1 = new ConcurrentBall(animator, WEST);
    (new Thread(cb1)).start();

    ConcurrentBall cb2 = new ConcurrentBall(animator, NORTH);
    (new Thread(cb2)).start();

    animator.setVisible(true);
  }
```

the lock for that object is held while the object sleeps. In this case, the ball thread is holding the lock on the Ball object the entire time it is sleeping. When the GUI thread then tries to get the synchronized lock on the Ball object on entering the draw method, it must wait until the sleep finishes, a new path is created, and the ball calls wait. In fact, because the GUI thread calls the draw method on both balls, it must wait until both ball threads call wait before continuing. So when both balls are waiting, and only when both are waiting, the GUI thread can move the Ball objects. This explains why both balls move together in the program and why the GUI components appear jammed. The GUI thread was forced to wait on a synchronized lock to enter the draw method while the ball threads slept.

This example shows that synchronizing the entire run method is not an appropriate way to get the synchronized lock on the Ball object. What is needed is for the ball thread not to hold the lock on the Ball object while the thread is sleeping. We have only two ways not to hold a synchronized lock; the first is via a call to wait, and the second is to run outside of the synchronized block, thus never obtaining the lock. The second approach is superior in most situations and is explored further in the rest of the chapter.

Another way to make Exhibit 2 (Program8.2) work without changing the scope of the synchronized block is to use a format for the wait call that takes a parameter that is the number of milliseconds to wait for a notify. It has the form "wait(int waitTime)." This wait call will wait waitTime milliseconds for a notify to occur. If a notify call does not occur within that period of time, then the wait call returns as if a notify had occurred. Like any wait call, it still drops the lock when it is executed and must re-obtain the lock before it can begin to run again. Exhibit 3 (Program8.3) uses this format of the wait method instead of sleep. Using this wait call to "sleep" drops the lock on the Ball object, thus allowing the GUI thread to run while the ball thread is "sleeping." This program does work correctly, but it is an inappropriate use of the wait call. This program uses the wait call to force the ball thread to drop the synchronized lock, but if the lock is not needed then why has the thread obtained it? Also, if it is actually needed because this is a critical section, the synchronization has been broken, which could result in a race condition.

Far better than using wait to drop the synchronized lock is to structure the program so that the synchronized lock protects the critical sections and the synchronized lock is not held in non-critical sections. This makes the locking used by the program explicit, as well as making it easier for a programmer to understand and see that it is correct.

8.6 A Solution with a Hidden Race Condition

As illustrated in Section 8.5, the correct approach to using a synchronized block in Java is often to lock less than an entire method. When trying to decide how much of a method to synchronize, a programmer should realize that a particular dynamic occurs with using synchronized locks. If too much of the object is locked, weird behavior (as described in Section 8.5), performance problems, or even deadlock can occur. If too little is locked, race conditions can occur. It is often crucial that the locking be done properly or the program will fail. Normally, a system should be designed to solve the user's problem,

Exhibit 3. Program8.3: Breaking Synchronization with a Call to Wait(waitTime)

```
import java.awt.*;
import java.util.*;
import animator.*;

/**
 *  This class animates a ball in a thread using the animator
 *  component by using a wait(int) call instead of sleep so that
 *  the object lock is dropped while the component is sleeping.
 */

public class ConcurrentBall implements DrawListener, Runnable {

  static final int EAST = 0;
  static final int WEST = 1;
  static final int NORTH = 2;
  static final int SOUTH = 3;
  int direction;

  boolean pleaseNotify = false;
  Path myPath;
  Random random;
  Animator animator;

  /**
   *  Constructor. Just save information for this ball.
   */

  public ConcurrentBall(Animator animator, int direction) {
    this.direction = direction;
    this.animator = animator;
    random = new Random(direction);
  }

  /**
   *  The run method simulates an asynchronous ball. The
   *  myPath variable is set here and used in the draw method
   *  and is intended to coordinate the ball thread running in
   *  this method and the GUI thread (from the animator)
   *  running in the draw method. This works but uses wait(int),
   *  which drops the object lock.
   */

  public synchronized void run() {
    animator.addDrawListener(this);
    try {
      while(true) {
        if (direction = = SOUTH) {
          myPath = new StraightLinePath(410, 205, 10, 205, 50);
          direction - NORTH;
        }
        else if (direction = = NORTH) {
          myPath = new StraightLinePath(10, 205, 410, 205, 50);
          direction = SOUTH;
        }
        else if (direction = = EAST) {
          myPath = new StraightLinePath(205, 410, 205, 10, 50);
```

(continued)

Exhibit 3. Program8.3 (Continued)

```
          direction = WEST;
        }
        else if (direction = = WEST) {
          myPath = new StraightLinePath(205, 10, 205, 410, 50);
          direction = EAST;
        }
      pleaseNotify = true;
      wait();
      pleaseNotify = false;
      wait(random.nextInt(10000));
      }
    } catch (InterruptedException e) {
    }
  }

  /**
   * Draw is called each time through the animator loop to draw
   * the object. It simply uses the path to calculate the
   * position of this object and then draws itself at that
   * position. When the end of the path is reached, it notifies
   * the ball thread.
   */
  public synchronized void draw(DrawEvent de) {
    Point p = myPath.nextPosition();
    Graphics g = de.getGraphics();
    g.setColor(Color.red);
    g.fillOval((int)p.getX(), (int)p.getY(), 15, 15);
    // Do not notify if the wait is for the wait that emulates
    // the sleep.
    if ((! myPath.hasMoreSteps()) && pleaseNotify) {
      notify();
    }
  }

  /**
   * The main method just creates the animator and
   * the ball threads and starts them running.
   */
  public static void main(String args[]) {
    Animator animator = new Animator();

    ConcurrentBall cb1 = new ConcurrentBall(animator, WEST);
    (new Thread(cb1)).start();

    ConcurrentBall cb2 = new ConcurrentBall(animator, NORTH);
    (new Thread(cb2)).start();

    animator.setVisible(true);
  }
}
```

but synchronization is so critical that there may be times when the locking scheme to be used might affect the design of the system.* In

* An example is the modifications to the Control Panel for the animator (see Chapter 9), which require the programmer to make sure that a wait call never occurs while the program is running in the GUI thread.

the case of Exhibit 2 (Program8.2), the problem was that too much of the run method was in the synchronized block; however, some portion of the run method must be synchronized to allow the wait method to be called. It is the job of the programmer to figure out how much actually needs to be locked and to lock only that portion of the program.

For the animated thread in Exhibit 2 (Program8.2), a programmer could naively say that, because the only statement in the run method that requires the lock is the wait statement, only the wait statement should be in the synchronized block. This solution is shown in Exhibit 4 (Program8.4). Because the sleep method, which was the problem in Exhibit 2 (Program8.2), is outside of the synchronized lock, the method will not have a problem with holding up the GUI thread. The only question left to answer is whether or not Exhibit 4 (Program8.4) is safe. When this solution is run, it does appear to behave correctly, and this program could be run for years without a problem. But, as has been continually stressed, you cannot test to show that a concurrent program is correct. Exhibit 4 (Program8.4) does, in fact, have a race condition. The race condition occurs if the path object is created before the wait method can be called in the run method. The GUI thread runs in the draw method, reaches the end of the path, and sends a notify to the thread. This notify would be lost, and the ball thread would be stuck at a wait for which a notify never occurs.

Because a Path object is required to have at least one step, the odds greatly favor that this program will run correctly close to 100% of the time. A programmer might argue, then, that because the problem is unlikely, the race condition can be ignored. Just because a problem seldom arises does not mean that it will *never* happen. What is likely is that this program will be maintained in the future by another programmer who does not understand the timing relationship between the creation of the path variable and the wait method call in the run method. This programmer might insert a time-intensive task between the creation of the path and the wait call, effectively destroying the timing interaction between the ball thread calling wait and the GUI thread calling notify. Doing so would lead to a much greater probability that the notify will occur before the wait, thus causing a bug that is difficult to reproduce and even more difficult to find and correct.

8.7 Solving the Race Condition

The problem in Exhibit 5 (Program8.5) is that the path can be created and finished before the ball thread can execute a wait on it. To solve this timing dependency, the creation of the Path object and the wait must be inside of the same synchronized block in the run method. This ensures that the draw method is not run and that the notify cannot

Exhibit 4. Program8.4: Concurrent Animation with a Race Condition

```
import java.awt.*;
import java.util.*;
import animator.*;

/**
 *  This class animates a ball in a thread using the animator
 *  component. It normally works but has a potential race
 *  condition.
 */

public class ConcurrentBall implements DrawListener, Runnable {

  static final int EAST = 0;
  static final int WEST = 1;
  static final int NORTH = 2;
  static final int SOUTH = 3;
  int direction;

  Path myPath;
  Random random;
  Animator animator;

/**
 *  Constructor. Just save information for this ball.
 */
public ConcurrentBall(Animator animator, int direction) {
  this.animator = animator;
  this.direction = direction;
  random = new Random(direction);
}

/**
 *  The run method, which simulates an asynchronous ball. The
 *  myPath variable is set here and used in the draw method,
 *  and is intended to coordinate the ball thread running in
 *  this method, and the GUI thread (from the animator)
 *  running in the draw method. But, the creation of the path
 *  before the synchronized lock means that the path could
 *  finish and the notify be called before the wait is
 *  called.
 */

  public void run() {
    animator.addDrawListener(this);
    try {
      while(true) {
        if (direction = = SOUTH) {
          myPath = new StraightLinePath(410, 205, 10, 205, 50);
          direction = NORTH;
        }
        else if (direction = = NORTH) {
          myPath = new StraightLinePath(10, 205, 410, 205, 50);
          direction = SOUTH;
        }
        else if (direction = = EAST) {
          myPath = new StraightLinePath(205, 410, 205, 10, 50);
          direction = WEST;
        }
```

(continued)

Exhibit 4. Program8.4 (Continued)

```
        else if (direction = = WEST) {
          myPath = new StraightLinePath(205, 10, 205, 410, 50);
          direction = EAST;
        }
        synchronized (this) {
          wait();
        }
        Thread.sleep(random.nextInt(10000));
      }
    } catch (InterruptedException e) {
    }
  }

  /**
   *  Draw is called each time through the animator loop to draw
   *  the object. It simply uses the path to calculate the
   *  position of this object and then draws itself at that
   *  position. When the end of the path is reached, it notifies
   *  the ball thread.
   */
  public synchronized void draw(DrawEvent de) {
    Point p = myPath.nextPosition();
    Graphics g = de.getGraphics();
    g.setColor(Color.red);
    g.fillOval((int)p.getX(), (int)p.getY(), 15, 15);

    if (! myPath.hasMoreSteps())
      notify();
  }

  /**
   *  The main method just creates the animator and
   *  the ball threads and starts them running.
   */
  public static void main(String args[]) {
    Animator animator = new Animator();

    ConcurrentBall cb1 = new ConcurrentBall(animator, WEST);
    (new Thread(cb1)).start();

    ConcurrentBall cb2 = new ConcurrentBall(animator, NORTH);
    (new Thread(cb2)).start();

    animator.setVisible(true);
  }
}
```

occur until the wait has been executed. This solution is shown in Exhibit 5 (Program8.5), which is a correct solution to this animation program. This procedure of creating a Path object, waiting in the run method, and coordinating with the GUI thread via a call to notify in the draw method can be used with the animator for any asynchronous object.

While this method of simply putting a synchronized block around the path creation and the notify method works, it is somewhat confusing as it encompasses a fairly large section of the code in the

Exhibit 5. Program8.5: Correct Concurrent Animation

```
import java.awt.*;
import java.util.*;
import animator.*;

/**
 * This class animates a ball in a thread using the animator
 * component. It is a correct solution.
 */

public class ConcurrentBall implements DrawListener, Runnable {

  static final int EAST = 0;
  static final int WEST = 1;
  static final int NORTH = 2;
  static final int SOUTH = 3;
  int direction;

  Path myPath;
  Random random;
  Animator animator;

  /**
   * Constructor. Note that we need to register with the
   * animator through the parent's class.
   */
  public ConcurrentBall(Animator animator, int direction) {
    this.animator = animator;
    this.direction = direction;
    random = new Random(direction);
  }

  /**
   * The run method simulates an asynchronous ball. The
   * myPath variable is set here and used in the draw method
   * and is intended to coordinate the ball thread running in
   * this method and the GUI thread (from the animator)
   * running in the draw method. This works correctly.
   */
  public void run() {
    animator.addDrawListener(this);
    try {
      while(true) {
        synchronized (this) {
          if (direction = = SOUTH) {
            myPath = new StraightLinePath(410, 205, 10, 205,
                50);
            direction = NORTH;
          }
          else if (direction = = NORTH) {
            myPath = new StraightLinePath(10, 205, 410, 205,
                50);
            direction = SOUTH;
          }
          else if (direction = = EAST) {
            myPath = new StraightLinePath(205, 410, 205, 10,
                50);
            direction = WEST;
          }
```

(continued)

Exhibit 5. Program8.5 (Continued)

```
          else if (direction = = WEST) {
            myPath = new StraightLinePath(205, 10, 205, 410,
                50);
            direction = EAST;
          }
          wait();
        }
      Thread.sleep(random.nextInt(10000));
      }
    } catch (InterruptedException e) {
    }
  }

  /**
   * Draw is called each time through the animator loop to draw
   * the object. It simply uses the path to calculate the
   * position of this object and then draws itself at that
   * position. When the end of the path is reached, it notifies
   * the ball thread.
   */
  public synchronized void draw(DrawEvent de) {
    Point p = myPath.nextPosition();
    Graphics g = de.getGraphics();
    g.setColor(Color.red);
    g.fillOval((int)p.getX(), (int)p.getY(), 15, 15);

    if (! myPath.hasMoreSteps())
      notify();
  }

  /**
   * The main method just creates the animator and
   * the ball threads and starts them running.
   */
  public static void main(String args[]) {
    Animator animator = new Animator();

    ConcurrentBall cb1 = new ConcurrentBall(animator, WEST);
    (new Thread(cb1)).start();

    ConcurrentBall cb2 = new ConcurrentBall(animator, NORTH);
    (new Thread(cb2)).start();

    animator.setVisible(true);
  }
}
```

method. Also, the steps, or procedure, of locking the code, creating the path, and doing a wait can occur many times in a program; simply copying the code in the program each time it occurs is time consuming, confusing, and prone to errors. Any time procedures occur more than once, the procedure is a good candidate to be abstracted for *reuse*. Because the procedure is abstracted, the type of reuse here is *procedural reuse*. The steps involved in moving the object are abstracted into a method named move, and the program is *refactored* to implement the move method. A move method is created in the class Car in Program8.7 (Exhibits 7 through 9) and is used to move the car as part of the animation.

Creating a move method is easy for a single object; however, abstracting out the behavior to apply it to multiple objects is not as easy as creating the method. Variables that are local to each object, such as the Path, must be manipulated in the move method, which means that a procedural function will be insufficient for a reusable move method. A stronger methodology is needed. Fortunately, two exist: classification and composition. These two methodologies are explained in Chapter 10.

8.8 Notification Objects

8.8.1 What Are Notification Objects?

At times, when implementing a concurrent program, a programmer may not want to wait on the "this" object and instead wants to wait on another object for a number of reasons. The "this" object might have a lock that cannot be dropped, or an object might be created and used as part of a cooperative synchronization that requires a significant amount of code between where it is created and used, as with the path object in Exhibit 5 (Program8.5). There might be a number of threads that are waiting on a component, and the component might want to notify a specific thread, as is shown in the readers/writers and first-in/first-out binary semaphore problems in Chapter 9. Generically, the object other than "this" that executes wait and notify is referred to as a *notification object* (NO). However, an NO is more than just the object itself; it is a mechanism needed to safely implement obtaining the lock on the object and notifying on the object. So, an NO is the object to be notified on and the pattern used to lock it. Even though the "this" object can be used to notify a specific thread, it will not be considered an NO. How to implement an NO is relatively straightforward, even if the logic behind each step is not. The next section describes how to implement an NO, and in Chapter 9 presents some examples of how they are used.

8.8.2 Implementing a Notifying Object

The implementation of an NO takes advantage of two properties of Java:

- In Java, a local identifier to a variable is on the stack and thus can only be referenced in the current context (i.e., thread); therefore, a thread can always safely access objects that are only referenced by a local identifier, because they have no scope outside of that method. However, a variable that is referenced by an identifier that is part of the class definition for an object has a scope of all methods in that object. Variables do not have a scope (they are just memory on the heap) but take on the scope of the identifier that references them. So, a variable created with a local identifier can later be given a classwide scope by setting it to an identifier defined as part of the class. This is consistent with Chapter 4, where a distinction is made between the identifier and the variable, and the fact that a variable which takes on the scope of the identifier that references it can be used to change the scope of a local variable to one that has scope in all the objects in a method.

- In Java, the synchronization lock for an object is on the variable, not the identifier; therefore, if a lock is obtained on a variable with a local identifier and that variable is then set to a reference for an identifier for an object, the thread has in effect co-opted the lock on the object identifier. When doing this, it is always safe to obtain the lock on the variable for the local identifier and then, in a synchronized block on the "this" object, to set that variable to an object identifier, giving the variable a larger, more permanent scope. It is generally not safe to set the variable with a local identifier to an object identifier outside of a synchronized block on the "this" object.

To understand the implications of these two properties, consider the following simple class. In this class, NotifyLockExample, the variable notificationObject is locked in both method1 and method2; however, in method1, an object is created with a reference to a variable temp, and a lock is obtained on that variable. The lock is obtained on the notificationObject by later setting the identifier notificationObject to the temp variable. In method2, the lock on the variable notificationObject is obtained on the variable directly referenced by the notificationObject identifier. If thread1 calls method1, thread2 calls method2, and thread2 runs first, it is possible in this program for thread1 and thread2 both to hold the lock for what appears to be the notificationObject. How? When we have two different objects, the notify in thread2 is simply lost because it is notifying on the old notificationObject variable, not the one on which thread1 is waiting:

```
public class NotifyLockExample {
  private Object notificationObject = new Object();
  public void method_1() {
    object temp = new Object();
    synchronized(temp) {
      notificationObject = temp;
      // temp and notificationObject are now the same
      // object, so it is safe to wait on notificationObject.
      notificationObject.wait();
    }
  }
```

```
    public void method_2() {
      synchronized(notificationObject) {
      // NOTE: This next statement can result in an
      // exception being thrown because the notify call
      // is not on the object for the synchronized block.
      // The notificationObject in the synchronized block is
      // is the original one, and the one here is the new one.
      notificationObject.notify();
      }
    }
  }
```

This behavior might be surprising to some, but it is a direct result of using the objects in the program. This behavior did not occur in any earlier programs because the object used was always the "this" object. When the "this" object was used, the reference could not be set to another object, so it was not possible to manipulate the objects on which the lock was held, thus the use of locking on the "this" object was safe. This example should make it clear that locking on an object other than the "this" object is inherently more complex. It should also reinforce why understanding the behavior of the JVM and how it manages memory is important to all programmers and why it can never be safely ignored.

Fortunately it is easy to get around the problems with notification objects. The following pattern always implements a safe notification object and is easy to implement:

- In the method that calls wait:
  - Create a temporary object of any type.
  - When ready to do the wait, synchronize on the temporary object.
  - Synchronize on the current object.
  - Set an instance object to the temporary object; the lock on the temporary object is still maintained, but it now has object scope.
  - End the synchronized block on the current object, dropping the lock on the current object.
  - Call wait on the temporary (now instance) object.
- In the method that calls notify:
  - Synchronize on the current object.
  - Synchronize on the instance object from step 1 above.
  - Call notify on the instance object.

This is shown in the following code fragment for two methods used in Exhibit 6 (Program8.6) to implement another correct version of the program that uses the animator with threads:

```
public class NOLockExample {

  private Object notificationObject = new Object();
  public void method_1() {
  object temp = new Object();
  synchronized(temp) {
    synchronized(this) {
    notificationObject = temp;
    }
    notificationObject.wait();
  }
  }
  public synchronized void method_2() {
  synchronized(notificationObject) {
    notificationObject.notify();
  }
  }
}
```

Exhibit 6 (Program8.6) shows the use of an NO with the ConcurrentBall program. The notification object is combined with state diagrams and the Java Event Model in Chapter 9 to enhance both of these techniques.

8.9 Animating the Gas Station Problem

The animator can easily be used with concurrent programs from Chapter 3 and the techniques used in Exhibit 5 (Program8.5), as shown in Program8.7 (Exhibits 7 through 9), for the Gas Station problem presented in Chapter 3 and animated here. One change has been made in the animation given in Exhibit 5 (Program8.5). As suggested in Section 8.7, the creation of the path and the wait have been abstracted into a single method, named move. This greatly decreased the amount of code needed and the complexity of the program.

To animate the gas station, the Pump class and the Car class were both made DrawListeners so that they could be drawn as part of the animation. They are both given a draw method. Because the Pump is passive and never moves, it does not need a thread to run, and its draw method is simply called from the animator; no path is needed. For the Car object, the run method has to be changed to produce an animated effect so that each major event that the Car has to process can be animated. When a car arrives (when it first wakes up from its sleep), it is put into the animation at an initial Parking Spot. When the car obtains the Pump (through the call to usePump), it is animated to move to the pump, and it pumps gas. When it is finished, it leaves the Pump and drives off the screen, opening up the pump for the next car.

Exhibit 6. Program8.6: Implementation of the Notification Object

```
import java.awt.*;
import java.util.*;
import animator.*;

/**
 *  This class animates a ball in a thread using the animator
 *  component. It shows how a notification object can be used
 *  to implement a correct coordination between the GUI and
 *  ball threads.
 */

public class ConcurrentBall implements DrawListener, Runnable {

  static final int EAST = 0;
  static final int WEST = 1;
  static final int NORTH = 2;
  static final int SOUTH = 3;
  int direction;

  Path myPath;
  Random random;
  Animator animator;

  /**
   *  Constructor. Just save information for this ball.
   */
  public ConcurrentBall(Animator animator, int direction) {
    this.animator = animator;
    this.direction = direction;
    random = new Random(direction);
  }

  /**
   *  The run method simulates an asynchronous ball. The
   *  coordination is via a notification object, which is
   *  explained in this function's header.
   */
  public void run() {
    Path tempPath;// Local variable to set to myPath; used as
         // part of a notification object.
    animator.addDrawListener(this);
    try {
      while(true) {
        if (direction = = SOUTH) {
          tempPath = new StraightLinePath(410, 205, 10, 205,
              50);
          direction = NORTH;
        }
        else if (direction = = NORTH) {
          tempPath = new StraightLinePath(10, 205, 410, 205,
              50);
          direction = SOUTH;
        }
        else if (direction = = EAST) {
          tempPath = new StraightLinePath(205, 410, 205, 10,
              50);
```

(continued)

Exhibit 6. Program8.6 (Continued)

```
          direction = WEST;
        }
        else {// direction = = WEST
          tempPath = new StraightLinePath(205, 10, 205, 410,
              50);
          direction = EAST;
        }

        synchronized(tempPath) {
          synchronized (this) {
            myPath = tempPath;
          }
          myPath.wait();
        }
        Thread.sleep(random.nextInt(10000));
      }
    } catch (InterruptedException e) {
    }
  }

  /**
   *  Draw is called each time through the animator loop to draw
   *  the object. It simply uses the path to calculate the
   *  position of this object and then draws itself at that
   *  position. When the end of the path is reached, it notifies
   *  the ball thread.
   */

  public synchronized void draw(DrawEvent de) {
    Point p = myPath.nextPosition();
    Graphics g = de.getGraphics();
    g.setColor(Color.red);
    g.fillOval((int)p.getX(), (int)p.getY(), 15, 15);

    if (! myPath.hasMoreSteps()) {
      synchronized(myPath) {
        myPath.notify();
      }
    }
  }

  /**
   *  The main method just creates the animator and
   *  the ball threads and starts them running.
   */
  public static void main(String args[]) {
    Animator animator = new Animator();

    ConcurrentBall cb1 = new ConcurrentBall(animator, WEST);
    (new Thread(cb1)).start();

    ConcurrentBall cb2 = new ConcurrentBall(animator, NORTH);
    (new Thread(cb2)).start();

    animator.setVisible(true);
  }
}
```

Exhibit 7. Program8.7a: Pump Class

```
import java.awt.Graphics;
import java.awt.Color;
import animator.*;

class Pump implements DrawListener {
  private static final int FREE = 0;
  private static final int BUSY = 1;
  private int state = FREE;

  /**
   * The draw method allows this class to be used with the
   * gas station animation.
   */
  public void draw(DrawEvent de) {
    Graphics g = de.getGraphics();
    g.setColor(Color.black);
    g.drawRect(325, 10, 100, 25);
    if (state = = BUSY)
      g.drawString("Pumping," 350, 30);
    else
      g.drawString("Pump Free," 350, 30);
    g.setColor(Color.gray);
    g.fillRect(350, 100, 50, 50);
    g.fillOval(350, 75, 50, 25);
  }

  /**
   * Method to call when a car first wishes to use a pump. It
   * adds a 1/2 second to the simulated time in the problem.
   */

  synchronized public void usePump() {
    try {
      // Pre-condition processing (guard)
      while(true) {
        if (state = = FREE)
          break;
        wait();
      }

      // Simulate pulling to the pump by waiting 1/2 second.
      Thread.sleep(500);

      // Post-condition processing, change state.
      state = BUSY;
      notifyAll();
    } catch (InterruptedException e) {
    }
  }

  /**
   * Simulate pumping the gas by waiting 5 seconds.
   */
  synchronized public void pumpGas() {
    try {
      // Pre-condition processing (guard)
      while(true) {
        if (state = = BUSY)
          break;
        wait();
      }
```

(continued)

Exhibit 7. Program8.7a (Continued)

```
      // Simulate pumping gas by waiting 5 seconds.
      Thread.sleep(5000);

      // Post-condition processing, no change state needed.
    } catch (InterruptedException e) {
    }
  }

  /**
   * Leave the pump, freeing it for the next customer.
   */
  synchronized public void leave() {
    try {
      // Pre-condition processing (guard)
      while(true) {
        if (state = = BUSY)
          break;
        wait();
      }

      // Simulate leaving the pump by waiting 1/2 second.
      Thread.sleep(500);

      // Post-condition processing, change state.
      state = FREE;
      notifyAll();
    } catch (InterruptedException e) {
    }
  }
}
```

Exhibit 8. Program8.7b: Car Class

```
import java.util.Random;
import java.util.Date;
import java.awt.Graphics;
import java.awt.Color;
import java.awt.Point;
import animator.*;

class Car implements Runnable, DrawListener {
  private static int totalTime = 0,// Total time spent by all
                                   // cars
    totalCars = 0;                 // Total number of cars
  private int customerNumber;      // The customer number to
                                   // set Random value and for
                                   // intermediate output.
  private Pump myPump;             // The pump the customer
                                   // should use.

  private Animator animator;
  private Path myPath;
```

(continued)

Exhibit 8. Program8.7b (Continued)

```
  private int parkingSpot;
  private static int ParkingSpots[] = {100, 175, 250, 325};
  private static int nextSpot = 0;

  private static int getFreeParkingSpot() {
    int returnValue = ParkingSpots[nextSpot];
    nextSpot = (nextSpot + 1)% ParkingSpots.length;
    return returnValue;
  }

  /**
   *  Constructor. Set the customerNumber and pump.
   */

  public Car(int customerNumber, Pump pump, Animator animator)
{
    this.animator = animator;
    this.myPump = pump;
    this.customerNumber = customerNumber;
  }

  /**
   * Static function to calculate average at the end of
   * the simulation.
   */
  public static float calcAverage() {
    return totalTime/totalCars;
  }

  /**
   *  This function implements the procedural mechanism for
   *  moving this object. It is synchronized, so in the
   *  synchronized block it sets up the path and then calls
   *  wait to stop the thread until the movement on the path
   *  has completed.
   */
  private synchronized void move(int startX, int startY, int
      endX,
    int endY,int numberOfSteps) {
    try {
      myPath = new StraightLinePath(startX, startY, endX, endY,
          numberOfSteps);
      wait();
    } catch(InterruptedException e) {
    }
  }

  /**
   *  The draw method allows this pump to be drawn as part of
   *  an animation.
   */
  public synchronized void draw(DrawEvent de) {
    // Get the Graphics to draw on.
    Graphics g = de.getGraphics();

    // Get where to draw. If at end of path notify the car.
    Point p = myPath.nextPosition();
    int x = (int)p.getX();
    int y = (int)p.getY();
```

(continued)

Exhibit 8. Program8.7b (Continued)

```
    if (! myPath.hasMoreSteps()) {
      notify();
    }

    // Draw the boxy car
    g.setColor(Color.red);
    g.fillRect(x, y, 100, 25);
    g.fillRect(x+20, y-20, 60, 20);
    g.setColor(Color.black);
    g.fillOval(x+10, y+20, 20, 20);
    g.fillOval(x+70, y+20, 20, 20);
    g.drawString("" + customerNumber, x+45, y);
  }

  /**
   * Thread that implements the pump.
   */

  public void run() {
    // Declare variables need for simulation.
    final int WAIT_TIME = 80000;
    long startTime, endTime;
    Random random = new Random(customerNumber);
    int waitTime = random.nextInt(WAIT_TIME);

    // Wait a random amount of time before coming to pump.
    try {
      Thread.sleep(waitTime);
    } catch (InterruptedException e) {
    }
    startTime = (new Date()).getTime();

    // Add To animation
    parkingSpot = getFreeParkingSpot();
    myPath = new StraightLinePath(50,  // This just ensures
      parkingSpot, 50, parkingSpot, 1);// the object is at
                       // a valid position
    animator.addDrawListener(this);

    // Use the pump, pump the gas, and leave.
    System.out.println("Customer " + customerNumber +
        " arrives at station");
    myPump.usePump();

    // Customer can now use the pump, so move customer to the pump.
    move(50, parkingSpot, 150, parkingSpot, 10);
    move(150, parkingSpot, 175, 175, 10);
    move(175, 175, 325, 175, 10);

    System.out.println("Customer " + customerNumber +
        " pumps gas");
    myPump.pumpGas();

    System.out.println("Customer " + customerNumber +
        " leaves pump");
    myPump.leave();
    move(325, 175, 400, 175, 10);
```

(continued)

Exhibit 8. Program8.7b (Continued)

```
    animator.removeDrawListener(this);
    endTime = (new Date()).getTime();
    System.out.println("Time = " + (endTime - startTime));

    // Update the variables to calculate the average. If this
    // is the last car, let the main() finish and print the
    // average. Note that to use the static variables we need
    // to get the lock on the class.
    synchronized(Car.class) {
      totalTime + = (endTime - startTime);
      totalCars++;
    }
  }
}
```

Exhibit 9. Program8.7c: Gas Station Class

```
import animator.*;

public class GasStation {
  static final int TOTAL_CARS = 10;

  public static void main(String args[]) {
    Animator animator = new Animator();
    Thread carThreads[] = new Thread[TOTAL_CARS];
    try {
      // Create the monitor (passive object).
      Pump pump1 = new Pump();
      animator.addDrawListener(pump1);

      // Start all the Car threads
      for (int i = 0; i < TOTAL_CARS; i++) {
        Car car = new Car(i, pump1, animator);
        (carThreads[i] = new Thread(car)).start();
      }

      // Start the animation
      animator.setVisible(true);

      // Now suspend and wait for simulation to finish.
      for (int i = 0; i < TOTAL_CARS; i++) {
        carThreads[i].join();
      }
    } catch (InterruptedException e) {
    }

    // Print average time at the end of the simulation.
    System.out.println("Average time to get gas = " +
      Car.calcAverage());
  }
}
```

Note that the ability to put the animation in a separate thread allows the thread to be a procedural definition of the behavior of an individual entity (in this case, the car). This makes writing descriptions of behaviors easier to follow, as the behavior is simply stated as what each individual object does, just like active objects in Chapter 3. The Car run method moves through the steps required to simulate its behavior. The ability to allow the GUI thread to coordinate with the Car threads makes the modeling of the system straightforward. This makes the use of cooperative synchronization a very nice addition to a programmer's toolbox.

8.10 Further Reading

The main topic here, cooperative synchronization, is defined in Sebesta [SEB99]; however, the level of detail that this chapter gives to the topic is not normally given in most texts. Notification objects and other concepts related to deadlock and other conditions are covered by Hartley [HAR98] and Lea [LEA00].

8.11 Problems

1. Animate the Bounded Buffer problem in Chapter 3 using the method described in Section 8.9.
2. Choose any other problem at the end of Chapter 3 and animate it using the method described in Section 8.9.
3. Show that the state diagrams in Problems 3.7, 3.8, and 3.9 are incorrect by animating them and running them long enough for the predicted anomalies to occur.
4. If you run the gas station simulation long enough, it shows that the wait and notify in Java are unfair. How does it show this? Does this happen frequently?
5. Create a type of path that can store two or more straight line segments and uses these segments sequentially to generate the points when nextPosition is called. Use this new type of path to move with one call from the Parking area to the pump.

Chapter 9

Combining Concurrent Techniques

9.1 Introduction

Each of the techniques that have been covered so far, such as the use of state diagrams, Java Events, and notification objects, as well as such concepts as race conditions and deadlock, is very powerful in its own right; however, it is when these are used together and combined with other object-oriented programming (OOP) concepts, such as confinement, that truly elegant yet simple program designs and implementations can be achieved. Problems that would be difficult, if not impossible, to effectively realize using other paradigms are easily decomposed into cooperating, asynchronous activities. This chapter solves four problems to illustrate some of the ways in which combining concurrent programming techniques can produce elegant and effective components. On first trying to understand these solutions, they may seem complex; however, when the interactions between the components and asynchronous activities are isolated and the components are seen as providing a single coherent service to those asynchronous activities, the complexity within the programs can be viewed as being much less than would be required with some other implementation mechanisms. These simple components can then be used as building blocks for larger, more complex systems.

The four programs covered in this chapter are:

1. *First-in/first-out binary semaphore*, which is a fair implementation of a binary semaphore. As was explained in Chapter 2 the wait/notify in Java is not fair (i.e., it does not necessarily give the semaphore to the thread that has been waiting the longest). This implementation of the binary semaphore is fair in that the thread

that has been waiting the longest is given the semaphore. It changes the way a state diagram is used to model a component by allowing the methods to work with Notification Objects to notify a specific thread.

2. *Readers/writers problem*, where a number of threads are simultaneously trying to read and write to a buffer. Because readers do not modify the buffer, an unlimited number of readers can read the buffer simultaneously but only one writer can use the buffer, and then only if there are also no readers. The solution to this problem takes advantage of a state diagram design of the system, as well as a notification object, object confinement, and a totally synchronized object, to ensure a safe implementation of this component.
3. An expansion of the *gas station simulation* from Chapter 3 has multiple pumps and one queue for cars waiting for a pump. This problem uses the Java Event Model and a state diagram for the design of a pump, as well as the ability to pass an object to other objects for processing.
4. A proper *controller* for the animator. The controller in the animator suffers from a number of problems. The worst problem is that the control of the animator from the control panel is really a hack that tightly couples the animator to the controller of the animator. This is fixed by using interfaces to separate the controller from the animator and by using the techniques from Chapter 3 to implement an object that defines and encapsulates the interactions required to control the animator.

9.2 Chapter Goals

After finishing this chapter you should be able to:

- Understand how a notification object can be used to create a fair component.
- Optimize a component by using a notification object to reduce the number of threads that are notified and moved from a wait queue.
- Relax the rules for synchronizing a monitor so that a component is faster as it allows more concurrency in the object.
- Understand the concept of confinement and how it can be used to control access to a component to ensure that it is safe to use the component concurrently even if some of the methods in the monitor are not synchronized.
- Create a thread-safe component by allowing the component to be given to one and only one thread at a time by using the Java Event Model.
- Implement an adapter to provide special handling of messages and events for other components and threads.
- Decompose a more complicated system into several simpler parts by using interfaces and intermediary components.

9.3 A First-In/First-Out Binary Semaphore

In Chapter 2, a binary semaphore was introduced to protect a critical region in the swap method of an object. The semaphore allowed a thread to obtain a lock when it entered a method and to release the lock when it left the method, thereby ensuring that only a single thread could be in that method at any one time. This scheme of locking and unlocking was used to illustrate the behavior of a synchronized block in Java; however, this semaphore was unfair in that if more than one thread was waiting for the semaphore the first thread to begin waiting was not necessarily the thread that would obtain the semaphore after another thread released it. This behavior mirrors the behavior of the Java synchronized statement, where the same unfair locking can occur.

The fact that a semaphore is unfair is normally not a problem. In fact, it allows the semaphore to be implemented more simply and to work well with thread priorities, but occasions arise when it would be nice to have a way to make sure that threads obtain the semaphore in the order in which they began waiting for it. Such a semaphore is a first-in/first-out binary semaphore (FIFOBS).

This section implements just such a FIFOBS using the type of monitor introduced in Chapter 3. However, because the rules on notify and notifyAll on an object do not allow the system to choose which thread will be given the semaphore, a notification object will be used for the notify in the state diagram so that a specific thread (the one waiting the longest) can be notified. This change shows how a notification object can be included in the simple monitor to greatly enhance the capabilities of the monitor object.

The rest of this section shows how to use a notification object in a monitor by using the example of the FIFOBS. The first step involves designing the state diagram for the component, as shown in Exhibit 1. The state diagram for this component is very similar to the state diagram for the unfair semaphore from Chapter 2. This is true because the basic

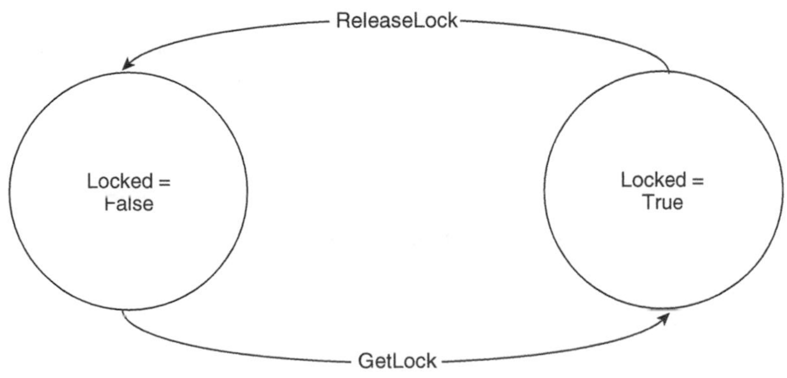

Exhibit 1. Binary Semaphore State Diagram

operations of the semaphore remain the same. In fact, it would be easy to define a binary semaphore interface and then simply instantiate the type of binary semaphore (fair or unfair) to be used at run time. The only thing that changes is the way in which the translations between the states for the monitor are handled in the program.

The code for the FIFOBS is given in Exhibit 2 (Program9.1). Because a specific thread is to be notified when the lock is free, the threads

Exhibit 2. Program9.1: FIFOBS implementation

```
import java.util.Vector;
import java.util.Random;

public class FIFOBS {
  private boolean locked;  // State of the semaphore
  private Vector waiting;  // Vector of notification objects
                           // Objects are released in the order
                           // in which they are entered into
                           // the vector.
  /**
   *  Public constructor. Set the monitor state and create the
   *  waiting object vector.
   */
  public FIFOBS () {
    locked = false;
    waiting = new Vector();
  }

  /**
   *  Get the lock on this semaphore if it is available. If the
   *  lock is not available, then put a notification object on
   *  the wait list to wait until the semaphore is free.
   */
  public void getLock(){
    Object waitObject = new Object();
    synchronized(waitObject) {
      synchronized(this) {
        if (locked) {
          waiting.addElement(waitObject);
        }
        else{
          waitObject = null;// No need to wait, get rid of
                    // object
        }
        locked = true;  // Note that this must be set
                        // while holding the semaphore
                        // object (this) lock.
      }

      if (waitObject ! = null) {
        try {
          waitObject.wait();
        } catch (InterruptedException e) {
        }
      }
    }
  }

  /**
   *  Release the lock on the semaphore. If any thread is
   *  waiting, notify the thread that has been waiting the longest;
```

(continued)

Exhibit 2. Program9.1 (Continued)

```
   * do not release the lock. This allows the lock to transfer
   * to the notified thread. Because the lock is never true, it
   * cannot be acquired by any other thread. If no threads are
   * waiting, set the semaphore to unlocked.
   */
  public synchronized void releaseLock() {
    if (waiting.size() > 0) {
      Object wakeObject = waiting.firstElement();
      waiting.removeElementAt(0);
      synchronized(wakeObject) {
        wakeObject.notify();
      }
    }
    else {
      locked = false;
    }
  }

/**
 * Main test program.
 */
public static void main(String args[]) {
    FIFOBS fifobs = new FIFOBS();
    Thread a[] = new Thread[10];
    for (int i = 0; i < 10; ++i) {
      (new Thread(new testP(fifobs, i))).start();
    }
  }
}

/**
 * This class simply creates the thread that allows us to test
 * the semaphore.
 */
class testP implements Runnable {
  FIFOBS fifobs;
  int id;
  Random random;
  public testP(FIFOBS fifobs, int id) {
    this.fifobs = fifobs;
    this.id = id;
    random = new Random(id);
  }

  public void run() {
    try {
      Thread.sleep(random.nextInt(500));
      System.out.println("Process "+ id + " Waiting");
      fifobs.getLock();
      System.out.println("Process " + id + " In Critical
         Section");
      Thread.sleep(500);
      System.out.println("Process " + id + " Free");
      fifobs.releaseLock();
    } catch(InterruptedException e) {
    }
  }
}
```

do not all wait on the monitor object, and all waiting threads are not notified to check the monitor when the state changes. Instead, each thread waits on a specific object, and the FIFOBS implements a queue of these objects. When the lock is freed, the FIFOBS takes the first object off of the queue and notifies that specific object. Because only one thread is waiting on that object, and that thread is the one that has been waiting the longest, that thread will be the one that is notified and will begin running. Thus, the FIFOBS is a fair semaphore.

In this program, the simpler test that the object is in the correct state as a precondition has been replaced by a more complex implementation that allows the object to wait and notify on a specific notification object. The reason for this complexity has to do with the format of the notification object. Because the notification object requires that the lock on the "this" object (in this case, the monitor object) be dropped before waiting on the notification object, accommodations must be made to make sure that all access to critical data (operations that must occur in a program critical region) only occur in the synchronized block on the "this" (monitor) object. Operations that occur while the notification object lock is held cannot be considered to be inside of the critical region, as the lock on the "this" object is what protects the critical region. Therefore, the presence of a notification object causes the critical section in the monitor to be broken between the checking of the precondition and the code and post-condition parts of the method.

The reason this was not a problem in the monitor as defined in Chapter 3 was that the lock on the monitor was obtained before the state of the monitor was checked, and no changes were made unless the monitor was in the correct state, allowing the lock to then be held through the rest of the method. If the monitor was not in the correct state, the lock was dropped, but the precondition was never part of the critical section of the program. With the notification object, the state can be checked and the thread allowed to enter the monitor with the lock on the "this" object not held. Attempting to obtain the lock with a later "synchronized(this)" block is also not sufficient, because a race condition can occur before the lock is obtained again.

To prevent this race condition, the FIFOBS in Exhibit 2 (Program9.1) handles the critical data in a more *ad hoc* fashion. First, if the lock is not set, the thread sets it inside of what is basically the precondition, while the lock on the "this" object is held. If the lock is already held by another thread, the current thread will do a wait on a notification object. When the running thread attempts to release the lock, it first checks to see if any threads are waiting on the lock. If so, it notifies the waiting thread and does not set the lock to false, in effect *transferring* the lock to the new thread and not allowing any other thread an opportunity to obtain the lock. If no threads are waiting, it would set the lock to false, in effect releasing the lock so that it can be obtained by any thread.

Exhibit 2 (Program9.1) shows how a notification object can be merged with a simple monitor; however, it lacks the simplicity and consistency of the monitors in Chapter 3, where all methods consisted of a precondition guard, the program code, the post-condition processing, and a return value. For simple situations, this *ad hoc* method of adding the notification object to a monitor is not difficult, but it would be nice to generalize a methodology for adding a notification object to a monitor. One example of doing this is found in Exhibit 3 (Program9.2). In this program, a new state is created from which the getLock method can be called. This new state is dependent on the number of threads waiting for this object. If the lock is taken or any thread is currently waiting, the thread will be forced to wait on the notification object's queue. The only other consideration necessary is to show that no harmful race condition exists between the time the "this" object's lock is dropped and it is reacquired in the getLock method. This is left for an exercise.

As shown in this section, notification objects can be combined with monitor objects to create fair components. They can also be used to optimize a component by getting rid of wasteful calls to the notifyAll method, as shown in Section 9.4.

9.4 Readers/Writers Problem

The readers/writers problem is a classical case of how the synchronization in a program can greatly affect the speed of the program. In the readers/writers problem, a number of activities must be read or written to a buffer. Obviously, one way to make the buffer safe would be to allow only one reader or writer in the buffer at a time; however, because the readers do not change the buffer, we have no reason to limit the number of readers accessing the buffer to one at a time. The possibility of a race condition does not exist, and allowing multiple readers to access the buffer concurrently allows for more concurrency in the program, thus allowing the readers to finish sooner and the program to run faster. On the other hand, the writers will modify the buffer, which could result in a race condition if any other reader or writer accessed the buffer concurrently with a writer; thus, only one thread can be allowed in the monitor if it is a writer.

A number of policies can be used to optimize a readers/writers program. One of the simplest is to allow readers to access the buffer until a writer requests the buffer to write to it. When the writer requests the buffer, readers currently using the buffer are allowed to finish using the buffer, but no new readers are allowed to start. When all the

Exhibit 3. Program9.2: Alternative FIFOBS Implementation with Pre- and Post-Conditions

```
import java.util.Vector;
import java.util.Random;

public class FIFOBS {
 private boolean locked;
 private Vector waiting;

  /**
   *  Public constructor. Initialize the locked variable and
   *  create waiting vector.
   */
  public FIFOBS () {
    locked = false;
    waiting = new Vector();
  }

  /**
   *  Get the lock on this semaphore if it is free. Note that
   *  here the method still has pre- and post-conditions, but
   *  extra code for locking has to be considered to make this
   *  work.
   */
  public void getLock(){

    // Pre-condition for the wait object.
    Object waitObject = new Object();
    synchronized(waitObject) {
      synchronized(this) {
        waiting.addElement(waitObject);
        if (! (locked || waiting.size() > 1))
          waitObject = null;
      }
      if (waitObject ! = null) {

        try {
          waitObject.wait();
        } catch (InterruptedException e) {
        }
      }
    }

    // Code section. Note the absence of a race condition here,
    // as a thread only comes through when no one is waiting
    // or the lock is free.
    synchronized (this) {
      locked = true;
      waiting.removeElementAt(0);

    // Post-condition. Note that the notifyAll here on the
    // monitor is useless as no threads are ever waiting on the
    // monitor itself. Also note that the synchronized block
    // from the code section should include the post-condition
    // processing.
    }
  }

  /**
   *  Release any locks held. If any threads are waiting,
   *  notify the one waiting the longest that this lock is
```

(continued)

Exhibit 3. Program9.2 (Continued)

```
   * now free. Note that the lock variable can be changed
   * in this method now.
   */
  public synchronized void releaseLock() {

    // Pre-condition is locked as "true," but this thread holds
    // the lock, so it must be true.

    // Code section
    locked = false;

    // Post-condition. Note you can only notify on notify object
    // if someone is waiting.
    if (waiting.size() > 0) {
      Object wakeObject = waiting.firstElement();
      synchronized(wakeObject) {
        wakeObject.notify();
      }
    }
  }

  /**
   * Main test program.
   */
  public static void main(String args[]) {
    FIFOBS fifobs = new FIFOBS();
    Thread a[] = new Thread[10];
    for (int i = 0; i < 10; ++i) {
      (new Thread(new testP(fifobs, i))).start();
    }
  }
}

/**
 * This class simply creates the thread that allows us to test
 * the semaphore.
 */
class testP implements Runnable {
  FIFOBS fifobs;
  int id;
  Random random;
  public testP(FIFOBS fifobs, int id) {
    this.fifobs = fifobs;
    this.id = id;
    random = new Random(id);
  }

  public void run() {
    try {
      Thread.sleep(random.nextInt(500));
      System.out.println("Process " + id + " Waiting");
      fifobs.getLock();
      System.out.println("Process " + id + " In Critical
          Section");
      Thread.sleep(500);
      System.out.println("Process " + id + " Free");
      fifobs.releaseLock();
    } catch(InterruptedException e) {
    }
  }
}
```

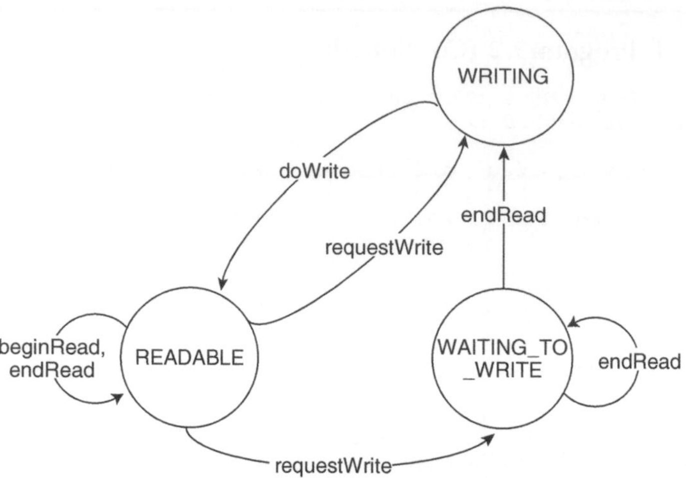

Exhibit 4. Readers/Writers State Diagram

current readers have finished, the writer uses the buffer and then releases it to allow readers and/or writers to access it again. Note that this is not an optimal strategy, as it only tracks one writer. Because the largest delay in the program is the time required to clear the buffer of readers before allowing a writer exclusive access, a more optimal strategy would be to allow not just one but all waiting writers to acquire the buffer before leaving the readers access to it again. However, the policy here is to inform only one writer when the buffer is free, and the more optimal solution is left as an exercise.

The state diagram necessary to implement the single writer policy is given in Exhibit 4. Note that the doRead method is not synchronized and so is not included in the state diagram. By not synchronizing the method, multiple readers can be accessing the object concurrently, but it also makes the doRead method unsafe. To safely access the doRead method, it should only be called after a successful call to beginRead, and endRead should always be called when it is completed; however, that policy is not enforced in any way in the buffer object. Also, a write should consist of a requestWrite followed by a doWrite method, but once again this policy is not enforced. If the state diagram is implemented so that it can be accessed directly from an implementing program, it becomes incumbent upon the programmer to follow the correct procedure of calling the methods in the proper order; however, it is not advised to rely on a programmer to implement a procedure consistently and correctly, particularly when the program is accessing a critical region. Exhibit 5 (Program9.3a) implements the buffer for this solution, and Exhibit 6 (Program9.3b) uses the buffer. The remainder of this section looks at how to handle this situation to ensure that the calls are correct and discusses why the actual implementation of the solution is not as simple as the steps laid out in Chapter 3.

Exhibit 5. Program9.3a: Readers/Writers Buffer Implementation

```
public class Buffer {
  private HiddenBuffer hb = new HiddenBuffer();
  // The actual buffer used. Access to this buffer is only
  // through the read and write methods.

  /**
   *  Read an object from the buffer. Note that to make this
   *  work the intention to read the buffer must first be
   *  declared by calling beginRead. The unsynchronized method
   *  doRead can then be called. Finally, the thread must say
   *  that it is finished by calling endRead.
   *

   *  Because this is all encapsulated in this method, the user
   *  of this buffer needs only to call this method as "Object
   *
   *  = buffer.read()," and the details will be handled.
   */
  public Object read() {
    System.out.println("Reader waiting for buffer");
    hb.beginRead();
    System.out.println("Reader got buffer");
    Object returnObject = hb.doRead();
    hb.endRead();
    System.out.println("Reader finished");
    return returnObject;
  }

/**
   *  Write an object to the buffer. Note that first the
   *  intention to write to the buffer must be declared by
   *  calling requestWrite. When the buffer is safe, the doWrite
   *  method is called, allowing the write to finish.
   */

public void write(Object o) {
    System.out.println("Writer requesting buffer");
    hb.requestWrite();
    hb.doWrite(new Object());
    System.out.println("Writer done with buffer");
  }

  /**
   *  This is the actual buffer object.
   */
  private class HiddenBuffer {
    // Buffer state variables.
    private static final int READABLE = 0;
    private static final int WAITING_TO_WRITE = 1;
    private static final int WRITING = 2;
    private int state = READABLE;

    private int numberOfReaders = 0;
    private Object notifyObject = new Object();
    // Note: Only a single notification object is used so only
    // a single writer can be notified. Also, note that we
    // cannot use the object to be written as the notification
    // object, as the user could have that one locked already.
```

(continued)

Exhibit 5. Program9.3a (Continued)

```
/**
 *  This method declares the intent of a thread to do a read.
 *  It protects the doRead method and returns when it is safe
 *  to call the doRead method.
 */
public synchronized void beginRead() {
  while(! (State = = READABLE) {
    try {
      wait();
    } catch(InterruptedException e) {
    }
  }

  numberOfReaders++;

  // No post-condition, as state will not change.
}

/**
 *  This method reads the data from the buffer and returns
 *  the object. Note this is only simulated here by a
 *  .5-second delay. Also note that this method is
 *  unsynchronized, allowing multiple simultaneous readers.
 */
public Object doRead() {
  try {
    Thread.sleep(500);// .5 second delay
  } catch(InterruptedException e) {
  }

  return new Object();
}

/**
 *  This method declares the thread to have completed
 *  reading the buffer. If any thread is waiting to write,
 *  when the numberOfReaders becomes 0, allow the writer
 *  thread to continue.
 */
public synchronized void endRead() {
  while (! ((state = = READABLE) ||
      (state = = WAITNG_TO_WRITE))) {
    try {
      wait();
    } catch(InterruptedException e) {
    }
  }

  numberOfReaders -- ;

  if ((numberOfReaders = = 0) && (state = = WAITING_TO_WRITE))
      {
    state = WRITING;
    synchronized(notifyObject) {
      notifyObject.notify();
    }
  }
}
```

(continued)

Exhibit 5. Program9.3a (Continued)

```
/**
 *  This method allows a writer thread to declare its intent
 *  to read from the buffer. This method will return when it
 *  is safe to call the doWrite method.
 */
public void requestWrite() {
    Object temp = new Object();
    synchronized (temp) {
      synchronized(this) {
        notifyObject = temp;
        // Can only requestWrite from state READABLE. This
        // means only one writer can be waiting at a time;
        // others must wait here.
        // Note that the wait drops the lock on the
        // HiddenBuffer object but holds it on the temp
        // object. This is not a problem, as the temp object
        // does not have scope outside of this method yet.
        while (! (state = = READABLE)) {
          try {
            wait();
          } catch(InterruptedException e) {
          }
        }

        // Post Conditions
        if (numberOfReaders = = 0) {
          state = WRITING;
          // notifyAll();     // Not needed.
          notifyObject = null;
        }
        else {
          state = WAITING_TO_WRITE;

          // notifyAll();// Not needed.
        }
      }

      // Note that we have to do the waiting to write here
      // while we still hold the notifyObject lock.
      if (notifyObject ! = null){
        try {
          notifyObject.wait();
        } catch(InterruptedException e) {
        }
      }
    }
  }

  /**
   *  This method writes the data from the buffer and returns
   *  the object. Note that this is only simulated here by a
   *  .5-second delay.
   */
  public synchronized void doWrite(Object o) {
    while(! (state = = WRITING)) {
      try {
        wait();
      } catch(InterruptedException e) {
      }
    }
```

(continued)

Exhibit 5. Program9.3a (Continued)

```
      // The write would be done here.
      try {
        Thread.sleep(500);
      } catch(InterruptedException e) {
      }

      // Post-condition

      state = READABLE;
      notifyAll();
    }
  }
}
```

9.4.1 Confinement

In order to implement the readers/writers buffer correctly, the read must always execute the methods beginRead, doRead, and finally endRead, in that order. The write must also execute the requestWrite and doWrite methods in order. If a programmer is allowed direct access to the readers/writers buffer, the programmer has to make sure to always execute the statements in this order. The most dangerous part of allowing a programmer direct access to this buffer is that the doRead method is not synchronized, but instead is protected by the calls to beginRead and endRead. If a programmer accesses this unsynchronized method directly, the possibility of a race condition is introduced into the program; therefore, this method should not allow programmers direct access.

One way to protect the unsynchronized method and ensure that it is not called incorrectly is to encapsulate or hide the buffer inside of another object that will implement the correct behavior. When this object is not able to leak information outside of the program, it is called *confinement*. In Exhibit 3 (Program9.2), the Buffer class is the external representation of the buffer, but the actual buffer represented by the state diagram in Exhibit 4 is the inner class called HiddenBuffer. Inner classes are covered in more detail in Chapter 12, but for now just realize that this class cannot be accessed except through objects of the Buffer class; hence, the HiddenBuffer is confined to the Buffer and is safe as long as the Buffer is implemented correctly.

Using this scheme, the Buffer class can implement a *read* method that correctly calls beginRead, doRead, and endRead on the HiddenBuffer, thus ensuring that the semantics of the read are correct. The method also ensures that the doRead method is not called unsafely, as no objects except the Buffer class can access this method.

This confinement has one other nice property. The calling program does not need to know more than what it wants to read or write to

Exhibit 6. Program9.3b: Using the Readers/Writers Buffer

```
import java.util.*;

public class ReadersWriters {
  public static void main(String args[]) {
    Buffer buffer = new Buffer();
    for (int i = 0; i < 50; i++)
      (new Thread(new Reader(buffer, i))).start();
    for (int i = 0; i < 3; i++)
      (new Thread(new Writer(buffer, i+50))).start();
  }
}

/**
 * This class implements a reader thread.
 */
class Reader implements Runnable {
  private Buffer buffer;
  private int readerNumber;
  private Random random;

  public Reader(Buffer buffer, int readerNumber) {
    this.buffer = buffer;
    this.readerNumber = readerNumber;
    random = new Random(readerNumber);
  }
  public void run() {
    try {
      while(true) {
        Thread.sleep(random.nextInt(5000));
        buffer.read();
      }
    } catch(InterruptedException e) {
    }
  }
}
/**
 * This class implements a writer thread.
 */
class Writer implements Runnable {
  private Buffer buffer;
  private int writerNumber;
  private Random random;
  public Writer(Buffer buffer, int writerNumber) {

    this.buffer = buffer;
    this.writerNumber = writerNumber;
    random = new Random(writerNumber);
  }

  public void run() {
    try {
      while(true) {
        Thread.sleep(random.nextInt(50000));
        buffer.write(new Object());
      }
    } catch(InterruptedException e) {
    }
  }
}
```

the Buffer. All the semantics of properly using the Buffer are contained in the read and write methods, so a calling program only needs to call a simple read or write to make the program work correctly. This makes using the buffer easier for the programmer, and the code for accessing the buffer is cleaner and clearer. It also means that if a more effective locking scheme is developed for accessing the buffer, the object using the buffer need only refer to this new object, as all the details are hidden.

9.4.2 Notification Objects

The other important property in the HiddenBuffer class is the use of notification objects to optimize the running of the buffer. This optimization involves carefully deciding what threads must be notified when states change and limiting the notification to only those threads that are affected. The reason this is an important and potentially large savings is that when a notify (or worse, notifyAll) call is made, a potentially large number of threads are moved from a wait list to the ready set. While on the wait list, these threads are idle and consume no processor time. When the threads are notified and moved to the ready set, these threads will have to be run, which causes a context switch for each thread. These threads must also attempt to regain the lock on the monitor object, as that is the first activity of a thread when it starts to run after a call to wait. Both of these operations have relatively high overhead, so calls to notify or notifyAll are fairly expensive. Further, if the only possible outcome of the call is for the thread to be put back in the wait state immediately, it is an expensive call that really does not need to be made. So, anytime a notify or notifyAll call can be removed safely from a program, it can represent a fairly substantial savings of resources. This is especially true in the case of the readers/writers problem, where a large number of readers might be waiting until a writer has written, so if they are notified their only action is simply to go back to a wait state.

The optimization done in the readers/writers problem is achieved by recognizing that, while having every thread wait on the monitor is a correct solution, it does incur significant useless overhead; therefore, only notify and notifyAll calls on the object will be done when they are specifically needed. In cases where only a single thread can run as the result of a state change, that thread will be notified specifically using a notification object.

This type of optimization can be used very effectively in the readers/writers problem. To see how this optimization can be done, consider first the transition (or method) endRead. If the endRead method is called when the HiddenBuffer monitor is in the state READABLE, there is no transition to another state so a notifyAll call does not need to be done. However, if the HiddenBuffer monitor is in the WAITING_TO_WRITE state, the only waiting thread that would ever be able to execute is the one writer thread that moved into the WAITING_TO_WRITE state, so it is notified specifically using a notification object when the numberOfReaders is zero. Because the notifyAll call in this method would have occurred once for each thread that needed to complete a read, and each notification could have potentially moved each thread waiting to read to the ready list, the savings in potential context switching and contention for the lock on the object could be quite large.

Next consider the requestWrite method. First, if no readers are currently using the buffer (numberOfReaders = 0), the Writer thread does not need to wait when running this method. Further, because this writer thread requires exclusive use of the buffer when running, any thread that might be notified would have to be put back to sleep immediately, so a notifyAll does not need to be done when moving to the WRITING state. Second, the only reader threads that are able to run once a requestToWrite call has been made are currently executing reader threads; therefore, no threads that are waiting can run. When moving to a WAITING_TO_WRITE state, then, no threads should have to be notified and a notifyAll is simply wasted.

This new version of the monitor is more complex than the one derived directly from the state diagram; however, the improvement in performance is probably worth the extra complexity if that complexity is implemented correctly. Doing so is not easy, though, and when improving the performance of a monitor it is best to start with one derived directly from the rules in Chapter 3 and then modify it carefully to improve performance. Keep in mind two old saws about programming:

> *Make it right then make it fast.*

and

> *It is easier to make a correct program fast than to make a fast program correct.*

Often a monitor with a notification object represents a good solution to a problem, but some more complex problems are more difficult, if not impossible, to implement. For example, it is difficult to write a program where a thread listens to two monitors for the first to become free. In these cases, designs using the Java Event Model are much better, as is shown in the improved gas station simulation in Section 9.5.

9.5 An Improved Gas Station Simulation

The gas station simulation that was written in Chapter 3 was limited in that the pump the car would wait on was assigned when the car was created. This was because the pump was modeled as a monitor object. The car had to wait for a pump object to move to the FREE state in the monitor before being able to move to the pump. Because a thread cannot be waiting on two monitors at the same time, the gas pump that was used had to be assigned before the car could begin waiting. If multiple pumps were to be used, the car would have to decide which pump to wait on before beginning to wait. In effect, a multiple pump solution involved lines at each pump with cars waiting for a specific pump. It was not possible to create a single queue of cars and allow them to go to the next available pump.

One other problem with using simple monitors is that the Java wait method is unfair, so it was not even possible to ensure that cars would be serviced in the order in which they arrived. This was graphically illustrated by Program8.7, where the animation showed cars moving to the pump before others that were waiting longer.

This section looks at how to simulate the gas station where all cars are in a single queue waiting for the next available pump. Because of the special problem of matching *m* pumps to *n* cars, a simple monitor solution, even with notification objects, just is not powerful enough to implement this simulation. Instead, the Java Event Model can be used with another object, known as an *adapter*, to create a solution.

The gas station simulation provided here still includes the pump, which has methods that are called in the same order as the methods in Program 3.2; however, these methods are not synchronized. Instead, when the pump is free it will pass a reference to itself to a listener on the pump. In this way, a copy of the pump object will be passed (eventually, as will be shown) to a car object. Because only one car object has a copy of the pump object at a time, the methods of the pump do not need to be synchronized.

If the gas station had only one pump or if a car could be forced to choose a pump when entering the gas station, the car objects could implement a pump listener directly; however, because we have many pumps and one queue of cars, an intermediary object, an instance of the class PumpManager, is used in the design. The purpose of the pump manager object is twofold. First, the pump manager is the pump listener and listens to many pumps. It this way, it de-multiplexes the pumps which effectively allows the cars to wait on more than one pump. The second purpose of the pump manager is to implement a notification object to process the cars in a first-in/first-out order. An object that sits between other objects to manage the interactions between those objects is called an adapter, and in this design the pump manager is an adapter between the pumps and the cars.

A graphic that shows how the gas station simulation works is shown in Exhibits 7 through 9. The overall program works in three steps. In the first step, shown in Exhibit 7, all the pumps notify the pump manager that they are free, and as part of that notification event pass

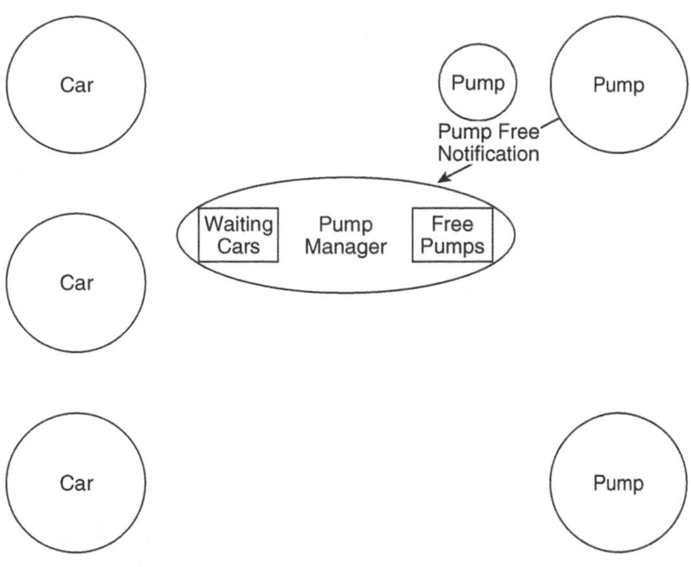

Exhibit 7. Pump Notifies Pump Manager It Is Free

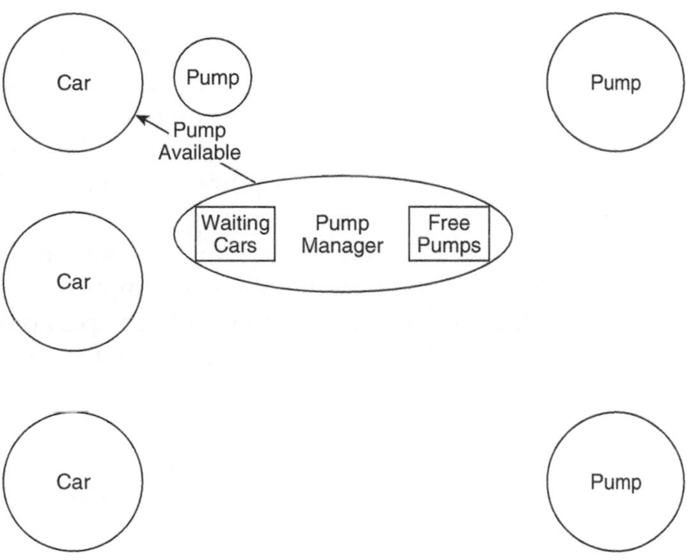

Exhibit 8. Pump Manager Gives Pump to a Waiting Car

a reference to the pump itself to the pump manager. When the pump manager receives the event from the pump, it places the pump in a vector of free pumps. It then sees if any cars are currently waiting on a pump. If one is, then the pump manager uses its notification object to let it know that a pump is now free for its use.

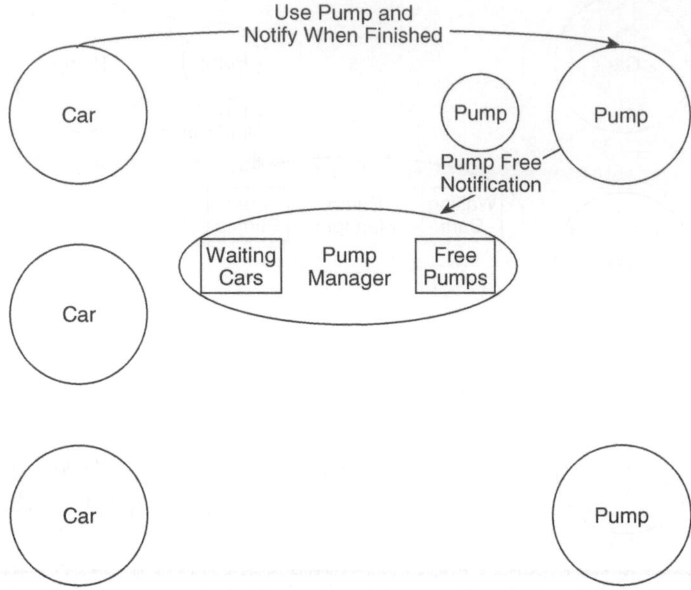

Exhibit 9. Car Uses Pump and Pump Notifies the Pump Manager When It Is Free Again

In the second step, shown in Exhibit 8, the car arrives and asks the pump manager, via a call to get Pump, for a pump to use. If one is available, the pump manager gives the pump object to the car; otherwise, the car is put in a wait queue using a notification object, and the car will be notified later when a pump becomes available via a message from the pump to the pump manager.

The final step is that the car now calls the methods on the pump object to complete the simulation. When the car completes, it calls the pump's leave method, which generates an event to the pump manager, freeing this pump and notifying the pump manager that it can now assign this pump to another car.

The code for implementing this gas station simulation is given in Program9.4 (Exhibits 10 through 15). Because the pump events are implemented using the Java Event Model, it was necessary to implement a listener interface (Exhibit 10 [Program9.4a]) and an event object (Exhibit 11 [Program9.4b]). The Pump, Car, and PumpManager classes are implemented in Exhibits 12 to 14 (Program9.4c, Program9.4d, and Program9.4e). Finally, the overall controlling program, the GasStation class, is implemented in Exhibit 15 (Program9.4f).

It should be noted that the only objects in this simulation containing threads are the cars. So, when the car calls the leave method, and the pump generates an event to the pump manager, the event in the pump manager runs in the car thread. This involves the thread going across two different passive objects. A much safer design would isolate this

Exhibit 10. Program9.4a: PumpListener Class

```
import java.util.EventListener;

public interface PumpListener extends EventListener {
  public void pumpReady(PumpEvent e) ;
}
```

Exhibit 11. Program9.4b: PumpEvent Class

```
import java.util.EventObject;

public class PumpEvent extends java.util.EventObject {
  private Pump pump;
  public PumpEvent(Object source, Pump pump) {
    super(source);
    this.pump = pump;
  }

  Pump getPump() {
    return pump;
  }
}
```

deep of a notification in a separate thread to prevent unforeseen delays or even possible deadlocks. This would be a particular problem if the pump manager could call back to the car that started the event; if the methods in the car were synchronized, then deadlock could occur. For this simulation this is not an issue, as the Car object is complete as soon as the event occurs, and in no methods could the car be called from the pump manager or pump; however, this level of indirection on a thread is generally not advisable. The chat program in Chapter 12 has such a deep calling structure and the possibility of just such a deadlock occurring.

We must mention here one more caveat regarding the pump manager that is often true of methods that use notification objects and return values. Because a notification object is used, the return value from the getPump method occurs outside of the synchronized block for the "this" object. This is very dangerous, and care should be taken when setting the return value. Technically, this program has a race condition. For example, suppose Car 1 arrives at the gas station followed by Car 2, and the pumps are then freed in the order of Pump 1 then Pump 2. Our intent is to give Pump 1 to Car 1, and Pump 2 to Car 2; however, in the program as written it is possible for Car 1 to get Pump 2 and Car 2 to get Pump 1. This is not a real problem in this simulation because the pump manager gives a free pump to the cars as pumps become free. However, it does show that a race condition is present because of the notification object locking.

Exhibit 12. Program9.4c: Pump Class

```
import java.util.Vector;
import java.util.Enumeration;

class Pump {
  private Vector pumpListeners = new Vector();

  /**
   * Method to add a listener to the pump
   */
  public void addPumpListener(PumpListener pl) {
    pumpListeners.addElement(pl);
  }

  /**
   *  Method to remove a listener from the pump
   */
  public void removePumpListener(PumpListener pl) {
    pumpListeners.removeElement(pl);
  }

  /**
   *  This is the process event method for the pump event. It is
   *  called when the pump is free.
   */
  public void notifyPumpIsFree() {
    PumpEvent evt = new PumpEvent(this, this);
    Vector v;

    synchronized(this) {
      v = (Vector) pumpListeners.clone();
    }

    Enumeration e1 = v.elements();
    while (e1.hasMoreElements()) {
      PumpListener P = (PumpListener)(e1.nextElement());
      P.pumpReady(evt);
    }
  }

/**
   *  Method that turns the pump on. It lets any listeners
   *  know that the pump is now available to use.
   */
  public void startPump() {
    notifyPumpIsFree();
  }

  /**
   *  Method to simulate pulling up to the pump
   */
  public void usePump() {
    try {

      // Simulate pulling to the pump by waiting .5 second.
      Thread.sleep(500);

    } catch (InterruptedException e) {
    }
  }
```

(continued)

Exhibit 12. Program9.4c (Continued)

```
  /**
   *  Method to simulate pumping the gas
   */
  public void pumpGas() {
    try {

      // Simulate pumping gas by waiting 5 seconds.
      Thread.sleep(5000);

    } catch (InterruptedException e) {
    }
  }

  /**
   *  Method to simulate leaving the pump
   */
  public void leave() {
    try {
      // Simulate leaving the pump by waiting .5 second.
      Thread.sleep(500);
      notifyPumpIsFree();
    } catch (InterruptedException e) {
    }
  }
}
```

In this case, if the pump given to a car did matter, another solution would have to be sought. For example, the notification object could be changed to store the correct pump, and that pump could be set in the synchronized block of the pumpReady method of the Pump manager. This pump could be retrieved in the getPump method. Because the notification object has a direct correspondence to a specific car thread, this would guarantee that the correct car is given to the correct thread. The details of actually implementing this are left as an exercise.

9.5.1 Adapters

The concept of an adapter was mentioned in the context of the PumpManager object. An adapter is a very important type of object in component programming. It is not a component, but an adapter is an object that changes the plumbing (so to speak) of an object so that the behavior of the object more closely matches the needs of the problem to be solved. Adapters have real-world uses, and most of these have analogs in OOP. For example, in plumbing a 1/2-inch pipe cannot be directly connected to a 1/4 pipe; an adapter would have to be used to change the diameter of one of the pipes. Another use for an adapter is to split a single input into multiple outputs, such as is accomplished by a cable splitter, which is used to break the input

Exhibit 13. Program9.4d: Car Class

```
import java.util.Date;
import java.util.Random;

publicclass Car implements Runnable {
  private static int totalTime = 0,// Total time spent by all
                // cars
                          totalCars = 0;// Total number of
cars
  private int customerNumber;
  private Pump myPump;
  private PumpManager pumpManager;

  /**
   * Public constructor. This constructor sets the
   * customerNumber for output and sets the pumpManager
   * so that it can talk to the adapter component.
   */
  public Car(int customerNumber, PumpManager pumpManager) {
    this.customerNumber = customerNumber;
    this.pumpManager = pumpManager;
  }

  /**
   * At the end of the simulation, this method is used to
   * calculate the average time taken by all the cars in the
   * simulation.
   */
  public static float calcAverage() {
    return totalTime/totalCars;
  }

  /**
   * Run method, where the behavior of the car in the
   * simulation is defined.
   */

  public void run() {
    final int WAIT_TIME = 30000;
    long startTime, endTime;
    Random random = new Random(customerNumber);
    int waitTime = random.nextInt(WAIT_TIME);

    // Wait a random amount of time before coming to pump.
    try {
      Thread.sleep(waitTime);

      startTime = (new Date()).getTime();
      // Wait for Pump Manager to tell me a pump is free.
      System.out.println("Customer " + customerNumber +
          " waiting in line");
      myPump = pumpManager.getPump();

      System.out.println("Customer " + customerNumber +
          " arrives at pump");
      myPump.usePump();
      System.out.println("Customer " + customerNumber +
          " pumps gas");
      myPump.pumpGas();
```

(continued)

Exhibit 13. Program9.4d: Car Class (Continued)

```
      System.out.println("Customer " + customerNumber +
          " leaves pump");
      myPump.leave();
      endTime = (new Date()).getTime();
      System.out.println("Time = " + (endTime - startTime));
      totalTime + = (endTime - startTime);
      totalCars++;
    } catch (InterruptedException e) {
    }
  }
}
```

from a single cable input line into multiple lines that can be used on multiple televisions in a home. Adapters can also bring multiple inputs together into a single output, such as all the drains in a home connecting to form one output line to the local sewer. A final example of an adapter is one that can take multiple input lines and filter them in some manner — for example, by choosing one of them, much as a radio or television selects from all the different radio wave or cable frequencies being received.

Before discussing adapters further, it is important to realize that the use of an adapter can result in other problems that have to be solved. For example, an adapter designed to connect a 1/2-inch pipe to 1/4-inch pipe would also have to handle problems associated with pressure differences resulting from the change in pipe diameter. The cable splitter may have to include a repeater to account for the loss of signal attenuation. Just as adapters have counterparts in OOP, adapters used in OOP also have problems that must be addressed when they are implemented.

Adapters have many uses in OOP that often correspond to the use of adapters in the real world. For example, to use an existing object in a new environment it might be necessary to map the interface methods of the existing object to the new methods that will work in the new environment. In this case, a separate adapter object could be created that would provide the connection between the object and the new environment, much as the plumbing adapter connects the 1/2-inch and 1/4-inch pipes. Another example of an adapter in OOP would be a single object that listens to the events generated from a process, such as the temperature controller on a chemical reactor. This object could filter the temperature events, looking for ones where the temperature exceeds some limit, and then could multicast that event to a number of listeners. This would save time, as only the events of interest would be generated to all the listeners, and the check for temperature deviations could occur once in a single object.

In the gas station example, the pump manager is an example of an adapter in that it listens to all of the possible pumps (acting as a de-multiplexer) and then assigns a car to the pump (acting as a filter

Exhibit 14. Program9.4e: PumpManager Class

```
import java.util.Vector;

public class PumpManager implements PumpListener {
  private Vector customers = new Vector();
  private Vector pumps = new Vector();
  private int pumpsAvailable = 0;

  /**
   * This method is called by a car thread to get a Pump object
   * that it can use. If no Pump object is available, the car
   * thread will wait until a pump manager has a pump
   * available. The car threads are notified in the order in
   * which they begin waiting.
   */
  public Pump getPump() {
    Object notifyObject = new Object();
    synchronized (notifyObject) {
      synchronized(this) {
          pumpsAvailable — ;
          if (pumpsAvailable < 0) {
            customers.addElement(notifyObject);
          }
          else {
            notifyObject = null;
          }
      }
      if (notifyObject ! = null)
        try {
          notifyObject.wait();
        } catch (InterruptedException e) {
      }
    }

    return (Pump)(pumps.remove(0));
  }

  /**
   * This method is called by the Pump object when it becomes
   * free (i.e., it starts or a car leaves). Note that this
   * method must consider the cases where a customer (car) is or
   * is not waiting.
   */
  public synchronized void pumpReady(PumpEvent e) {
    pumps.addElement(e.getPump());
    pumpsAvailable++;
    if (!customers.isEmpty()) {
      Object notifyObject = customers.remove(0);
      synchronized(notifyObject) {
        notifyObject.notify();
      }
    }
  }
}
```

Exhibit 15: Program9.4f: GasStation Class

```
public class GasStation {
  public static final int NUMBER_OF_CUSTOMERS = 10;

  public static void main(String args[]) {
    Pump pump1 = new Pump();
    Pump pump2 = new Pump();

    PumpManager pm = new PumpManager();
    pump1.addPumpListener(pm);
    pump2.addPumpListener(pm);

    pump1.startPump();
    pump2.startPump();

    Thread threadArray[] = new Thread[NUMBER_OF_CUSTOMERS];
    for (int i = 0; i < NUMBER_OF_CUSTOMERS; i++) {
      threadArray[i] = new Thread(new Car(i, pm));
      threadArray[i].start();
    }

    for (int i = 0; i < NUMBER_OF_CUSTOMERS; i++) {
      try {
        threadArray[i].join();
      } catch(InterruptedException e) {
      }
    }

    // Print average time at the end of the simulation.
    System.out.println("Average time to get gas = " +
      Car.calcAverage());
  }
}
```

on the pumps). This use of an adapter to the pump event is important, as otherwise the cars would have to listen to all the events from all the pumps and choose from among themselves who will be allowed to act in response to the event. This scenario would be complicated to program and would result in significant runtime overhead.

9.6 Improving the Animator

The last program developed in this chapter shows how multiple paradigms can be applied to create more effective solutions. In the animator in Chapter 7, a control panel was included as part of the animator object. This control panel allowed the animator to start, stop, and single step an animation. It also allowed an animation to be sped up or slowed down. This was a useful enhancement, but the control panel was pretty much hacked into the animator. This is obvious because the control panel had to manipulate shared variables internal to the animator to get the control to perform correctly. A good design

Exhibit 16. Program9.5a: DrawListener Interface

```
import java.util.EventListener;

public interface DrawListener extends EventListener {
  public void draw(DrawEvent e);
}
```

would decouple the control panel from the animator. The example given here does this. The source code for all parts of this program is contained in Program9.5 (Exhibits 16 through 23).

9.6.1 Decoupling the Animator from the Control Panel

The first step in this process is to decouple the animator and control panel. When doing this, an intermediate interface, the Controller interface in Exhibit 19 (Program9.5d), is created. The purpose of the controller interface is to allow the animator to work with any generic controller. Thus, the controller given here is only one possible controller for the animator. Another controller could be developed that controls both the animator and the application that is being animated, or a controller could be developed to control multiple animators. Decoupling the controller from the animator raises many more possibilities for how the controller can be implemented.

The controller interface is defined with only a single method, a doRedraw method. This method is called each time a repaint occurs. The controller can only schedule a repaint event if it does not know when that event takes place. The purpose of the doRedraw method is for the animator to notify the controller that the scheduled redraw has taken place. This is the only interaction that the animator needs to have with the controller. Thus, by making this interface with one call, the animator is independent from the controller except when the controller schedules repaint events and the animator informs the controller that the event has taken place.

Other than allowing different controllers to use the animator, another advantage is offered by interfacing the controller and the animator in this manner. In the design presented here, the animator only has to call the controller to let the controller know that it has responded to the paint event. This is significantly less complicated than when the controller was built into the animator and a number of variables were shared. Now the concerns of the different parts of the program are well defined, and problems should be easier to understand and fix, as they should be isolated to smaller parts of the program.

Exhibit 17. Program9.5b: DrawEvent Class

```
import java.util.*;
import java.awt.*;
import java.io.Serializable;

public class DrawEvent extends EventObject implements
    Serializable {
  Graphics myGraphics;
  boolean doMove;

  /**
   * Public constructor that takes all the possible options
   * needed for this event
   */
  public DrawEvent(Object source, Graphics graphics, boolean
      doMove) {
    super(source);
    myGraphics = graphics;
    doMove = doMove;
  }

  /**
   * Public constructor that sets the doMove variable to the
   * default value of true
   */
  public DrawEvent(Object source, Graphics graphics) {
    this(source, graphics, true);
  }

  /**
   * Accessor method to return the value of the myGraphics
   * variable
   */
  public Graphics getGraphics() {
    return myGraphics;
  }

  /**
   * Accessor method to return the value of the doMove
   * variable
   */
  public boolean getDoMove() {
    return doMove;
  }
}
```

Exhibit 18. Program9.5c: ControllerAlreadyStartedException

```
public class ControllerAlreadyStartedException extends Exception
    {
  public ControllerAlreadyStartedException() {
  }

  public ControllerAlreadyStartedException(String s) {
    super(s);
  }
}
```

Exhibit 19. Program9.5d: Controller Interface

```
public interface Controller {
  public boolean doRedraw();
}
```

Exhibit 20. Program9.5e: ControllerImp Class

```
public class ControllerImpl implements Controller {
  // States for this monitor.
  private static final int WAITING = 0;
  private static final int MOVING = 1;
  private static final int DRAWING = 2;
  private static final int STOPPED = 3;

  private int controllerState = STOPPED;
  private int stateAfterDoRedraw = WAITING;

  /***************/

  private int waitTime = 100; // Time to wait between drawing.

  private Animator animator;  // Animator to be used with this
                              // controller.

  /**
   * Public constructor. This just hooks this controller up to
   * the animator.
   */
  public ControllerImpl(Animator animator) {
    this.animator = animator;
  }

  /**
   * This method is called by the animator's paint method to
   * reset this controller object and to return to the
   * animator whether or not the event that caused this repaint
   * was from the animator or some other event, such as a
   * reSize event. Because it is run from the GUI thread, it
   * cannot do a wait in the method.
   */
  public synchronized boolean doRedraw() {
    boolean returnValue;

    if (controllerState = = DRAWING)
      returnValue = true;
    else
      returnValue = false;
    if (controllerState = = DRAWING) {

      controllerState = stateAfterDoRedraw;
      notifyAll();
    }
    return returnValue;
  }
```

(continued)

Exhibit 20. Program9.5e (Continued)

```
/**
 * This method is called from the GUI's controller thread
 * to do the wait for the amount of time between redraws.
 * Because it cannot run in the GUI thread, it can execute a
 * wait inside of the method.
 */
public synchronized void doWait() {
  try {
    while (! (controllerState = = WAITING)) {
      wait();
    }

    controllerState = MOVING;
    notifyAll();

    wait(waitTime); // Post-processing; this hangs the
                    // controller thread for waitTime but
                    // also allows any notify to get it to
                    // start.
  } catch(InterruptedException e) {
  }
}

/**
 * This method is called from the GUI's controller thread
 * to signal that the thread is doing a move.
 */
public synchronized void doMove() {
  try {
    while (! ((controllerState = = MOVING) ||
        (controllerState = = WAITING))) {
      wait();
    }

    stateAfterDoRedraw = WAITING;
    animator.repaint();

    if (controllerState = = MOVING) {
      controllerState = DRAWING;
      notifyAll();
    }

  } catch(InterruptedException e) {
  }
}

/**
 * Called from the Controller GUI to stop the animator.
 * Because it runs in the thread, wait cannot be called from
 * this method. Also, when a button is pressed, the controller
 * notifies all waiting threads (in this case, only the GUI
 * controller thread).

 */
public synchronized void doStop() {
  stateAfterDoRedraw = STOPPED;
  controllerState = STOPPED;
  notifyAll();
}
```

(continued)

Exhibit 20. Program9.5e (Continued)

```
  /**
   *  Called from the Controller GUI to start the animator.
   *  Because it runs in the thread, wait cannot be called from
   *  this method. Also, when a button is pressed, the controller
   *  notifies all waiting threads (in this case, only the GUI
   *  controller thread).
   */
  public synchronized void doStart() {
    stateAfterDoRedraw = WAITING;
    animator.repaint();
    controllerState = DRAWING;
    notifyAll();
  }

  /**
   *  Called from the Controller GUI to step the animator.
   *  Because it runs in the thread, wait cannot be called from
   *  this method. Also, when a button is pressed, the controller
   *  notifies all waiting threads (in this case, only the GUI
   *  controller thread).
   */
  public synchronized void doStep() {
    stateAfterDoRedraw = STOPPED;
    animator.repaint();
    controllerState = DRAWING;
    notifyAll();
  }

  public synchronized void setWaitTime(int waitTime) {
    this.waitTime = waitTime;
    notifyAll();
  }
}
```

Exhibit 22 (Program9.5g) shows the animator that is implemented with the Controller interface. Note that now the animator consists only of the paint, addDrawListener, and removeDrawListener methods, and that the paint method is significantly simpler than before.

9.6.2 Correcting the Repaint Problem

The doRedraw method also allows a fix for a problem by calling the repaint method. When the repaint method is called from the controller thread, it creates a repaint event in the GUI thread; however, this repaint event is also created when another window passes over the animator or if the animator is resized. In fact, a number of things can cause a repaint event. When the animator from Chapter 7 is run, any of these redraw events could cause the animator to move all the objects in the animation.

To get around this, the doRedraw method returns a Boolean when called. The purpose of this Boolean is to allow the animator to determine whether or not the repaint event being processed originated

Exhibit 21. Program9.5f: ControlPanel Class

```
import java.awt.*;
import java.awt.event.*;
import java.util.*;
import javax.swing.*;

public class ControlPanel extends JPanel {
  private ControllerImpl controllerImpl;
  private boolean controllerStarted = false;

  /**
   *  Public constructor. This constructor hooks to the
   *  ControllerImp for control and then creates the panel with
   *  all the controls to run the animator.
   */
  public ControlPanel(ControllerImpl controllerImpl) {
    this.controllerImpl = controllerImpl;
    createPanel();
  }

  /**
   *  This method creates all the controls for the animator and
   *  hooks all the actions to the controls.
   */
  private void createPanel() {
    setLayout(new FlowLayout());
    final JButton startButton = new JButton("Start");
    startButton.addActionListener(new ActionListener() {
      public void actionPerformed(ActionEvent e) {
        JButton jb = (JButton)(e.getSource());
        String s = jb.getText();
        if (s.equals("Start")) {
          controllerImpl.doStart();
          startButton.setText("Stop");
        }
        else {
          controllerImpl.doStop();
          startButton.setText("Start");
        }
      }
    });
    add(startButton);

    final JButton stepButton = new JButton("Step");
    stepButton.addActionListener(new ActionListener() {
      public void actionPerformed(ActionEvent e) {
        controllerImpl.doStep();
        startButton.setText("Start");
      }
    });
    add(stepButton);

    JButton exitButton = new JButton("Exit");
    exitButton.addActionListener(new ActionListener() {
      public void actionPerformed(ActionEvent e) {
        System.exit(0);
      }
    });
    add(exitButton);
```

(continued)

Exhibit 21. Program9.5f (Continued)

```
    add(new Label("Animator Speed"));
    final JScrollBar speedControl = new JScrollBar(JScrollBar.
       HORIZONTAL, 500, 25, 100, 1000);
    speedControl.addAdjustmentListener(new AdjustmentListener()
       {
      public void adjustmentValueChanged(AdjustmentEvent e) {
        controllerImpl.setWaitTime(1000 - e.getValue());
      }
    });
    add(speedControl);
  }

  /**
   *  Display the control panel. Note that if by this time the
   *  control panel is not associated with an animator, it is a
   *  mistake. Throw control an exception if this happens.
   */
  public void startControlPanel() throws ControllerAlready
      StartedException {

    if (controllerStarted) {
      throw new ControllerAlreadyStartedException();
    }

    setVisible(true);
    controllerStarted = true;
    (new Thread(new ControlThread())).start();
  }

  /** Thread that runs the animator. This thread sleeps for some
   *  amount of time specified by sleepTime, then calls repaint,
   *  which forces a call to the paint method, but in the GUI
   *  thread. Note that the animatorStopped button allows the
   *  animator to single step and pause the animation. The
   *  notify is done in the control frame from the button.
   */

  private class ControlThread implements Runnable {
    public void run() {
      while (true) {
        controllerImpl.doWait();
        controllerImpl.doMove();
      }
    }
  }
}
```

from the animator. If the repaint event did not originate with the animator, this fact is recorded as part of the DrawEvent, and the application program can then choose to ignore the need to actually move an object as part of the animation. The new DrawEvent is shown in Exhibit 17 (Program9.5b) and now includes a Boolean field doMove that tells the application whether or not the DrawEvent is intended to move the animation a step.

The decision to delegate to the application the decision of what to do with a DrawEvent not generated from the animator was made for

Exhibit 22. Program9.5g: Animator Class

```
import java.awt.*;
import java.awt.image.*;
import java.awt.event.*;
import java.util.*;
import javax.swing.*;

public class Animator extends JPanel {

  private Vector elementsToDraw = new Vector();
  private Controller controller;

  /**
   * A static method to create an instance of the animator
   * using a frame for the animator and a frame for the
   * controller.
   */
  public static Animator createAnimator() {
    Animator animator = new Animator();
    JFrame animFrame = new JFrame("Generic Animator");
    Container animContainer = animFrame.getContentPane();
    animContainer.add(animator);
    animFrame.setSize(700,450);
    animFrame.setLocation(0,100);
    animFrame.setVisible(true);

    ControllerImpl controllerImpl = new ControllerImpl(animator)
        ;
    animator.setController(controllerImpl);
    ControlPanel controlPanel = new ControlPanel(controllerImpl)
        ;
    JFrame controlFrame = new JFrame("Control Panel");
    Container controlContainer = controlFrame.getContentPanel();
    controlContainer.add(controlPanel);
    controlFrame.setSize(500,100);
    controlFrame.setVisible(true);
    try {
      controlPanel.startControlPanel();
    } catch (ControllerAlreadyStartedException e) {
    }

    return animator;
  }

  /**
   * Public constructor. If this constructor is used,
   * the controller must be set at some point using
   * the setController method.
   */
  public Animator() {
  }

  /**
   * Public constructor. This constructor hooks the animator to
   * a controller.
   */
  public Animator(Controller controller) {
    this.controller = controller;
  }
```

(continued)

Exhibit 22. Program9.5g (Continued)

```
  /**
   *  Accessor method that sets the controller for this object.
   */
  public void setController(Controller controller) {
    this.controller = controller;
  }

  /**
   *  This method implements the equivalent of the processEvent
   *  method for the Java Event Model.
   */
  public void paint(Graphics g) {
    DrawEvent de;
    super.paint(g);

    if ((controller ! = null) && (!controller.doRedraw()))
      de = new DrawEvent(this, g, false);
    else
      de = new DrawEvent(this, g, true);

    Vector v;
    synchronized(this) {
        v = (Vector) elementsToDraw.clone();
    }

    Enumeration e = v.elements();
    while (e.hasMoreElements())
      ((DrawListener) e.nextElement()).draw(de);
  }
  /**
   *  addListener method for the Java Event Model
   */

  public synchronized void addDrawListener(DrawListener d) {
    elementsToDraw.addElement(d);
  }

  /**
   *  removeListener method for the Java Event Model
   */
  public synchronized void removeDrawListener(DrawListener d) {
    elementsToDraw.removeElement(d);
  }
}
```

a number of reasons. For example, the application might be written simply to display the state of the object, not to animate it. If that is the policy when a repaint event is generated, the application might always want to be redrawn to show its current state.

Another application could be interested in drawing its icons based on the size of the current window, which is contained in the Graphics object. So, if a reSize event on the window generated the repaint call, the application may want to redraw itself at a new size; however, the repaint event might not move the object a step on the path. The animator does not know what the policies of the application are or

Exhibit 23. Program9.5h: Concurrent Ball Program To Run the New Animator

```
import java.awt.*;
import java.util.*;

/**
 *  This class animates a ball in a thread using the animator
 *  component. It is a correct solution.
 */

public class ConcurrentBall implements DrawListener, Runnable {

  static final int EAST = 0;
  static final int WEST = 1;
  static final int NORTH = 2;
  static final int SOUTH = 3;
  int direction;

  Path myPath;
  Random random;
  Animator animator;

  /** Constructor. Note that we need to register with the
   *  animator through the parents class.
   */
  public ConcurrentBall(Animator animator, int direction) {
    this.animator = animator;
    this.direction = direction;
    random = new Random(direction);
  }

  /**
   *  The run method simulates an asynchronous ball. The
   *  myPath variable is set here and used in the draw method
   *  and is intended to coordinate the ball thread running in
   *  this method and the GUI thread (from the animator)
   *  running in the draw method. This works correctly.
   */
  public void run() {
    animator.addDrawListener(this);
    try {
      while(true) {
        synchronized (this) {
          if (direction = = SOUTH) {
            myPath = new StraightLinePath(410, 205, 10, 205,
                50);
            direction = NORTH;
          }
          else if (direction = = NORTH) {
            myPath = new StraightLinePath(10, 205, 410, 205,
                50);
            direction = SOUTH;
          }
          else if (direction = = EAST) {
            myPath = new StraightLinePath(205, 410, 205, 10,
                50);
            direction = WEST;
          }
          else if (direction = = WEST) {
```

(continued)

Exhibit 23. Program9.5h (Continued)

```
            myPath = new StraightLinePath(205, 10, 205, 410,
                50);
            direction = EAST;
          }
          wait();
        }
      Thread.sleep(random.nextInt(10000));
      }
    } catch (InterruptedException e) {
    }
  }

  /**
   *  Draw is called each time through the animator loop to draw
   *  the object. It simply uses the path to calculate the
   *  position of this object and then draws itself at that
   *  position. When the end of the path is reached, it notifies
   *  the ball thread.
   */
  public synchronized void draw(DrawEvent de) {
    Point p = myPath.nextPosition();
    Graphics g = de.getGraphics();
    g.setColor(Color.red);
    g.fillOval((int)p.getX(), (int)p.getY(), 15, 15);
    if (! myPath.hasMoreSteps())
      notify();
  }

  /**
   *  The main method just creates the animator and
   *  the ball threads and starts them running.
   */
  public static void main(String args[]) {
    Animator animator = Animator.createAnimator();

    ConcurrentBall cb1 = new ConcurrentBall(animator, WEST);
    (new Thread(cb1)).start();

    ConcurrentBall cb2 = new ConcurrentBall(animator, NORTH);
    (new Thread(cb2)).start();
  }
}
```

how the application might implement them, so it simply makes the information on what caused the event available to the application and lets the application decide what it wants to do.

9.6.3 Designing the Controller

A control panel and controller can now be designed that implements the basic functionality of the controller in Chapter 7. The controller is designed using the techniques given in Chapter 3, with some additions because of constraints in using the GUI threads. The first constraint is

Exhibit 24. Psuedo-Code Design of the Three Active Objects

Controller Thread	ControlPanel Thread (GUI)	Animator Thread (GUI)

```
Controller Thread:
while(true) {
  call doWait
  sleep for waitTime
  call doMove
}

ControlPanel Thread (GUI):
while (true) {
  select
  when (stopped &&
    start button)
    call doStart
  when (running &&
    stop button)
    call doStop
  when (step button)
    call doStep
}

Animator Thread (GUI):
while(true) {
  call doMove
  createEvent
call each listener
}
```

that the GUI thread is physically one thread, but it will present itself to the controller as two active objects: the animator and the control panel. Even though they are both run in the GUI thread, it is easier to talk about them as different active objects. A third thread, the control thread, generates the timer repaints as shown in Chapter 7. The pseudo-code design of the three active objects is given in Exhibit 24.

The pseudo-code implemented here is not implemented in a thread as in Chapter 3, because the control is not actually coming from the thread itself. In the case of the ControlPanel, the active process is the user. In the case of the animator, the active process is generated in response to repaint events, which can come from any number of conditions; however, it is possible to capture these behaviors and abstract them to appear as threads in relation to the passive control component. Also note that a "select" statement with "when" clauses is used in the ControlPanel to show that the control panel acts like an infinite loop that can select one of the three options. The "when" clause then tells when each option can be selected.

Now the passive object can be designed to interact with these active tasks. When designing the passive object (in this case, the controller), it is important to keep in mind that the GUI thread can never execute a wait or do anything else that uses a potentially large or indeterminate amount of time, in the monitor. This places some constraints on the state diagram. A method that is called from the GUI thread must always be able to execute, which means that either the transition that runs in the GUI thread must emanate from every state (such as the doRedraw method) or must never be called from a given state (such as the doStart method, which logically cannot be called from the WAITING or MOVING states). The state diagram for implementing the controller object is given in Exhibit 25. The program to implement this new ControllerImpl object is given in Exhibit 22 (Program9.5g), and the ControlPanel that uses this object is shown in Exhibit 23 (Program9.5h).

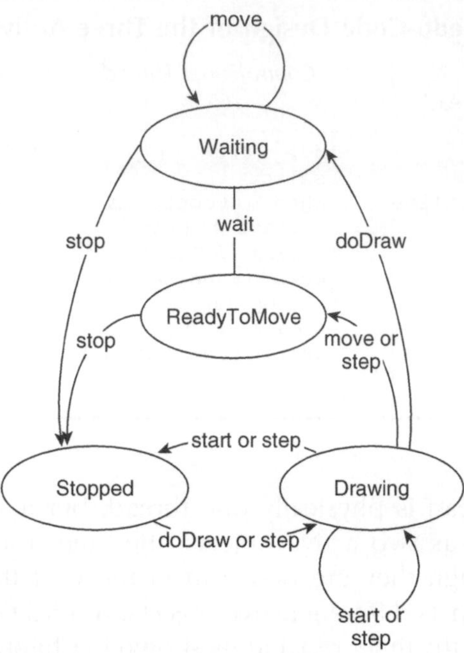

Exhibit 25. ControllerImpl Stat Diagram

This design raises one last design issue. If the controller thread is waiting and a doStep, doStart, doStop, or setWaitTime method is called, the controller thread should be notified so that it can begin waiting again or respond to the correct state in the monitor. If the waiting time was done with a sleep in the controller thread, there would be no easy way to wake this thread up from one of the calls; therefore, the sleep call has been moved into the monitor and is achieved through the use of a timed wait method call. Now the controller thread can sleep normally but can be notified by a normal notify or notifyAll call in the monitor if the monitor changes state.

9.7 Conclusion

This chapter has shown how a number of concurrent programming techniques can be combined to create even more powerful components; however, the components that can be created are only as powerful as the techniques that are employed. Once again, trying to reason through these techniques is difficult, so it is in the best interest of the programmer to learn as many techniques for concurrent programming, design patterns, and adapters as possible to be able to recognize when they can be used effectively.

9.8 Further Reading

The problems presented in this chapter are either classic problems of concurrency (the readers/writers and first-in/first-out binary semaphore problems) or specific to situations covered in this text (the gas station simulation and the animator). The classic problems can be found in any number of books (see, for example, [HAR98]). Adapters as covered in this chapter are different from adapters as implemented in the Java AWT. The adapters given here are covered in [SUN96] or most books on Java Beans, such as that by Englander [ENG97].

9.9 Problems

1. Extend the first-in/first-out binary semaphore (FIFOBS) to be a counting semaphore (a so-called first-in/first-out counting semaphore, or FIFOCS).
2. The following code fragment is in Exhibit 3 (Program9.2):

   ```
   if (! (locked || waiting.size() > 1))
   waitObject = null;
   ```

   If the object was locked or objects were already waiting, the current thread's wait object would not be null, and the thread would be forced to wait. In Exhibit 3 (Program9.2) are both needed to implement this test? If not, which part of the check can be removed? Can the "if" test always be reduced, as in this case? For example, consider the general case when multiple states could be present in the program.
3. Show that no harmful race condition will occur as a result of dropping and reacquiring the synchronized lock on the "this" object in the getLock method of Exhibit 3 (Program9.2). Does the same hold if the FIFOCS in Problem 9.1 is implemented following the same basic design?
4. Exhibit 3 (Program9.2) suggests a way to generalize the implementation of notification objects. Formalize this methodology. What are some of the limits placed on the state diagrams when this is done?
5. Change the readers/writers object to implement the notification object using the methodology you developed in Problem 9.4.
6. Rewrite the readers/writers buffer so that it does not have an inner class for confinement but is a single object. This can be done by making the beginRead, endRead, doRead, requestWrite, and doWrite methods private, so that the only access to the object is through the read and write methods. Compare this solution with the one using a separate private object and confinement.

7. Change the readers/writers object in Program9.3 (Exhibits 5 and 6) to handle multiple writers after all readers have been processed.
8. Change the gas station simulation in Program9.4 (Exhibits 10 through 15) to handle three pumps. Change it to handle four pumps. Change it to handle 100 cars. What is required for these changes?
9. What are magic numbers, and why should they not be used in a program? How can you get around using a magic number?
10. In the gas station simulation in Section 9.5 it was pointed out that, if multiple pumps became free at once, the pumps might not be given to the cars in the order in which they were freed. A solution was also proposed involving storing the pump with the notification object. Implement this solution.
11. Why did the methods of the Pump class not have to be synchronized in Program9.4 (Exhibits 10 through 15)? How are the threads guaranteed to be safe when used by multiple car threads if the methods are not synchronized?
12. Explain why it is a bad idea to allow a thread to run through several components. Put a separate thread in the pump object to do the notifications when the pump is free. Explain why this is a better solution to this problem.
13. Complete the animator to handle repaint events correctly. This requires changing the application object.
14. Change the ControlPanel so that if the speed controller is reset it does not automatically call move if the timeout has not occurred.
15. Change the gas station program so that the pump manager can turn the pumps off at the end of the day. Make sure that no cars remain at a pump before turning it off.
16. Change the gas station program so that multiple pump listeners (instances of pump manager) are listening on a pump. When a pump becomes free, the pump notifies all pump managers. When the pump is taken, the pump should notify all pump managers. However, to prevent a race condition where more than one pump manager tries to allocate the pump, the pump manager should first check the pump to see if it is taken. If not, the pump manager locks the pump before giving it to the next car. This is similar to the hardware TSET instruction. Before the car leaves, it should notify that the pump is now free.
17. Implement a solution to the readers/writers problem using the Java Event Model, similar to the one used in the gas station simulation.
18. Implement the gas station simulation assuming that the use of the pumps can have a priority bias.
19. Section 9.5 discussed the race condition involving pumps being given to the cars and suggested that a solution would be to put the correct pump in the notification object. Implement this solution to the problem.

Chapter 10

Organizing the Problem for Reuse: Reuse of Utility Classes

10.1 Introduction

The first nine chapters of the text have been concerned with creating the framework for the solution to a problem that is to be implemented on a computer using components. Once the framework of a problem solution has been specified, we still must decide how to organize the pieces that will be used within that framework. This involves figuring out how to organize the data and methods in the program and is called *problem decomposition*. Decomposition can involve either not saving a state between invocations of a method (procedural functions) or saving a state between invocations of a method (using objects).

Objects can be organized according to *composition* or *classification*. Composition and classification are techniques that define the relationships between the classes used in the program, allowing methods and variables for one class to be used as part of the definition of other classes. The ability to use part of the definition of one object in another object is called *reuse* and was one of the original reasons why object-oriented programming (OOP) was developed.

When designing the objects in a program, classes are defined and used in two ways. In the first, classes in the program are designed around entities in the problem specification after properties intrinsic to a specific problem have been identified. This allows reuse but is really part of the design of the system and as such is treated as object-oriented design (OOD) (covered in Chapter 11). In the second, classes are based on functionality that is extrinsic to the problem and thus can be used in many problems; the classes can be created to be used in a number of systems, or existing classes or methods can be identified that have the desired functionality. These methods and objects provide a service to be utilized by the current program; therefore, this type of object design is called *utility reuse*. Examples of utility classes are Vector or StringTokenizer objects, and examples of utility methods are Integer.parseInt or Math.random.

This chapter specifically covers utility reuse. Because utility reuse deals with methods, classes, algorithms, and components that are not specific to a problem, but occur across a wide variety of problems, this chapter is not concerned with designing objects in the problem; rather, it focuses on identifying and reusing functionality that occurs across a wide range of applications and making that functionality generally available. This chapter explains the four major types of utility reuse: reuse by copy, method reuse, and the two types of object reuse, composition and classification. The two types of object reuse are examined in detail using the move method (introduced in the gas station simulation in Chapter 8) to illustrate each type of reuse and how code can be *refactored* to take advantage of the reuse. The chapter then contrasts the two types of object reuse and uses the criteria of cohesion and coupling to show why composition is nearly always superior to classification designing for reuse of utility objects.

The chapter concludes by examining two components, the animator component from Chapter 6 and the java.util.Stack class, to show why a design using composition is superior. Once again, this discussion emphasizes why compositional design is nearly always superior when implementing reuse of what is essentially a utility object.

10.2 Chapter Goals

After completing this chapter, you should be able to:

- Understand the concept of reuse and the difference between procedural reuse and object reuse.
- Identify the difference between composition and classification, and show how each is used in Java.
- Implement reuse of procedural methods, as well as methods that rely on a state.
- Evaluate designs based on cohesiveness and coupling.

10.3 Types of Reuse

When implementing a computer program, functional or data commonality exists in the program and across many programs. It is generally accepted that this commonality should be found, factored out, implemented once, and then reused throughout the program. Entire development methodologies, such as extreme programming, invest heavily in the idea that large improvements in a program are achievable if common functions and classes are refactored, implemented, and stored once and then reused throughout one or more programs.

Reuse can occur in a program in two ways. The first type of reuse occurs when an algorithm, object, or component is built to operate on a generic data type. This type of reuse, which we call *generic reuse*, builds an algorithm or component around an interface (generic type) and then reuses the algorithm or component with types defined at runtime. This type of reuse is used in the GUI components in the Java AWT, the animator from Chapter 7, and the SortedPrintTable from Chapter 5. It can also be used in algorithms, such as a generic sort algorithm, and is often used in components. This has already been covered in detail and is not examined further in this chapter. The second type of reuse occurs when existing functionality is used as building blocks to create other procedures or objects. For example, a common method, such as Integer.parseInt, might be used to convert input data from a string to an int; a vector might be used to store objects as part of the Java Event Model; or a problem-specific data type, such as a car, could be defined and extended by a number of different car type objects. In each of these cases, some base functionality has been implemented, and that base functionality is extended to create larger methods or objects.

Decomposing objects when implementing reuse of functionality is done for two reasons. The first is to look at objects and methods that are specific to the current problem, to factor out the commonality between these objects and methods, and finally to implement these objects in ways that will allow them to be reused to solve the current problem (this is what we refer to as object-oriented design and is covered in Chapter 11). The second reason is to be able to look at the objects and methods that are not part of the current problem definition but which are needed to actually implement the program. For example, a problem may have to store a set of employees. While the set of employees is problem specific, the mechanism to store a collection is much more common than just its use in the current program. The storage can therefore be accomplished using an object, such as a Vector object, that is not problem specific. The Vector object is not part of the current problem but is simply a helper object necessary to implement the program. These helper objects and methods provide utilities to handle commonly recurring tasks; hence, these objects and methods are referred to as *utility objects*, and this type of reuse is called *utility reuse*. Utility reuse is the subject of the remainder of the chapter.

Utility reuse falls into two main categories. The first is when a series of statements, or a method with no state data, is reused in a program. In this case, no variables are used to store values between invocations of the method. The method does calculations on the current input data, producing results that are only dependent on the input parameters. Examples are converting strings to numbers (e.g., Integer.parseInt) or creating random numbers (e.g., Math.random). In these methods, the only thing being reused is the procedure, or a series of statements that does the actual calculation; hence, this type of reuse is referred to as *procedural reuse*, which can be achieved in two ways. The first is to find a section of code in a program that does basically what is needed, copy that code to a new place in the program, and modify the code to fit the current problem, a process known as *reuse by copy*. The second approach to procedural reuse is to find a section of code in a program that does basically what is needed and use it to create a method; parameters can then be added to the method to make it work in a number of different situations. This type of reuse is called *method reuse*. Because these methods do not require data, or state, to be maintained between their invocations, they are often referred to as *stateless methods* and are implemented as static methods in Java.

Utility reuse can also occur when a state needs to be maintained between invocations of a method. For example, in the Vector class, when an add method is called the object sent as a parameter must be stored so that it can be accessed in subsequent calls. The objects that are stored represent a state for the Vector object, and the methods required to encapsulate, store, and retrieve objects in the vector must save and access this state between invocations. So, a program reusing methods that must maintain a state has to create objects to keep that state, thus we call this type of reuse *object reuse*. To achieve object reuse in a program, objects must be extended in some way, either by classification or composition. These two methodologies are nearly interchangeable, but each has its own advantages and disadvantages. This chapter examines these advantages and disadvantages and draws conclusions about criteria for choosing one method over the other, particularly for utility reuse. Chapter 11 looks at this question in more detail as it relates to OOD.

The remainder of this chapter examines the reuse utility, particularly regarding the question of using composition or classification for reusing objects. The move method introduced in the gas station simulation in Chapter 8 is used to explain the concepts, but, to simplify the example, a program that simply moves a ball in a thread will be used. The move method is implemented procedurally first by copy and then as a method. The shortcomings of procedural reuse for this situation are explained, and objects are created to allow the move method to be used in more than one object. Both a composition and two classification solutions are presented, and the relative merits and problems of them are discussed.

10.4 Finding Commonality in Code

Before reuse can occur, commonality in the program must first be identified so that it can be abstracted into a function or an object. Finding common code that is present multiple times in a program is something that is obvious to an experienced programmer but for some reason is often not recognized by the novice programmer, who can blissfully repeat the exact same code, perhaps with variable names changed, over and over again not realizing that they just finished doing the same thing two statements before in the program. Inexperienced programmers will copy blocks of code within a program and never think to abstract it into a method. How to begin to recognize that code is appearing time and time again and can be abstracted is not something that is easily taught and appears to require experience. However, it is well recognized in computer science that when common code occurs the programmer should abstract that common behavior out and create a single implementation that can be used multiple times in the program. Abstracting out this behavior could be as simple as writing a subroutine in C or as complicated as making an entire Java class.

Most computer scientists generally agree that this abstraction of common functionality is a good thing. That it does not happen often enough is also generally agreed. For some reason, programmers often seem loath to implement a prepackaged solution for their programs, instead choosing to "roll their own" solutions. Why this is true is the subject of many debates, studies, and conjecture in the computer science field and is not an appropriate topic for this book. Instead, the way that these methods can be reused are discussed here.

10.5 Reuse by Copy

Reuse by copy is perhaps the most prevalent way that reuse of common functionality is accomplished. It is not magical; a programmer finds some lines of code in a program that achieves some necessary behavior and copies the block of code, possibly modifying it slightly for the new situation, to another place in the program or even to a completely different program. The example of reuse by copy shown in Exhibit 1 (Program10.1) is similar to the programs that move balls in Chapter 8, but in this case we have only one ball. The ball simply sets up a path to move from the top of the screen to the bottom of the screen and then back again. Note that the code to wait for the ball to finish moving

Exhibit 1. Program10.1: Reuse by Copy

```
import java.awt.*;
import java.util.*;
import animator.*;

public class ConcurrentBall implements DrawListener, Runnable {

  private Path myPath;
  private Animator animator;

  /** Constructor. Note that we need to register with the
   *   animator through the run method.
   */
  public ConcurrentBall(Animator animator) {
    this.animator = animator;
  }

  /**
   * The run method simulates an asynchronous ball. The
   * myPath variable is set here and used in the draw method
   * and is intended to coordinate the ball thread running in
   * this method and the GUI thread (from the animator)
   * running in the draw method. This works correctly.
   */
  public void run() {

    // Set an initial point to draw this object, and then add it
    // to the animator.
    myPath = new StraightLinePath(10, 205, 10, 205, 1);
    animator.addDrawListener(this);
    Random random = new Random(System.currentTimeMillis());

    try {
      // Note that this block of code is copied twice in this
      // program. All that is changed is the actual path that
      // is created. It would be best to abstract out this
      // behavior.
      while(true) {
        synchronized(this) {
          try {
            myPath = new StraightLinePath(410, 205, 10, 205,
              50);
            wait();
          } catch(InterruptedException e) {
          }
        }

        Thread.sleep(random.nextInt(10000));

        synchronized(this) {
          try {
            myPath = new StraightLinePath(10, 205, 410, 205,
              50);
            wait();
          } catch(InterruptedException e) {
          }
        }
        Thread.sleep(random.nextInt(10000));
      }
```

(continued)

Exhibit 1. Program10.1 (Continued)

```
      } catch (InterruptedException e) {
      }
    }

    /**
     *  Draw is called each time through the animator loop to draw
     *  the object. It simply uses the path to calculate the
     *  position of this object and then draws itself at that
     *  position. When the end of the path is reached, it notifies
     *  the ball thread.
     */
    public synchronized void draw(DrawEvent de) {
      Point p = myPath.nextPosition();
      Graphics g = de.getGraphics();
      g.setColor(Color.red);
      g.fillOval((int)p.getX(), (int)p.getY(), 15, 15);

      if (! myPath.hasMoreSteps())
        notify();
    }

    /**
     *  The main method just creates the animator
     *  and the ball threads and starts them running.
     */
    public static void main(String args[]) {
      Animator animator = new Animator();
      ConcurrentBall cb1 = new ConcurrentBall(animator);
      (new Thread(cb1)).start();
      animator.setVisible(true);
    }
}
```

is copied twice in the program, an obvious case for abstracting this behavior into a function.

In Exhibit 1 (Program10.1), we now have two copies of the code to move the ball in the run method, each one doing largely the same thing. Later, if the procedure is needed again, another copy can be made. This continues until this same piece of code is spread throughout a program or, worse, many programs. It might be changed slightly in each of its incarnations, even in such minor details as variable names used, so it could be difficult to even identify all of the places in the program it is being used.

This type of reuse, while common, is not a good method for reusing code. It has a number of disadvantages:

- Every time a new copy of a method is made, it must be managed. The more copies of redundant code that exist, the bigger the problems in managing the overall program or systems.
- If a bug is ever found in the copied code, that bug must be fixed everywhere that code is used. This can become a daunting task, as there is likely no documentation on all the places this code is

used. Also, because it could be modified slightly each time it is used, it might be very difficult to find and fix all the occurrences of this bug.

- Frequently used behaviors can often be used effectively if the programmers know they exist; however, the presence of reuse by copy hides these commonly used behaviors in the actual program code, so they are difficult to find and catalog. Therefore, many programmers on a project will not know that a problem has been previously solved and will redevelop a solution to an already solved problem. These solutions will vary greatly in effectiveness and efficiency and, because they are very different, cannot be easily optimized. By abstracting this frequently used code out into separate methods or objects, it is easier to identify, catalog, use, and optimize the behaviors in these methods.
- Poorly structured programs often result. Instead of a single function call, the copied code could be several dozen lines of code, sometimes with complex logic, branches, or looping inside of it. Copying it into an already complex program can make the program longer and further obfuscate the purpose and procedure of the program. Being able to summarize a section of code with a single method call often makes it easier to understand the role it plays in an algorithm and the overall role of the algorithm in which it is used.

Reuse by copy is not a good solution to the reuse problem. Much better ways to achieve reuse are covered in the next three sections and provide better reuse characteristics than reuse by copy.

10.6 Procedural Reuse in Java

Method reuse is achieved by taking a number of procedural statements and putting them into a method that can be called from a number of places in a program. Exhibit 2 (Program10.2) is an example of method reuse to implement the move method to solve the moving of the concurrent balls problems in Exhibit 1 (Program10.1). A move method is defined that does the correct locking on the object, thus removing the need for synchronized and try blocks inside of the run method. This cuts down a lot on the amount of code, making it more readable. It also abstracts out the coordination of the two threads so the code is better cataloged and thus more usable. Finally, it also implements the code in one place so that any bugs or optimizations can be addressed in a single method in the program.

Method reuse allows sets of procedural statements to be abstracted, implemented as methods, and reused. By changing the parameters to the methods, the actual behavior can be modified to fit specific programming problems. In the case of the move method, the path that is used can be changed. The Java API has numerous examples of

Exhibit 2. Program10.2: Method Reuse

```
import java.awt.*;
import java.util.*;
import animator.*;

public class ConcurrentBall implements DrawListener, Runnable {

  private Path myPath;
  private Animator animator;

  /** Constructor. Note that we need to register with the
   *  animator through the run method.
   */
  public ConcurrentBall(Animator animator) {
    this.animator = animator;
  }

  /**
   * The run method simulates an asynchronous ball. The
   * myPath variable is set here and used in the draw method
   * and is intended to coordinate the ball thread running in
   * this method and the GUI thread (from the animator)
   * running in the draw method. This works correctly.
   */
  public void run() {

    // Set an initial point to draw this object, and then add it
    // to the animator.
    myPath = new StraightLinePath(10, 205, 10, 205, 1);
    animator.addDrawListener(this);
    Random random = new Random(System.currentTimeMillis());

    try {
      while(true) {
        move(new StraightLinePath(410, 205, 10, 205, 50));
        Thread.sleep(random.nextInt(10000));

        move(new StraightLinePath(10, 205, 410, 205, 50));
        Thread.sleep(random.nextInt(10000));
      }
    } catch (InterruptedException e) {
    }
  }

 /**
   * This method allows a thread to move to completion before
   * it continues. A Path variable is defined and then a wait is
   * done. This wait is matched by a notify in the draw method
   * when this thread has reached the end of the path,
   * releasing the thread to continue running.
   */
  public synchronized void move(Path path) {
    myPath = path;
    try {
      wait();
    } catch (InterruptedException e) {
    }
  }
```

(continued)

Exhibit 2. Program10.2 (Continued)

```
  /**
   *  Draw is called each time through the animator loop to draw
   *  the object. It simply uses the path to calculate the
   *  position of this object and then draws itself at that
   *  position. When the end of the path is reached, it notifies
   *  the ball thread.
   */
  public synchronized void draw(DrawEvent de) {
    Point p = myPath.nextPosition();
    Graphics g = de.getGraphics();
    g.setColor(Color.red);
    g.fillOval((int)p.getX(), (int)p.getY(), 15, 15);

    if (! myPath.hasMoreSteps())
      notify();
  }

  /**
   *  The main method just creates the animator
   *  and the ball threads and starts them running.
   */
  public static void main(String args[]) {
    Animator animator = new Animator();

    ConcurrentBall cb1 = new ConcurrentBall(animator);
    (new Thread(cb1)).start();
    animator.setVisible(true);
  }
}
```

procedural reuse; for example, Integer.parseInt would be called to parse a String to get an int, and Math.random would be called for a random number. What these methods have in common is that they are *static* methods in a class. They do not rely on an object, and in fact do not use any data associated with an object. They simply perform a procedural service in the program. Because these procedural methods do not use any data from an object, and thus do not rely on the state of an object to work correctly, they are sometimes called *stateless* methods, which is just another way of saying that the method is a procedural method.

From the discussion of stateless methods in the previous paragraph, it should be obvious that the move method as it is implemented has a problem. The move method is not stateless, and it cannot be static as it has a state that is maintained between calls to the move method and the draw method. This state is kept in two places in the object: the myPath variable and the synchronized lock for the object. Both of these variables are needed to make the move method work correctly. To see this, consider Exhibit 3 (Program10.3), which implements movement of objects of two different classes: a Ball class and a Square class. Each of these classes must contain its own move methods so that objects of both types have access to a unique object lock and myPath

Exhibit 3. Program10.3: Ball and Square Classes, Each Implementing Its Own Move Method

```
import java.awt.*;
import java.util.*;
import animator.*;

public class MoveObjects {

  /**
   *  The main method just creates the animator and the ball
   *  threads and starts them running.
   */
  public static void main(String args[]) {
    Animator animator = new Animator();

    (new Thread(new Ball(animator))).start();
    (new Thread(new Square(animator))).start();
    animator.setVisible(true);
  }
}

class Ball implements DrawListener, Runnable {

  private Path myPath;
  private Animator animator;

  /** Constructor. Note that we need to register with the
   *   animator through the run method.
   */
  public Ball(Animator animator) {
    this.animator = animator;
  }

  /**
   *  The run method simulates an asynchronous ball. The
   *  myPath variable is set here and used in the draw method
   *  and is intended to coordinate the ball thread running in
   *  this method and the GUI thread (from the animator)
   *  running in the draw method. This works correctly.
   */
  public void run() {

    // Set an initial point to draw this object, and then add it
    // to the animator.
    myPath = new StraightLinePath(10, 205, 10, 205, 1);

    animator.addDrawListener(this);
    Random random = new Random(System.currentTimeMillis());

    try {
      while(true) {
        move(new StraightLinePath(410, 205, 10, 205, 50));
        Thread.sleep(random.nextInt(10000));

        move(new StraightLinePath(10, 205, 410, 205, 50));
        Thread.sleep(random.nextInt(10000));
      }
    } catch (InterruptedException e) {
    }
  }
```

(continued)

Exhibit 3. Program10.3 (Continued)

```
  /**
   * This method allows a thread to move to completion before
   * it continues. A Path variable is defined and then a wait is
   * done. This wait is matched by a notify in the draw method
   * when this thread has reached the end of the path,
   * releasing the thread to continue running.
   */
  public synchronized void move(Path path) {
    myPath = path;
    try {
      wait();
    } catch (InterruptedException e) {
    }
  }

  /**
   * Draw is called each time through the animator loop to draw
   * the object. It simply uses the path to calculate the
   * position of this object and then draws itself at that
   * position. When the end of the path is reached, it notifies
   * the ball thread.
   */
  public synchronized void draw(DrawEvent de) {
    Point p = myPath.nextPosition();
    Graphics g = de.getGraphics();
    g.setColor(Color.red);
    g.fillOval((int)p.getX(), (int)p.getY(), 15, 15);

    if (! myPath.hasMoreSteps())
      notify();
  }
}

class Square implements DrawListener, Runnable {

  private Path myPath;
  private Animator animator;

  /** Constructor. Note that we need to register with the
   *  animator through the run method.
   */
  public Square(Animator animator) {
    this.animator = animator;
  }

  /**
   * The run method simulates an asynchronous ball. The
   * myPath variable is set here and used in the draw method
   * and is intended to coordinate the ball thread running in
   * this method and the GUI thread (from the animator)
   * running in the draw method. This works correctly.
   */
  public void run() {

    // Set an initial point to draw this object, and then add it
    // to the animator.
    myPath = new StraightLinePath(10, 205, 10, 205, 1);
```

(continued)

Exhibit 3. Program10.3 (Continued)

```
    animator.addDrawListener(this);
    Random random = new Random(System.currentTimeMillis());

    try {
      while(true) {
        move(new StraightLinePath(10, 205, 410, 205, 50));
        Thread.sleep(random.nextInt(10000));

        move(new StraightLinePath(410, 205, 10, 205, 50));
        Thread.sleep(random.nextInt(10000));
      }
    } catch (InterruptedException e) {
    }
  }

  /**
   * This method allows a thread to move to completion before
   * it continues. A path variable is defined and then a wait is
   * done. This wait is matched by a notify in the draw method
   * when this thread has reached the end of the path,
   * releasing the thread to continue running.
   */
  public synchronized void move(Path path) {
    myPath = path;
    try {
      wait();
    } catch (InterruptedException e) {
    }
  }

  /**
   * Draw is called each time through the animator loop to draw
   * the object. It simply uses the path to calculate the
   * position of this object and then draws itself at that
   * position. When the end of the path is reached, it notifies
   * the ball thread.
   */
  public synchronized void draw(DrawEvent de) {
    Point p = myPath.nextPosition();
    Graphics g = de.getGraphics();
    g.setColor(Color.red);
    g.fillRect((int)p.getX(), (int)p.getY(), 15, 15);

    if (! myPath.hasMoreSteps())
      notify();
  }
}
```

variable. It is not possible to make this method static and available to both classes, thus it really is not stateless.

Because the move method is not stateless, it is not procedural and thus not a good candidate for method reuse. The only way to implement this type of state-dependent reuse is to create object definitions that allow the method requiring the state to be included in the object that uses it. The need to maintain a state to implement reuse is a common problem in OOP languages such as Java. Many objects need to maintain a state. As was shown in Chapters 3 and 7, this is always true of components, but it is also true of many utility objects that are not components. For example, a StringTokenizer needs to keep track of its current position in parsing a string, and a Vector needs to keep track of what elements are currently stored. When these objects are reused it is necessary to find a way to include the state of the reused object inside of the object that is using the utilities provided. This can be done in two ways in OOP, by composition or classification. Section 10.7 shows how classification can be used to allow object reuse for the move method, and Section 10.8 shows the same move method reuse using composition.

One last note about the state needed by the move method: As mentioned earlier, the state that must be maintained not only is kept by a variable (in this case, the myPath variable), but also involves the lock on this object. This second dependency on the object lock might not be obvious, as the variable that implements it is hidden. As will be seen later, though, it impacts the way the methods in this object are designed.

10.7 Classification: Reuse by Extension

The first way to reuse methods that require state data is to create a base class that can be used as part of the definition of the class for the object to be created. Thus, the class being defined consists of the base class and a class that *extends* the properties of the base class, creating a class with properties from both the base and extended class. Objects that instantiate this extended class have all the properties of the base and extended class. This is called *inheritance*, or classification, and is achieved in Java using the extends clause. It is important to remember that when classification is used, two objects (one for the base class and one for the extended class) are not created; rather, a single object is created that has the properties of both objects.

Exhibit 4 (Program10.4a), the MoveController object, is an example of how the move method can be included in the current object through classification. Exhibit 5 (Program10.4b) is an example of a program that uses the MoveController object of Exhibit 4 (Program10.4a). Here, the move method is in the MoveController object. Because the ConcurrentBall object extends the MoveController object, all of the methods and variables for the MoveController object become part of the ConcurrentBall object. Thus, the myPath variable and the object lock used by the MoveController are also used in the draw method for the ConcurrentBall class. Because the myPath and object lock are shared between the MoveController and the Concurrent Ball, the move method now has a state that can be kept between invocations. This allows the

Exhibit 4. Program10.4a: MoveController Utility Object Showing Reuse by Classification

```
import java.awt.Graphics;
import java.awt.Point;
import animator.*;

abstract public class MoveController {
  Path myPath;

  /**
   *  The move method simply saves the parameter path into the
   *  variable myPath and does the wait, much like its
   *  procedural cousin.
   */
  public synchronized void move(Path path) {
    myPath = path;
    try {
      // Note that this wait is wrong, as it could
      // unintentionally drop a lock on the object that is held
      // by an enclosing synchronized block.
      wait();
    } catch (InterruptedException e) {
    }
  }
}
```

MoveController class to be extended by any object, and the move to be reused without being copied to those objects.

This type of reuse has the advantage that every data item and method in the base class (in this case, the MoveController class) can be available when using the extended object; therefore, extra methods do not have to be created to delegate actions to the utility object. This increases the possibility for reuse of the base class. Such a potential for simple reuse is one of the reasons why classification is favored by a number of programmers.

Using classification in object reuse does have a number of significant drawbacks, however. First, the details of the base class must be known and taken advantage of by the class that extends it. This means that the behavior of the base class cannot be encapsulated.* Encapsulation occurs when the variables of an object are all declared private; access to them is hidden inside the object and is only accessible through a well-defined method. This means that the programmer does not need to know the details of the object being used, and the object is protected from the programmer accidentally or intentionally creating invalid states in the object; however, in the case of the MoveController implemented in Exhibit 4 (Program10.4a), the programmer writing a class that uses the MoveController has to know how it works and is expected to

* It can be argued that encapsulation is possible for a base class, but it would have no advantage over composition and in fact would have several disadvantages, as is shown in Section 10.8.

Exhibit 5. Program10.4b: Program That Uses a MoveController Object

```
import java.util.Random;
import java.awt.Graphics;
import java.awt.Point;
import java.awt.Color;
import animator.*;

public class ConcurrentBall extends MoveController
      implements DrawListener, Runnable {

  private Animator animator;

  /** Constructor. Note that we need to register with the
   *   animator through the run method.
   */
  public ConcurrentBall(Animator animator) {
    this.animator = animator;
  }

  /**
   *  The run method simulates an asynchronous ball. The
   *  myPath variable is set here and used in the draw method
   *  and is intended to coordinate the ball thread running in
   *  this method and the GUI thread (from the animator)
   *  running in the draw method. This works correctly.
   */
  public void run() {
    animator.addDrawListener(this);
    Random random = new Random(System.currentTimeMillis());
    try {
      while(true) {
        move(new StraightLinePath(410, 205, 10, 205, 50));
        Thread.sleep(random.nextInt(10000));

        move(new StraightLinePath(10, 205, 410, 205, 50));
        Thread.sleep(random.nextInt(10000));
      }
      } catch (InterruptedException e) {
    }
  }

  /**
   *  Draw is called each time through the animator loop to draw
   *  the object. It simply uses the path to calculate the
   *  position of this object and then draws itself at that
   *  position. When the end of the path is reached, it notifies
   *  the ball thread.
   */
  public synchronized void draw(DrawEvent de) {
    if (myPath = = null)
      return;

    Point p = myPath.nextPosition();
    Graphics g = de.getGraphics();
    g.setColor(Color.red);
    g.fillOval((int)p.getX(), (int)p.getY(), 15, 15);

    if (! myPath.hasMoreSteps())
      notify();
  }
```

(continued)

Exhibit 5. Program10.4b (Continued)

```
  /**
   *  The main method just creates the animator and
   *  the ball threads and starts them running.
   */
  public static void main(String args[]) {
    Animator animator = new Animator();

    ConcurrentBall cb1 = new ConcurrentBall(animator);
    (new Thread(cb1)).start();

    animator.setVisible(true);
  }
}
```

provide the extra code in the draw method to complete the execution of the move method.

Because the data for the MoveController object is accessible to the extending class, it is even possible for the programmer to break the object by improperly changing data that they should probably not have access to. For example, they could reset the path in the middle of a movement without doing a notify, possibly deadlocking the programming. The data for the MoveController class can be misused in an even more insidious way. Because the move method calls the wait method, the object lock is released, but the lock that is released is not simply the lock for the MoveController object. The one object in this case is an instance of the class created by combining the MoveController and the ConcurrentBall classes; therefore, when the wait method is called for this object, the lock is dropped for the entire object. If the method calling wait is itself called from a synchronized method, then the object lock is dropped for all the synchronized blocks. To see this, consider the following code fragment using the swap method from Chapter 2:

```
public void synchronized swap(SwapObject a, SwapObject b) {
  tmp = a.val1;
  move(100,100,200,200,10);
  val2 = val1;
  val1 = tmp;
}
```

Here, the swap method was synchronized to protect against a race condition when using the tmp variable. However, if the class implementing the swap method extends the MoveController object to gain access to the move method, the same object is used for the move and swap methods, even though the methods are in different classes. This means that when the move method is called the programmer has unintentionally done a wait in a critical section (as move calls wait), dropping the object's lock and introducing a race condition into their program. This unintended side effect shows that, when using classification to extend an object, the programmer must understand the details of the object being extended. Worse, the programmer must understand things that are implied in the implementation, such as what it means to drop a synchronized lock in a base class.

This example of how the synchronized block can cause unexpected side effects points out another problem with classification. Classification can result in the OOP version of *spaghetti code*. Because variables can be accessed in subclasses, control over where variables are changed is no longer clear. Methods that are overridden can result in the programmer not being able to easily tell what method is actually being called. Variables that are redefined can lead programmers to make invalid assumptions about what variables are accessed, and the deeper the inheritance hierarchy in the program the more convoluted these relationships can become.

All of the problems with classification aside, it is still a much better mechanism for utility reuse than copying procedures between programs. And, if a better solution did not exist, object reuse by classification would still be a good solution; however, for utility reuse a better mechanism for object reuse does exist: composition.

10.8 Composition: Reuse by Delegation

A second way to accomplish object reuse is called composition. Composition requires that we first create a class that will instantiate a utility object that is completely unattached to any other class. The utility class is then included as a variable in any encapsulating class. When the encapsulating class is instantiated, the resulting object is composed of other objects, hence the term *composition*.

Because this utility class is not part of the definition of the implementing class, the data for the utility object represents an entirely different object than for the object that uses this class. Therefore, the utility object is completely separate from the enclosing object, and the utility object can be completely encapsulated, thus protecting the utility object from interactions with the using object. Reuse of the utility object is accomplished when the methods of the utility object are called from the encapsulating object, a process that is known as *delegation*.

To see how composition works, consider Exhibit 6 (Program10.5a), which implements the MoveController using composition, and Exhibit 7 (Program10.5b), which is a ConcurrentBall program using this MoveController. In Exhibit 7 (Program10.5b) the ConcurrentBall program defines a variable, mc, which is a MoveController object that is a completely separate object from the ConcurrentBall object. The

Exhibit 6. Program10.5a: MoveController Utility Object Showing Reuse by Composition

```
import java.awt.Graphics;
import java.awt.Point;
import animator.*;

public final class MoveController {
  private Path myPath;
  private boolean doNotify = false;

  /**
   * The move method simply saves the parameter path into the
   * variable myPath and does the wait, much like its
   * procedural cousin.
   */
  public synchronized void move(Path path) {
    myPath = path;
    try {
      doNotify = true;
      wait();
    } catch (InterruptedException e) {
    }
  }
  /**
   * Check if the path has more steps in it. Note that it is
   * not necessary to call this method in the using class, as
   * the notification is handled in the nextPosition call, but
   * because the myPath variable is encapsulated, this delegate
   * call allows the program to still have access to this
   * method if it needs it.
   */
  public boolean hasMoreSteps() {
    return myPath.hasMoreSteps();
  }

  /**
   * This method gets the nextPosition from the myPath variable
   * and does a notify if the end of the path has been reached.
   * Note that this method does more than simply get the
   * nextPosition; the name was kept from the Path to simplify
   * adding MoveController objects into existing programs.
   */
  public synchronized Point nextPosition() {
    if (myPath ! = null && myPath.hasMoreSteps()) {
      return myPath.nextPosition();
    }
    else if (myPath ! = null) {
      if (doNotify) {
        doNotify = false;
        notify();
      }
      return myPath.nextPosition();
    }
    else
      return new Point(0,0);
  }
}
```

Exhibit 7. Program10.5b: Program That Uses a MoveController Object

```
import java.util.Random;
import java.awt.Graphics;
import java.awt.Point;
import java.awt.Color;
import animator.*;

public class ConcurrentBall implements DrawListener, Runnable {

  private Animator animator;
  private MoveController mc;

  /** Constructor. Note that we need to register with the
   *   animator through the run method.
   */
  public ConcurrentBall(Animator animator) {
    this.animator = animator;
    mc = new MoveController();
  }

  /**
   *  The run method simulates an asynchronous ball. The
   *  myPath variable is set here and used in the draw method
   *  and is intended to coordinate the ball thread running in
   *  this method and the GUI thread (from the animator)
   *  running in the draw method. This works correctly.
   */
  public void run() {

    animator.addDrawListener(this);
    Random random = new Random(System.currentTimeMillis());

    try {
      while(true) {
        mc.move(new StraightLinePath(410, 205, 10, 205, 50));
        Thread.sleep(random.nextInt(10000));

        mc.move(new StraightLinePath(10, 205, 410, 205, 50));
        Thread.sleep(random.nextInt(10000));
      }
      } catch (InterruptedException e) {
    }
  }

  /**
   *  Draw is called each time through the animator loop to draw
   *  the object. It simply uses the path to calculate the
   *  position of this object and then draws itself at that
   *  position. When the end of the path is reached, it notifies
   *  the ball thread.
   */
  public synchronized void draw(DrawEvent de) {

    Point p = mc.nextPosition();
    Graphics g = de.getGraphics();
    g.setColor(Color.red);
    g.fillOval((int)p.getX(), (int)p.getY(), 15, 15);
  }
```

(continued)

Exhibit 7. Program10.5b (Continued)

```
  /**
   *  The main method just creates the animator and the ball
   *  threads and starts them running.
   */
  public static void main(String args[]) {
    Animator animator = new Animator();

    ConcurrentBall cb1 = new ConcurrentBall(animator);
    (new Thread(cb1)).start();

    animator.setVisible(true);
  }
}
```

ConcurrentBall object in this case is composed of the MoveController object, and it reuses the MoveController by delegating to the MoveController methods the behaviors it wishes to use — in this case, the move, hasMoreSteps, and nextPosition methods.

The important thing to remember is that, unlike classification, where the MoveController and ConcurrentBall shared an object, in composition the MoveController object is a separate object from the ConcurrentBall object. The variable myPath and the object lock are not shared with the ConcurrentBall object. This is important in that it solves many of the problems of classification. First, the anomaly of the wait call unexpectedly freeing a lock on the object is avoided because there are two locks, and the lock that is freed will be the one limited to the MoveController object. Second, the problem of the program having access to the variables or needing to know details of the utility class is avoided because the details are completely encapsulated in the MoveController object, and the program using the utility method, the ConcurrentBall program, has no access to these details. This greatly enhances the safety of the program. Finally, the spaghetti that could result from overriding methods and variables is avoided because the methods and variables are clearly contained in the proper objects and can be referred to in those objects.

However, some costs are associated with using composition. The first is that, with classification, an object can be done with one allocation (as it is a single object), but with composition each object must be allocated separately, although the overhead for doing this is normally small when compared to the overall overhead involved in running a program, and separation of the parts of an object using composition can have some beneficial aspects, particularly if parts of the object could be run in a distributed computing environment such as RMI. The second cost is that to use a method in the utility class, it must be referred to with the variable representing the utility class object if you are in the method (e.g., mc.move vs. simply move). If objects other than the enclosing object are to have access to methods in the utility object, a separate method must be created in the enclosing object that simply delegates the work to the utility object. These problems indicate that reuse of the class requires slightly more code, and, while no practical difference in the ability to reuse the object exists, the argument is that the increase in the amount of code required could limit the amount of reuse that is actually implemented. To my mind, this is a poor argument for classification, considering its drawbacks for utility reuse.

One last point about composition must be considered. It is possible to argue that the same type of reuse that is done with composition can be implemented using classification. To do this, all of the variables in the class are made private, and all of the methods are made protected, as shown in Exhibit 8 (Program10.6a) and used in Exhibit 9 (Program10.6b). This is the equivalent of private inheritance in C++. While this classification solution appears to be the equivalent of the composition solution of Exhibit 6 (Program10.5a), there are two differences, one small and one very important. The first difference is that the MoveController class in Exhibit 8 (Program10.6a) requires that the program that implements it must use up its single extends clause that is allowed by Java. This probably in and of itself is enough to argue against this solution, particularly in Java.

The second problem is much more critical. The classification solution in Exhibit 8 (Program10.6a) does not solve the problem of the two classes making one object which first appeared in Exhibit 4 (Program10.4a). For example, because the two classes make up one object, the solution in Exhibit 8 (Program10.6a) had to add another variable for the synchronization lock because the lock for the object is still shared, as they are still the same object. This shows that if the actual object that is used is shared (as in classification), it is not possible to implement a properly encapsulated object. Leakage of object information will always occur between the classes in Java.

All of this leads to the general rule that a programmer should never subclass what is essentially a utility object. The reason for doing classification is to create type hierarchies, where objects are actually made of attributes from several classes, as is covered in Chapter 11. It is the essence of the "is-a" and "has-a" relationships of objects. That type of hierarchy is not present when using a utility class. It will always be as valid to say a Button *has* a vector as saying a Button *is* a Vector, and it is all meaningless for utility classes. The question is not one of applying an inappropriate rule, but rather what works best in the design and implementation of a program. As we have seen already, utility classes should generally be implemented using composition, not classification, because it generally results in better programs.

Exhibit 8. Program10.6a: New Classification Implementation Using Encapsulation

```
import java.awt.Graphics;
import java.awt.Point;
import animator.*;

abstract public class MoveController {
  private Path myPath;
  private boolean doNotify = false;
  private Object notifyObject = new Object();
  protected void move(Path path) {
    synchronized(notifyObject) {
      myPath = path;
      try {
        doNotify = true;
        notifyObject.wait();
      } catch (InterruptedException e) {
      }
    }
  }

  protected boolean hasMoreSteps() {
    return myPath.hasMoreSteps();
  }
protected Point nextPosition() {
    if (myPath ! = null && myPath.hasMoreSteps()) {
      return myPath.nextPosition();
    }
    else if (myPath ! = null) {
      if (doNotify) {
        synchronized(notifyObject) {
          doNotify = false;
          notifyObject.notify();
        }
      }
      return myPath.nextPosition();
    }
    else
      return new Point(0,0);
  }
}
```

10.9 Defining the Java Event Model by Extending a Vector

The Java Event Model used in the animator in Chapter 7 (and defined in the Sun Java Beans Spec [SUN96]) used a utility class to store the listeners, a Vector. This was done using by including the vector of listeners as a variable in the animator class; hence, the reuse was achieved using composition. It could be argued, however, that the animator is a case where the use of classification would have worked better. For example, the addDrawListener and removeDrawListener methods do nothing except delegate the responsibility for adding and

Exhibit 9. Program10.6b: Concurrent Ball Program Using MoveController from Problem10.5a

```
import java.util.Random;
import java.awt.Graphics;
import java.awt.Point;
import java.awt.Color;
import animator.*;

public class ConcurrentBall extends MoveController
       implements DrawListener, Runnable {

  private Animator animator;

  /** Constructor. Note that we need to register with the
   * animator through the run method.
   */
  public ConcurrentBall(Animator animator) {
    this.animator = animator;
  }

  /**
   *  The run method simulates an asynchronous ball. The
   *  myPath variable is set here and used in the draw method
   *  and is intended to coordinate the ball thread running in
   *  this method and the GUI thread (from the animator)
   *  running in the draw method. This works correctly.
   */
  public void run() {
    animator.addDrawListener(this);
    Random random = new Random(System.currentTimeMillis());

    try {
      while(true) {
        move(new StraightLinePath(410, 205, 10, 205, 50));
        Thread.sleep(random.nextInt(10000));
        move(new StraightLinePath(10, 205, 410, 205, 50));
        Thread.sleep(random.nextInt(10000));
      }
    } catch (InterruptedException e) {
    }
  }

  /**
   *  Draw is called each time through the animator loop to draw
   *  the object. It simply uses the path to calculate the
   *  position of this object and then draws itself at that
   *  position. When the end of the path is reached, it notifies
   *  the ball thread.
   */
  public synchronized void draw(DrawEvent de) {
    Point p = nextPosition();
    Graphics g = de.getGraphics();
    g.setColor(Color.red);
    g.fillOval((int)p.getX(), (int)p.getY(), 15, 15);
  }

  /**
   *  The main method just creates the animator and
```

(continued)

Exhibit 9. Program10.6b (Continued)

```
   *  the ball threads and starts them running.
   */
  public static void main(String args[]) {
    Animator animator = new Animator();

    ConcurrentBall cb1 = new ConcurrentBall(animator);
    (new Thread(cb1)).start();

    animator.setVisible(true);
  }
}
```

removing the listener by calling the method in the vector. If the animator had extended class Vector, then the addElement and removeElement methods could be called directly, and these routines would not have had to be written, saving the programmer the necessity of writing these two methods.

This argument has two problems. The first is that the animator already extends a JPanel, giving it the ability to be placed on a frame. This uses up the single inheritance allowed by Java, which shows why it is important to consider what an object inherits from in Java. Second, while it is obviously true that extending class Vector would save the programmer a very small amount of time writing add and remove methods, the more important question is which design is safer and more extensible. These are the qualities that make the program more useful. The animator developed with composition in Chapter 7 offers four advantages compared to the classification method, all of which are much more important than the savings incurred by not having to implement the addDrawListener and removeDrawListener methods:

1. In Java, only single inheritance is allowed, and because the animator already extends JPanel it is impossible to create the animator by extending class Vector. This is generally true of classification in Java. Because Java allows only single inheritance, the programmer needs to decide carefully what one class should be extended.
2. The purpose of the objects in the vector is to store objects that are DrawListeners, as they will eventually be cast to a DrawListener and have their draw methods called. By creating an addDrawListener method that takes only DrawListeners as parameters, it is guaranteed that only objects of type DrawListener will ever be stored in the vector. If a programmer attempts to add anything that is not a DrawListener then an error will be produced at compile time; however, if the addElement method of the vector is used directly it is possible for objects that are not DrawListeners to be added to the vector. This will cause a runtime ClassCastException when an attempt is made to cast the object to a DrawListener to

call the draw method. It is a generally accepted principle that it is always best to catch a problem as early as possible in the software development process, when it is easier and less expensive to fix. Even if only one situation ever occurs where software is released and some set of logic allows a non DrawListener object to be added to the animator's vector, the cost of fixing that bug and reissuing the software (not to mention the ill will that is caused) will be many orders of magnitude greater than the cost involved in writing the addDrawListener and removeDrawListener methods.

3. The animator has not made any external promises to the programs that use it as to how the listeners are stored, so it can change the class that is used to define the container for the listeners without any impact on the programs that use it. This was important in the case of the Java Event Model. The Java Event Model originally defined listeners as being stored in vector classes, and the vector was cloned when processing the event; however, because the listeners vector is cloned when the events are processed, but the add and remove methods are called less frequently, it is better to clone this vector as part of the add and remove method, rather than when the events are processed. EventMulticaster classes, such as the DrawEventMulticaster class used in Program 7.6, were created and the Java AWT was changed to use these EventMulticasters. Because the class used to store the listeners is private, this type of change can be made without affecting the programs that used the AWT classes.
4. We might not want all of the functionality of the Vector class to be available for manipulating the listener's vector. The vector in the animator is not as good an example as the classic mistake made when implementing the Stack class in the java.util package. A stack needs to store elements in a collection, so the Stack class in Java was implemented to extend the Vector class. This made all the methods of the Vector class accessible to stack objects, so programs could misuse the stack by doing things like adding objects at places other than the top of the stack. This poor behavior is shown in Exhibit 10 (Program10.7), where an object is added at the bottom of the stack.

Sections 10.8 and 10.9 provided a number of reasons why using classification to extend what is basically a utility class results in poor designs; however, problems like these often are apparent only after the program has been implemented. What is needed is some way to evaluate a design using basic principles that would predict whether or not a design is likely to result in problems such as those in Sections 10.8 and 10.9. The principles we will use are cohesion and coupling.

Exhibit 10. Program10.7: Improper Use of Stack Object

```
import java.util.Stack;

public class UseStack {
  public static void main(String args[]) {
    try {
      Stack stack = new Stack();
      stack.push("Element 1");

    // The next statement is invalid for a stack.
      stack.add(1, "Element 2");
    // Note that the items in the stack are in the wrong order
      System.out.println(stack.pop());
      System.out.println(stack.pop());
    } catch(Exception e) {
      e.printStackTrace();
    }
  }
}
```

10.10 Using Cohesion and Coupling to Evaluate Designs

A program is a very complex logic puzzle. If a program is regarded as a simple state machine, and every statement is allowed to access every data item, then the complexity of a program is all the possible values in memory that every variable can have multiplied by every statement in a program. So, if a program has N memory variables, each having M possible values, a line of code that can access any of those values would have $N * M$ possible consequences. If we multiply this by the number of statements executed in a program (S), we get $N * M * S$ possible results for a program, a number which while finite is probably not manageable by a person for a program of any significant size.

This is what makes it very easy to write programs that are impossible to understand. Languages that allow addressing of any piece of data, such as C/C++, immediately make the maximum level of complexity of the program obtainable and is one of the reasons the use of pointers was eliminated in Java. The same problem existed in older FORTRAN programs, where all the data values were kept in a single common block and could be accessed anywhere in a program. Structured programming was supposed to solve these problems but, unfortunately, structured programming by itself did not limit the scope of the data. A great description of a program given to me was that "the program is very well structured, but it is like the data was just poured into it."

To get around this program of unstructured data, the concept of *encapsulation* was introduced by Parnas [PAR72]. With encapsulation, if data is hidden inside of a function and only allowed to be acted on in well-defined ways by program statements in that function, the data and the function could be treated as a single entity in the program, thus reducing the amount of data each statement can act on and decreasing the overall program complexity. This idea of encapsulation is applied to OOP in that the data is now encapsulated in the object, and only methods for that object can act on that data. If the encapsulation is complete, then the object can be treated as a single entity in the program, not as a number of separate values and statements, thus reducing the overall complexity significantly.

How well the encapsulation has been achieved can be evaluated by looking at the cohesiveness and coupling of an object. Cohesion and coupling have already been introduced in the discussion of how to do exception handling in Chapter 6; here, the concepts are further developed and applied to methods and objects. Cohesion for a method is the property of doing a limited number of things, ideally just one thing. If a method must implement more than one behavior, other objects or methods should be created and used for those behaviors. Cohesion for an object requires that the object represent one entity, even though that one entity could be made up of numerous other entities, such as a car having an engine and tires. Still, the object is one thing, a car. Coupling is concerned with how much of the internal details of the object or method must be known by other methods or objects for the object to be implemented. For methods, coupling means that the data that will be used by the method has a well-defined path into that method. For procedural methods, this means that no data is sent to the method except via parameters. For methods that are part of objects, some of the data can be part of the object, but the data used is limited and access to it is controlled and well understood as part of the object state. For objects, coupling means that no other object has access to its state (variables and data) except through well-controlled access, such as methods.

The basic principles here are that, as an object or a method does more things, its cohesion goes down, and as the access to it becomes more intertwined with other objects its coupling goes up. The ideal is to raise cohesion while lowering coupling. Doing so will better isolate the data, and hopefully make the program less complex.

It was already shown that cohesion and coupling can be used to evaluate the error handling in the SortedPrintTable objects of Chapter 5. In these objects, when an error occurred it was printed to the terminal from within the object itself. Chapter 6 suggested that this was a bad idea, as this procedure locked the object to a specific execution environment and showed that exceptions were a better way to handle this situation. Cohesion and coupling can be used to explain this further. First, the objects tried to do two things: handle requests for the object and handle errors for the object. Second, they were too tightly coupled to the environment in which they were run; in this case, they relied on the fact that the program would be terminal based. The use of exceptions was an attempt to break this coupling of the object to the environment and to allow the object to be concerned with how to handle the table, not what to do with errors.

Cohesion and coupling do not find errors, but they are at the root of many errors, so they are good indicators of designs that are likely to be more error prone. For example, the classification implementation of the MoveController object in Exhibit 6 (Program10.5a) is more tightly coupled because the two classes that are present, the MoveController and the ConcurrentBall, both are represented by the same object. This might or might not cause a problem, but it suggests a higher probability of error in the classification design than the composition design. This, indeed, proved to be the case, as was shown with call to wait in the move method. Generally, designs that use composition have higher cohesion and lower coupling than designs that use classification. So, if no other factors are influencing the decision, as is generally true with utility classes, the decision about which approach to use should always favor composition.

This does not mean that classification should never be used, as it really depends on the problem that is being solved. For example, the Java AWT creates components by extending the Component class. In this case, the AWT components really are just types of components, and they must extend components to be used properly. An external factor also influences the design, as the Component class is not a utility class in the AWT, thus making classification the best choice for design of the AWT. Many AWT classes also extend Container, in which case whether or not classification is the best design is less clear. Problem 10.3 looks further at this issue.

10.11 Conclusion

This chapter has looked at different methods of reuse. If no state needs to be saved, then procedural reuse, creating a method, works fine; however, if a state must be saved for the reuse, then some form of object reuse is necessary. Object reuse means that a class definition must be implemented so that an object can be instantiated to store the state. If the only purpose of the object is to provide for reuse, then the object is called a utility object. The two ways to implement object reuse are composition and classification. If the object that is providing the reuse is a utility object, then the only consideration regarding how to design the object is to make the properties of the object available. If this is true, then composition is preferred over classification, as composition designs generally have higher cohesion and lower coupling.

10.12 Further Reading

The idea that object design can be separated into utility reuse and OOD is largely based on Coad and Mayfield [COA99]. Most of the arguments presented here are from that text, and this chapter adds more examples to simply flesh out the arguments. Information about extreme programming and refactoring can be found at [XP02] or at any number of other sites that can be found by doing a search on the Web for either term.

10.13 Problems

1. The MoveController object in both the Composition and Classification programs cannot be used with procedural programs such as the MoveObjects in Program 7.5d. Why? Suggest modifications to the class so that the MoveController object's move method can be used with either procedural or concurrent programs.
2. Show that all of the problems with using classification identified in Sections 10.8 and 10.9 are a result of the classification design increasing coupling and decreasing cohesion relative to the composition design.
3. All of the Java AWT components (Button, TextField, etc.) are created by extending class Component and many also extend Container. Discuss the relative merits of this design, especially considering whether or not the Component class and Container classes are utility classes with respect to the AWT components. Also, consider the behavior of some components, such as adding a Layout Manager or component to a JFrame, and the methods that are overridden in the various classes. Is the design of the Java AWT a good one?
4. Compare the animator control panel in Chapter 7 with the control panel in Chapter 9. Show that the one in Chapter 9 is superior using the arguments of cohesion and coupling.
5. Applying the concepts of coupling and cohesion, discuss the relative merits of the design of the Java AWT. By these criteria, is the design of the AWT a good one?

Chapter 11

Object-Oriented Design

11.1 Introduction

The first nine chapters of the book discussed how to structure the objects in a problem, and Chapter 10 addressed how to organize the relationships between objects for utility objects. The discussion in Chapter 10 suggested that composition should always be preferred over classification when designing and constructing utility objects; however, most objects used in a program are not utility objects but represent parts of the problem definition. When the objects are part of the problem definition, should composition or classification be used when constructing an object?

The choice of composition or classification can normally be determined by answering the question, "Is the relationship between the objects an 'is-a' or a 'has-a' relationship?" "Is-a" relationships are always implemented with classification, and "has-a" relationships are implemented with composition. This simple test is often used by designers as an acid test to determine if objects should be constructed by composition or classification. This chapter argues that as with any simple test it is simply not powerful enough to be applied indiscriminately. Care must be taken to consider the results of an "is-a" or "has-a" test in light of the context. How are the objects used in the problem definition? Do object design criteria other than if the relationship is one of "is-a" or "has-a" affect the choice between composition or classification? Do considerations involving how the program needs to be implemented impact the choice of composition or classification?

This chapter looks at how to construct objects that are part of the problem definition. It first looks at how to apply "is-a" and "has-a" relationships to the design of a program. It then examines how the problem and program contexts must be considered before implementing the design.

11.2 Chapter Goals

When you have completed this chapter, you should understand:

- The difference between "is-a" and "has-a" relationships and how to implement these relationships.
- The difference between an abstract class and an interface.
- How to use classification to "composite" an object, and why this is a bad idea.
- Why "is-a" and "has-a" relationships are dependent on the problem context.
- Why classification should not be used to represent the state of an object.
- Why roles should not be represented using classification.
- How composition and classification can be used to extend not only representation, but also behavior.

11.3 Organizing Objects

Abstraction is the process of factoring out commonality in a program, storing it once, and reusing it. Once this commonality has been factored out, some way must be found to organize it so that it can be used. As was pointed out in Chapter 10, if the abstraction involves only stateless methods, static methods can be created and added to a library class and called as needed. Often, however, the commonality will require that a state be maintained between invocations of a method, and this will result in the need for object-oriented programming (OOP) techniques to maintain this state. OOP involves organizing objects around information (data) and behavior (methods that act on that data). The objects created to organize the data and methods are generally structured around objects that exist in the problem definition, with the objects in the problem definition being decomposed into objects in the program, thus this process is often called *decomposition*. In Chapter 10, the topic of how to handle this reuse of object state and behavior in utility classes was covered. This chapter addresses the reuse of an object state and behavior for objects represented in the problem to be solved. As will be shown, this type of design is more concerned with representing the objects to match their use in the problem definition than in the reuse possibilities, but the end result is still a design that factors out commonalities and enhances reuse.

As was pointed out in Chapter 10, information and behavior for objects can be organized in two ways: (1) build an object by including instance of other objects as variables, referred to as *composition*; or (2) build an object by using the Java extends clause to extend the behavior of some base object, called *classification*. Composition is normally thought of as a "has-a" relationship (see Section 11.3.1); the two major types of composition, aggregation and association, are defined and illustrated below. Classification is often thought of as an "is-a" relationship (see Section 11.3.2) and often involves using what are called *abstract classes*. Abstract classes are often confused with interfaces, but Section 11.3.3 demonstrates how they are different. Finally, Section 11.3.4 shows how classification can be used to implement an object that is made up of data and methods from other objects, using what are essentially "has-a" relationships that should be implemented as composition. Section 11.3.4 also discusses how this approach can result in an incorrect design and why this use of classification should normally be avoided.

Section 11.4 looks at why the simple "is-a" vs. "has-a" test must be carefully applied to a program design. Section 11.4.1 shows that an "is-a" relationship is really dependent on the definition of the problem to be solved. Section 11.4.2 goes on to show that, even when an object relationship is a true "is-a" relationship, mutable objects are not handled well in classification. When this occurs the "is-a" relationship really represents a state, which is better stored in a variable using composition rather than classification. Section 11.4.3 suggests that if classification is used to represent a role then it is best to use composition. Section 11.4.4 points out problems that can occur with objects if an object can take on multiple roles, which causes the number of possible classes needed to represent the possible objects to grow exponentially. Finally, Section 11.4.5 deals with how the choice of classification or composition can be impacted by the design of the program.

11.3.1 Composition: "Has-a" Relationships

Objects can be built by including information about the object as variables that are declared as part of the class definition for the object. These variables can be objects or primitives. For example a car "has an" engine size, "has a" driver, "has" four tires, "has a" model name, and "has an" ability to calculate the expectedTimeToService. The definition for this class is shown in Exhibit 1 (Program11.1a). Note that the composition relationship allows an object to be built from primitives (a float for engine size), other objects (a driver), collections of objects or primitives (an array of tires), and methods (expectedTimeToService).

At some point during the life of the object, often when it is constructed, these values are set. This mechanism of building an object is referred to as *composition* because an object is composed of the objects and primitives. Composition can be used anytime a "has-a"

Exhibit 1. Program11.1a: Composition Example for a Car Class

```
/**
 * A class to build a Car class
 */
class Driver {
}

/**
 * A class to build a Car class
 */
class Tire implements Clonable {
  protected Object clone() {
    return new Tire();
  }
}

/**
 * An interface used to build the Car class
 */
interface ServiceTimeCalculator {
  public int expectedTimeToService();
}

/**
 * A class to instantiate the interface
 */
class myCarsCalculator implements ServiceTimeCalculator {
  public int expectedTimeToService(){
    return 0;
  }
}

/**
 * This shows a class created using composition. All of the
 * different mechanisms for composition are included:
 *     driver: association
 *     modelName: aggregation (using immutable objects)
 *     stc: composition using an interface
 *     engineSize: aggregation (using a primitive)
 *     tires[]: aggregation (using an encapsulated variable)
 */
public class Car {
  private Driver driver;
  private String modelName();
  private ServiceTimeCalculator stc;
  private int engineSize;
  private static final int NUMBER_OF_TIRES = 4;
  private Tire tires[];

  /**
   * Public constructor. It sets the values for the
   * variables. Note that the driver is association because
   * the driver object passed was saved. The tires are
   * aggregation, because new objects are created that do not
   * have scope outside of this object. Finally, methods can
   * be composited using interfaces.
   */
  public Car(Driver driver, ServiceTimeCalculator stc, Tire[]
      tires) {
    this.driver = driver;
    this.stc = stc;
    this.engineSize = 350;
```

(continued)

Exhibit 1. Program11.1a (Continued)

```
    for (int i = 0; i < NUMBER_OF_TIRES; i++) {
      this.tires[i] = (Tire) tires[i].clone();
    }
  }

  /**
   * Accessor method for tires, which are aggregate variables
   * using cloning of the object.
   */
  public void setTire(int tireNo, Tire tire) {
    this.tires[tireNo] = (Tire)tire.clone();
  }

  /**
   * Accessor method for modelName, which is an aggregate
   * variable using an immutable object.
   */
  public void setModelName(String modelName) {
    this.modelName = modelName;
  }

  /**
   * Accessor which returns the model name. Because the object is
   * immutable, this does not violate the aggregate property of
   * the object.
   */
  public String getModelName() {
    return modelName;
  }
  /**
   * Accessor method for engineSize, which is an aggregate
   * variable using a primitive.
   */
  public void setEngineSize(int engineSize) {
    this.engineSize = engineSize;
  }
  /**
   * Accessor method to return engineSize. Because it is a
   * primitive, this does not violate the aggregate property of
   * the object.
   */
  public int getEngineSize() {
    return engineSize;
  }

  /**
   * Accessor method for the driver, an association variable.
   * Note that the actual mutable object is stored, meaning
   * that the object is shared with the calling method.
   */
  public Driver getDriver() {
    return driver;
  }

  /**
   * Accessor method for driver, an association variable.
   * Note that the actual mutable object is returned.
   */
  public void setDriver(Driver driver) {
    this.driver = driver;
  }
}
```

relation exists. For example, a paragraph has at least one sentence, which has one or more words, or a person has an age. To build an object using composition, a variable is created to represent the property needed, and then an instance of that property is assigned.

One interesting thing to note is that not only is composition implemented for properties represented by data values, but it is also possible for properties that need to be calculated, in this case with the expectedTimeToService interface. Because each car object could have differing requirements for service that needs to be done, a class can be created that simply implements this function. An object instance of this class can then be stored with the car object, and the expectedTimeToService method in the car object can delegate the actual calculation to that object. *Delegation* is the way in which reuse occurs in composite objects and simply means that a method in the encapsulating object calls the method in the encapsulated object to do the actual calculation. This relationship can be polymorphic, as shown in the car object through the use of interfaces.

Composition can be used in two ways to build an object, aggregation or association. These topics are discussed in the next three sections.

11.3.1.1 Aggregation

Aggregation applies to data for an object that is completely encapsulated inside of the object. This means that the data item cannot be changed outside of the object, and the data item exists only while the object exists. For example, a Car object has an Engine. The Engine is created when the Car is created and is only accessed from within the Car class. It has no existence or presence outside of the Car class. One big advantage of using aggregation is that, because the aggregated object cannot be modified outside of the object that encapsulates it, the encapsulating object can control any changes to the aggregated object. This is useful for monitoring any changes to the aggregated object or for providing synchronized access to an encapsulated aggregated object, as in the readers/writers program in Chapter 9.

Aggregate properties are normally maintained in a program in one of three ways. The first two ways are similar and use primitives and immutable variables. If primitives or immutable objects are used with private identifiers, it is not possible to change the values of these variables outside of the object in which they are contained. Exhibit 1 (Program11.1a) illustrates these two ways to specify an aggregate property using the engineSize and modelName identifiers. The engineSize is a primitive and thus can only be referenced from within the current object; it is copied when it is returned to the calling program via the getEngineSize method. The modelName is an instance of a string and is thus immutable; it can be safely returned via the getModelName method.

The third way to specify an aggregate property is to create a new object for each aggregate property and to limit the scope of these objects to the encapsulating object. This means that only the methods in the encapsulating object have access to these aggregated objects, thus the encapsulating object can be used to control access to them. Exhibit 1 (Program11.1a) illustrates this concept through the array of tires. When the tires are stored in the Car object, the program always creates a new Tire object to represent it (via a call to the clone method). Unlike the use of primitives or immutable objects, no getTire method is used, because returning a copy of the Tire breaks the encapsulation (confinement) of the Tire object, so it can be changed outside of the Car object. In this way, the Tire object used by the Car object is always specific to the Car and has no visibility outside of the Car object.

Finally, note that all three types of aggregation can use *setter* methods (such as setModelName). This in no way breaks the encapsulation of the object; however, it can come with its own problems. For example, consider the case when an aggregated object is used as a notification object. If setter methods are used in an object, it is possible for a thread to wait on the aggregated notification object but then the variable in the encapsulating object to be changed. This leaves the thread waiting on the de-referenced object for a call to notify that will never happen. So, while the use of setter methods does not violate aggregation, it should be carefully considered.

11.3.1.2 Association

Association applies to data for an object that might have existence outside of an object. For example, the objects stored in a vector will be created externally to the vector, and then added to the vector. The object can later be modified, and this modification will be reflected in the object in the vector. Objects will thus only be associated with the vector. In Exhibit 1 (Program11.1a), association is illustrated by the driver of a car. A Car object could have multiple Driver objects over its lifetime, and the Driver object is normally maintained in the program outside of the Car object. Thus, attributes of the driver of the Car can be changed outside of the control of the Car object.

When association is used in a design it impacts concurrent operations. When an object is associated with the encapsulating object (in this case, the Driver with the Car), the encapsulating object cannot be used to ensure synchronized accessed to the associated object. Just because the Driver object is referenced in a synchronized method in the Car does not mean that some other thread that obtained a reference other than through the Car cannot change the Driver object and create a race condition.

As was shown, the choice between aggregation and association has important consequences when used with concurrent operation. It also affects other design considerations. For example, aggregate objects are garbage collected when the containing object goes out of scope, but the status of an associate object is unknown as there could be other references to it. When an object is created and exported by some mechanism, it could outlive the object that creates it. Likewise, if an object was created outside of the object and imported by some mechanism, the reference to it in the calling object could keep it from being garbage collected. All of this leads to the question of when to use aggregation and when to use association. Generally, this choice hinges on how the object is used in the program design.

11.3.1.3 Using Aggregation and Association

It seems obvious when to use aggregation or association. For example, it is obvious that when modeling a car, tires are always tracked with a car, are only of interest when they are part of the car, and thus should be aggregated. The driver of a car is created outside of the Car class, should be modifiable outside of the Car class, and thus should be associated with the car. That this design is obviously true can be shown by considering the modeling of a car rental company. Because drivers are changed each time the car is rented and because the driver record must be accessed outside of when the driver is renting the car (for functions such as billing), the driver must be associated (not aggregated) with the car. Likewise, the tires on a car are only of interest when they are on the car, and so represent an aggregation with the car object. This agrees with our basic intuition of how to model a car, that these relationships must always hold, and it stands to reason that a car is modeled with an associated driver and aggregate tires. But, is it really so obvious? Consider the problem of modeling a race car. A race car is always associated with a particular driver; however, during a race the tires on the car might be replaced several times, and these tires must be tracked when they are off the car to make sure that they are not accidentally used again. In this case of a race car, where the driver is an aggregate item and the tires are associated items, our preconceived notions about how to model a car really do not apply. A good rule that cannot be repeated enough is to *solve the problem you are given, not the one you want to solve.*

As this example shows, no easy rules exist for implementing a design. Designers need to understand the problems they are trying to implement and should remember that OOP is not about modeling the real world or, worse, the designer's intuition about how the real world behaves. A good design must reflect the realities of the problem being solved.

Exhibit 2. Program11.1b: Classification Example for a Car Class

```
class SUV extends car {
}

class Convertible extends car {
}
```

11.3.2 Classification: "Is-a" Relationships

Classification involves putting things into class hierarchies. A common example is in biological classification of living organisms, such as: "A human 'is-a' mammal 'is-an' animal 'is-a' living thing." Just as composition uses "has-a" relationships to build objects, classification uses "is-a" relationships to build objects. The difference is that in composition, an object is a composite of other objects that are included as variables in the definition of the larger object. In classification, a larger object is built by extending the properties of other base objects.

Classification is accomplished in Java using the extends clause, which tells a subclass to keep the functionality and data from a super class and add new functionality to it, extending the base class with the data and functionality of the new class. For example, Exhibit 2 (Program11.1b) shows an example of how the Car class in Exhibit 1 (Program11.1a) can be extended into specific types of cars. In this case, we have two types of cars, an SUV and a convertible. Both of these types have all the attributes of a car, but both extend that functionality to create more specific types of cars. Because each subclass inherits the functionality from the base class, classification is also called *inheritance*.

Many novice programmers believe that because they can directly access data and methods from the super class in the subclass that classification designs are better than composition designs. However, the first rule should always be to implement a design consistent with the problem to be solved and within any constraints that might be imposed by the implementation details for the program. As will be shown, such an approach generally favors composition.

11.3.3 Abstract Classes versus Interfaces

Often, the base classes in a classification hierarchy are not meant to be instantiated as there is no instance of something that is strictly the base type. In the biological example, there are no animals that are just a mammal, but there are many different types of animals (such as dogs and people) which all share the characteristic of being a mammal. In Java, when a class is created to simply represent commonality between all objects that are subtypes of that class, the class created is declared to be abstract.

For example, consider the employee example provided in Exhibit 3 (Program11.2). Here, the base class Employee is created to define some variables and methods that are common to all types of employees, such as name, dependents, and calculating their weekly pay using the calculatePay method. The ability to calculate the pay of each employee is an important part of the definition of an employee; however, we have a number of different types of employees, and the way to calculate the salary is different for each type. It is not possible, then, to have an object that is an instance of a generic employee. The objects must be specific types of employees, so the employee class and calculatePay methods are declared as abstract, indicating that they must be defined in a subclass before objects of this type can be declared. In this case, each type of

Exhibit 3. Program11.2: Employee Class

```
/**
 *  The base class to define a person.
 */
class Person {
  private String name;

  publicPerson(Stringname) {
    this.name = name;
  }

  public Person(Person person) {
    this.name = person.name;
  }

  public void setName(String name) {
    this.name = name;
  }

  public String getName() {
    return name;
  }
}

/**
 *  The base class for an employee. The data to define an
 *  employee, as well as the methods that must be defined in the
 *  subclasses, are defined here.
 */
abstract class Employee extends Person {
  protected Employee(String name) {
    super(name);
  }

  protected Employee(Employee employee) {
    super(employee);
  }

  abstract public float calculatePay();
```

(continued)

Exhibit 3. Program11.2 (Continued)

```
  public static void main(String args[]) {
    Employee employee = new HourlyEmployee("Cindy," 12.23f,
        40.00f);
    System.out.println(employee.calculatePay());
    // Here the employee is changed to a SalariedEmployee.
    // Note that a new object was created.
    employee = new SalariedEmployee(employee, 2075.00f);
    System.out.println(employee.calculatePay());
  }
}

/**
 *  A type of employee that is paid based on the number of hours
 *  worked. To calculate the pay, the hours worked and the rate
 *  per hour need to be entered.
 */
class HourlyEmployee extends Employee {
  private float ratePerHour;
  private float hoursWorked;

  public HourlyEmployee(String name, float ratePerHour,
    float hoursWorked) {
    super(name);
    this.ratePerHour = ratePerHour;
    this.hoursWorked = hoursWorked;
  }

  public HourlyEmployee(Employee employee, float ratePerHour,
    float hoursWorked) {
    super(employee);
    this.ratePerHour = ratePerHour;
    this.hoursWorked = hoursWorked;
  }

  public float calculatePay() {
    return ratePerHour * hoursWorked;
  }
}

/**
 *  A type of employee that is paid a fixed amount each week
 */
class SalariedEmployee extends Employee {
  private float weeklySalary;

  public SalariedEmployee(String name, float weeklySalary) {
    super(name);
    this.weeklySalary = weeklySalary;
  }

  public SalariedEmployee(Employee employee, float weeklySalary) {
    super(employee);
    this.weeklySalary = weeklySalary;
  }

  public float calculatePay() {
    return weeklySalary;
  }
}
```

employee, salaried or hourly, has its own calculatePay method and variables necessary to support their pay type (salaried or hourly).

This implementation of the Employee class shows that just as with interfaces, classification using extends clauses is polymorphic. The specific calculatePay method that is called is not determined until the program is actually run and the specific object type chosen. So, what is the difference between an abstract class and an interface? In C++, no difference exists, so why did Java make the distinction? The first reason why the distinction is made is that abstract classes and interfaces are not semantically the same. Abstract classes are used when some base functionality can be extended using the Java extends clause. This base functionality is found in either variable definitions or implementation (not definition) of methods. An interface does not have any functionality to be extended, as it is simply an agreement between objects that some behavior will be available. What is nice about the Java keywords *extend* and *implement* is that they make this distinction clear.

The second reason to make the distinction is that it makes handling of objects easier. In Java, multiple interfaces can be implemented in a single object; however, because these interfaces are simply agreements, if two interfaces define the same method the implementing class must implement the method only once to meet the requirements of both interfaces. Thus, no confusion exists as to which method is to be used, as one method satisfies all interfaces. When some functionality, be it data or methods, is extended in Java, only single inheritance is allowed, so it is not possible to have conflicts regarding what behavior to use.

If, however, abstract classes are used for interfaces, subclasses must be able to extend (not simply implement) multiple super classes, even if those abstract classes are only used to implement true interfaces. This is because the abstract class could implement variables and methods, as there is no restriction to doing this in the language. Because multiple parent classes can define the same variables and methods, the language must implement the capability to decide how to clarify the methods and variables. Other problems, some very complex, including possible inheritance structures, lead to rules for handling conflicts that can be very confusing. Thus, the use of abstract classes to define a base behavior and interfaces to define promises of behavior in objects is actually a very nice feature in Java. It more correctly defines the semantics of what is happening and is much easier to implement and understand.

11.3.4 Using Classification to Mimic Composition

This section closes with an example of how not to use classification in a program. Nearly every problem that can be solved with

Exhibit 4. Program11.3: Club

```
/**
 *  A class to define a name for a person
 */
class Name {
  String firstName;
  String lastName;
}

/**
 *  A class to define a person who has a name and age
 */
class Person {
  Name name;
  int age;
}

/**
 *  A class to define a building
 */
class Building {
  String streetAddress;
  String city;
  String state;
}

/**
 *  This class shows that a club has a clubhouse,
 *  a president, and a list of members.
 */
class Club {
  Person president;
  Building clubHouse;
  Person members[];
}
```

classification can be solved with composition, and vice versa, but that does not mean that the solutions are equally as good. This was made clear to me in a class when I gave a design problem similar to the following to be done during a break in class. The problem, intended to illustrate composition, was to design a program for a social club. This club was to have a president, who was a person, and a roster of members, and it was to be headquartered in a building that had an address consisting of a street address, city, and state, all stored as strings. Each person was to have a name, consisting of a first name and last name, and an age. I thought this would be a trivial assignment and anticipated designs similar to the one in Exhibit 4 (Program11.3).

When the groups of students presented their designs, one stood out, which is shown in Exhibit 5 (Program11.4). This design used inheritance to collect all the data values needed to create the social club. This struck me as wrong. After all, the relationships were obviously "has-a" relationships, yet the students had implemented them as

Exhibit 5. Program11.4: Club

```
/**
 *  A class that defines a name, consisting of a first name and
 *  a last name
 */
class Name {
  String firstName;
  String lastName;
}

/**
 *  A person object still has a name and age, but the
 *  name comes to the object through inheritance.
 */
class Person extends Name {
  int age;
}

/**
 *  A building is still an address, but because of single
 *  inheritance we include the attributes of a person so
 *  that a club can be built from a building.
 */
class Building extends Person {
  String streetAddress;
  String city;
  String state;
}

/**
 *  All the data needed for a club is now present except
 *  the list of members. Note that this class has the same
 *  data as the class presented in Program11.3.
 */
class Club extends Building {
  Person members[];
}
```

"is-a" relationships. Further, they had created a very deep inheritance hierarchy that I felt was confusing. No amount of discussion, however, could convince even one student that Exhibit 5 (Program11.4) was a better design than Exhibit 4 (Program11.3). They felt that the classification design allowed for more reuse and felt that the deep hierarchy was more a result of Java not allowing multiple inheritance, which would have allowed the social club to directly extend the Building class and the Person class.

When it was pointed out that this example would also be limited if the application were to be changed to add an address to the person class, the students argued that this was more a limitation of Java than a valid criticism of their design. Having thought long and hard about this problem, I still feel that classification is an invalid solution to this problem that leads to a more confusing and potentially less extensible solution; however, the issue is left open to discussion as a problem at the end of the chapter.

11.4 Choosing Composition or Classification

As with deciding whether to use aggregation or association, trying to figure out whether to use classification or composition is not as straightforward as figuring out whether the relationship is a "has-a" or an "is-a" relationship. As with everything, the best answer is to do what produces the best solution to the problem to be solved. As stated before, nearly any problem that can be implemented as a "has-a" relationship can be implemented as an "is-a" relationship, and vice versa. So, the choices made should reflect what is most appropriate for the problem.

As discussed in Chapter 10, solutions that use classification allow easier access to the underlying definition in the base class but lead to less robust designs. So, a good general rule to follow is to first look at the problem to determine the presence of "is-a" or "has-a" relationships. For "has-a" relationships, choose composition, as composition has very few problems as compared to classification. Examine "is-a" relationships more closely. Make sure that choosing classification does bring with it hidden problems; if no problems appear to exist, classification should be used, as it will provide the easiest reuse for the underlying class.

This section describes five checks to identify problems in classification relationships. If these problems exist, using classification will likely result in poor designs. The first check is to make sure the relationship being described is, in fact, an "is-a" relationship in the context of the problem being solved. The second is to make sure that that the object type is not mutable, that it cannot change its type. The third check is to make sure that the class is created to represent a true type and not simply a role for an object. The fourth check is to make sure that an object cannot take on multiple types. Finally, a check should be made to ensure that no other constraints in the problem definition or program implementation would be hindered by using classification.

11.4.1 Check to Ensure That the Relationship Is an "Is-a" Relationship

The "is-a" and "has-a" checks on a relationship are useful because they are so easy to understand. The larger question is whether they are generally correct when applied to a problem. For example, in the employee problem shown in Exhibit 3 (Program11.2), it might seem obvious that an hourly employee (HourlyEmployee) "is an" employee, thus classification should be used in the design. To suggest that HourlyEmployee "has an" employee flies in the face of the intuition and experience of most designers, and so is simply discarded out of hand. However, are the intuition and experience of a designer relevant to the question of how to design this particular program? The answer should obviously be "no," as it is the context of the problem that should determine the approach. Too often designers and programmers bring their own view of the world into solving problems and make choices based on their preconceived ideas and biases. This is what makes this check so easy to ignore, but absolutely vital.

For example, consider the HourlyEmployee and SalariedEmployee example. Some company (a temporary employment firm) might need to solve a problem where a certain number of employee slots (some hourly and some salaried) are allocated to a particular project; when an employee is assigned to a slot, his pay is determined by the slot he occupies. In this problem context, an employee is not hourly or salaried; instead, HourlyEmployee "has an" employee who will be paid for doing the work. In the context of the specific problem to be solved, the bias of programmers to create a designs that represent how they view the problem must be overcome to produce a design that actually represents the problem to be solved.

This shows why the "is-a" and "has-a" rule must be carefully applied. A designer needs to understand the problem to be solved, and any preconceived notions about how the world works must be set aside. If "is-a" does apply to the relationship, then the next step is to make sure that no other constraints suggest using composition rather than classification.

11.4.2 Be Sure the Object Type Is Not Mutable

Once a relationship is determined to be an "is-a" relationship, the next check is to be sure that the object type is not mutable. A mutable object type occurs when an object can change type, such as when HourlyEmployee is promoted to a SalariedEmployee position. To understand why this is a problem, remember that inheritance objects that instantiate the subclass actually represent a single object (allocation of memory), not a collection of objects. Therefore, when changing the object type from HourlyEmployee to SalariedEmployee, the employee part of the object must be copied to create a new SalariedEmployee object, and the HourlyEmployee object is then discarded. Depending on how the problem is defined and how the application is implemented, this might or might not be a problem, but it should be considered.

A classification solution to the employee program was given in Exhibit 3 (Program11.2); a composition solution is given here in Exhibit 6 (Program11.5). Note that the simplicity of the classification solution is somewhat lost, as the composition solution requires a static constructor to be used in an abstract factory pattern to produce the object of the correct type. Thus, some of the elegance of the object models is lost, but now the type of employee can be changed without losing the reference to the original employee object.

Exhibit 6. Program11.5: Composition Solution to Modeling Employees

```
/**
 *  This class shows how to create an employee when the
 *  employee is a basic "abstract" type. In this case, the
 *  constructor for the employee is private, so the employee
 *  can only be created by calling one of the static methods to
 *  create a specific employee type. This use of a static method
 *  to create a specific type of employee is sometimes called a
 *  "factory pattern."
 *
 *  Note that because we use a composition design, it is easy
 *  to change the object from an hourly to a salaried employee
 *  without losing track of the employee object.
 */
class Employee extends Person{
  private PayType payType;

  private Employee(String name) {
    super(name);
  }

  public static Employee createHourlyEmployee(String name,
    float ratePerHour, float hoursWorked) {
    Employee employee = new Employee(name);
    employee.payType = new HourlyPayType(ratePerHour,
        hoursWorked);
    return employee;
  }

  public static Employee createSalariedEmployee(String name,
      float weeklySalary) {
    Employee employee = new Employee(name);
    employee.payType = new SalariedPayType(weeklySalary);
    return employee;
  }

  public void changeToSalaried(float weeklySalary) {
    payType = new SalariedPayType(weeklySalary);
  }

  public void changeToHourly(float ratePerHour, float
      hoursWorked) {
    payType = new HourlyPayType(ratePerHour, hoursWorked);
  }

  public float calculatePay() {
    return payType.calculatePay();
  }

  public static void main(String args[]) {
    Employee employee = createHourlyEmployee("Cindy," 12.23f,
        40.00f);
    System.out.println(employee.calculatePay());
    // Here the employee is changed to a SalariedEmployee.
    // Note that no new object is created.
    employee.changeToSalaried(2075.00f);
    System.out.println(employee.calculatePay());
  }
}
```

(continued)

Exhibit 6. Program11.5 (Continued)

```
/**
 * The base class for an employee
 */
class Person {
  private String name;

  public Person(String name) {
    this.name = name;
  }

  public Person(Person person) {
    this.name = person.name;
  }

  public void setName(String name) {
    this.name = name;
  }

  public String getName(String name) {
    return name;
  }
}

/**
 *  An interface that sets the employee to the correct type
 *  and allows the employee's pay to be calculated
 */
interface PayType {
  public float calculatePay();
}

/**
 *  A class that specifies an hourly employee
 */
class HourlyPayType implements PayType {
  private float ratePerHour;
  private float hoursWorked;
  public HourlyPayType(float ratePerHour, float hoursWorked) {
    this.ratePerHour = ratePerHour;
    this.hoursWorked = hoursWorked;
  }

  public float calculatePay() {
    return ratePerHour * hoursWorked;
  }
}

/**
 *  A class that specifies a salaried employee
 */
class SalariedPayType implements PayType {
  private float weeklySalary;
  public SalariedPayType(float weeklySalary) {
    this.weeklySalary = weeklySalary;
  }

  public float calculatePay() {
    return weeklySalary;
  }
}
```

Changing an object's reference, as is done in the classification solution, produces two problems. The first occurs in the case of many references to the object. For example, an Employee object could be stored in a Hashtable to be looked up in a human resources system and as a vector of dependents for another employee. When the object reference is stored in multiple places in a program, whenever it is changed it must be updated everywhere it is stored; for the employee, in this case, both the human resource's Hashtable and the dependent's vector must have the object reference changed. This type of problem results in many knock-on effects. If not done correctly it can result in multiple copies of the "same" object existing in the program. Options that worked in one release of the program may not work in the next release, and it quickly becomes nearly impossible to track down the errors or to ensure that all of the relevant structures are updated. Because composition leaves the reference to the employee object unchanged, these problems are avoided.

A less significant but still important concern regarding creating new objects when the type changes is performance. Allocating and deallocating objects can be expensive operations in a computer, and problems could occur if the object is changed frequently in the program. Generally speaking, unless the use of the object is limited and well defined, it is best to avoid these problems with mutable object types and to use composition when an object can change type.

The third consideration is that objects that are mutable are often used to store the history of the object. For example, if the problem definition calls for storing a history of the pay types for an employee, there is no easy way in a classification design for an employee to keep track of the former object type. The pay type is part of the object and thus cannot be separated from the object. If a history of the type changes is needed, it is almost always necessary to use composition in a design. This does not mean that if objects can change their types that classification should not be used; however, care should be taken in considering the design because of the problems that could arise. All things being equal, if an object type can be changed, a design using composition should be seriously considered.

11.4.3 Check If the Type Simply Represents a Role

This check is very similar to the one used in Section 11.4.3. The problems that result from mutable object types are often the result of inheritance being used to represent a role for the object in a program. For example, the pay type of an employee (hourly or salaried) might not be an intrinsic quality of an employee, but simply a state that the employee is in while the program is running. It is the fact that the state is changeable (hence, the role that the object plays in the program is

Exhibit 7. Program11.6: Amphibious Vehicle Designed Using Multiple Inheritance

```
abstract class Vehicle {
  abstract public float getMaxSpeed();
}

class LandVehicle extends Vehicle {
  float maxSpeed;
  public float getMaxSpeed() {
    return maxSpeed;
  }
}

class WaterVehicle extends Vehicle {
  float maxSpeed;
  public float getMaxSpeed() {
    return maxSpeed;
  }
}

public class AmphibiousVehicle extends LandVehicle, WaterVe-
hicle
  {
}
```

changeable) that caused problems with the employee type in Section 11.4.2. When a type is simply used to represent a role for an object, it is normally best to represent it not with a type but with a state variable. In the case of the employee in Section 11.4.2, a better design for the program is provided in Exhibit 6 (Program11.5). Here, composition is used to implement the payType state using an interface to call the correct calculatePay method. This question of role can also be used to explain some cases where a design uses multiple inheritance and to suggest alternative designs. Multiple inheritance occurs when a type extends more than one base class. For example, consider Exhibit 7 (Program11.6), which shows the design of an AmphibiousVehicle as inheriting from a LandVehicle and a WaterVehicle (note that this example does not compile in Java, as Java does not allow multiple inheritance). Some programmers would argue that an amphibious vehicle is a combination of vehicles that can run on land and ones that can run on water, so this is a natural design. However, note that LandVehicle and WaterVehicle both have a maxSpeed method. In the case of the AmphibiousVehicle, which method should be used? The answer obviously depends on whether the AmphibiousVehicle is on land or in water, which is a state of the vehicle. Noting this fact leads to the compositional design with an explicit state shown in Exhibit 8 (Program11.7).

11.4.4 Check for Subclasses with Multiple Roles

As was stated in Section 11.4.2 and 11.4.3, if an object can change type or represents a role in a program that can change, it should be

Exhibit 8. Program11.7: Amphibious Vehicle Designed Using Composition and Explicit State

```
abstract class Vehicle {
  abstract public float getMaxSpeed();
}

class LandVehicle extends Vehicle {
  float maxSpeed;
  public float getMaxSpeed() {
    return maxSpeed;
  }
}

class WaterVehicle extends Vehicle {
  float maxSpeed;
  public float getMaxSpeed() {
    return maxSpeed;
  }
}

public class AmphibiousVehicle {
  public static final int ON_WATER = 0;
  public static final int ON_LAND = 1;
  private int myState = ON_LAND;

  WaterVehicle waterVehicle = new WaterVehicle();
  LandVehicle landVehicle = new LandVehicle();

  public float getMaxSpeed() {
    if (myState = = ON_WATER)
      return waterVehicle.getMaxSpeed();
    else
      return landVehicle.getMaxSpeed();
  }
}
```

designed using composition. This type of behavior can also cause problems when an object can take on multiple roles. To illustrate this, an example of the jobs people have in a town is used. In this town, people are doctors, lawyers, mayors, and programmers. To make the problem easier, assume that, once an object of a given type is created, it will never change. Also assume that a person can have multiple roles. For example, the mayor might also be a doctor. A new type, Doctor-Mayor, would have to be created to represent objects of this type. But, instead, what if the mayor was also a lawyer? The type Lawyer-Mayor would have to be created. And, if the lawyer was a doctor *and* a mayor, a Lawyer-Mayor-Doctor class would be needed. In fact, for this simple example, 16 different classes would have to be created. In general this type of problem requires 2^n different classes and is not supportable. The point is that, even when the classes do not represent roles and the object types are not mutable, if the types can be combined it is possible for the system to require a large number of classes. When this happens, it is best to rewrite the design using composition.

11.4.5 Check for Compatibility with the Program Implementation

The final consideration in choosing a design is to make sure that someone will actually be able to implement it. This might sound inane, as what designer would ever design a system that could not be implemented? It should take most programmers only a few years of experience to realize that often the design is isolated from the implementation, and that designers often make decisions based on what they feel would make a nice system. This leads to designs with serious flaws when it actually comes time to implement them.

To see how implementation details can be impacted negatively by a design, the design of the simple expression tree program from Chapter 5, Exhibit 14 (Program5.5), is again considered; however, in this example, the program simply takes operators and operands and performs a calculation on them. The main focus here is the design of the operator object. Because the operator can occur many times in a program, a single instance of each type of operator is created, greatly reducing the number of objects the program needs to create. Each time an instance of that operator type is needed, that single static instance is returned.* This can be accomplished using either composition or classification, and the designs are largely equivalent. Examples of both designs are provided in Exhibit 9 (Program11.8) and Exhibit 10 (Program11.9).

Using this single instance of each operator type can result in a problem if at a later time it is decided that what is actually needed is to be able to use this operator class with an expression tree, as implemented in Program 5.5. If the designer specifies a composition relationship (an OperatorNode has an operator and two child nodes), the design is easy to implement** and is shown in Program11.10 (Exhibit 11 and Exhibit 12). Many designers, though, will get to the point of asking the "is-a/has-a" question, will determine that an OperatorNode "is-an" operator, and will feel that settles the issue; however, a much larger issue than if the OperatorNode "is-an" or "has-an" operator must be acknowledged. The Operator part of the object only has one instance in the entire program for each operator type, but OperatorNode exists for each occurrence of an operator in a tree. Therefore, the relationship between Operator and OperatorNode is one to many. This leads to a logical contradiction when classification is used to create an object. There is only one instance of the object

* This design pattern is referred to as a *factory pattern*. When used with the classification classes, the objects are called *singletons*, as there is only one instance of the class. The purpose of this book is not to define design patterns or to comment on their use; however, because these patterns occur here, they are identified for the benefit of readers doing further research into this area.

** This design is an example of a *flyweight pattern*.

Exhibit 9. Program11.8: Operator

```
import java.util.Hashtable;

/**
 * The operator class.  Other than defining the static methods to
 * retrieve the operator type, this method does nothing except
   define
 * the abstract method "calculate" which all operators must
   define.
 */
abstract public class Operator {
     private static Hashtable operators;

     static {
          operators = new Hashtable();
          operators.put("+", new AddOperator());
          operators.put("-", new SubtractOperator());
     }

    public static Operator getOperator(String operatorSymbol) {
          return((Operator) operators.get(operatorSymbol));
     }

     public static boolean isOperator(String operatorSymbol) {
          return operators.containsKey(operatorSymbol);
     }

     abstract public double calculate(double d1, double d2);

     // Unit Test Application
     public static void main(String args[]) {
          // Calculate 3+5-2
          System.out.println( getOperator("-").calculate(
                              getOperator("+").calculate(3.0,
                              5.0), 2.0));
     }

     /**
      *  class to define an operator that does addition.
      */
     static private class AddOperator extends Operator {
          public double calculate(double d1, double d2) {
              return (d1 + d2);
          }

          public String toString() {
               return "+";
          }
     }

     /**
      *   class to define an operator that does subtraction
      */
     static private class SubtractOperator extends Operator {
          public double calculate(double d1, double d2) {
               return (d1 - d2);
          }

          public String toString() {
               return "-";
          }
     }
}
```

Exhibit 10. Program11.9: Add and Subtract Operator Classes Using Composition

```
import java.util.Hashtable;

/**
 * This class defines the operator. Note that unlike program
   11.8,
 * delegation is used to do the calculation.  An interface
   is created
 * which defines how an operation works, and that interface
   is called
 * from the operators calculate method.
 */
public class Operator {
     private static Hashtable operators;

     private String operatorSymbol;
     private Evaluator evaluator;

     static {
          operators = new Hashtable();
          operators.put("+", new Operator
                       ("+", new AddEvaluator()));
          operators.put("-", new Operator
                       ("-", new SubtractEvaluator()));
     }

    private Operator(String operatorSymbol, Evaluator evaluator) {
          this.operatorSymbol = operatorSymbol;
          this.evaluator = evaluator;
     }

     public static boolean isOperator(String operatorSymbol) {
          return operators.containsKey(operatorSymbol);
     }

    public static Operator getOperator(String operatorSymbol) {
          return((Operator) operators.get(operatorSymbol));
     }

     public double calculate(double d1, double d2) {
          return evaluator.calculate(d1, d2);
     }

     public String toString() {
          return (operatorSymbol);
     }
     // Unit Test Application
     public static void main(String args[]) {
          // Calculate 3+5-2
          System.out.println( getOperator("-").calculate(
                              getOperator("+").calculate
                                  (3.0, 5.0), 2.0));
     }

     /**
      *  interface for define how to do a calculation.
      */
     private interface Evaluator {
          public double calculate(double d1, double d2);
     }
```

(continued)

Exhibit 10. Program11.9 (Continued)

```
/**
     *  Class to do an add calculation
     */
    static private class AddEvaluator implements Evaluator {
        public double calculate(double d1, double d2) {
            return (d1 + d2);
        }
    }

    /**
     *  Class to do a subtract calculation
     */
   static private class SubtractEvaluator implements Evaluator
{
        public double calculate(double d1, double d2) {
            return (d1 - d2);
        }
    }

}
```

that contains all the data and methods for the object, both from the super class and from the child class, but the Operator requires one instance of that object, and the OperatorNode requires many instances of that same object. It cannot be both one and many, so classification cannot be used to implement the OperatorNode class.

As this example shows, anytime a class must be extended composition is nearly always a safer choice than classification. As shown in Program11.10 (Exhibit 11 and Exhibit 12), composition could be used to create the OperatorNode from either Exhibit 9 (Program11.8) or Exhibit 10 (Program11.9). (Note that Program11.10 [Exhibits 11 and 12] will work with either Exhibit 9 [Program11.8] or Exhibit 10 [Program11.9] without any changes, but classification could not.) If the final use of a class is not known in a design, it is almost always better to use composition, as it will allow the most latitude in later modifications of the design.

11.5 Conclusion

It is important to write a conclusion for this chapter, as it might appear that the message is always to use composition when designing objects. If only one of the two mechanisms, composition or classification, is available, then this would be true. However, in many instances classification leads to better answers, and when it is used appropriately it is very powerful. Keep in mind, though, that it is easy to misuse classification. When designing a program, the designer must carefully think through how the implementation will be impacted by the design and not simply apply simple-minded tests such as the “is-a/has-a” test. The art of designing and implementing a program is not a simple task;

Exhibit 11. Program11.10a: Add and Subtract Operator Classes Using Classification

```
import java.util.Hashtable;

/**
 *  This class defines the operator. Note that, unlike Program11.8,
 *  delegation is used to do the calculation. An interface
 *  is created that defines how an operation works, and that
 *  interface is called from the operator's calculate method.
 */
public class Operator {
  private static Hashtable operators;

  private String operatorSymbol;
  private Evaluator evaluator;

  static {
    operators = new Hashtable();
    operators.put("+," new Operator("+," new AddEvaluator()));
    operators.put("-," new Operator("-," new SubtractEvaluator
        ()));
  }

  private Operator(String operatorSymbol, Evaluator evaluator)
{
    this.operatorSymbol = operatorSymbol;
    this.evaluator = evaluator;
  }

  public static boolean isOperator(String operatorSymbol) {
    return operators.containsKey(operatorSymbol);
  }

  public static Operator getOperator(String operatorSymbol) {
    return((Operator) operators.get(operatorSymbol));
  }

  public double calculate(double d1, double d2) {
    return evaluator.calculate(d1, d2);
  }

  public String toString() {
    return (operatorSymbol);
  }
  // Unit Test Application
  public static void main(String args[]) {
    // Calculate 3 + 5 - 2

    System.out.println(getOperator("-").calculate(
                         getOperator("+").calculate(3.0, 5.0),
                                                      2.0));
  }
}

/**
 *  Interface for defining how to do a calculation
 */
interface Evaluator {
  public double calculate(double d1, double d2);
}
```

(continued)

Exhibit 11. Program11.10a (Continued)

```
/**
 * A class to do an add calculation
 */
class AddEvaluator implements Evaluator {
  public double calculate(double d1, double d2) {
    return (d1 + d2);
  }
}

/**
 * A class to do a subtract calculation
 */
class SubtractEvaluator implements Evaluator {
  public double calculate(double d1, double d2) {
    return (d1 - d2);
  }
}
```

Exhibit 12. Program11.10b: Implementing an Operator Node Using Classification

```
import java.util.Hashtable;

interface Node {
  public void printTree();
  public double evaluate();
}

public class OperatorNode implements Node {
  Operator operator;
  Node left, right;
  public OperatorNode(String operatorSymbol,
        Node left, Node right) {
    this.operator = Operator.getOperator(operatorSymbol);
    this.left = left;
    this.right = right;
  }

  public void printTree() {
    System.out.print(" (");
    left.printTree();
    System.out.print(" " + operator.toString());
    right.printTree();
    System.out.print(")");
  }

  public double evaluate() {
  return operator.calculate(left.evaluate(), right.evaluate
      ());
  }

  public static void main(String args[]) {
    Node root;
```

(continued)

Exhibit 12. Program11.10b (Continued)

```
    // ((5 - 3) + 1)
    root = new OperatorNode("+",
      new OperatorNode("-",
        new OperandNode(5), new OperandNode(3)),
      new OperandNode(1));
    root.printTree();
    System.out.println(" = " + root.evaluate());

    // (5-(3+1))
    root = new OperatorNode("-",
        new OperandNode(5),
        new OperatorNode("+",
          new OperandNode(3), new OperandNode(1)));
    root.printTree();
    System.out.println(" = " + root.evaluate());
  }
}

class OperandNode implements Node {
  double value;
  public OperandNode(float value) {
    this.value = value;
  }

  public void printTree() {
    System.out.print(" " + value);
  }

  public double evaluate() {
    return value;
  }
}
```

if it were, we would have no need for programmers. So, the bottom line in any design is to implement a solution to the problem that you need to solve, not the one you want to solve or ones you create while solving the real problem. Be flexible. Not all problems can be solved with obvious solutions, and many attempts might be necessary to come up with a good design.

11.6 Further Reading

The material found in this chapter also forms the nucleus of most books on OOP; as such, the topics in this chapter will be covered in most books on OOP (see, for example, [COA99] or [BUD00]).

11.7 Problems

1. You are to design account objects for a bank application. The accounts in this bank contain a name (string) and balance data (float). The two types of accounts are checking and savings. A

checking account is an account that also has a current check number (int), which is the number of the next check to be written. The savings account is an account that has a data field for the account and an interest rate used to calculate the amount of interest to add to the account each month. (Note that only data is given here, not the methods that will be needed for the accounts.)

- For the checking and saving accounts, what type of design should be used? Are both accounts obviously "is-a" relationships, are both "has-a" relationships, is one an "is-a" relationship and one a "has-a" relationship, or can both be designed using either "is-a" or "has-a"? Justify your answer.
- Implement the solution to this problem using *both* classification and composition. Give advantages and disadvantages for both solutions.

2. Program11.3 and Program11.4 gave two different designs for a social club. Discuss these two designs. Is one superior to the other? Why? What types of problems would you expect from working with each of these designs?
3. Program11.2 and Program11.5 showed two designs for employee objects, one using composition and one using classification. Change the definition of the Employee class by adding a vector of dependents to the class. The dependents should be objects of type Person, so write addDependent(Person p) and removeDependent(Person p) methods to add and remove dependents from the Employee object. Implement these methods for both the classification and composition solutions. For this problem, an employee can also be a dependent (for example, a husband and wife both work for the company). As an example, the following pseudo-code should work in your program. Discuss the advantages and disadvantages of each approach.

```
Employee Cindy = new SalariedEmployee("Cindy," 2073.00f);
Employee Roger = new HourlyEmployee("Roger," 12.23f, 40.00f);
Cindy.addDependent(Roger);
Roger.addDependent(Cindy);
```

4. The new Employee class (with dependents added) is to be used in a human resources (HR) system. The employee records are to be added to a hash table to be tracked by employee number. For example, Cindy's employee number is 123 and Roger's is 456. As part of the system, the HR department wants to know the family income paid to all employee families. This is done by the following pseudo-code:

```
Enumeration e = employees.elements();
while(e.hasMoreElements) {
  Employee emp = (Employee)e.nextElement();
  totalPay = emp.calculatePay();
  Enumeration e1 = emp.dependents.elements();
  while(e1.hasMoreElements) {
    Object o = e1.nextElement();
```

```
    if (o instanceof Employee)
      totalPay = totalPay + ((Employee)o).calculatePay();
  }
}
```

Assume that the history of Cindy and Roger objects is as follows:

```
Employee cindy = new SalariedEmployee("Cindy," 2073.00f);
employees.add("123," cindy);
Employee roger = new HourlyEmployee("Roger," 12.23f, 40.00f);
employees.add("456," roger);
cindy.addDependent(roger);
roger.addDependent(cindy);
roger.changeToSalaried(1073.00f);
```

Implement two programs that store the employees in a hash table, one using the employee objects with classification, one using composition. Use the pseudo-code for Cindy and Roger above. Show that you have written a correct solution to this program by calculating the family income before and after Roger's pay status changes. Which solution was easiest to implement and verify?

5. Are Exhibits 13 and 14 (Problem 5a: Java and Problem 5b: Java) both correct? If they are different, why are they different?
6. What types of problems (other than concurrent programming) can happen when association is used?
7. Animated Swap Problem (in Section 11.4.5).
8. The problem with using classification to design an operator node is that there was only a single instance of the operator object. In the following two programs, that restriction has been removed. Problem8.a gives the composition solution for the node, and Problem8.b gives a classification solution. For both of these, implement an OperatorNode, as in Program11.10 (Exhibits 11 and 12). Which was easier to implement? Why? Which design (if either) would force changes that could affect programs that already use Operator class objects?
9. In this problem, you are going to model a simple bank with an ATM. The bank will have two kinds of accounts, checking and savings. These accounts both have the name of the customer, an account number, a balance in the account, and a vector of all transactions that have occurred on that account. Transactions are the things that change the account balance and will be discussed in more detail later. The savings account also has an interest rate to be used to calculate the monthly interest, and the checking account has a current check number, which is the number of the next check from that account. The designs of the methods required for each account are given as interfaces below (you do not have to use these interfaces in your program, as they are provided here to define the methods you will need). The bank will keep a database of accounts using any Java key map container object (for example, a Hashtable). The key will be the account number. When a transaction is to be processed the account is retrieved and the

Exhibit 13. Problem 5a: Java

```
public class Problem5a implements Runnable {
  SwapObject swapObject;

  public Problem5a(SwapObject swapObject) {
    this.swapObject = swapObject;
  }

  public void run() {
    swapObject.swap();
    System.out.println(swapObject.toString());
  }

  public static void main(String args[]) {
    SwapObject swapObject = new SwapObject(5, 7);
    (new Thread(new Problem5a(swapObject))).start();

    try {
      Thread.sleep((int)(Math.random() * 100));
    } catch (InterruptedException e) {
    }
    swapObject.temp = 22;
  }
}

class SwapObject {
  int val1, val2, temp;

  public SwapObject(int val1, int val2) {
    this.val1 = val1;
    this.val2 = val2;
  }

  public void swap() {
    temp = val1;
    try {
      Thread.sleep((int)(Math.random() * 100));
    } catch (InterruptedException e) {
    }
    val1 = val2;
    val2 = temp;
  }

  public String toString() {
    return ("val1 = " + val1 + " val2 = " + val2);
  }
}
```

appropriate action applied to the object. (*Note:* The object does not have to be stored back into the container, but why not?) The bank will only be accessible by the interface below. This interface allows only transactions to be sent to the bank. Transactions represent actions to take on accounts. The accounts themselves should not be given any scope outside of the bank, but the bank should process transactions for each account. Transactions will contain the date and time the transaction was made and the account number. The three types of transactions are credit, debit, or balance.

Exhibit 14. Problem5b: Java

```
public class Problem5b implements Runnable {
  SwapObject swapObject;

  public Problem5b(SwapObject swapObject) {
    this.swapObject = (SwapObject)swapObject.clone();
  }

  public void run() {
    swapObject.swap();
    System.out.println(swapObject.toString());
  }

  public static void main(String args[]) {
    SwapObject swapObject = new SwapObject(5,7);
    (new Thread(new Problem5b(swapObject))).start();

    try {
      Thread.sleep((int)(Math.random() * 100));
    } catch (InterruptedException e) {
    }
    swapObject.temp = 22;
  }
}

class SwapObject implements Clonable{
  int val1, val2, temp;

  public SwapObject(int val1, int val2) {
    this.val1 = val1;
    this.val2 = val2;
  }

  public Object clone() {
    Object o = null;
    try {
      o = super.clone();
    } catch (CloneNotSupportedException e) {
      throw new RuntimeException("Invalid Cloning Operation");
    }
    return o;
  }

  public void swap() {
    temp = val1;
    try {
      Thread.sleep((int)(Math.random() * 100));
    } catch (InterruptedException e) {
    }
    val1 = val2;
    val2 = temp;
  }

  public String toString() {
    return ("val1 = " + val1 + " val2 = " + val2);
  }
}
```

A credit transaction decreases the balance of the account, and a debit increases the balance, so both the credit and debit transactions require an amount field. All three types of transactions return the balance of the account once the transaction is made. Finally, one or more ATMs send transactions to the bank. The ATM will not directly access the bank but should communicate with the bank through the Bank interface. The ATM will present a graphical user interface (GUI) to the customer that asks for account number, type of transaction, and amount. It will use this information to build the transaction and send the transaction to the bank. The bank will then pass the transaction to the account for processing, and return back to the ATM the new balance on the account. Note that each account should store all transactions that are made on that account. Design the bank in this problem. You can (and probably should) use Java objects to do so. For which objects do you use classification? For which objects do you use composition? Which objects represent aggregation vs. association? Finally, once your design is complete, implement your design.

Chapter 12

Program Management in Java

12.1 Introduction

Too many designers believe that if they have laid out the basic framework and the objects that will be used in a program that the job of actually implementing the program is trivial; however, once a design for a program has been developed the job has only started. Actually, implementing any design, even a very good and complete design, as a program requires trade-offs when it is matched to very real physical constraints that might be present. These constraints often involve details that are not part of the problem being solved but are a result of a need to manage the complex interactions between files, objects, and variables that make up a program.

Management of a program is a separate issue from design of the program itself. This is important to remember, as aspects of managing the system are often added as part of the program design. Issues such as what packages an object should belong to or what classes should be final or inner classes, if addressed too early can severely hamper the ultimate implementation of the program. While these issues should be handled before implementation of the program begins, management of the program should be put off as long as possible so as not to limit how the program is designed. One important aspect of program management is that it is here that the power of a language becomes a help or a hindrance. It is also here that the use of external tools, such as integrated development environments (IDEs) and utility programs, become very important.

12.2 Chapter Goals

When you have completed this chapter, you should understand:

- The difference between program management and design
- How to categorize program management utilities
- How program management can be supported in a programming language
- How tools, such as IDEs and other utilities, can be used to assist in program management
- How program management issues are handled in different languages
- Examples of issues to be considered in program management

12.3 What Is Program Management?

When the functional and object relationships needed to solve a problem have been designed, as well as the objects that will be used, many programmers believe that the design process is complete, and they begin to implement the system. However, an important part of the implementation has not yet been considered. When a program representing a virtual entity (a design) is actually created, the objects that have been designed must be implemented and a physical artifact (a program) produced. This process of creating the physical artifact carries with it a host of implementation concerns not present in the design — for example, naming conventions; object, method, and variable scope; organization of the files necessary to create the program; or source code management and control. These are not part of the design of the system, which is what the system does and how it does it. Instead, these are issues of how to manage the product that is being created. These concerns create the physical infrastructure that allows the program to be implemented in a way that allows it to be easily manipulated and controlled by the programmer. They also create limitations on the design that must be addressed before implementing the program.

Booch [BOO91, p. 51] states that, "Modules serve as the physical containers in which we declare the classes and objects of our logical design." Creating and managing the modules is what we wish to do and what obviously must be done for all programs and systems. An important question is, "How does the creation of these modules affect implementation of the design?"

When considering how implementation of the physical program into modules affects the design, a question is raised regarding to what degree the implementation details for the modules are formalized and enforced. The best design can still result in a mess that is not properly modularized and controlled, but excess control can limit the ability of the programmer to make decisions and can affect the design badly. The question we want to answer, then, is, "What degree of formalization and control should be placed on a program?"

To better understand this, the process of managing a program can be thought of as a two-dimensional matrix. One dimension is the degree of formalization, which can be none, informal, or formal. The second dimension is the way in which formalization is controlled, which can be none or by management fiat, external system validation, or internal system validation. This matrix can be applied to each implementation attribute (such as naming or source code control), and choices can be made regarding how to manage that attribute. For example, consider naming conventions in a program. The naming of variables could be left completely up to the programmer (no formalization), it could be done according to "best practices" but with no precise definition of the best practices (informal), or the naming convention could be explicitly defined for every variable (formal). In order to ensure that these practices are followed, the programmer could simply be told to follow a standard (no control), the manager could ask for periodic code samples to review (management fiat), a code walk-through could be done on every module to identify incorrect variable names (external system validation), or, finally, a precompiler could be written that automatically checks each variable name to ensure that it follows standards (internal system validation). Exhibit 1 shows these options. In Exhibit 1, the combinations of options that are not marked with an X are not possible; for example, without a formal definition of naming standards it is possible to identify bad names in a code walk-through, but it is impossible to automate the procedure for finding bad names.

Which of the options in this chart is the best? It depends on how tightly the particular implementation attribute is to be controlled. This is not something that will be the same for all attributes, or for any one attribute for every program that is implemented. What is clear is that the more important the control of an implementation detail is to the success of the program, the more formally it should be defined and the more rigorous the control placed on it. In fact, some of these attributes were considered so important that when the Java language was defined control of these attributes was placed in the language itself; for example, all Java source codes must exist in a file with a ".java" extension.

The rest of this chapter is divided into two sections. Section 12.4 covers implementation attributes not defined in the Java language, and Section 12.5 discusses implementation attributes that are defined in Java. In Section 12.5, the implementation attributes are compared to C++, where the definition and control of these attributes tend to be less formal and less rigorously enforced, with the intent to show why the particular attribute was formalized and included in the Java language.

Exhibit 1. Standards

Formalization Technique	Degree of Formalization: No Formalization (Programmers Choose Names for Variables)	Informal (Programmers Agree to Use "Best Practices")	Formal (Formal Programmers Document Details Naming Standards)
None: no control			
Management fiat: Manager checks code and bases part of evaluation on standards followed.	X		
External program validation: Code walk-through, rules in an IDE	X		
Internal system validation: Pre-compiler check of variable names that must be passed to compile code.	X	X	

12.4 Implementation Attributes Not Defined in Java

A number of implementation attributes have a generally accepted format in Java but are not enforced as part of the language or language definition. This section looks at some of them — specifically, naming conventions, indenting style, accessor methods, integrated development environments (IDEs), and source code management systems.

12.4.1 Naming Conventions

Naming conventions define standards for naming variables in a program. Naming conventions allow an identifier in a program to be easily associated with its type. In Java, it is generally accepted that classes start with an upper-case letter, and objects (variables that are instances of classes or primitives) start with a lower-case letter. This allows a programmer to quickly identify the Integer.parseInt method as being

Exhibit 2. Naming Identifiers

Type of Identifier	*How to Name*
Primitive type	Use all lower-case letters (e.g., float, int).
Class or interface	Begin name with an upper-case letter, and begin each new word with an upper-case letter (e.g., TextArea).
Variable or method	Begin name with a lower-case letter, and begin each new word with an upper-case letter (e.g., myTextArea).
Constant	Use all upper-case letters and an underline (_) between each word (e.g., MAXIMUM_VALUE).
Package name	Use all lower-case letters (e.g., java.util); remember these names map to directory names, and so the package name must be able to be mapped to a directory name on the target system.

a static method in the class Integer and the myFrame.setSize method as being a method on the object myFrame. This is useful when trying to understand code fragments in a program. Exhibit 2 gives a list of the type of names used in Java, the rules for naming them, and an example of each type of name.

12.4.2 Indenting Style

Indenting style is the way that code appears between a start brace, "{", and an end brace, "}". The one correct style for indenting a program should be obvious to every programmer; unfortunately, programmers cannot agree on what that one correct style actually is. Indenting style is an issue of religion, where each person is absolutely convinced of the rightness of his cause. I will not try to put forth any one style as right or wrong, as it would add little to the debate, but I will offer the following council: *Be consistent and be flexible.* By being consistent I mean choose an indenting style and use it consistently. If you indent three spaces, *always* indent three spaces. If you put a start brace on a separate line, *always* put the start brace on a separate line. No matter what way you format an inner class or catch clauses, *always* format them that way. Nothing is more aggravating then reading a program with inconsistent indenting. It is extremely difficult to read and makes the programmer who wrote it look incompetent.

The second point is related to the first, be consistent *and* flexible. If you need to modify a program for which a programmer used the "wrong" indenting style, adopt that style for changes to the program. This will be extremely difficult for some readers to stomach, but all the other possible options are worse. As mentioned before, mixing indenting styles makes the program difficult to read, and, unless you have a very understanding boss, blowing a budget to rewrite what you consider invalid indenting could be detrimental to your career, especially if your boss uses the "wrong" indenting style and is equally religious about its use.

Finally, when indenting in an editor or IDE, you should consider using the option of saving tabs as blanks. The reason is simple in that most editors and IDEs handle tabs differently; when your source is moved to a new development environment, all your careful indenting will go for naught.

12.4.3 Accessor Methods

Accessor methods are used in Java to set and get properties (data values) in an object. They are also called *setters* and *getters*. In some languages, such as C#, these methods are formally defined and their use validated as part of the language definition. In Java, an informal definition for these methods can be enforced, especially when an object is used as a Java Bean. Accessor methods work on properties for an object — for example, the name variable for a Person class. This property is declared as a private identifier in the object. To access this variable, two methods are defined: one to set the property and one to get the property. These methods are named by adding the prefix "set" or "get" to the name of the property; for example, consider the name property in the Person class below:

```
class Person {
  private String name;
  public void Person(String name) {
    this.name = name;
  }
  public void setName(String name) {
    this.name = name;
  }
  public String getName(String name) {
    return name;
  }
}
```

This is a standard way to handle properties in Java. One thing should be noted about this definition. In the setName method, the instance identifier "name" has been redefined by the local parameter identifier "name," requiring the use of the "this" qualifier to access the correct name. Many programmers react very badly to redefining an instance variable in a method and would force the parameter to use another name (for example, inputName); however, the redefinition of instance variable names is common in Java for constructors and accessor methods.

12.4.4 Interactive Development Environment (IDE)

An IDE is a program that includes an editor and specific functions for manipulating, compiling, and executing Java programs. Typical examples include Forte, Eclipse, Visual Café, or JBuilder. In Java, no one IDE is considered standard, as Java was written to work with any number of IDEs. This is not true of some languages, such as C#, which is designed to work with Visual Studio. The main thing to remember when using an IDE is that some IDEs provide nonstandard extensions to the language. These generally are not in the language definition, but in the implementation details. For example, an IDE might not use the standard Java compilation sequence and instead implement projects that behave differently than standard Java. Without a formal definition of what the IDE must do, a programmer must exercise care when using an IDE to ensure that the implementation attributes defined by working in that environment are actually what the programmer requires.

12.4.5 Source Code Control

No production project is complete until the issues involved in source code control are answered. How are changes to the system tracked? What backup/recovery mechanisms are in place? How are multiple accesses to source files controlled? What mechanisms are in place for distributing major and minor software releases? A number of tools are available to provide external system control over these source code issues, but many projects do not consider source code control problems until they have been adversely affected.

12.5 Implementation Attributes Defined in Java

While many details of implementing a program have been left purposely ambiguous in Java, the language designers felt that some aspects were important enough to include in the language definition. This section deals with some of the implementation attributes that are included in Java.

12.5.1 Source File Names

As difficult as it is to believe, often the source code for a program gets lost. One cause of this is good source code control not being in place; as programmers come and go on a project, files get moved to the wrong places. Another problem is that programmers jealously protect their right to name programs *creatively* or to store them in places such as their homes or other directories. Some languages even allow programmers to name files with any extension they choose or allow arbitrary files to be included inside of a source program. When this happens, often all that is left is the executable code (in Java the ".class" files) used to run the program.

For example, C/C++ allows a programmer to include a header file (".h" file) in a program to allow the variables and function prototypes to be defined; however, the include feature does not limit a programmer to including valid C/C++ file type. In fact, any arbitrary file can be included in a C/C++ source program. To see how this results in lost files, consider the following example. A programmer decides that standard library functions should be in files named "lib1.std" and "lib2.std," where "std" means standard definitions. These files can now be included in a C/C++ source program that compiles all libraries, and a file that compiles all the libraries for a system, called library.c, could look as follows:

```
#include <lib1.std>
#include <lib2.std>
```

This is all that is needed in library.c, as it includes the two source files that contain the actual C source for the program. It is now impossible, though, based on the file names alone, for a programmer unfamiliar with the project to even guess where the source code for the system is stored.

To make matters worse, the programmer can now effectively hide where these source files are located. They do not have to be in the current directory, as the format of the #include used here allows the files to exist anywhere on the system as long as the directory is included in an "-I" command line option (e.g., cc -I/usr/anywhere). The programmer who has done this then finds another job, and someone else must make sense of this, which is nearly an impossible task. C/C++ leaves the issue of how to store and control source code open, which allows great flexibility for programmers, for good or ill.

To avoid this situation, an implementation attribute of Java requires that the format for the name for all source files must have the extension ".java." Also, the #include statement has no equivalent in Java. This forces all files that are potential Java source files to have the suffix ".java" and makes it easier to find Java source files. The formal naming scheme in Java is internally verified so it cannot be circumvented. This does not mean that source code cannot be lost if a good source code control system is not in place; it simply means that programmers have to try harder to lose the programs.

12.5.2 Definition Files

One problem in every modern programming language is defining a way to include program definitions for objects and methods that are defined outside of the current source file. Ada has a formal definition, called a *specification*, that defines how this works. C/C++ has an informal mechanism, called a *header* (".h") file. The concept behind a header file is that functions and classes are defined in the header file, and the implementation is defined in C/C++ source files. In the hands of a disciplined and experienced programmer, this approach works well. The problem is that not all (in fact, not even most) programmers are disciplined and experienced.

The C/C++ header files rely on the programmer using them properly, but nothing in the language forces the name to have an ".h" suffix, and programmers can often become creative with their naming. Even worse is that no good rule exists for what goes in the files. They should contain prototypes and definitions only; implementation details should not be in them. This informal rule, though, not only is not enforced, but in some cases cannot be achieved; for example, #define and inline methods must be defined in a header file so that they can be included in the source program when it is compiled. This all leads to a situation where it is easy to misuse header files and implement poor programs.

In Java, this problem was handled by including the definition as part of the executable (".class") file. When a program is compiled, prototypes for all of the methods and definitions for all of the structures are written and maintained in the ".class" files, so header files or specifications are not needed.

12.5.3 Stateless Methods

Stateless methods are methods that do not maintain any data between executions but use only the parameters for the current invocation to do their calculations. Examples are Integer.parseInt or Math.sin. In Java, even though the class the methods are in does not maintain any state for them, they must still be included as static methods within a class, and the name of the class is necessary to resolve their references. Because stateless methods do not need a context, many languages, including C/C++, allow them to exist simply as freestanding methods. These methods can exist in any file that is compiled as part of a valid C/C++ source file, and they do not need to reference anything but their name. This makes "grep" (a UNIX utility for searching for strings in a file) an absolute necessity for maintaining any reasonably sized C/C++ program. The need to store a stateless method with a class and to reference that class might seem an unnecessary hassle in Java, but it makes it easier to find the actual definitions of methods.

12.5.4 Final Classes and Methods

Sometimes when implementing a class, we want to limit the ability of a programmer to extend a class or redefine a method. For example, an immutable class might be declared final to ensure that no subclass can be created that could break the encapsulation and make the class mutable. One example of this is the String class. Some programmers want to extend the String class in order to directly call methods that use strings as parameters; however, the classes that they create are not always immutable. As was pointed out in Chapter 11, one way to make aggregate data thread safe is to use immutable classes; however, this type of design breaks encapsulation and can make an aggregate relationship into an association relationship, thus causing problems when the class is used in a concurrent program. Methods might be declared final for a number of reasons. For example, methods that perform essential services in a base case could be declared final to ensure that they are not overridden, with the result that their behavior is inadvertently (or maliciously) changed. Another reason why a method could be declared final is if it is to be sent through the network to execute on a remote computer. Making a method final ensures that a class does not override the existing methods and thus fool the remote programming into executing unsafe code.

12.5.5 Inner Classes

Inner classes are Java classes that are defined inside of other program structures, such as other classes or methods. Because they are defined as part of another program, they have scope just like a variable. For example, an inner class can be local, instance, or static. These classes can also have scooping resolution modifiers, such as private and public (these scope resolution modifiers are covered in more detail in the section on packages). This leads to a number of interesting uses for inner classes. For example, consider Program11.8 (see Chapter 11, Exhibit 9), where only the Operator class is meant to be accessible. The specific type of operator (AddOperator or SubtractOperator) is declared as a private inner class inside of the operator and cannot be used outside of the Operator class. Likewise, in Program11.9 (see Chapter 11, Exhibit 10), the interface Evaluator is declared private so classes implementing it must be inner classes of the Operator class.

The scope resolution modifier can also be used to get around the rule that only a single public class can be inside of a ".java" source file. Consider Exhibit 3 (Program12.1), where a Stack class is defined

Exhibit 3. Program12.1

```
import java.awt.*;
import java.awt.event.*;
import javax.swing.*;

public class InnerClassExample {
     static int counter;

     public static void main(String args[]) {
          JFrame frame = new JFrame();
          Container container = frame.getContentPane();
          container.setLayout(new FlowLayout());

         // Note that counter cannot be declared here as it
         // will not exist when the main method is exited.
         // Since the button uses this value, and possibly
         // exists after the method is exited, the variable
         // must be given a lifetime that outlives this method.
         // This can be done by declaring the variable final,
         // or declaring it as part of the class (as is done
         // in this example). Both actions move the variable
         // off of the stack, allowing this variable to be
         // used in the listener.  Note however the declaring
         // the variable final here means that it cannot be
         // incremented, hence the decision to declare it as
         // part of the class itself. int counter = 0;

          JButton incrementButton = new JButton("Increment");
          container.add(incrementButton);
          incrementButton.addActionListener
             (new ActionListener() {
                public void actionPerformed(ActionEvent ae) {
                     counter++;
                }
          });

          JButton exitButton = new JButton("Exit");
          container.add(exitButton);
          exitButton.addActionListener(new ActionListener() {
                public void actionPerformed(ActionEvent ae) {
                     System.exit(0);
                }
          });

          frame.setSize(300,300);
          frame.show();
     }
}
```

that can throw Stack.Empty and Stack.Full exceptions. In a normal Java program, these exceptions would only be related informally to the Stack class that throws them by their name (for example, they might be called StackEmpty and StackFull). Further, they must be public classes themselves and so must be contained in a source code file separate from the Stack class; however, because these exceptions are public inner classes of the public class Stack, they are now formally associated with the Stack class, are contained in the same physical file as the Stack class, and have internal system validation to ensure that they are used correctly. While these uses of inner classes to structure a program seem useful, they do not follow standard coding practices in Java and should only be used after careful consideration of the impacts on the overall implementation of the system. Generally, this type of use of inner classes to structure a program should probably be avoided.

12.5.6 "Making" a Program

One of the most common questions asked by students and faculty who have programmed in C/C++ is how to create a makefile for compiling a Java program. Make is a program utility in C/C++ that allows the program dependencies to be defined in a file, normally named makefile. It also ensures that, when a program is created, any dependency needed to create the program that has been changed since the last time the program was made is recompiled and thus current. For example, consider the makefile example below:

```
test.exe: test.c libs.o
  cc -o test.exe test.c libs.o
libs.o: libs.c
  cc -c libs.c
```

This simple makefile states that the program test.exe is dependent on two other files, test.c and libs.o. If either has changed, then the command "cc -o test.exe test.c libs.o" must be rerun to remake test.exe; however, the file libs.o also has a dependency on libs.c. So, before test.exe can be made the make program checks to see if libs.o must be recompiled.

This makefile utility is extremely useful in C/C++, thus most programmers coming from a C/C++ environment want to know how to apply it to Java. The simple answer is that it has no place in Java because Java already (correctly) handles dependencies. The problem with a makefile is that it once again represents an informal way to handle an implementation problem that is externally validated. First, we do not have a standard as to how the dependencies in the makefile must be encoded for a language. What actually makes up dependencies might be generally agreed upon, but there is no guarantee that a program will follow those guidelines. Even more problematic is the fact that a programmer must maintain the dependencies in the makefile, and that is often a prescription for something that will not happen consistently. Finally, the makefile is not required to make a program, or programmers will keep multiple makefiles around for development, testing, production, etc. The validation that a program is correct for a particular environment is thus an externally applied one and is dependent on the programmer updating and using the correct makefile.

Java has borrowed from Ada to correct these problems with the make utility. At its core, the problem with make is that it relies on external factors to ensure that a makefile is current and used correctly. At best, however, the makefile is only a guess regarding the actual dependencies, and the only place where the actual dependencies are present is in the source code for a program. Because the program does contain the actual dependencies, the compiler is able, as part of the compiler process, to build the dependency list and ensure that it is correct and current. This is a formal definition of the dependencies, and it is internally verifiable. The dependencies are generated and checked as part of the Java compilation, and Java will automatically do the equivalent to a "make" on a Java program.

12.6 Packages

Packages are considered in a separate section because they represent the major structural element for source code in Java. Many concepts such as scope resolution modifiers and program distribution using *Java ARchive* (JAR) files are built around packages. Packages are covered here in three parts. Section 12.6.1 gives an overview of packages, Section 12.6.2 talks about scope resolution modifiers in relation to packages, and Section 12.6.3 discusses distribution of a program and the use of JAR files and the CLASSPATH environment variable.

12.6.1 What Are Packages?

A package is a collection of the ".class" files for related classes that are stored and distributed together in a program. For example, the classes that make up the Java AWT are all part of the java.awt package, and all the classes that make up the Java utilities are in the class java.util package. All files containing classes that are part of a package must be in the same directory and have the "package" clause as the first statement in the file. All packages that are used by a program must be referenced as an offset from a directory contained in the CLASSPATH system variable. By using classes, Java has forced programmers to distribute programs using a standard structure. In Java, a class that is being used outside of a package must also be declared public, forcing the source file to have the same name as the ".class" file that is created. This makes it easier to manage the final artifact program and maintain the source files for the program.

To see how this works, first look at the useAnimator.bat file that comes with the source code for this text and is shown in Exhibit 4

(Program12.2). In this batch file, the CLASSPATH is set to the parent directory of the animator package used in Chapters 7 to 9. Later, when the Java source files contain the statement "import animator," the directories under all entries in the CLASSPATH variable are searched for a directory named "animator". The first such directory found is assumed to be the animator package, and any classes in the animator package will resolve to a public class file in this directory. (See Exhibit 5.)

This organization also applies to the source files for the animator. All source files must be in a directory named "animator" that is in the CLASSPATH for the program to compile. This means that the source code for all classes used outside of a package must be in a file named the same as the class and in a directory with all other files from that package. This means that Java programs have enforced order, making it more difficult (but possible) to misplace source code.

12.6.2 Scope Resolution Modifiers

Another reason to use packages in Java is that they form the basis for the scope of variables outside of classes. Java has four values for scope of a variable. The scope modifiers are listed below in decreasing order of restrictiveness:

- *Private* — A private scope for a variable means that this variable, method, or inner class/interface cannot be used outside of the current class. Note that a normal class/interface cannot be declared private, as it could never be used.
- *Friendly* — Friendly scope is the default scope if no scope modifier is used. *Friendly* is not a keyword in Java and so cannot be used explicitly in Java. Friendly scope says that this variable, method, inner class/interface, or class/interface can be referenced in any other class in the current package.
- *Protected* — Protected scope indicates that the variable, method, or inner class/interface can be accessed in the current package or in any descendent of the current class. Note once again that it would not make sense to allow classes/interfaces to be declared protected.
- *Public* — Public scope allows a variable, method, inner class/interface, or class/interface to be used anywhere in a program.

12.6.3 Distributing Source Programs

Packages serve one more very useful purpose in Java as the basis for distributing the applications. Most applications in Java are packaged into JAR files, which are basically zip files that have some extra information about the Java classes they contain. The files inside of the

Exhibit 4. Program12.2

```
public class IntStack {
     int sizeOfStack;
     int elements[];
     int currentElement;

     /**
      *  The exception to be thrown if this stack is full
and an element is
      *  to be added.
      */
     public class FullException extends Exception {
          public FullException() {
               super();
          }
          public FullException(String message) {
               super(message);
          }
     }
     /**
      *  The exception to be thrown if this stack is empty
and an element
      *  is to be retrieved.
      */
     public class EmptyException extends Exception {
          public EmptyException() {
               super();
          }
          public EmptyException(String message) {
               super(message);
          }
     }

     /**
    *  Public constructor that creates a stack of "sizeOfStack"
ints.


*/
     public IntStack(int sizeOfStack) {
          this.sizeOfStack = sizeOfStack;
          this.elements = new int[sizeOfStack];
          this.currentElement = -1;
     }

/**
     *  Default public constructor, creates a stack of 10 ints.
      */
     public IntStack() {
          this(10);
     }

     /**
      *  Look at the item at the top of the stack.
      */
     public int peek() throws IntStack.EmptyException {
          if (currentElement < 0)
               throw new IntStack.EmptyException();
          return elements[currentElement];
     }
```

(continued)

Exhibit 4. Program12.2 (Continued)

```
/**
     *   Put a new item on the stack.
     */
    public void push(int newElement) throws IntStack.FullEx-
ception {
         int tmpElement = currentElement + 1;
         if (tmpElement >= sizeOfStack)
              throw new IntStack.FullException();
         elements[++currentElement] = newElement;
    }

    /**
     *   Remove and return the item at top of the stack.
     */
    public int pop() throws IntStack.EmptyException {
         if (currentElement < 0)
              throw new IntStack.EmptyException();
         return elements[currentElement--];
    }

    /**
     *   Test program.
     */
    public static void main(String args[]) {
         try {
              IntStack intStack = new IntStack(5);
              intStack.push(5);
              intStack.push(2);
              System.out.println(intStack.pop());
              System.out.println(intStack.pop());
              intStack.peek();
         } catch (Exception e) {
              e.printStackTrace();
         }

         try {
              IntStack intStack = new IntStack(5);
              intStack.push(5);
              intStack.push(2);
              System.out.println(intStack.pop());
              System.out.println(intStack.pop());
              intStack.pop();
         } catch (Exception e) {
              e.printStackTrace();
         }

         try {
              IntStack intStack = new IntStack(5);
              intStack.push(1);
              intStack.push(2);
intStack.push(3);
              intStack.push(4);
              intStack.push(5);
              intStack.push(6);
         } catch (IntStack.FullException e) {
              e.printStackTrace();
}
    }
}
```

Exhibit 5. useAnimator.bat

```
set CLASSPATH=%CLASSPATH%;.;%cd%
```

JAR file are stored in directories representing the packages in the file. The CLASSPATH environment variable is then set to the JAR file, and the program can be distributed. This can also be made to work with the code base for an applet and is used in Chapter 13 with RMI.

12.7 Further Reading

This chapter deals with topics that are mostly specific to the Java language, so books that cover the Java language well (see, for example, [FLA02]) would be good references.

Chapter 13

Distributed Programming Using RMI

13.1 Introduction

A distributed program is one that runs on multiple computers. These types of programs are concurrent because parts of them are run on physically different CPUs; therefore, these systems can often be modeled as components and can use the techniques described in the text. Distributed programming has evolved from very simple mechanisms using technologies such as Unit-to-UNIX Copy (UUCP) and sockets into techniques that take advantage of the higher-level languages in which the programs are written. Perhaps the best example of this is Java *remote method invocation* (RMI), which uses the Java interfaces and exceptions to create distributed programs that almost completely hide the complexity of a distributed program.

This chapter presents distributed programming using RMI. It first gives a simple example of a "HelloWorld" program that covers the basics of RMI, how to set up a simple RMI program, and how to actually make the program run. The chapter then shows how objects can be created to run on the computer where they were created or to be physically transferred to a remote computer and run on the remote system. This behavior is then combined with the Java Event Model to create a chat program, such as the UNIX "talk" command or AOL Instant Messenger.

13.2 Chapter Goals

When you have completed this chapter, you should be able to:

- Describe the parts of RMI and how each part is used in creating a program.
- Implement and run a program using RMI.
- Create objects that are run on the computer where they were created or are sent to a remote process to execute.

13.3 A Brief History of Distributed Computing

With the advent of large computer networks and the Internet, many of the resources that are to be used by a program no longer exist on a single computer. For example, a credit card might need to be validated on a bank's computer, with the program on the current computer being responsible only for sending the data to the bank's computer and then processing any return information. Another example would be a program that interfaces with a legacy system, such as a large employee database written using Common Business Oriented Language (COBOL) and possibly running on a mainframe. A final example would be any program running on the World Wide Web (WWW) that sends messages to a Web server on a remote computer to process requests and receives back a reply. It is improbable to think that a programmer starting a career today could work his entire career without ever writing a program that uses distributed programming in some manner. Programs that run on remote computers are by definition concurrent, so all of the current methodologies that have been studied to this point will apply to various parts of the concurrent programming model.

To better understand the current technology that is used to implement distributed computing, it is helpful to know a little about how distributed computing evolved over time. Original distributed systems were implemented using "sneaker net," which involved walking tapes containing files of data to the different computers running the programs processing this data. An improvement over sneaker net occurred when programmers built scripts using standard utilities, such as ftp or uucp, to copy these files between the various computers; however, these types of solutions were batch oriented, so one or more times a day files were transferred between the systems and executed.

Eventually, real-time access to remote systems was required. Early on this meant that programmers had to create their own protocols for accessing remote systems, building on low-level primitives such as sockets. While sockets provided an easy way to write data between the systems, it read and wrote simple streams of bytes, and it was up to the program to handle issues such as varying data types between computers (e.g., how to represent floating point numbers and questions of big-endian vs. little-endian) and reconstructing the byte streams into meaningful program data. This made any real-time interaction between programs expensive to implement because the programmer had to deal with low-level primitives and write and debug their own protocols for sending and receiving data.

As the need for more network services became apparent, high-level tools to implement network services became available. One of the first such tools was *remote procedure calls* (RPCs), which allowed a computer to effectively call (or invoke) a function on a remote computer. Built into RPC was the ability to ensure that the data sent between the systems was correct, so all the programmer needed to do to make a request of a remote system was to instantiate the RPC environment and then call the method as if it was running on the local computer. The RPC engine handled all the details of implementing the protocol to send and receive the data across the network.

One problem with RPC was that it did not work with objects, only with methods. Other methodologies, such as the Common Object Request Broker Architecture (CORBA) or the XML-based simple object access protocol (SOAP), were developed to allow objects to be accessed across networks. Java implemented its own method of transferring and accessing objects over a network, called remote method invocation (RMI), which builds on the strengths of the Java language to implement network-accessible objects.

The rest of this chapter shows how to implement a program using RMI and how objects can be accessed on the network using RMI. Section 10.4 gives a simple overview of RMI and how the different parts of RMI work to communicate across the network. Section 10.5 presents a simple HelloWorld program to introduce the basic capabilities of RMI. Section 10.6 shows how RMI can be used to send objects across the network (migrating objects) or to keep objects on a local computer that are to be accessed from a remote computer (non-migrating objects). An example program that illustrates the power of RMI is presented, and Section 12.7 implements a chat program that shows how the Java Event Model can be combined with RMI.

13.4 Overview of RMI

The purpose of using RMI is to allow objects that exist on remote computers (or in a separate process on the same computer) to be accessed as if they are local objects. This section describes the process that is involved in creating an RMI program. It first describes the components required to run an RMI program and then describes the steps for making a program run using RMI. A simple example of a program that illustrates these concepts is given in Section 10.5.

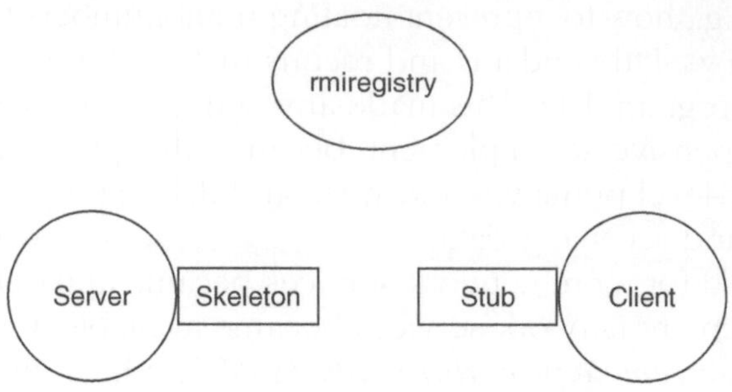

Exhibit 1. Components That Make Up RMI

The simplest type of RMI program is a client/server program. A client/server program is really a program with two separate programs. The first is the server that provides a resource to a client program, and only runs in response to requests from the server; thus, the server is normally a component. The second is the client program that implements the program to solve the user's problem. Because these two pieces are separate programs, they need some mechanism to pass messages back and forth. If this mechanism supports messaging over a network, the program can be distributed to remote computers, as in RMI.

The five basic components required to run this type of program using RMI, as illustrated in Exhibit 1, are:

1. *Server*, which is simply a passive object that sits on a remote computer and waits for requests to come to it from client computers
2. *Client*, which is an active process and makes requests of the server by calling the methods of the server using the RMI protocols
3. *rmiregistry*, which is a program that allows the client to find server objects with which it can communicate
4. *Skeleton class*, which is a Java class used by the server to handle the communications with the client
5. *Stub class*, which is a Java class used by the client to handle the communications with the server

RMI uses these classes as follows. First, rmiregistry is run; rmiregistry is used to store a handle to the server object so that the client can retrieve these handles and begin communicating with the server. Once rmiregistry is running, the server calls the method Naming.rebind to register a handle that is associated with a name for this server object. The Server object then suspends its execution and waits for a client object to access one of its methods. This process is shown in Exhibit 2. When the server is running and registered with rmiregistry, the second step is for the client program to start and to call Naming.lookup with the name of the server object. If the name of this object exists

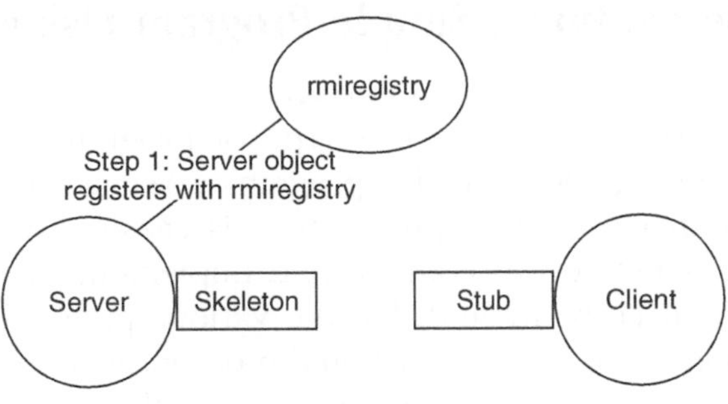

Exhibit 2. Registering the Server Object

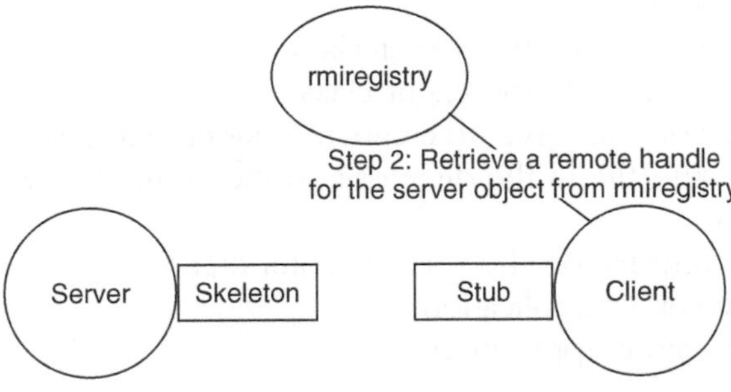

Exhibit 3. Retrieving the Handle for the Server Object

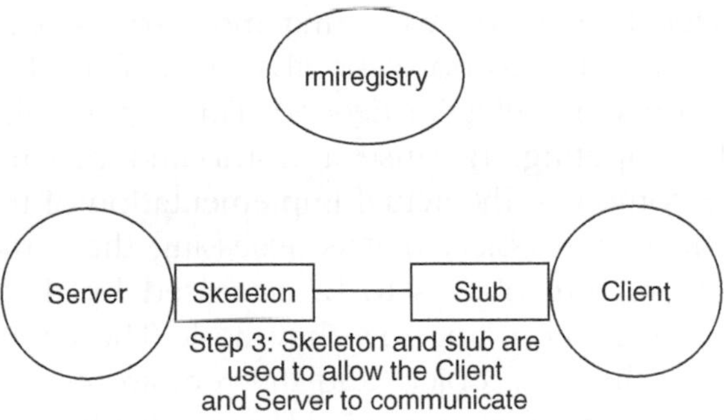

Exhibit 4. Client and Server Communicating

in rmiregistry, the handle for the server object registered with the name is returned. This is shown in Exhibit 3. When the client has the handle for the object, the client and the server communicate using the stub and skeleton classes (see Exhibit 4). Note, however, that in this scenario all messages must originate from the client when it makes calls to methods on the server.

13.5 Implementing a Simple Program Using RMI

The first program to write when encountering any new technology is a simple HelloWorld program. This type of program simply prints a string to a terminal. Because the program does not implement any complex logic that can cause problems, it is easier to make sure that the components needed to compile and implement the program are present and used correctly and that the various parts of the program are correctly placed to be found when the program is run. This section gives step-by-step instructions for how to implement a simple HelloWorld program in Java. The steps needed to implement RMI are:

1. Create the interface that will be used to allow the objects to communicate.
2. Write and compile the server class.
3. Write and compile the client class.
4. Run rmic on the server to create the skeleton and stub files for RMI.
5. Put the stub file in the directory on the computer where the client will run.
6. Run rmiregistry on the server's computer.
7. Run the server application.
8. Run the client application.

13.5.1 Implement the RMI Interface

Chapter 5 presented the use of interfaces. In subsequent chapters, we have emphasized that interfaces permit more robust designs as they allow what the object is to do to be abstracted from how the object actually implements the behavior needed. This is particularly important in distributed computing. Because a distributed program is run on more than one computer, the actual implementation of the class might not be available to the object that is accessing the remote resource. Interfaces allow remote objects to be accessed by the definition of what they are going to do, not how they do it. The interface provides the link between the local object and the remote resource.

Some form of an interface is needed for any distributed architecture; for example, CORBA, which can be used for any number of languages (e.g., C/C++, Ada), implements a language called Interface Definition Language (IDL) to allow interfaces to be written that can work for all of these languages. However, Java has an advantage over a number of these older languages in that it already has the concept of an interface built into the language, so RMI simply uses the Java interface language facility.

While the interface definition used for RMI is a standard Java interface, some particular features must be included in an interface that runs remotely using RMI. The first is that the interface must extend

Exhibit 5. Program13.1a: HelloWorld Interface

```
import java.rmi.Remote;
import java.rmi.server.UnicastRemoteObject;

/**
 *  This is an RMI interface. To work with RMI the
 *  following must occur:
 *    1 - The interface must extend java.rmi.Remote.
 *    2 - All remote methods must be declared to throw
 *        java.rmi.RemoteException.
 *        Note that the exception does not have to be thrown
 *        when the Server implements the method, as rmic adds
 *        the exception to the method in the stub class.
 *
 *  This interface is needed by both the client and the server
 *  and defines how they communicate with each other; however,
 *  the client only needs the class file to compile, so only the
 *  ".class" file should be put with the client code.
 */

public interface HelloWorld extends java.rmi.Remote {
  public void PrintHello()
    throws java.rmi.RemoteException;
}
```

java.rmi.Remote, which simply tells java that any class implementing this interface may be run remotely using RMI. The second is that any method that is to be called remotely needs to be defined in the interface, and these methods need to throw the exception java.rmi.RemoteException. The reason this exception must be thrown is that any RMI will automatically handle any communication-related exceptions that might occur when the method is called. This allows the programmer to call the remote method as if it were a local method and not to be concerned with such issues as how to ensure that messages are properly sent to the remote methods.

The interface needed to run the HelloWorld program is shown in Program13.1a (Exhibit 5). Note that this interface (or at least its class file) must be present on both the client and server when compiling the program.

13.5.2 Implement the RMI Server Class

Once the interface is implemented which specifies how messages will be passed between the client and server, a server to implement the behavior for that interface can be written. The server class is a normal Java class that has the following four characteristics:

1. The server class must extend java.rmi.server.UnicastRemoteObject. This is necessary to allow an object to set up the infrastructure to respond to messages from remote clients.

2. The server class must implement the interface defined in step 1 to ensure that the promises made in the interface are kept when the Server is called from the Client.
3. The constructor method for the Server class must throw java.rmi.-RemoteException. This exception is thrown by the default constructor for the UnicastRemoteObject, and because the default constructor for that object is automatically called, this exception propagates to this method. Note that it is not possible to catch this exception in the constructor and then try to handle it, as Java forces an explicit call to a super constructor to be the first statement in a constructor. To implement a try block violates this, so a try block cannot be put around a call to a super constructor; therefore, at least one constructor must be created to throw this exception.
4. Even though the Server will be called as a passive object, it must have a main that calls Naming.rebind to register the object with rmiregistry. This main class needs only to create the object to register and then to register it with a name. The main thread can then suspend, as the object will run in threads created when the objects methods are called.

An example of a Server class for the HelloWorld program is provided in Exhibit 6 (Program13.1b). A few details about the implementation of the Server class should be emphasized. First is the convention for naming the Server class the same as the interface with a suffix of "Imp" (for implementation), which was followed here. Obviously, this convention could not be used if several different servers were implemented for a single interface. Second, even though the method that is defined in the interface must throw RemoteException, the actual implementation of this method does not. The reason is that proxies for these methods will be created for these methods in the skeleton and stub classes, and these proxy methods will throw these exceptions, but, because the method as defined in the Server does not throw the exception, there is no need to put it in the signature for the method.

The last thing to look at is the call to Naming.rebind. To use this method, an object instance of this class must first be created, then the object, along with a name, is passed to the Naming.rebind method. The name for the object is a URL-formatted name just like those typed into a browser window. In the Server defined for this project, a port other than the standard port for RMI is used to run rmiregistry, so the computer (localhost) and the port (5012) are specified as part of the name as "/ /localhost:5012." The rest of the string is the name associated with that object in the rmiregistry program associated with that computer and port.

13.5.3 Implement the RMI Client Class

The client class that will interface with the server should now be implemented. The client class is a normal Java class except that one

Exhibit 6. Program13.1b: HelloWorld Server Class

```
import java.rmi.*;
import java.rmi.server.UnicastRemoteObject;
import java.io.*;

/**
 *  This class is a simple RMI server. To be a server using RMI,
 *  this class implements the following:
 *
 *   1 - It extends the remote interface, in this case
 *       interface HelloWorld.
 *   2 - It extends UnicastRemoteObject.
 *   3 - The constructor must throw java.rmi.RemoteException,
 *       as the parent constructor for UnicastRemoteObject
 *       throws this exception.
 *   4 - It sets up the security manager (if needed). It is not
 *       used here, so it is commented out. To use it, the
 *       policytool program must be run to set the policy
 *       before running this application.
 *   5 - The object is created and registered with rmiregistry
 *       using the Naming.rebind() call. Note that, in this
 *       example, to show that the default RMI port does not
 *       have to be used, port 5012 is used. Be careful when
 *       starting this program to use the correct port.
 */

class HelloWorldImp extends UnicastRemoteObject
    implements HelloWorld {

  /**
   *  Public constructor, which simply runs
   *  the parent constructor.
   */
  public HelloWorldImp() throws java.rmi.RemoteException {
    super();
  }

  /**
   *  Method from the remote interface. Note that this method is
   *  called remotely from the client. Also note that this
   *  method does not throw java.rmi.RemoteException, even
   *  though the interface defines it for this method. The
   *  exception will be added when rmic is run.
   */
  public void PrintHello() {
    System.out.println("Hello from Local");
  }

  /**
   *  The main method, which creates the object
   *  and registers it with rmiregistry.
   */
  public static void main(String argv[]) {
    try {

      // The security manager is only needed if the class is to
      // be loaded across the network. This code is commented
      // out because we will distribute the classes before
      // starting the client and the server.
      /******
      if (System.getSecurityManager() = = null) {
```

(continued)

Exhibit 6. Program13.1b (Continued)

```
        System.setSecurityManager(new RMISecurityManager());
      }
      */

      HelloWorldImp thisExample = new HelloWorldImp();
      Naming.rebind("// localhost:5012/HelloGuy," thisExample);

      // This is not needed, but it tells us the rebind worked.
      System.out.println("HelloGuy bound in registry");
    } catch (Exception e) {
      System.out.println("HelloGuy err: " + e.getMessage());
      e.printStackTrace();
    }
  }
}
```

of the objects, the server object, is retrieved from the remote rmiregistry by calling Naming.lookup. A name is passed to Naming.lookup that matches the name used by the server to register with rmiregistry. The object returned is an instance of an object that allows methods of the server to be called, so the object is cast to the interface on the client computer. The client class for the HelloWorld program is shown in Exhibit 7 (Program13.1c).

13.5.4 Creating and Distributing the Skeleton and Stub Files

The next step is to produce skeleton and stub files. These files are used by RMI to perform what is called *marshaling* and *unmarshaling* of the data. Basically, this means that the skeleton and stub files translate the data into a format that can be transferred across the network and can then be reconstituted into proper objects. How it does this is not important to understand here because it always works. If an object or primitive is sent across the network as a parameter or return value, it will be correct when it is used on the remote computer, or an exception will be thrown which can then be handled.

To create skeleton and stub files, the rmic program is run on the Server ".class" file. For example, in the HelloWorld program, the command "rmic HelloWorldImp" will produce the files HelloWorldImp_Skel.class and HelloWorld_Stub.class. These are the skeleton and stub files for the HelloWorld program. In more recent versions of rmic, the skeleton file is simply included in the Server ".class" file; however, the command as shown here will create both the skeleton and stub files.

Take note, however, that normally in Java objects are passed by reference (actually, the reference is copied so it is a call by value, but the effect is a call by reference); therefore, the values of an object can

Exhibit 7. Program13.1c: HelloWorld Client Class

```
import java.rmi.*;

/**
 *  Client program for an RMI program. To be a server, the
 *  program must do the following:
 *
 *    1 - Set the security manager to allow the stub class to be
 *        loaded from the server (if needed). It is not used here,
 *        so it is commented out.
 *    2 - Retrieve the remote object from the rmiregistry
 *        programming running on the server computer. Note that in
 *        this example, to show that the default RMI port does not
 *        have to be used, port 5012 is used. Be careful when
 *        starting this program to use the correct port.
 *    3 - Call the object using the interface as if it were local.
 */
class HelloWorldClient {
  public static void main(String argv[]) {
    try {

      // If the stub class was loaded across the network, this
      // would have to be set, but we are distributing all the
      // class files to the right directories, so this is not
      // needed here. See the Server code for more details.
      /***********
      if (System.getSecurityManager() = = null) {
        System.setSecurityManager(new RMISecurityManager());
      }
      */

      HelloWorld H = (HelloWorld)Naming.lookup(
        "// localhost:5012/HelloGuy");
      H.PrintHello();
    } catch(Exception e) {
      e.printStackTrace();
    }
  }
}
```

be changed in the method and reflected in the object when the method returns to the calling program. Because RMI does not have access to remote memory, all calls treat objects as call by value, meaning that the object itself, and not simply its reference, must be copied, and changes made in the remote method will not be reflected in the object when control is returned to the calling program. It also means that passing large composite objects, such as vectors and arrays, can require many more resources than a similar call to a local method, and passing of such structures should be carefully considered before being initiated.

13.5.5 Distributing and Running the Program

Now that all the parts of the program are ready, the pieces can be distributed and the program tested and run. The example here shows how to run the program on a single computer running MS Windows, but the same principles apply to running RMI on any computer. The first thing to do is to create two directories, one for the server and the other for the client. In the server directory should be the HelloWorld interface, the HelloWorldImp server, and both the skeleton and stub files. In the client directory should be the HelloWorld interface, the HelloWorldClient, and the stub file. Now start three DOS command prompts, and change the directory for two of them to the directory for the server, and one to the directory for the client. In one of the server directories, type "rmiregistry 5012". This starts the rmiregistry program and tells it to listen to port 5012. In the second server directory, start the server application. It should tell you that it is registered with rmiregistry. Finally, in the client directory run the client application. Each time you run the client application, a message should appear in the server window telling you that the client has contacted the server. When this happens, you have gotten a simple RMI program to run. The next step is to see some ways RMI can be used to solve larger problems.

13.6 Migrating and Non-Migrating Objects

Before describing how to use RMI in an application, an important concept in RMI is that some objects can be sent across the network to run on a remote computer, and some of them can be run on a local computer. I will call objects that run on a remote computer *migrating objects* because they move (migrate) from one computer to another computer. Objects that run on the computer on which they are created are called *non-migrating objects* because they do not move across the network; instead, they are called remotely from the system that uses them.* Because migrating objects must move across the network, they must have a representation that can run on any computer and hence must be serializable. Non-migrating objects do not have to be serializable, but must follow the rules for creating a server object, as discussed in Section 12.5.2.

Program13.2 (Exhibits 8 through 12) and Program13.3 (Exhibits 13 and 14) illustrate the difference between a migrating and a non-migrating object. In both of these programs, a server is created that implements a sendMessage method. This method takes a printMessage

---

* The Java references refer to non-migrating objects as *remote* and migrating objects as *non-remote*. This is because a non-migrating object stays on the computer on which it was created and is thus called remotely when it is called. A migrating object moves to another computer, so when its methods are called they are called non-remotely. I will use the terminology of migrating and non-migrating because it seems more intuitive to talk about what happens to the objects, not the semantics of the method call. It also helps to make the difference between objects that must be serializable vs. objects that implement UnicastRemoteObject more understandable.

Exhibit 8. Program13.2a: Server Interface

```
interface Server extends java.rmi.Remote {
  public void sendMessage(PrintMessage pm)
    throws java.rmi.RemoteException;
}
```

Exhibit 9. Program13.2b: ServerImp Class

```
import java.rmi.*;
import java.rmi.server.UnicastRemoteObject;
import java.io.*;

class ServerImp extends UnicastRemoteObject
      implements Server, Serializable {

  public ServerImp() throws java.rmi.RemoteException {
    super();
  }

  public void sendMessage(PrintMessage pm) {
    try {
      pm.print();
    } catch (Exception e) {
      e.printStackTrace();
    }
  }

  public static void main(String argv[]) {
    try {
      ServerImp thisExample = new ServerImp();
      Naming.rebind("/Server," thisExample);
      System.out.println("bound in registry");
    } catch (Exception e) {
      System.out.println("HelloGuy err: " + e.getMessage());
      e.printStackTrace();
    }
  }
}
```

object created on the client computer and sent via the sendMessage method to the server. The only difference between Program13.2 (Exhibits 8 through 12) and Program13.3 (Exhibits 13 and 14) is that in Program13.2 (Exhibits 8 through 12) the PrintMessage object is a migrating object, so it is serializable and runs in the remote server's process (the message will print in the DOS window where the server was started). In Program13.3 (Exhibits 13 and 14), the PrintMessage object is a non-migrating object. When the PrintMessage object is passed to the server, it continues to run on the client and only passes a reference to the PrintMessage object to the server. The PrintMessage object thus runs on the client, and when the print method is called on the server it will run in the client's process (the message is printed in the window where the client is running).

Exhibit 10. Program13.2c: Client Class

```
import java.rmi.*;

class Client {
  public static void main(String argv[]) {
    try {
      Server server = (Server)Naming.lookup(
        "// localhost/Server");
      server.sendMessage(
        new PrintMessageImp("Created on Client"));
    } catch(Exception e) {
      e.printStackTrace();
    }
  }
}
```

Exhibit 11. Program13.2d: PrintMessage Interface

```
public interface PrintMessage {
  public void print();
}
```

Exhibit 12. Program13.2e: PrintMessageImp Class

```
import java.io.Serializable;

public class PrintMessageImp implements
    PrintMessage,Serializable {
  String message;
  public PrintMessageImp(String message) {
    this.message = message;
  }

  public void print() {
    System.out.println(message);
  }
}
```

Exhibit 8 (Program13.2a), Exhibit 9 (Program13.2b), and Exhibit 10 (Program13.2c) show the implementation of the Server interface, ServerImp, and Client classes for the migrating object. These classes are exactly the same for the non-migrating object and will not be shown with Program13.3 (Exhibits 13 and 14). As with the HelloWorld program, the Server object simply registers with rmiregistry and waits for the client to call its methods. The Client object retrieves the Server object from rmiregistry and calls the sendMessage method on the Server object, sending the PrintMessageImp object.

Exhibit 13. Program13.3a: PrintMessage Interface for Migrating Object

```
public interface PrintMessage extends java.rmi.Remote {
  public void print() throws java.rmi.RemoteException;
}
```

Exhibit 14. Program13.3b: PrintMessageImp Class for Non-Migrating Object

```
import java.rmi.*;
import java.rmi.server.UnicastRemoteObject;

public class PrintMessageImp extends UnicastRemoteObject
      implements PrintMessage {
  String message;

  public PrintMessageImp(String message) throws java.rmi.
      RemoteException {
    this.message = message;
  }

  public void print() throws java.rmi.RemoteException {
    System.out.println(message);
  }
}
```

The differences between Program13.2 (Exhibits 8 through 12) and Program13.3 (Exhibits 13 and 14) are completely in the PrintMessage and PrintMessageImp objects, and these are examined here. In Program13.2 (Exhibits 8 through 12), the PrintMessage interface and PrintMessageImp class are normal serializable objects in that they do not use any of the RMI infrastructures; therefore, when the object is created on the client and passed to the server, the actual object is sent to the server. Thus, the PrintMessageImp class must exist on the server (not just the interface and stub classes) because the actual PrintMessageImp object will be run on the server. When the print method is called, the message prints out in the window running the server process. The PrintMessage interface and PrintMessageImp class are shown in Exhibit 11 (Program13.2d) and Exhibit 12 (Program13.2e).

Program13.3 (Exhibits 13 and 14) is similar to Program13.2 (Exhibits 8 through 12), but the PrintMessage and PrintMessageImp classes now implement the infrastructure to use RMI. Also, when compiling these programs rmic must be run on PrintMessageImp, and the PrintMessageImp_Stub.class file (not the PrintMessageImp.class file) must be copied to the directory containing the server. This is because the PrintMessageImp class is only run on the client, not the server, so the PrintMessageImp.class file need only exist on the client, but the stub file must be accessible to the server so that it can call back to the client. When the print method is called on the server, the message is passed back to the client, and the message comes out in the window running the client. Exhibit 13 (Program13.3a) and Exhibit 14 (Program13.3b) show the implementation of the PrintMessage interface and PrintMessageImp objects for the migrating objects example.

One last note is that the PrintMessageImp object did not need to register with rmiregistry, because rmiregistry is only used to find an object. In this case, the object was passed as a parameter to the server, so it is already known and it does not have to be looked up in rmiregistry. The actual communications are not handled by rmiregistry, so in that sense it is not really an *object request broker* (ORB). The communications are handled completely in the stub and skeleton classes.

This behavior of allowing objects to migrate or not has many uses; for example, it can be used to create agents that can roam across the network looking for computers on which they can run. In the next section, the dichotomy between a migrating and non-migrating object is used to implement a simple chat program.

13.7 Chat Program

We now use RMI and the ability to send objects or object references to write a simple chat program. This chat program allows multiple users to connect to a chat server; when any user types text in the text box and hits the "Send" button, the text will be sent to the server, and the server will then send the message out to all the users currently registered with the chat server. The design of this server requires that some objects must be migrating and some non-migrating. For example, the text string that the user types in must be able to transfer to the server and then to each of the clients; hence, it must be a migrating object. The chat client, however, will register with the chat server but will run on the client computer; hence, it will be a non-migrating object. It will also require the use of the Java Event Model from Chapter 7 to implement the server, with a slight twist to take care of a possible deadlock situation.

13.7.1 The Chat Server

The chat server will be presented first, as it is the heart of the system. Also, because it uses interfaces to interact with the chat clients, it is really a separate entity, and the design of the interfaces it uses will drive the design of the chat client. Because the chat server is simply an implementation of the Java Event Model, it draws upon just three methods to deal with requests from clients: add listeners, remove

Exhibit 15. Program13.4a: The ChatListener

```
interface ChatListener extends java.rmi.Remote,
java.util.EventListener {
  public void chatEventSent(ChatEvent cme)
    throws java.rmi.RemoteException;
}
```

Exhibit 16. Program13.4b: The ChatServer Interface

```
public interface ChatServer extends java.rmi.Remote {
  public void addChatListener(ChatListener A)
    throws java.rmi.RemoteException;
  public void removeChatListener(ChatListener cl)
    throws java.rmi.RemoteException;
  public void sendChatMessage(String message)
    throws java.rmi.RemoteException;
}
```

Exhibit 17. Program13.4c: The ChatEvent

```
public class ChatEvent extends java.util.EventObject {
  String message;
  public ChatEvent(Object source, String message) {
    super(source);
  this.message = new String(message);
  }

  public String getMessage() {
    return message;
  }
}
```

listeners, and process the events. One main method is used to create the object and register it with rmiregistry. However, to be a true event program, it also must define the listener and the event. Also, to implement RMI, the remote interface must be defined. The listener, a ChatListener, is shown in Exhibit 15 (Program13.4a), the ChatEvent is shown in Exhibit 16 (Program13.4b), and the ChatServer interface is shown in Exhibit 17 (Program13.4c). Implementation of the ChatServer is shown in Exhibit 18 (Program13.4d).

This implementation is short and should be immediately recognizable to anyone who understood the Java Event Model that was implemented in Chapter 7. Listeners are added to the server using the addChatListener and removeChatListener methods. The method that processes the event in the server is sendChatMessage, which receives messages from the clients and sends the text out to all of the listeners using the chatEventSent method putting the text of the message in the event object that is sent.

Exhibit 18. Program13.4d: The ChatServer

```
import java.rmi.*;
import java.rmi.server.UnicastRemoteObject;
import java.util.*;

public class ChatServerImp extends UnicastRemoteObject
    implements ChatServer {

  Vector chatListeners = new Vector();

  public ChatServerImp() throws RemoteException {
  }

  public void addChatListener(ChatListener cl)
      throws java.rmi.RemoteException {
    System.out.println("Adding Listener");
    chatListeners.add(cl);
  }

  public void removeChatListener(ChatListener cl)
      throws java.rmi.RemoteException {
    System.out.println("Removing Listener");
    chatListeners.remove(cl);
  }

  public void sendChatMessage(String message)
      throws java.rmi.RemoteException {
    Vector v;
    synchronized(this) {v = (Vector)chatListeners.clone();}

  try {
    for (Enumeration e = v.elements(); e.hasMoreElements();) {
      ChatListener cl = (ChatListener)e.nextElement();
      cl.chatEventSent(new ChatEvent(this, message));
    }
  } catch(Exception e) {
    e.printStackTrace();
  }
  }

  public static void main(String argv[]) {
    try {
      ChatServerImp thisExample = new ChatServerImp();

      Naming.rebind("// localhost/ChatServer," thisExample);
    } catch (Exception e) {
        System.out.println("ChatServer err: " + e.getMes-
sage());
        e.printStackTrace();
    }
  }
}
```

It is interesting to note that the client program does not ever get a copy of the server; instead, all of the methods to be called are placed in an interface. This is different from how the Java Event Model is implemented in the Java AWT, where, for instance, a program would have direct access to the JButton and not an interface representing a JButton. However, this does not change how the event source is implemented and in fact helps to isolate the actual source from the client program.

The server should help to show that the models of components that have been developed so far in the text are applicable when new concurrency mechanisms, such as distributed programming, are used. The actual implementation details of the asynchronous activities (in this case, processes on a remote computer) and the details of how the objects are accessed (here, via skeleton and stub files) do not change the details of how the components work.

13.7.2 The Chat Client

Using the definition of the chat server from Section 13.7.1, the client is designed to meet the requirements of the event model it uses. First, a GUI is designed that allows the user to type messages that are sent to the server and to see the messages that are typed by the other users. Developing this GUI is relatively straightforward and is provided in Exhibit 19 (Program13.4e). Once the GUI is designed, messages must be sent to the server so that they can be relayed to all the ChatListeners registered with the server. To do this, the client program must retrieve the server from the rmiregistry and then register itself with the server. Care must be taken to ensure that all the objects are run on the correct computers, so the concept of migrating and non-migrating object is very important. It is important that the programmer keep in mind each object, how it is used, and where it will be run.

Because the client is the interface for the user, it must stay on the user's computer; thus, the chat client must be a non-migrating object that registers with the server. The actual message that is sent, however, is just a text string and thus is a migrating object that is sent to the server. The event that is sent to each listener should once again be a migrating object that is unwrapped on the client computer.

This all needs to be accounted for in the design. Note that some of this was part of the server's event model design. For example, the ChatListener interface extends java.rmi.Remote. The following table outlines what must be done for each class in this system to make it work:

What Must Be Extended or Implemented	*Affected Classes or Interfaces*
java.rmi.Remote	ChatServer, ChatListener
java.rmi.UnicastRemoteObject	ChatServerImp, ChatClient
java.io.serializable	ChatEvent

Exhibit 19. Program13.4e: The ChatClient Program

```
import java.rmi.*;
import java.rmi.server.UnicastRemoteObject;
import java.util.*;
import java.io.*;
import java.awt.event.*;
import java.awt.*;
import javax.swing.*;

public class ChatClient extends UnicastRemoteObject
     implements ChatListener, Serializable {

  private ChatServer chatServer;
  private TextArea messageBox;

  public ChatClient() throws java.rmi.RemoteException {
    createFrame();
    try {
      chatServer = (ChatServer)Naming.lookup(
       "// localhost/ChatServer");
      chatServer.addChatListener(this);
    } catch(Exception e) {
      e.printStackTrace();
    }
  }

  public void createFrame() {

    JFrame chatFrame = new JFrame("Chat Program");
    Container chatContainer = chatFrame.getContentPane();

    JScrollPane sp = new JScrollPane(messageBox = new TextArea
        (40, 10));
    messageBox.setEditable(false);
    chatContainer.add(messageBox, BorderLayout.CENTER);

    JPanel controlPanel = new JPanel();
    final TextField inputText = new TextField(40);
    controlPanel.add(inputText);

    JButton sendButton = new JButton("Send");
    sendButton.addActionListener(new ActionListener() {
      public void actionPerformed(ActionEvent e) {
        try {

          chatServer.sendChatMessage(inputText.getText() +
            "\n");
        } catch (Exception ex) {
          ex.printStackTrace();
        }
        inputText.setText("");
      }
    });
    controlPanel.add(sendButton);

    JButton exitButton = new JButton("Exit");
    exitButton.addActionListener(new ActionListener() {
      public void actionPerformed(ActionEvent e) {
```

(continued)

Exhibit 19. Program13.4e (Continued)

```
        try {
          chatServer.removeChatListener(ChatClient.this);
          System.exit(0);
        } catch (Exception ex) {
          ex.printStackTrace();
        }
      }
    });
    controlPanel.add(exitButton);

    chatContainer.add(controlPanel, BorderLayout.SOUTH);

    chatFrame.setSize(500,400);
    chatFrame.setVisible(true);
  }

  public void chatEventSent(ChatEvent ce)
      throws java.rmi.RemoteException {
    messageBox.append(ce.getMessage());
  }

  public static void main(String argv[]) {
    try {
      ChatClient chatClient = new ChatClient();
    } catch (Exception e) {
      e.printStackTrace();
    }
  }
}
```

To make this program work, the following files must be on the client:

- ChatListener.class
- ChatServer.class
- ChatEvent.class
- ChatServerImp_Stub.class
- ChatClient_Stub.class
- ChatClient_Skel.class

and the following files must be on the server:

- ChatServer.class
- ChatListener.class
- ChatServerImp.class
- ChatServerImp_Stub.class
- ChatServerImp_Skel.class
- ChatClient_Stub.class

When these files are in place, rmiregistry is run from the ChatServerImp directory, and the ChatServerImp is run, followed by the Chat Client.

This will bring up the chat program correctly. Note that multiple clients can be run with a single server.

This should make it plain that care must be taken in designing distributed components. If a programmer is simply hacking to implement the component and not using simple and tested methods, it is likely that other details will be missed, such as what parts of the model run on what computers and what race conditions or deadlock conditions are possible. That this can happen is illustrated by the fact that this simple chat program has a fairly obvious deadlock condition in it. If the actionListener for the "Send" button and the chatEventSent method both have a synchronized lock on the same object, the program will deadlock. Resolving this deadlock is left for an exercise at the end of the chapter.

13.8 Conclusions

Once the details of how to create and distribute the objects are worked out, distributed computing using RMI is almost as simple as writing a threaded program running on a single process. However, because distributed computing is essentially concurrent computing, the best way to develop distributed programs is to use some form of the component models that were presented in this text. The extra details of properly structuring a distributed program make it especially essential that clean component models that are well thought through are used to ensure that the programs will work correctly.

13.9 Further Reading

The definitive source for information on RMI is on the Sun Microsystems Web site [SUN02e]. A number of good books can complement this site, such as Pitt et al. [PIT01]; also, Flanagan et al. [FLA990] and Ayers et al. [AYE99] have good sections on RMI programming. Readers might also be interested in CORBA, a more universal and industrial-strength distributed programming environment. Information on CORBA can be found at [OBJ02], or a good book is that by Vogel and Duddy [VOG97].

13.10 Problems

1. Explain each part of RMI. Include the programs (rmiregistry, rmic), the interfaces and classes needed, and all the files produced. Explain how each is used.

2. For each program in Chapter 13, delete all the ".class" files, leaving only the ".java" files. Rebuild the programs, moving each of the class files as needed. (*Note:* You do not need to move any ".java" files; even for interfaces, you can simply copy the ".class" files.) Explain why each file must be moved.
3. The Web page at [SUN02d] explains how to use the code base property to automatically download the ".class" file for the stub file when calling a remote object. Make the HelloWorld program work with the code base so that the stub file does not have to be put in the client directory.
4. For the chat program, first put up a dialog box that will prompt the user to log in using a user name. Change the ChatEvent and the sendChatMessage to handle inclusion of the user's name. Include the user's name when each message is displayed. Add an option to the ChatClient that allows users to disable receiving messages from a specific user.
5. Using the user name changes from Problem 4, change the way the ChatServer Event Source Object stores the Listeners to use some type of a map (e.g., a ListMap or HashTable). The key should be the user name, and the object is as in Program13.4 (Exhibits 15 through 19). Now create an administrator interface that can:
   - Send a message to a specific user.
   - Log a user out of the chat system.
6. Fix the race condition in the chat program that was described in Section 13.7.2.
7. Implement the bank and the ATM programs from Problem 11.9 using RMI. Make the Bank object the server with one or more ATM clients.
8. Exhibits 10 through 15 in Chapter 9 (Program9.4) implemented a gas station simulation where a pump manager was used to register open pumps and to give those pumps to customers when they asked to pump gas. Make this program distributed using RMI using the following criteria:
   - The pump manager is a server object. It stores pump objects which it then sends to the customers when they request a pump.
   - The pump object itself is a non-migrating object, as it does not move to another process when it is included in the PumpEvent. This means that a proxy is included with the PumpEvent. To do this, the pump object should extend UnicastRemoteObject, it will need to run rmic, and a remote interface will have to be defined.
   - The car objects will be processes instead of threads. You can start cars anytime in another process, and they will request a pump from the pump manager. Note that because the cars are now separate processes, the static variables are no longer stored and shared between the cars. Move the static variables for the totalTime and totalCars to the pump manager, and define an

RMI method call to update them when the car has completed pumping gas.

9. Often, when running a distributed program such as a bank or reservation system, several servers can be run, and one or more "load balancing" programs will take a user request and give it back to one of the servers. Starting with Problem 13.8, design a load balancing program. Extend the design to include multiple load balancing front ends. Implement your design with the bank from Problem 13.7. (*Note:* This implies that there will be several separate banks, but for this simulation this is all right.)
10. Move the storage of the data for the bank in Problem 13.9 outside of the bank object to a data storage object that is shared by several bank objects using RMI. Discuss how this architecture is three tiered. What are some of the advantages and disadvantages of this type of architecture?

Appendix A

Key Words

Activation Record: A record for each method call on the program stack.

Active Object: An object that is an asynchronous activity. In terms of threads it is an object that has a run method and is run as a thread.

Activity: A series of steps that is implemented to do a task.

Adapter: Software that provides an interface allowing a component to be used in a manner.

Animation: A technique where pictures are changed slightly and displayed on a terminal so fast that the eye perceives movement.

Asynchronous Activity: When the steps involved in the two or more sub-tasks are being executed independently, or asynchronously, from each other.

Born (thread state): The initial state of a thread before it can be run.

Cache: A special place to store data, often hidden from either the other objects or in some cases the program. In the case of computer architecture, it is very fast memory that the program cannot directly manipulate. In a sense it is hidden from the program.

Checked Exception: An exception that the compiler forces the program to explicitly handle in either a try block or by using a throws clause in the current method. These exceptions extend Exception.

Child Thread: A thread that was started by the current thread.

Classification: An OOP design methodology where objects are designed by extending other objects, using the "extends" clause in Java. Classification is also called inheritance.

Cohesion: The degree that an object or method does a specific task, and only that task.

Common Gateway Interfaces (CGI): A way to process Web requests that was initially dependent on using a separate process for each request.

Competitive Synchronization: When two or more asynchronous activities coordinate around a resource.

Complete Synchronization: An object with all of its methods synchronized and no waits in any methods.

Component: Used in this text to mean concurrent component.

Composition: An OOP design methodology where objects are created by using instances of other objects or primitives, hence they are "composites" of other objects.

Concurrency: The presence of asynchronous activities that interact and thus must at some point in their execution implement either competitive or cooperative synchronization.

Concurrent Component: A passive object that controls interactions between two or more asynchronous activities.

Concurrent Programming: A program that contains asynchronous activities which synchronize at one or more points or on one or more resources during execution.

Confinement: Complete encapsulation of an object inside of another object.

Context Switch: The switching between the thread to be run.

Control Object: An object used to build all the active and passive objects in a concurrent program and start them.

Cooperative Synchronization: When two or more asynchronous activities coordinate around an event.

Coupling: How tightly integrated two objects or methods are integrated together.

Critical Section: A section of a program (for example a method) where the existence of a race condition could cause the program to be incorrect.

Data Type: A set of data values and operations on those data values.

Dead (thread state): The state of a thread after it has finished running but before it can be gotten rid of.

Deadlock: When one or more threads have not completed and cannot make progress to completion.

Delegation: This occurs when composition is used. It is when the enclosing class calls a method on an encapsulated class, delegating the work of actually implementing that behavior to the encapsulated class.

Ensembles: Collections of objects that work together to solve a problem.

Event: A way for a component to notify a specific asynchronous activity that something of interest has occurred.

Expression Tree: A binary tree representation of an arithmetic expression.

Garbage Collection: A process where Java reclaims memory for objects that are no longer used.

Generic Components: Components that are written so they can work with many different data types. This is normally done in Java using interfaces.

Heap: A portion of memory, shared between threads, where objects are stored.

Identifier: The name of the variable that is in the source code for the program.

Immutable: Used to describe an object whose value is set when it is constructed, and after that the value cannot be changed.

Java Event Model: A standard pattern for sending events between threads. It is used in the Java AWT.

Java Virtual Machine (JVM): The program used to simulate a computer architecture that runs Java ".class" files.

Liveness: A property of a program that says the program can eventually complete.

Method Area: A portion of memory, shared between threads, where the executable statements for the program are stored.

Method Reuse: When common code is abstracted into a method and called from a number of places in a program.

Monitor: A data structure much like an object with all of its methods synchronized so that only a single thread can be executing in any method on at that time.

Nondeterminism: The property of a concurrent program that says there are multiple total orderings consistent with the valid partial ordering in the program.

Notification Object: An object other than the "this" object that has a wait and notify performed on it. Normally, notification objects need some infrastructure in the program, in the way locks are obtained and used, to be correctly implemented.

notify (Method): A method in class object that releases a thread waiting on the object specified in the notify call.

notifyAll (Method): A method in class object that releases all threads waiting on the object specified in the notify call.

Object Oriented Programming: Programming in a language that supports objects.

Object Reuse: Extracting commonality in a program that requires some state to be maintained, and using an object to maintain that state.

Parent Thread: The thread that started the current thread.

Passive Object: An object used to control interactions between active objects. Because it runs only when a service is requested by an active object, this type of object is often called a reactive object. Passive objects are generally components.

Procedural: Executing serially (step by step).

Procedural Reuse: Extracting commonality in a program and putting it in a procedural method.

Process: The heap, method area, and program contexts for all threads needed to run a program. Often it is the program being run.

Program Context: The stack, PC, and state stored in memory and used to define a thread.

Program Counter (PC): The address of the current instruction to execute next. In the SVM this is a line of code, as it does not contain instruction addresses.

Program Stack: A FIFO list of information (activation records) to execute methods. This is contained in the program context.

Propagating an Exception: Allowing an exception to continue up the call stack until it is caught in a catch block.

Race Condition: A condition where, if a thread can complete a critical section without interference, the program will be correct, but the possibility exists that interference can occur, in which case the program would be incorrect.

Reactive Object: An object that "reacts" to messages from active objects. Also often called a passive object.

Ready (thread state): A state of a thread that says the thread can be run when the CPU is available.

Refactoring: Modifying the code base to ensure that each thing is done once and only once.

Reuse: The abstracting of common code and applying it to several situations in a program or programs.

Reuse by Copy: When a block of code is copied within, or between, programs and modified to fit the current needs of a program.

Running (thread state): A state of a thread that says the thread is currently executing on the CPU.

Safety: A property of a program that says if a concurrent program finishes, the answer produced will be correct. This normally means that the program does not contain race conditions.

Servlets: A way to use Java to process requests from the Web in a Web server using threads instead of processes.

Simple Memory Model (SMM): The simple model of memory used by the SVM.

Simple Virtual Machine (SVM): A simple computer architecture used to explain how concurrent programs run.

Stateless Methods: Methods that do not have to maintain state (i.e., keep variables with values) between invocations.

Synchronization: When two or more asynchronous activities coordinate.

Synchronized Blocks: A block of code that can only be entered (or executed) by one method at a time.

Synchronous Activity: An activity where the order of the steps is determined by a single activity.

Tagged Interface: An interface with no methods, used as a runtime type tag.

Thread: The results of executing a program context.

Thread Safe: An object that is safe to use in a multithreaded environment.

Unchecked Exception: An exception that does not have to be explicitly handled in the program. These Exceptions extend Error or RunTime-Exception.

Unwinding the Stack: A process whereby an exception executes a return from the program stack until the exception is handled.

Utility Reuse: Reuse of functionality that is extrinsic to a problem, and thus common to more than one problem.

Variable: The actual memory that is allocated at run time.

Wait (method): A method in class Object that is called to suspend the execution of a thread until a notify call has been made on this object.

Web Server: A program that processes requests from the Web, normally from browser clients.

XML: A human readable, hierarchical representation language for representing objects.

References

[ADA95] *Ada 95 Reference Manual* (1995), ISO/IEC 8652.

[AHO93] Aho, A., Hopcroft, J., and Ullman, J. (1983), *Data Structures and Algorithms*, Addison-Wesley, Reading, MA.

[AYE99] Ayers, D. et al. (1999), *Java Server Programming*, Wrox Press, Birmingham, U.K.

[BAC98] Bacon, J. (1998), *Concurrent Systems, Operating Systems, Database and Distributed Systems: An Integrated Approach*, Addison-Wesley, Reading, MA.

[BAR96] Barnes, J. (1996), *Programming in Ada 95*, Addison-Wesley, Reading, MA.

[BEN90] Ben-Ari, M. (1990), *Principles of Concurrent and Distributed Programming*, Prentice Hall, New York.

[BOO91] Booch, G. (1991), *Object-Oriented Design with Applications*, Benjamin/Cummings Publishing, New York.

[BOO99] Booch, G., Rumbaugh, J., and Jacobson, I. (1999), *The Unified Modeling Language User Guide*, Addison-Wesley, Reading, MA.

[BRO95] Brooks, F. (1995), *The Mythical Man-Month, Anniversary Edition*, Addison-Wesley, Reading, MA.

[BUD00] Budd, T. (2000), *Understanding Object-Oriented Programming with Java*, Addison-Wesley, Reading, MA.

[CAR01] Carpinelli, J. (2001), *Computer Systems Organization and Architecture*, Addison-Wesley, Reading, MA.

[COA99] Coad, P. and Mayfield, M. (1999), *Java Design*, 2nd ed., Yourdon Press, Upper Saddle River, NJ.

[DAL99] Dale, N. (1999), *C++ Plus Data Structures*, Jones and Bartlett Publishers, Sudbury, MA.

[DEI02] Deitel, H. and Deitel, P. (2002), *Java: How to Program*, Prentice Hall, Upper Saddle River, NJ.

[ECK98] Eckel, B. (1998), *Thinking in Java*, Prentice Hall, Upper Saddle River, NJ.

[ENG97] Englander, R. (1997), *Developing Java Beans*, O'Reilly & Associates, Sebastopol, CA.

[FLA99] Flanagan, D., Farley, J., Crawford, W., and Magnusson, K. (1999), *Java Enterprise in a Nutshell*, O'Reilly & Associates, Sebastopol, CA.

[FLA02] Flanagan, D. (2002), *Java in a Nutshell*, O'Reilly & Associates, Sebastopol, CA.

[GAM95] Gamma, E., Helm, R., Johnson, R., and Vlissides, J. (1995), *Design Patterns: Elements of Reusable Object-Oriented Software*, Addison-Wesley, Reading, MA.

[GEH88] Gehani, N. and McGettrick, A., Eds. (1988), *Concurrent Programming*, Addison-Wesley, Reading, MA.

[GEH89] Gehani, N. and Roome, W. (1989), *The Concurrent C Programming Language*, Silicon Press, Summit, NJ.

[GEL92] Gelernter, D. and Carriero, N. (1992), Coordination languages and their significance, *Commun. ACM*, 35(2), 97–107.

[HAR98] Hartley, S. (1998), *Concurrent Programming: The Java Programming Language*, Oxford University Press, New York.

[HAT88] Hathorn, F. (1998), Structured Concurrent Processes and Automatic Intermediary Process Generation in Operations-Oriented Concurrent Programming Languages, doctoral dissertation, The George Washington University, Washington, D.C.

[HEL99] Heller, P. and Roberts, S. (1999), *Complete Java 2 Certification Study Guide*, Sybex, Oakland, CA.

[HOA74] Hoare, C. (1974), Monitors: an operating system structuring concept, *Commun. ACM*, 21(8), 666–677.

[HOR02] Horton, I. (2002), *Beginning Java 2 SDK 1.4 Edition*, Wrox Press, Inc.

[JIA00] Jia, X. (2000), *Object-Oriented Software Development Using Java*, Addison-Wesley, Reading, MA.

[KAN01] Kann, C. (2001), Don't get stuck in the GUI thread, *JavaPro,* January.

[LAM80] Lampson, B. and Redell D. (1980), Experience with processes and monitors in Mesa, *Commun. ACM*, January.

[LEA97] Lea, D. (1997), *Concurrent Programming in Java: Design Principles and Patterns*, Addison-Wesley, Reading, MA.

[LEA00] Lea, D. (2000), *Concurrent Programming in Java: Design Principles and Patterns*, 2nd ed., Addison-Wesley, Reading, MA.

[LEW03] Lewis, J. and Loftus, W. (2003), *Java Software Solutions*, Addison-Wesley, Reading, MA.

[LIN99] Lindholm, T. and Yellin, F. (1999), *The Java Virtual Machine Specification*, 2nd ed., Addison-Wesley, Reading, MA.

[MAG99] Magee, J. and Kramer, J. (1999), *Concurrency, State Models and Java Programs*, John Wiley & Sons, New York.

[MAN93] Mano, M. (1993), *Computer System Architecture*, 3rd ed., Prentice Hall, Upper Saddle River, NJ.

[MEY88] Meyer, B. (1988), *Object-Oriented Software Construction*, Prentice Hall, Upper Saddle River, NJ.

[OAK97] Oaks, S. and Wong, H.(1997), *Java Threads*, O'Reilly & Associates, Cambridge, MA.

[PAR72] Parnas, D.L. (1972), On the criteria to be used in decomposing systems in modules, *Commun. ACM*, 15(9), 1053–1058.

[PIT01] Pitt, E., McNiff, K., and McNiff, K. (2001), *java(TM).rmi: The Remote Method Invocation Guide*, Addison-Wesley, Reading, MA.

[ROB99] Roberts, S., Heller, P., and Ernest, M. (1999), *Complete Java 2 Certification Study Guide*, Sybex, San Francisco, CA.

[RUM91] Rumbaugh, J., Blaha, M., Premerlani, W., Eddy, F., and Lorensen, W. (1991), *Object-Oriented Modeling and Design*, Prentice Hall, Upper Saddle River, NJ.

[SAN94] Sandon, B. (1994), *Software Systems Construction with Examples in Ada*, Prentice Hall, Englewood Cliffs, NJ.

[SAV98] Savage, J.E. (1998), *Models of Exploring the Power of Computing*, Addison-Wesley, Reading, MA.

[SEB99] Sebesta, R. (1999), *Concepts of Programming Languages*, Addison-Wesley, Reading, MA.

[STA01] Stallings, W. (2001), *Operating Systems*, 4th ed., Prentice Hall, Upper Saddle River, NJ.

[VAN01] van der Linden, P. (2001), *Just Java 2*, Prentice Hall, Upper Saddle River, NJ.

[VAN97] van der Veer, E. (1997), *Java Beans for Dummies*, IDG Books Worldwide, Foster City, CA.

[VOG97] Vogel, A. and Duddy, K. (1997), *Java Programming with CORBA*, John Wiley & Sons, New York.

[WEI99] Weiss, M. (1999), *Data Structures and Algorithm Analysis in Java*, Addison-Wesley, Reading, MA

URLs

[MAG02] MageLang Institute (2002), *Introduction to the Collections Framework Short Course*, http://developer.java.sun.com.

[OBJ02] Object Management Group (2002), http://www.omg.org.

[SUN96] Sun Microsystems (1996), *Java Beans Specification*, http://java.sun.com.

[SUN02a] Sun Microsystems (2002), *Reflection*, http://java.sun.com.

[SUN02b] Sun Microsystems (2002), *Object Serialization,* http://java.sun.com.

[SUN02c] Sun Microsystems (2002), *The Java Tutorial*, http://java.sun.com.

[SUN02d] Sun Microsystems (2002), *Dynamic Code Downloading Using RMI* (using the java.rmi.server.codebase property), http://java.sun.com.

[SUN02e] Sun Microsystems (2002), *Java Remote Method Invocation (RMI)*, http://java.sun.com.

[SUN02f] Sun Microsytems (2002), *JSR 14: Add Generic Types to the Java Programming Language*, http://www.jcp.org.

[VEN98] Venners, B. (1998), *Exceptions in Java: The Full Story of Exceptions in the Java Language and Virtual Machine Exceptions in Java*, http://www.artima.com.

[XP02] *Extreme Programming: A Gentle Introduction*, http://www.extremeprogramming.org/.

Index

A

B

C

D

E

F

G

H

I

N

O

P

R

S

T

U

V

W

X